The Works of
Ralph Vaughan Williams

$16.80

The Works of
Ralph Vaughan Williams

MICHAEL KENNEDY

CLARENDON PRESS · OXFORD

Oxford University Press, Walton Street, Oxford OX2 6DP

Oxford New York
Athens Auckland Bangkok Bombay
Calcutta Cape Town Dar es Salaam Delhi
Florence Hong Kong Istanbul Karachi
Kuala Lumpur Madras Madrid Melbourne
Mexico City Nairobi Paris Singapore
Taipei Tokyo Toronto
and associated companies in
Berlin Ibadan

Oxford is a trade mark of Oxford University Press

Published in the United States by
Oxford University Press Inc., New York

First published as a Clarendon Paperback 1992
Reprinted 1995

ISBN 0-19-816330-4

Printed in Great Britain by
Bookcraft Ltd., Midsomer Norton, Avon

Preface to the Second Edition Reissue

THIS book was written between 1960 and 1963. Its appearance in a new impression, therefore, coincides more or less with its thirtieth anniversary. I have pondered whether I should revise the text and re-write some of my conclusions. But I have decided to leave things as they are for two reasons: there have been no major revelations which would affect the biographical sections, and my opinions about the music have changed hardly at all. If I were writing now, I might possibly modify some of my enthusiastic superlatives—but, equally, I might not. I would lay more stress on the influence of Ravel, which I believe to be of prime importance, and I would perhaps commit myself to the belief that *A Pastoral Symphony* is the most original of the nine. On the whole, though, I stand by my judgements. Others will, surely, write books which examine Vaughan Williams's working methods in far more analytical detail than I could attempt, even if I wanted to. But I hope the following pages will stand as a testament to what Vaughan Williams's music meant to someone who lived during the composer's lifetime. It gives me immense pleasure and satisfaction today to know that *The Pilgrim's Progress* and the Ninth Symphony have at last come to be valued as the great and important works they are. Writing this book was a task laid on me by the composer, but I would have written it anyway, as a labour of love. My love of this music has not diminished but intensified in the three decades since I first put pen to paper in the aftermath of his death.

M.K.

March, 1992

Preface to the Second Edition

FOR this new edition of a book first published in 1964 as a companion volume to *R.V.W.*, Ursula Vaughan Williams's biography of her husband, a few minor amendments of the text have been made. These either correct errors or are necessitated by the discovery of new information. I have also added a new appendix, a comprehensive chronological list of works, not as detailed as Appendix I of the original hardback edition but giving the most important information about most of the published works, and I have repaired the omission of an index.

It is now over twenty years since Vaughan Williams died and the passage of time has not affected his reputation or place in English music. If one judges simply from the figures of royalties and performing rights, then it is incontrovertible that performances have continued to increase. Although in the years just before and after his death there was a critical reaction against him, this seems to have levelled out and, since 1972, the centenary of his birth, he has been recognized as a great composer of strong individuality, with more emphasis placed on the remarkable variety and power of his music than on the nationalist aspects of his style. With the majority of his works available on records, certain hitherto neglected pieces have been reassessed. I have, however, decided not to alter any of the views I expressed when I first wrote this book. Possibly I am more enthusiastic now about this particular work, less about that, but not enough to justify any departure from the text published fifteen years ago. I said then that I held to the faith that Vaughan Williams was a very great composer. I am unshaken in that faith.

M.K.

1980

Contents

'The man who serves humanity best is he who, rooted in his own nation, develops his spiritual and moral endowments to their highest capacity, so that growing beyond the limits of his own nation he is able to give something to the whole of humanity, as the great ones of all nations have done.'

GUSTAV STRESEMANN

CHAPTER ONE

The Land Without Music?

W HEN Ralph Vaughan Williams was born at Down Ampney on 12 October 1872, English music was still drifting down the years of the Victorian era, leaderless and bereft of a sense of purpose. Music in England, on the other hand, was thriving. August Manns, at his Crystal Palace concerts, and Charles Hallé, at his Manchester concerts, were introducing new works and had changed the nature of symphony concerts from a miscellaneous selection of music of varying types into a more selective and substantial evening's listening. Christine Nilsson, Emma Albani, Trebelli, Santley, Reeves, and Tietjens—these were among the singers at festivals and the opera. London was still a vital port of call for all the great celebrities of the day. Joachim, von Bülow, and Rubinstein were among the frequent visitors from the ranks of the virtuoso instrumentalists. Anton Bruckner played at the inauguration of the Royal Albert Hall organ. If the Germans' jibe that England was the land without music ever had any truth it can only have accurately referred to the state of our native creative production. To understand the background of Vaughan Williams's youth, it is necessary to look closely at the generation of composers which preceded him.

Today we look back complacently upon the early part of Victoria's reign as the nadir of English musical composition. Perhaps it was, but the tastes of the day were well satisfied. We are probably surprised that Balfe should have been accorded a status not far below that of Auber and Donizetti, but Continental opinion encouraged this estimate. Sterndale Bennett's links with Schumann were taken seriously in Leipzig as well as in London. As the new reign dawned there seemed to be hopes that a musical era might also begin which would revive the glory of Purcell and Byrd. Alas, there can be no golden age without genius. Balfe and Macfarren, Bennett and

Benedict, could not withstand the competition of the Continent from Berlioz, Mendelssohn, Chopin, Wagner, Liszt, and Verdi. As the young Queen's reign wore on, it became increasingly evident that its musical prowess would not begin to compare with the originality of its literature, the gusto of its politics, the intensity of religious controversy, or the ingenuity of its scientists and engineers.

With the advent of the 1860s the first signs of what we now call the English musical renascence were manifest. Like all important movements in art, it was to be a slow and gradual process, with many by-ways and diversions along the road. The first new and original talent to appear in English composition was Arthur Sullivan. His music for *The Tempest*, written when he was 20 in 1862, had an immediate vogue. Two years later a ballet, *The Enchanted Island*, was produced at Covent Garden and a cantata *Kenilworth* was sung at the Birmingham Festival. The greatest cellist of the day, Piatti, played Sullivan's cello concerto at the Crystal Palace in 1866, the year in which the composer was appointed Professor of Composition at the Royal Academy of Music. In 1871 he wrote a comic opera, *Thespis*, to a libretto by W. S. Gilbert. It was a failure, but a great partnership had begun, and over the next twenty-five years the two men produced the brilliant series of operettas which will un-doubtedly earn them lasting fame. Yet, the temper of the age being what it was, Sullivan himself and his friends regarded the Savoy operas as inferior products of his genius. They encouraged him to think that his true musical worth lay in symphonies and oratorios. And so he added *The Prodigal Son*, *The Golden Legend*, and others like them to the long and dismal list of post-Mendelssohnian choral works with which English composers sealed their own doom at this period. Though he must have known it in his heart, Sullivan would not admit that in *The Yeomen of the Guard* and *The Gondoliers* he had produced works which were, and still are, unique. Their invention, their apt and skilful orchestration (rarely heard to its best advantage), and their rhythmical resourcefulness have a vitality sufficient to carry their composer's name to generations yet unborn.

Sullivan had studied at Leipzig. Alexander Mackenzie was sent when only ten to study the violin there. A Continental musical education was still considered *de rigueur* despite the existence of the Royal Academy of Music. English music was English by proxy, and there were still families which did not regard music as a proper profession for their sons. In Bradford the young Frederick Delius encountered stubborn opposition to his musical ambitions from a father who was host to all the great players of the day when they went to play at Hallé's concerts in the Yorkshire town. Delius was ten when Vaughan Williams was born. A boy of fifteen, Edward Elgar, was feeding his innate passion for music on the knowledge he could acquire in his father's music shop in Worcester. At Oxford, that year, Charles Hubert Parry, with another undergraduate, Charles Lloyd, founded the Oxford University Musical Club; and at Cambridge Charles Villiers Stanford was organ scholar and, in 1873, became Trinity College organist. Here, then, was a concentration of bright promise for the future. Wider horizons were opening before the youth of the day. A Bach revival, which may be dated from Barnby's performance of the *St. Matthew Passion* in Westminster Abbey and his annual performances of the *St. John Passion* at St. Anne's, Soho, was under way. From abroad the great schism in music caused by the disciples of Wagner and Brahms sent its echoes here. Interest in the deeper aspects of music as an art rather than merely as fashionable entertainment led to the establishment in 1874 of the Musical Association. Two years later an important training college, the National Training School for Music, opened with Sullivan as principal. In 1883 the school became the Royal College of Music. Its first director was Sir George Grove, and on its professorial staff were Jenny Lind, J. F. Bridge, Walter Parratt, Hubert Parry, and Charles Villiers Stanford. Sir George Grove had written the programme-notes from 1856 for Manns' Crystal Palace concerts. In 1879 the first edition of his *Dictionary of Music and Musicians* was published.

Thus was our musical life beginning to be more integrated, to show more signs of concern for a national musical tradition. Yet, not unnaturally, it was still dominated by the great Continental figures. Wagner returned in 1877 to the London whose public, though not its leading critics, had welcomed him in 1853. On this visit, nearly a quarter of a century later, he came as the outstanding musician of his time, still controversial, still arrogant, but indisputably the greatest single influence on music for generations. With him as assistant conductor came Hans Richter, his friend from earlier times who in 1876 had conducted *The Ring* at the first Bayreuth Festival. Richter began a series of regular concerts in London which were to revolutionize standards of orchestral playing. At the time of his first visit he was thirty-three. For the next twenty-three years his name was familiar to London audiences not only in the concert-hall but at Covent Garden. In the 1880s he introduced *Tristan* and *Die Meistersinger* to London. He conducted the Birmingham Festival from 1885 until 1909, supervising the first performances of many English works. In 1899 he left the Vienna Opera and settled in Manchester, where for the next twelve years, the last active period of his career, he was conductor of the Hallé Orchestra. In 1904 he became also principal conductor of the newly-formed London Symphony Orchestra. He and Georg Henschel were the foremost of the alien musicians who exercised a powerful and on the whole beneficial effect on English musical life in the late Victorian and Edwardian eras. They never neglected to foster and encourage such native talent, among composers and instrumentalists, as was available. And, in the early 1880s, there was striking evidence that, now that the soil was being more systematically tilled, the seeds of composition were not all falling on stony ground. The most depressing feature of the musical scene at this period was the gap between musician and man-in-the-street. In the schools musical instruction was rudimentary. In the home the drawing-room ballad was a flaccid debaucher of taste. In the church the favoured hymn tunes were of a quite appallingly sentimental or insipid type. The enlightened minority existed then, of course, as in every other generation, but, as far as the general public was concerned, in an age when to hear music demanded some real effort, not merely the turn of a switch, the most virile and honest music which it encountered was in the music-hall.

For those who had ears to hear, however, the achievements of Parry and Stanford, Mackenzie and Cowen were a considerable advance on anything produced in Great Britain earlier in the nineteenth century. The two first-named were the first important British composers for very many years who were, so to speak, home-grown and had not spent their whole apprenticeship in Germany. Parry was educated at Eton and Oxford. He spent one long vacation in Stuttgart studying with H. H. Pierson, who in any case was an Englishman (born Pearson) who had adopted Germany as his home. Parry's *annus mirabilis* was 1880, from which it is convenient to date the true start of the English Renascence. Edward Dannreuther played the F sharp minor piano concerto at two successive Richter concerts at the Crystal Palace (3 and 10 April). At the Gloucester Festival of that year the *Scenes from 'Prometheus Unbound'*, though pronounced a failure by the critics, heralded a new epoch in English choral music. Its sensitivity to the accentuations of the English language, its basic sincerity, its richer melodic content—these were, in 1880, a novelty. Voice and verse were once again wedded with a poet's instinct. In 1881 Parry published the first of his twelve sets of *English Lyrics*, settings of some of the greatest poems in the language, many of which are still unrivalled. The mid-twentieth century has no time for Parry's music. His invention is written off as unoriginal, mere watered-down Brahms, and his orchestration as dull and colourless. How many of those who scoff at the mention of Parry's name have heard the choral works, the *English Lyrics* or the symphonies? A century has not yet passed since the zenith of his fame, and a hundred years is no time in which to assume that a composer's work is dead for all time. His music did not strike his contemporaries as merely imitative or unduly influenced by Brahms. Vaughan Williams, as a boy deeply moved by music, remarked to his brother on the 'peculiarly English' quality of Parry's music. No one has yet satisfactorily defined what 'English' quality in music is. To some it merely means an oboe with muted strings as background, but that does not fit Parry nor Elgar. This national spirit in music is surely capable of many forms whose basic structure, or element, is that, perhaps subconsciously, the composer expresses some deeply-felt national characteristic with roots far back in social and cultural evolution. Parry, in fact, was truly Victorian in the best sense of the term. He tried to relate music to life, philosophy, and science. He admired the ideas of Herbert Spencer and this led to his book *The Evolution of the Art of Music* in which he traced music back to its primitive folk origins. It is important in assessing this great man's place in English musical history to give prominence to Vaughan Williams's reminder (in his 1955 lecture to the Composers' Concourse) that the often propagated view of Parry as a jovial country squire is wrong, even though he looked the part. 'The fact is,' Vaughan Williams said, 'that Parry had a highly nervous temperament. He was in early days a thinker with very advanced views.' He was an early champion of Ibsen, and he at once appreciated the magnitude of Wagner. The essay on Wagner, published in 1887 in *Studies of Great Composers*, anticipated the more widely publicized encomium by Bernard Shaw. It is obvious from his relationship with his pupils that Parry never closed his ears to what the young had to say, and as an old man he listened to the music of Schoenberg.

Hubert Parry was undoubtedly a great man and a great influence for good on the future of English music at a time when it needed such an influence desperately. It cannot be said at this date whether he was a great composer. He certainly composed great works. It is no mean achievement to have written *Blest Pair of Sirens* and *Jerusalem*. Vaughan Williams, even allowing for his lifelong loyalty to Parry's memory, was not a man to allow sentiment to cloud his judgement. He regarded *Job* and *De Profundis* as magnificent music and rebuked Michael Tippett for taking a cue from Bernard Shaw and describing *Job* as a product of 'academic mediocrity'. Vaughan Williams wrote:[1] 'Parry was never mediocre. . . . Parry was potentially a great composer, but he often failed because there was some hitch in the process of artistic incubation. But this is not mediocrity. When he succeeded he did so magnificently. . . . *Job* seems to me to contain some of the best (as well as, I admit, the worst) of Parry: witness the superb exordium, which later develops into a great coda; Job's lament, and the splendid choral passage "Hath the rain a father?" '

Parry's name is inseparably linked with Stanford's, although the two men differed in almost every respect both in their music and their personalities. Where Parry was kindly and patient, Stanford was brusque and irascible, though no less kindly. Where Parry's music was mainly in the 'purer' forms, Stanford was attracted by the dramatic possibilities of the opera-house.

Born in Dublin in 1852, Stanford received his musical education at Cambridge, where from 1873 he conducted the University Musical Society and laid the foundations of its high reputation. First English performances of works by Brahms, including the C minor symphony, were given there. He made three short visits abroad to study, in Leipzig with Reinecke and in Berlin with Kiel. A symphony in F major was played in Berlin and at a Crystal Palace concert in January and February 1879, and Richter conducted a setting of the 46th Psalm. His first opera, *The Veiled Prophet of Khorassan*, was performed for the first time in 1881 at Hanover. It did not reach Covent Garden until 1893, although another opera, *Savonarola*, first produced in Hamburg, was conducted at Covent Garden by Richter on 9 July 1884. Germany also heard the first performances of works by Alexander Mackenzie. Since there was no organization of operatic activity in England during Stanford's lifetime it is hardly surprising

---

[1] *The Listener*, 9 August, 1956.

that none of his works entered the repertoire although they were well received by public and press. *Shamus O'Brien* ran for several weeks, but more serious works—*Much Ado About Nothing, The Critic*, and *The Travelling Companion*—were never accorded their due. More easily accessible, because they could be performed by the choral societies throughout the land, were his incomparable settings of Irish melodies and his own extremely beautiful songs and part-songs of which 'The Blue Bird', 'The Fairy Lough', 'A Soft Day', and the *Songs of the Sea* and *Songs of the Fleet* are outstanding examples. Like Parry, Stanford was alive to the possibilities for music of settings of the great poets. He went for his texts to Tennyson, Bridges, Swinburne, and Sheridan, where too many other English composers were still content with the versifying of minor parsons and hack journalists. 'In such works as the *Stabat Mater* and the *Requiem*,' Vaughan Williams wrote, 'we find Stanford thinking his own beautiful thoughts in his own beautiful way'—not, that is to say, in Brahms's way, which is the criticism most easily levelled against his work—'His very facility prevented him from knowing when he was genuinely inspired and when his work was routine stuff.' Both Parry and Stanford paid the price of their enthusiasm for their art—they did too much. They conducted, they taught, they administered, they travelled, they wrote, and they composed. 'Academic' is the sneer they encountered, yet could there have been two more *practical* academicians? There is a popular misconception that only in the 1950s and 1960s has one been able to observe the novelty of youth at the helm. As far as music is concerned let these facts speak for themselves: Stanford was thirty-five when he was elected Professor of Music at Cambridge University. Parry was thirty-five on his appointment as Professor of Composition at the Royal College of Music. William Henry Hadow was lecturer in music at Worcester College, Oxford, at the age of twenty-six. J. A. Fuller Maitland was appointed chief music critic of *The Times* at thirty-three. Whatever may be said of English music towards the end of the Great Queen's reign, it was not in the hands of old men with outworn ideas. The subject of this book defined genius as 'the right man in the right place at the right time'. Parry and Stanford were the right men in the right places as far as teaching was concerned. As far as composition of music was concerned, they were to be outshone by another, Edward Elgar, whose appearance in English music is often represented as a strange and unexpected manifestation. I have been trying to show in these pages that the whole climate of English musical life had developed from 1870 to 1900 so that a genuine native talent could flourish. Parry's words to the inaugural meeting of the Folk Song Society in 1898 are highly relevant:

'True style comes not from the individual but from the products of crowds of fellow-workers who sift and try and try again till they have found the thing that suits their native taste. . . . Style is ultimately national.'

It might be thought that Elgar was a contradiction of this theory. He is in a sense a 'sport', as biologists used to say. He was born at Broadheath, Worcester, in 1857, away from fashionable musical circles. His father owned a music-shop in Worcester and the boy grew up amid musical talk and activity. Worcester may have seemed far from London, but it was not a musical backwater. Then, as now, the Three Choirs Festival dominated the city; Birmingham, with Stockley's orchestra and visits from Hallé's, was easily reached. There was not enough money to send Edward to a college of music. His musical education, therefore, was of a haphazard but practical kind. While still at school he deputized for his father at the organ of St. George's Roman Catholic Church. He learned the violin and the bassoon. It had been hoped to send him to Leipzig when he left school, but circumstances forbade this. He taught himself, with help from his father, from books—Crotch's *Elements of Musical Composition*, Reicha's *Orchestral Primer*, Cherubini's *Counterpoint*—and by a remarkable system of self-imposed composition exercises. Best of all, he continued his practical experience. In 1878 he played among the second violins of the Festival Orchestra at Worcester. The following year he became conductor of the orchestra at the Worcester Lunatic Asylum at Powick, an early example of the use of music as a therapeutic influence on mental illness. Elgar inserted his own compositions into his programmes. In 1883 he paid a brief visit to Leipzig where he heard a great deal of Wagner, Brahms, and Schumann. By now he was also a member of Stockley's orchestra at Birmingham and on 13 December 1883 his *Sérénade Mauresque* was played, and appreciated, at a Stockley concert. Another six years of formative local work—as conductor of the Worcester Amateur Instrumental Society and, from 1885, as organist of St. George's— were to follow before Elgar's marriage in 1889 and his removal to London, where only August Manns took any interest in the young composer. But in 1890 the overture *Froissart*, played at the Worcester

Festival, brought his name into greater prominence. Dispirited by life in London, Elgar returned to Worcestershire. At first he worked fitfully, convinced that his compositions would never penetrate far beyond local circles. But there was encouragement in the production of the cantata *The Black Knight* in 1893. On summer holidays abroad he heard Wagner's operas at Munich and at Bayreuth. This led to a spate of activity, and in 1896 his *Scenes from the Bavarian Highlands* was produced at a concert in Worcester, the cantata *King Olaf* at the North Staffordshire Musical Festival at Hanley (and a year later by Manns at the Crystal Palace), and *The Light of Life*, his first oratorio, at the Worcester Festival. Now his name was made. *Caractacus* was commissioned for the 1898 Leeds Festival. And in 1899, with the performance under Richter of the *Enigma Variations*, English music at last produced a European masterpiece.

It has been suggested that the unsatisfactory nature of the early choral works of Elgar such as *King Olaf* and *Caractacus* was due to the lack of an English operatic tradition: they belonged properly to the stage. There is something in this theory. But the truth surely is that England had at last produced a composer whose natural medium was the orchestra. The temper of the age demanded choral music and Elgar tried to supply it. It is significant that only one of his choral works, *The Dream of Gerontius*, has kept a regular, un-challenged position in the repertoire. But *Gerontius* is a masterpiece because, for one thing, it is an intense personal declaration of belief and faith, and for another the orchestra is the protagonist. As in *King Olaf*, Elgar used the Wagnerian *leitmotif* principle, but with a far greater subtlety and spontaneity than he had hitherto commanded.

Elgar, perhaps, was not the English genius in the form which Parry and Stanford might have expected. But they recognized and acknowledged him. Although the folk-song revival began in the late 1880s, culminating in the foundation of the Folk Song Society in 1898, Elgar owed nothing to folk music except as part of his natural evolution. He was a true child of his time. He was, as anyone can hear, much influenced by the music that was in the air at the time of his full flowering, by Brahms, Wagner, Liszt, and Franck. He took as much of this as he needed, and he transformed it, by his own inventive mind, into music of such originality that the adjective 'Elgarian' has come to be a recognized and authentic description. Thus we have the paradox that Elgar's music appealed at once to those bred in the European tradition who recognized its accent as part of the mainstream of Western musical art. That is why Richter, Brodsky, Kreisler, and Richard Strauss were among Elgar's earliest champions. Yet to the English Elgar's music was 'peculiarly English' and still seems to be. An un-English English composer? Not really, for how can one describe the opening of the slow movement of the violin concerto as anything but an intense aspect of English art? The answer is that Parry's words were true: 'Style is ultimately national.' Moreover, although Elgar's career marked the beginning of a new golden age of English music, his work, like that of so many great men, closed an epoch. He was no pioneer. He came from nowhere and he broke most of the rules. He stands in relationship to English music much as Mahler stands to Austrian. It was only right that the genuine and devoted labours of the lesser men towards a new English musical vitality should be rewarded by an Elgar. And only to be expected.

The years from 1880 to 1900 have been examined in some detail because they were the years in which Ralph Vaughan Williams was developing from childhood to manhood. Other aspects of the musical nineties should be borne in mind: Mahler's visits to conduct *Tristan* at Covent Garden, the emergence of a brilliant young English conductor, Henry J. Wood, and of several fine English (or British) singers, Agnes Nicholls, Robert Radford, Clara Butt, Plunket Greene, Kirkby Lunn, Muriel Foster, Ffrangcon Davies. Shaw was writing, for *The World*, devastating criticisms of Parry and Stanford, Brahms and Dvořák. The music of Tchaikovsky, Dvořák, and Rimsky-Korsakov was entering the repertoire. Besides Elgar a new generation of English composers was claiming a hearing—Bantock, Delius, Ethel Smyth, Coleridge-Taylor. In the realm of light opera Edward German, Alfred Cellier, Sydney Jones, and Leslie Stuart enjoyed considerable success. Since 1892 Dan Godfrey had been championing new music at Bournemouth. Cowen was holding the fort at Manchester, after Hallé's death in 1895, until Richter took over. Henschel since 1893 had been conductor of the Scottish Orchestra, formed to provide Glasgow and Edinburgh with a musical life. Most important of all, a new London concert-hall, the Queen's Hall, was opened in 1893 and there, in 1895, Wood began his Promenade Concerts under Robert Newman's management.

Much remained unsatisfactory about England's music in 1899, but it could face the Twentieth Century with a sense of bustle and purpose.

CHAPTER TWO

1872–1895

I

VAUGHAN WILLIAMS has written, inimitably, his own account of his musical upbringing.[1] No great composer ever had a stranger one. His first composition, which still exists, was a four-bar pianoforte piece called 'The Robin's Nest'.[2] This was shown to some musically inclined visitors to Leith Hill Place, one of whom inquired whether Ralph had learned any thorough bass. Shortly after this, his aunt—his 'very maiden maiden aunt' as Frances Cornford put it—Sophy Wedgwood, instructed him in this mystery from *The Child's Introduction to Thorough Bass in Conversations of a Fortnight between a Mother and her Daughter aged 10 Years Old* (1819). Next was Sir John Stainer's *Harmony* and, when he was eight, he took a correspondence course in music at Edinburgh University and passed two examinations. He was taught the piano, which he did not like, and the violin. His first violin lessons were from 'a wizened old German called Cramer' and they were continued at his preparatory school at Rottingdean by the Brighton teacher W. M. Quirke. Pianoforte lessons continued from a visiting teacher, C. T. West, to whom Vaughan Williams was always grateful for the gift of Novello's *Bach Album*. Bach was not played at Leith Hill Place. At a concert at Rottingdean, Ralph played Raff's *Cavatina*, but it was Bach's music which must even then have filled his mind.

Another memory of these days is contained in a letter written to a friend in about 1947 by Adeline Vaughan Williams in which she

[1] In 'Chapter of Musical Autobiography', reprinted in *National Music and Other Essays* (London, 1963).
[2] Mr. Roy Douglas tells me that Vaughan Williams once played to him 'the first music I ever wrote, called "The Robin's Nest" '. It was quite different from the actual composition found among his effects!

said: 'R. at his private school was asked by a fellow schoolboy to write incidental music to a play he was writing on "The Rape of Lucretia". R. wrote an opening drinking chorus but the plan got no further. His friend was quite innocent of the full meaning—R. not quite.'

In January 1887, 'Williams R.V. minor' entered the headmaster's house at Charterhouse. The school had moved to Godalming in 1872. Here he joined the school orchestra and played the second violin. Later he changed to viola. He has recalled that his first practical lesson in orchestration came during a performance of Beethoven's first symphony when he heard the holding note on the horn which accompanies the violas during the slow movement. For a time, too, he sang in the choir which, as he recalled in *The Carthusian* in 1952, 'practised in the time otherwise devoted to Extra French and was therefore very popular'.

But the most important event of his Carthusian career was in early August 1888, when he approached Dr. William Haig Brown, the headmaster, for permission to use the school hall for a concert of compositions by his friend, H. Vivian Hamilton, a pianist, and himself. 'Dr. Haig Brown was a formidable man,' Vaughan Williams wrote, 'and in later life I should never have dared to make the request, but leave was obtained and we gave the concert.'[1] The work of Vaughan Williams's was a Pianoforte Trio in G. It was performed after a Spohr duet and a song by Sullivan, and there was an early and characteristic disregard of convention because the trio was played by four performers. The composer persuaded a friend to share the violin part with him. 'All I remember about it is that the principal theme was distinctly reminiscent of César Franck, a composer whose name I did not even know in those days, and whom I have since learned to dislike cordially. I must have got the theme from one of the French or Belgian imitators of Franck, whose salon music was popular in those days. I remember that after the concert James Noon, the mathematical master, came up to me and said in that sepulchral voice which Carthusians of my day knew so well, "Very good, Williams, you must go on". I treasured this as one of the few words of encouragement I ever received in my life!'[2]

There was never any doubt but that young Ralph should make his career in music, however strange an occupation it may have

[1] *The Carthusian*, December, 1952.
[2] 'Chapter of Musical Autobiography.'

appeared to the Wedgwoods at Leith Hill Place. At any rate there seems to have been no family opposition, for even though Victorianism might have shadowed it for a time, the Wedgwood-Darwin tradition was liberal and the only rule was that if something was undertaken it must be done to the best of one's ability. Even the Darwin Aunt Etty was reconciled to Ralph's ambition when she wrote of 'that foolish young man Ralph Vaughan Williams who will go on working at music when he is so hopelessly bad at it. He has been playing all his life, and for six months *hard*, and yet he can't play the simplest thing decently. They say it will simply break his heart if he is told that he is too bad to hope to make anything of it'.[1] Perhaps that was why he *was* allowed to 'go on'. An employee at Leith Hill Place, J. Ellis Cook, recalls that on holiday from Charterhouse, Ralph would ask workmen on the estate to sing to him. He would write the notes down and ask for the same song again and note any difference.[2] There was fun at Leith Hill Place when he sang comic duets with his cousin Diana Massingberd, later Lady Montgomery-Massingberd. Another cousin, Diana's brother Stephen Massingberd, introduced him to Parry's great book *Studies of Great Composers*. ' "This man Parry," he said, "declares that a composer must write music as his musical conscience demands." This was quite a new idea to me, the loyalty of the artist to his art. Soon after that I got to know some of his music, especially *Judith*.'[3]

Aunt Sophy had brought up the three Vaughan Williams children on a strictly classical diet—Handel, Mozart, Haydn and early Beethoven. Later Schubert's marches and Haydn's symphonies were added to the pianoforte duets. Haydn set Ralph a problem. Aunt Sophy considered waltzes to be vulgar and the second subject of the first movement of Haydn's E flat symphony was a waltz. How could Haydn, a great composer, be vulgar? Further problems of vulgarity awaited him when it was decided at Charterhouse that the organ was a "safer" choice than the violin, for he must then have encountered the Victorian hymn-writers at close quarters.

He moved from the headmaster's house, after two years, into Mr. G. H. Robinson's. Robinson was the school organist. For his last four terms Ralph was head of the house. It seems that a boy

---

[1] *Period Piece*, by Gwen Raverat (London, 1952).
[2] *R.C.M. Magazine*, Easter Term 1959, Vol. LV, No. 1.
[3] 'Chapter of Musical Autobiography.'

whose primary concern was music and who had no interest in games was not, at Charterhouse at any rate, condemned to perdition. At home at Leith Hill Place an organ was installed in the entrance hall at which Ralph could practise. Practise he did, though he considered himself unsuited to the instrument and was proud of the 'distinction' of being the only pupil ever entirely to baffle Sir Walter Parratt. One cannot imagine that he was ever able to co-ordinate brain, hands and feet, especially feet. But he passed the F.R.C.O. examination while at the Royal College of Music.

Vaughan Williams left Charterhouse at the end of the summer term, 1890; in the summer holidays, before going on to the Royal College of Music, he went to Munich, where he heard for the first time Wagner's *Die Walküre*. He experienced no surprise from the music, 'rather that strange certainty that I had heard it all before. There was a feeling of recognition as of meeting an old friend which comes to us all in the face of great artistic experiences'. So began an admiration for Wagner's operas which lasted all his life. 'Oh, you young people who run down Wagner,' he would mutter.

In September 1890, a month before his eighteenth birthday, Vaughan Williams entered the Royal College of Music with the ambition to study composition under Hubert Parry. At that date study of composition was forbidden until the entrant had passed Grade 5 in harmony. For his first two terms Vaughan Williams did theory with Dr. F. E. Gladstone who made him undertake every exercise in Macfarren's *Harmony*. Some of the tasks he undertook for Dr. Gladstone still exist among his unpublished manuscripts. They include an overture for organ and an organ sonatina in E flat, both dated 1890, some tunes for a ballet and sketches for a string quartet.

The Grade 5 hurdle was overcome, and early in 1891 Vaughan Williams became Parry's pupil. Never throughout the next sixty-seven years did he cease to remember this experience with pride and gratitude. 'Parry could hardly believe that I knew so little music': an example was the *Appassionata* sonata. So Parry played the finale to his pupil. He lent him the scores of works by Wagner and Brahms and explained to him the greatness of Bach and Beethoven in relation to Handel and Mendelssohn—radical teaching according to the methods of some colleges at that time. Parry was intensely keen to discover whether his pupils had character and would study even the poorest efforts at composition to try to find a distinctive voice. Once through carelessness Vaughan Williams wrote out a scale passage with one note repeated and then a gap. Parry would keep his pupils' compositions after the official lesson in order to look at them during the week. When next he saw R.V.W. he said: 'I have been looking at this passage for a long time to discover whether it was just a mistake or whether you meant anything characteristic.'

Vaughan Williams himself confesses that at this time he was 'suffering from an overdose of Gounod' and 'hated Beethoven'. Parry made him study the late Beethoven quartets and also advised him to 'write choral music as befits an Englishman and a democrat'. Early efforts—'the horrible little songs and anthems which I presented for his criticism'—betray a preoccupation with Brahms's *Requiem*. An anthem for tenor and organ, 'I heard a voice from heaven', written in the summer term of 1891, has some melodic charm of the kind usually associated with Mendelssohn and Sterndale Bennett. The 'characteristic' which emerges is a lack of consideration for the tenor's resources. There is nothing in these works to suggest the composer we know now. What is apparent is the boy's industry—his capacity for sheer hard work.

These first years at the College were also particularly valuable in broadening his knowledge of music not only through Parry's guidance but by contact with fellow-students, chief among them Richard Walthew. Vaughan Williams visited Walthew's home at Highbury to play pianoforte duets, including Stanford's Irish Symphony. It was Walthew who took his friend to hear *Carmen*. 'By that time,' Vaughan Williams has written, 'I had quite recovered from my Gounod fever and had become the complete prig. Bach, Beethoven (*ex officio*), Brahms and Wagner were the only composers worth considering so I went to *Carmen* prepared to scoff; but Walthew won the day and I remained to pray.'

An even more important experience at this time was his first encounter with Verdi's *Requiem*. Once again Vaughan Williams's own words are sufficiently eloquent:

'At first I was properly shocked by the frank sentimentalism and sensationalism of the music. I remember being particularly horrified at the drop of a semitone on the word "Dona". Was not this the purest "village organist"? But in a very few minutes the music possessed me. I realized that here was a composer who could do all the things which I, with my youthful pedantry, thought wrong— indeed would be unbearable in a lesser man; music which was sentimental, theatrical, occasionally even cheap, and yet was an overpowering masterpiece. That day I learnt that there is nothing in itself that is "common or unclean"; indeed, that there are no canons of art except that contained in the well-worn tag "To thine own self be true".[1]

How well he learned and practised that lesson his whole career exemplified. His reaction to this work is also an indication of his essentially romantic temperament. Another clue to his inner nature is given by Dr. G. F. McCleary[2] in describing their first meeting at Charing Cross Station on 15 June 1892, after a performance of *Tristan* conducted by Gustav Mahler, with Rosa Sucher as Isolde and Max Alvary as Tristan. McCleary writes: 'Vaughan Williams in his comments on *Tristan* was not enthusiastic and I gathered that the work did not appeal much to him. In this, however, I was mistaken. Many years later, on talking over our first meeting, he assured me that *Tristan* had profoundly impressed him. He added: "In those early days I remember not being able to sleep after a performance of it." ' Even at the age of nineteen, Vaughan Williams had evidently mastered the art of concealing the violent emotional disturbances of his nature. His temperament was passionate and eruptive. This is obvious enough in a great deal of his music. It also showed in his sudden outbursts of white-hot anger at rehearsals which he was conducting—terrifying but as swift to subside as they had been to arise.

In October 1892 Vaughan Williams entered Trinity College, Cambridge, with the intention of obtaining his degree as Bachelor of Music and to read history. He continued weekly lessons at the R.C.M. At Cambridge he had lessons from Charles Wood, Fellow of Caius, who had had a brilliant career at the R.C.M. and achieved some distinction as a composer. His description[3] of Wood is illuminating:

'Wood was the finest technical instructor I have ever known. I do not say necessarily the greatest teacher. I do not think he had the gift of inspiring enthusiasm or of leading to the higher planes of musical thought. Indeed, he was rather prone to laugh at artistic ideals, and would lead one to suppose that composing music was a trick anyone might learn if he took the trouble. But for the craft of

---

[1] 'Musical Autobiography.'
[2] *R.C.M. Magazine*, Easter Term 1959, Vol. LV, No. 1.
[3] 'Chapter of Musical Autobiography.'

composition he was unrivalled, and he managed to teach me enough to pull me through my Mus.Bac. I also had organ lessons from Alan Gray. Our friendship survived his despair at my playing.' Wood admitted in later years that he had sustained few hopes for Vaughan Williams's future as a composer. These early years were a hard internal struggle for him, a struggle to master his craft and a profound searching struggle for his own means of self-expression. Few either at Cambridge or the Royal College of Music expected eminence from him. Yet all knew, as Aunt Etty had perceived, that music was his life whether it proved heart-breaking or not.

Vaughan Williams entered wholeheartedly into Cambridge life, musical and otherwise. This was a remarkable period in the university's history. A list of the undergraduates between 1890 and 1895 makes memorable reading. Among them were Bertrand Russell, Crompton and Theodore Llewelyn Davies, McTaggart the philosopher, Roger Fry, Lowes Dickinson, Edward Marsh, G. E. Moore, Charles, George and Robert Trevelyan, not to mention K. S. Ranjitsinhji. Here, indeed, was a society of the elect. Vaughan Williams's cousin, Ralph Wedgwood, (father of the historian C. V. Wedgwood), was a contemporary and so was Maurice Amos. G. E. Moore, George Trevelyan, Amos, Ralph Wedgwood and Vaughan Williams met for reading parties, in the vacation, at Seatoller, in Borrowdale. In later years Vaughan Williams would say that he felt intellectually inferior to these companions. It is unlikely that they were conscious of any such gap. With strangers a natural shyness and diffidence meant that he was not a fluent talker. What he had to say was to the point and original. Among friends his gaiety would reveal itself, his shrewd wit and the laugh which shook his whole body. The friendships they formed lasted in many cases for their lifetimes and many of them kept faith with the beliefs and philosophies which they formed in their university days.

Vaughan Williams quickly joined the University Musical Club at which the members played chamber music and discussed it afterwards. A new member contemporary with R.V.W. was Hugh P. Allen, who was elected organ-scholar of Christ's College. He was within two months of his twenty-third birthday, older than the average undergraduate, and had already taken his B.Mus. degree at Oxford. Allen at once took a leading part in the club's activities and he and R.V.W. became firm friends. Vaughan Williams introduced the music of Brahms to Allen; and Allen rehearsed the club members in Brahms's and Schumann's pianoforte quintets, playing the pianoforte part himself, and Schubert's string quintet. He liked to have Vaughan Williams present to hear his criticisms; and R.V.W. for his part recorded that he 'got much musical instruction in listening to the rehearsal of these works, which I came to know nearly by heart'. Allen performed one of his friend's compositions at these concerts. This was a quartet for men's voices—a setting of 'Music when soft voices die'—and during the performance the second tenor got a bar out and stayed out. Allen seized the opportunity for an encore and the work was repeated correctly. 'The audience disliked it the second time even more than the first,' according to Vaughan Williams, whose testimony is supported by Dr. McCleary. But McCleary records that Haydn Inwards, a violinist on the teaching staff of the R.C.M., who regularly led the Cambridge orchestra, told the dissenters: 'You are all wrong. That is real good stuff.' It is worth recording here that the club concerts were often followed by informal performances of comic songs for which Vaughan Williams always remained. He had a repertoire of comic songs and enjoyed singing them, with appropriate accents and *panache*, to the end of his life.

Vaughan Williams formed his own choral society at Cambridge. They met on Sundays to sing the Masses of Schubert which were then considered rarities, as indeed they are still. Here he learned the first principles of conducting. He was also active in the affairs of the University Musical Society, of which he was honorary secretary for the three terms of 1894. McCleary recalls his taking a collecting-box round at a club meeting to raise enough money for a bassoon player's fee to travel from London to play the double-bassoon part in Beethoven's C minor symphony. The Society had decided to save the expense by omitting the instrument. This proposed mutilation, in the name of economy, enraged Vaughan Williams, who promptly acted to prevent it.

Very little music of this Cambridge period survives in manuscript, although the quartet for men's voices is preserved. A piano suite for four hands dated 4 October 1893 contains a diminished seventh.

In the autumn of 1895 Vaughan Williams returned to the Royal College of Music. Sir George Grove had resigned his Directorship in October 1894, and had been succeeded by Parry. Vaughan Williams, therefore, went to Stanford for composition lessons, and there began the strange, stormy, and affectionate relationship

between those two idiosyncratic personalities. Vaughan Williams
has left some vivid descriptions of their lessons; and he attributed
Stanford's greatness as a teacher to his intolerance and narrow-
mindedness—'if a thing was right it was right; if it was wrong it was
wrong, and there was no question about it'. But R.V.W. was un-
teachable and he fought his teacher. He regarded Stanford's views,
especially his condemnation of all music since Brahms as 'ugly',
with contempt. Moreover, as he admitted later, in his obstinacy he
insisted upon obtruding his personality into the simplest harmony
exercises.

But Vaughan Williams at any rate stood up to Stanford. Several
more sensitive pupils transferred to kinder teachers, unable to
withstand the cruel judgements and the curt 'All rot, me bhoy,' with
which, for instance, he demolished a string quartet slow movement
on which Vaughan Williams had expended hours of agonized
concentration.

In one respect Vaughan Williams was a radically altered musician
during his second spell at the R.C.M. For in 1893 he had discovered
the folk song 'Dives and Lazarus' in *English County Songs*, which
Lucy Broadwood and Fuller Maitland had published in that year.
In his own words: 'Here, as before with Wagner, I had that sense of
recognition—"here's something which I have known all my life—
only I didn't know it!" ' But in a sense he did, for as a boy in the
1880s he had responded in a strong and deep-rooted manner to
'The Cherry Tree Carol' in Stainer and Bramley's *Christmas Carols,
New and Old*. Thus he went to Stanford deeply involved in his mind
with the uses of the modes. Stanford himself, who was forty-two at
this time, had himself been studying (in 1890) 'modal counterpoint'
under W. S. Rockstro,[1] and therefore made his pupils write motets
and masses in strict modal counterpoint as an antidote to their
growing preoccupation with the richer textures of Tchaikovsky and
Dvořák. But he recognized that Vaughan Williams was 'too far
gone' with the modes and he was concerned at the young composer's
thickness of texture. His exercise for R.V.W., therefore, was to
write waltzes. The result was modal waltzes. They still exist.

However hard the teacher was on the pupil in their lessons, he
appreciated the younger man's worth. A Serenade for small
orchestra by Vaughan Williams had been played through in 1899.
Stanford called it 'a most poetical and remarkable piece of work'.

[1] Stanford undertook this work with Rockstro in preparation for his *Eden* (1891).

Another potent influence on Vaughan Williams at the College was S. P. Waddington, three years his senior and a brilliant student from 1883–9. Though he never gave R.V.W. formal lessons he would look over and criticize his work and also play it to him. He had 'uncanny' powers of sight-reading from a manuscript. One of his criticisms of the young Vaughan Williams was 'You try to run before you can walk'. According to R.V.W. this was true—'I had not sufficient practice or application to study. I have learnt by trial and error; I have drawers full of these errors—attempts to run, with a fatal stumble almost every other bar'. In the long run this was surely the best method for Vaughan Williams to undertake. It is almost certainly what gives his music its special flavour of deliberate power and effect. Throughout his writings one finds this self-deprecatory attitude which, though it reveals the stature of the man, does him less than justice. Because he carved his own path and because he did not possess facility, he pretended to regard his work as 'amateurish' in technique. Unfortunately, his critics have seized upon this word in order to disparage the later music, but, as will be shown, all Vaughan Williams's orchestral and choral effects were carefully calculated.

Vaughan Williams, although his potential was recognized by Stanford and Waddington, was overshadowed by most of his fellow pupils. Among them were Thomas Dunhill, John Ireland, Fritz Hart and Evlyn Howard-Jones. They used to meet in a Kensington tea-shop and 'discuss every subject under the sun, from the lowest note of the double bassoon to the philosophy of *Jude The Obscure*. I learnt more from these conversations than from any amount of formal teaching, but I felt at a certain disadvantage with these companions: they were all so competent and I felt such an amateur.'

The Kensington tea-shop was Wilkins'. Dunhill recalled that at the end of the formal debates in Room 46 of the College, someone would rise from his seat and sing, to the main theme of the scherzo of Brahms's fourth symphony, 'Shall we go to Wilkins'? Shall we go to Wilkins'?—*YES*', the last sforzando word being declaimed by the whole assembly.

One of the companions was to have the most powerful influence of anyone on Vaughan Williams's music—Gustav von Holst. Holst, of Swedish descent, was born in Cheltenham on 21 September 1874. He entered the Royal College of Music as a student in May 1893, and was awarded an open scholarship for composition in February

1895. It was in 1895 that Holst and Vaughan Williams met. Holst quoted from Sheridan's *The Critic* and this, as Vaughan Williams said in a broadcast in 1954, 'broke the ice and seemed to seal our friendship'. Almost at once they began to give each other composition lessons. They played the earliest sketches of their works and would then criticize them, with complete candour, and re-write passages together. Often they disagreed and would find their own way to solution of the problem either because of, or in spite of, the criticisms. These sessions they called their 'Field Days'. They continued for nearly forty years, until Holst's death. 'I think he showed all he wrote to me,' R.V.W. has written,[1] 'and I nearly all I wrote to him. I say "nearly all" advisedly, because sometimes I could not face the absolute integrity of his vision, and I hid some of my worst crimes from him. I regret now that I did not face even his disapproval. . . . He would not rest till he had found a solution for the problem which not only satisfied him, but one which my obstinacy would accept.'

This is Vaughan Williams's characteristic voice. He attributed his inner conviction to obstinacy, amateurishness or inferiority complex. In fact, he had a great natural pride combined with an innate realization of when he had found the way in which he wished to express himself. He would always listen to criticism or advice, but if he himself was convinced by his own work no amount of criticism would make him alter it. Those passages which he did alter were nearly always those over which he himself felt dubious.

II

After Vaughan Williams's death it was discovered that most of his childhood and student compositions had been preserved, first by his mother and then, no doubt, by the composer himself and his first wife. They can now be studied in the British Museum. It is not proposed to probe into them for obscure hints and foreshadowings of the great composer of later years. They are juvenilia, significant mainly for their touching evidence of a whole lifetime devoted to music and also for the light they shed on Vaughan Williams's extreme self-discipline. He worked hard to be a composer and the exercises he set himself—'doing his stodge'—proved their value in

[1] 'Musical Autobiography.'

later years. His industry is itself an example to future generations. Because so many early works were suppressed there is a tendency to imagine that the composer suddenly and surprisingly burst forth in about 1907. That certainly was when he emerged as a musician of positive and idiosyncratic character. But the years in the chrysalis were not barren and fruitless.

CHAPTER THREE

Folk Song and Nationalism

IT is convenient to date the beginning of the English folk-song revival from 1843, when the Rev. John Broadwood, who at the time was living in Worthing,[1] published his *Old English Songs as now sung by the Peasantry of the Weald of Surrey and Sussex.*[2] He had noticed the beauty of the songs sung by the country people at harvesting and other rustic festivities. His volume, which was published privately, contained sixteen songs harmonized by George A. Dusart, organist to the Chapel of Ease at Worthing. Dusart, unused to flattened sevenths, protested that the tunes contained wrong notes, but Broadwood told him: 'Musically it may be wrong, but I *will* have it exactly as my singers sang it.' But Broadwood was not the first in the field. In 1812 R. Topliff had published twenty-four popular songs of Tyneside, some of them genuine folk songs, and William Chappell's *National English Airs* of 1838 contained several folk tunes. The Percy Society issued *Ballads and Songs of the Peasantry* in 1866. The methodical collection of folk songs may be said to have begun in 1889, coincident with the expanded reprint of Broadwood's book. This was now called *Sussex Songs.* It had ten more songs added by Miss Lucy Etheldred Broadwood, niece of the Rev. John, and arranged by H. F. Birch Reynardson. In the same year, the Rev. Sabine Baring-Gould published the first part of his

---

[1] He did not become 'squire' at Lyne, the Broadwood family's country house at Capel and Newdigate, until 1851 when his father died.

[2] It is worthwhile to quote the historic book's full title, set out by the publisher, Balls and Co., of Oxford Street, London, with a virtuoso display of typography:

'Old English Songs, as now Sung by the Peasantry of the Weald of Surrey and Sussex, and collected by one who has learnt them by hearing them Sung every Christmas from early Childhood by The Country People, who go about to the Neighbouring Houses Singing or "Wassailing", as it is called, at that season. The Airs are set to Music exactly as they are now Sung to rescue them from oblivion and to afford a specimen of genuine Old English Melody and the words are given in their original rough state with an occasional slight alteration to render the sense intelligible.'

Songs and Ballads of the West, the result of his collecting in Devon and Cornwall. In collaboration with H. Fleetwood Sheppard he published three more parts of this important work between 1889 and 1901, containing 110 songs. Other significant collections published at this time were Frank Kidson's *Traditional Tunes* (1891), which contained 109 songs without accompaniment obtained in Yorkshire and Southern Scotland, Dr. W. A. Barrett's *English Folk Songs* (1891, 54 songs) and Lucy Broadwood's and J. A. Fuller Maitland's *English County Songs* (1893, 95 songs). On 16 June 1898 the Folk Song Society was founded, with Parry, Stanford, Mackenzie, and Stainer among the vice-presidents. This was an 'official' acknowledgement of the new interest in folk song, but the Society's affairs were at first of rather a dilettante nature.[1] The whole movement blazed into life with the advent of Cecil Sharp. He had become aware of folk-music through the dancing of the traditional Morris 'side' at Headington, near Oxford, in 1899. In September 1903, at Hambridge, Somerset, he collected his first folk song, 'The Seeds of Love'. The Vicar of Hambridge, the Rev. C. L. Marson, collaborated with Sharp in his researches into the folk songs of this one county. The outcome was the five parts of *Folk Songs from Somerset*, the first three of them with Marson, published between 1904 and 1919 and containing 130 songs.[2] In all in Somerset he noted nearly 1,500 tunes, and by the time of his death on 23 June 1924 he had noted about 3,300 (including variants and dance tunes) in England and about 1,700 in the Southern Appalachian mountains of North America where he and Maud Karpeles spent 46 weeks in 1916–18.

Sharp's work, and that of his fellow-collectors, was done at the eleventh hour. He estimated that the last generation of folk singers was born about 1840 and he found that it was nearly always useless to obtain a song from anyone who was under the age of fifty. The younger people's songs, even if traditional, were already showing signs of adulteration. The practice of singing folk songs seems to have begun to fade in the second half of the nineteenth century. This

[1] The committee included Lucy Broadwood, Mrs. Laurence Gomme (later Lady Gomme), A. P. Graves (father of Robert), Frank Kidson, J. A. Fuller Maitland and W. Barclay Squire. The adoption of its first report, in 1899, was moved by 'Mr. Edward Elgar'.

[2] The first three volumes date from 1904–6. The last two, without Marson's name appeared between 1906 and 1919. The friendship between the two men came to an unhappy end in November 1906 after 17 years. They never met again, but Sharp went to Marson's funeral at Hambridge in 1914. (See *Cecil Sharp* by Fox Strangways and Karpeles, second edition 1955, pp. 31–32.)

may have been due to the increased ease of transport and the spread of popular education, so that people were able to travel out of their villages to the larger towns and obtain ready-made entertainment instead of providing it for themselves. The new generations just did not take the trouble to learn the tunes. Vaughan Williams attributed the decline to the 1871 Education Act. Or it may have been a deeper symptom of a fundamental though unconscious realization by the people that they had reached a new stage of development. England had become an industrial nation.[1] Already by 1907 many of the folk singers who had provided Sharp with his songs were dead. By the same date all from whom Baring-Gould had collected were dead. There are still a few traditional singers living even at the present day (1964), but the situation both as regards quantity and quality of songs has greatly deteriorated during the last fifty years. The achievements of the folk-song collectors at the turn of the century are a miracle which has never, perhaps, received its due in wonder from their fellow-countrymen.

Why, it may be asked, if this national treasury of song was still a living art in the mid-nineteenth century, did no one take any notice of it? Why, when so many educated people presided over the country districts, was folk song allowed almost to die unrecorded? Cecil Sharp's experience was that if he had made several exciting discoveries in a village and informed the vicar of his success, his story was at first disbelieved and then, when proof was shown, greeted with amazement. A country vicar, unless he was a Baring-Gould, was not likely to be very musical, and when he heard the folk songs sung with rough accents, unaccompanied, at a harvest-home or the annual Club Feast, he would be most unlikely to recognize artistic gems beneath such crude trappings.[2] Moreover the

---

[1] An aspect of this situation is also to be found in a letter from Thomas Hardy to Rider Haggard in 1902, when the latter was investigating the conditions of agricultural labourers:

'The consequences [of migration to the towns] are curious and unexpected. For one thing village tradition—a vast mass of unwritten folk-lore, local chronicle, local topography and nomenclature—is absolutely sinking, has almost sunk, into eternal oblivion. I cannot recall a single labourer who still lives on the farm where he was born, and I can only recall a few who have been five years on their present farms. Thus you see, there being no continuity of environment in their lives, there is no continuity of information.' *The Life of Thomas Hardy*, by F. E. Hardy, Vol. II (London, 1930).

[2] Marson himself, a clergyman out of the ordinary, wrote in the Preface to *Folk Songs from Somerset*, Vol. I:

'The folk song is like the duck-billed platypus in this particular, you can live for years within a few yards of it and never suspect its existence. . . . Eight years of constant

village folk regarded their songs as an intimate personal possession which might be ridiculed by the 'educated folk'. They recognized, all too rightly, that the ballad songs of the gentry were a very different kettle of fish. So it was that Carl Engel in his *Literature of National Music*, published in 1879,[1] could write:

'It seems rather singular that England should not possess any printed collection of its national songs with the airs as they are sung at the present day; while almost every other European nation possesses several comprehensive works of this kind. . . . Some musical enquirers have expressed the opinion that the country people in England are not in the habit of singing while at their work in the fields. . . . However, this opinion would probably be found to be only partially correct if search were made in the proper places. . . . There are, in some of the shires, rather isolated districts in which the exertions of a really musical collector would not be entirely resultless.'

If any English musician had taken up this challenge, had decided to test the truth of this paragraph, he could have walked into any village and collected folk songs by the dozen, for Engel wrote at a time when folk singing was still a living art. But obviously everyone believed that Britain had no folk songs. Yet all the old people to whom Sharp spoke in the early years of the twentieth century told him that everyone of their kind sang on the way to work, at work, and while returning home in the evenings. 'The evidence is overwhelming,' Sharp wrote,[2] 'that as recently as thirty or forty years ago [i.e. 1867–77] every country village in England was a nest of singing-birds. It seems impossible to believe that this was unknown to the squires or to the clergy. We had rather conclude, I think, that they did know it, but that they failed to appreciate its significance.'

It is also significant that Engel, writing at the time to which Sharp refers, did not use the term 'folk song', which is a German compound. Himself of German extraction, he would not have used the phrase 'national music' if 'folk song' had been in popular usage. The latter term entered the language in 1847, and mainly referred to

---

residence in the small village of Hambridge in Somerset had left him [the writer] in Stygian ignorance of the wealth of art which that village contained.' (*Cecil Sharp*, op. cit., p. 33.)

[1] Reprinted from the *Musical Times* in which it appeared in the monthly numbers from July 1878 to March 1879.

[2] *English Folk Song: Some Conclusions*, by Cecil J. Sharp, rev. M. Karpeles. (London, 1954.)

verse. In the latter years of the nineteenth century, specialists restricted its meaning to 'the songs of the unlettered classes'. Others applied it to all popular songs whatever their origin, thereby spoiling a good precise term, for 'popular song' covered the wider meaning adequately. Engel clearly defined his 'national music' as folk song in the specialist sense. He writes:

'The great majority of the airs printed in Ritson's *English Songs* can evidently not be regarded as national airs in a strict sense of the term, although the tunes may have been for some time in popular favour. The same remark applies to the airs in almost all the English collections of old songs. The difference between a national song (German, Volkslied) and a merely popular song (German, Volksthümliches Lied) is not always distinctly observed by the English musicians.'

It would often be found that the term 'folk song' was applied to songs founded upon folk airs and set to words by ballad-mongers ('Begone, Dull Care', 'The Vicar of Bray'), or to folk songs freely edited by professional musicians ('Polly Oliver'). These, excellent in themselves, were often corrupted in the process of adaptation. 'The Vicar of Bray', for instance, lacks the genuine sparkle of the Morris dance tune 'Country Gardens' from which it derives. As a result of the work of Sharp and others it is possible to compare the authentic folk song with the professionalized version and to see why the edited folk song never penetrated into the villages. The very qualities which the editors removed—irregular rhythm, strange modal cadences and lack of modulations, and unexpected intervals—are the qualities which give English folk song its native charm.

The 'authenticity' of the collected folk song is a vexed question. Critics of the movement in the early 1900s argued that the collectors' work was spurious because the tunes were corrupt: 'decaying survivals of something better' which had, by the oral tradition, been minimized as each generation passed them on to the next. This argument had some justification in regard to the words of the songs. As to the tunes, the best answer was Vaughan Williams's: 'If "Bushes and Briars" is a corruption, what must the original have been like?'

Variants are an essential feature of the evolution of folk song. Vaughan Williams defined folk song in 1912[1] as 'a series of individual variations on a common theme.

[1] *English Folk Songs*, by R. Vaughan Williams (London, 1912).

'A folk song is like a tree, whose stem dates back from immemorial times, but which continually puts out new shoots. . . . There is evidence of the extraordinary accuracy of tradition . . .; on the other hand many folk songs which are collected show evidence of the personal characteristics of their singer. . . . In one aspect the folk song is as old as time itself; in another aspect it is no older than the singer who sang it. The question of antiquity does not seem to me important; *it is the question of the nature of the song which is of interest* [my italics]. . . . The scoffer comes along, and he says "I expect the old chap was having you on. I believe he made it up himself". To which I answer that it is quite possible that to a large extent he did, and that for that reason it is all the more valuable to me. . . . The more I see of folk song the more important I believe the impress of the individual to be.'

Vaughan Williams believed that a stage had been reached when the evolution of folk song by oral transmission was no longer possible. In his 1912 lecture he said:

'We must take the folk songs we have recovered as they now are; we must not venture to alter or "improve" them; as we find them we must keep them. We may have found them at the highest point of their development, or they may have passed their climax and have begun the downward path when they were recovered. That we can never tell. It is on their face value that we must judge them.'

The collectors were fascinated by their discovery that a large group of English folk songs was constructed in the ancient modes. These had been discarded by musicians as archaic when the major/minor system of scales was evolved, yet in the folk songs the modes, far from sounding archaic, had a vitality which attracted and interested the collectors and presented to composers greater melodic possibilities.

Most English folk songs are in the Dorian, Mixolydian, and Aeolian modes. Sharp discovered only one in the Lydian mode, and only about six Phrygian have been discovered.

The modes came easily and naturally to country singers. This spontaneity surprised some of the more scholastic folk-song collectors, one of whom remarked to Vaughan Williams that some notations taken down from a village singer must be wrong because 'nobody's going to tell me that an uneducated villager sings correctly in the Dorian mode when, as often as not, even our trained musicians don't know what the Dorian is'.[1]

[1] *Penguin Book of English Folk Songs*, Ed. R. Vaughan Williams and A. L. Lloyd, 1959.

It is clear that Vaughan Williams sub-consciously also responded to modality and to the sense, in folk song, of a living and flexible tradition. He was deeply impressed because, as he put it in his 1912 lecture, 'folk songs seem to take kindly to the harmony of any period at which a skilled musician may happen to treat them harmonically. Now this is not the case with "composed" music. It would be ridiculous and out of keeping to try and harmonize a melody by Gluck in the style of Richard Strauss; the anachronism would be apparent at once. But in folk song there is no anachronism—it seems to defy the ravages of time.' His view on the accompaniment to a folk song was that 'the harmony should be subsidiary and above all impersonal'.

Vaughan Williams began to collect in earnest on 4 December 1903, three months after John England—wonderfully appropriate name!—the vicar's gardener at Hambridge, had sung 'The Seeds of Love' to Cecil Sharp while mowing the vicarage lawn. The tune in Vaughan Williams's case was the beautiful 'Bushes and Briars', and he found it at Ingrave, near Brentwood, where he had been invited to an old people's tea-party. According to the version recounted in his lecture nine years later, 'after tea we asked if any of them knew any of the old songs, whereupon an old man, a shepherd [Mr. Charles Pottipher] began to sing a song which set all my doubts about folk song at rest'.

Until the discovery of 'Bushes and Briars' Vaughan Williams said that he was 'entirely without first-hand evidence' about folk song—'I knew and loved the few English folk songs which were then available in printed collections, but I only believed in them vaguely . . . my faith was not yet active.' Oddly, although Vaughan Williams had met Sharp in 1900, folk song was not mentioned and when he began collecting in earnest in 1903 and telling his friends about his discoveries, he excluded Sharp 'because I thought he would not be interested'.[1] From 1903 to 1913 he collected over 800 songs and variants. They are listed in full in the hardback edition of this book. But what were the 'doubts' which he had about folk song? His first published article,[2] 'A School of English Music', gives the answer. Answering the question of how to re-awaken English music, he cast doubt on 'the pioneers of the English School' whose

---

[1] 'A Musical Autobiography.'
[2] The Vocalist, Vol. I, No. 1, April 1902, p. 8.

'universal remedy was to be the folk song'. Just because folk song had been exploited on the continent, he wrote,

'it is surely doubtful if any good result will follow the extremely artificial course of setting before a composer music which is entirely foreign to his temperament. . . . A musician who wishes to say anything worth saying *must first of all express himself* [my italics]—in fact his music must be the natural utterance of his own natural emotions. These natural emotions need not necessarily be those of the peasant. . . . English composers do not spring from the peasantry. Indeed, in England there are no true peasantry for them to spring from. Why, then, should an English composer attempt to found his style on the music of a class to which he does not belong, and which itself no longer exists? . . . In former times, musical England came to grief by trying to be foreign; no less surely shall we now fail through trying to be English. It is useless to invent a style and then model individual utterances upon it. The national English style must be modelled on the personal style of English musicians. Until our composers will be content to write the music that they like best, without an ulterior thought, not till then shall we have a true School of English Music.'

These views are not inconsistent with any which he expresses later. They emphasize merely that Vaughan Williams's style, so hard-won, is the man himself. But a further study of folk song, before he became an active collector, helped him to achieve his own salvation. This is made clear by press reports of the Oxford University extension lectures which he gave in the autumn of 1902[1] at Pokesdown Technical School, Bournemouth. Many of the phrases and metaphors are forerunners of more famous versions in *National Music* (1934). There were six lectures in the series under the general title of 'The History of the Folk Song'. The first two dealt with that history; the remainder were:

3. The characteristics of National Song—On the Continent.
4. The characteristics of National Songs in the British Isles.
5. Religious folk songs.
6. The importance of folk song.

The lectures were illustrated by singers, among them the lecturer himself, and instrumentalists. Song, he told his audiences (which, at Bournemouth, grew to a maximum of 112) was the most universal

---

[1] The *Eastern Morning News* of 10 January 1903, speaking of a forthcoming recital by A. Foxton Ferguson, mentions that he will sing three arrangements of folk melodies by R. Vaughan Williams—11 months before R.V.W. first collected a folk song himself.

form of music 'because it is the most direct expression of personal
and intimate emotions.

'It is the natural development of excited speech. I was once at an open-air
service in the Isle of Skye, where a sermon was being preached in Gaelic.
. . . At first the preacher spoke in a rather monotonous voice—a sort of
sing-song—as he had to raise his voice a good deal to make himself heard.
But as he became more and more excited over his discourse his speaking
gradually changed to a sort of irregular chanting on four distinct musical
tones. Here, then, you have the rough beginnings of song—excited speech
gradually becoming distinct musical tone.'

He described folk songs as 'springing up like wild flowers among the
people of a nation. . . . To those of you who say that you like country
tunes but do not care about classical music—whatever that might mean—I
would ask you to remember that there is absolutely no difference between
the two. If a piece of music is good, sincere and beautiful then it does not
matter if it is sung in an out-of-the-way part of Sussex, or Hampshire, or
performed at a Queen's Hall concert; but if it is bad and insincere it does
not matter where it is sung—it is not worthy of your attention'.

The third lecture dealt with the difference in styles and characteristics of Magyar and German music, and included some
Hungarian dances arranged by Francis Korbay among the illustrations. For the more extensive fourth talk the songs were sung by
Lucy Broadwood, who was afterwards presented with a bouquet
'composed chiefly of chrysanthemums, maidenhair fern, etc., with
orange coloured streamers attached'. That this must have been a
highly amusing as well as invigorating talk is clear enough even
from the indirect speech of the local paper's long report—a good
deal fuller and more accurate report than a comparable occasion
would be likely to receive today. Vaughan Williams, at the age of
thirty, was riding the hobby-horses which gave him a good gallop
all his life.

His sympathies were obviously more strongly engaged by English
than by Scottish, Welsh, or Irish songs. He passed over entirely
'those songs which are supposed to be the songs of England—the
songs which sprang up in Elizabethan and Stuart times.

'Those were very fine tunes but he always felt they belonged to the town
rather than to the country. . . . Those tunes which had only begun to be
collected in comparatively late years were what he believed to be the
genuine English folk music—the music which represented the true English
spirit. As would be seen from the examples which were to be sung, they

had nothing to do with that false joviality and glorification of over-eating which was usually supposed to be typical of English music. Indeed he did not suppose that the people who originally sang those songs had much opportunity for over-eating. . . .'

The conclusion of this lecture is worth full quotation because it bears strongly upon the whole ethos of Vaughan Williams's special brand of nationalism which was far from being a chauvinistic insularity:

'It is always asserted that England is an unmusical nation, and I cannot exactly say that the accusation is unjust. I do not mean to say that there is not always a lot of music going on in England; I do not mean to say that there are not a great many people who can sing, compose and play very well up to a point, but that is not enough. When it comes to the subtle point of difference which marks the distinction between the very clever craftsman and the real artist—just that which really displays the musicianship—then in 99 cases out of 100 I think English people fail. On the other hand there can be no doubt, when we look at those English, Scots, Irish and Welsh songs, that there must be a lot of real music hidden somewhere amongst us. I think it has been crushed very largely by the false ideals of English respectable life: by the desire always not to make fools of ourselves, or not to do anything which is out of the way. There was a time in the period of Queen Elizabeth when England was always reckoned a most musical nation, and even since that time occasionally a Purcell, a Parry or an Elgar has come along and broken those cramping bonds, whatever they may be, and has given us some real music. . . . I think we have a lesson to learn from the inventors of those folk songs. Why did the singers and the inventors of folk songs sing them and invent them? It was not because they wanted to produce a novelty; it was not because they wanted to get up an entertainment to pay off the debt on the organ; and neither was it because there was going to be a festival and everybody was going to be there. The reason why those early musicians sang, played, invented and composed was simply and solely because they wanted to; and I think the lesson we can learn from them is that of sincerity. When English musicians learn to do that—to write and play for the sake of the music and for the sake of nothing else, then I think that the music which is latent amongst us will come to the front.'

The fifth lecture, on religious music, was equally indicative of Vaughan Williams's lifelong approach to this subject. It shows the strength of his feelings on the matter and, therefore, why, two years later, he agreed to edit the music for a new hymnal. He reminded his listeners of the powerful links between the folk song and the church, in all countries, exemplified by the Christmas carol. But in England 'publishers of church music are doing their best to supersede them [the genuine carols] by the sentimental effusions of the Barnby school'. If ever, he continued, there was music invented for the people and sung by the people it was found in the congregational hymn tunes.

'The Salvation Army make hymn-singing an important part of their services. Some of those hymns they have borrowed from the Established Church, some they have invented for themselves, and many they have adapted from the popular songs of the moment—keeping, it should be observed, not only the music but also the catch-phrase or characteristic words of the original song.

'The Salvationists were following a great leader, as the Lutheran hymns emanated from three sources: (1) adaptations of melodies from the Roman Church; (2) original tunes; and (3) adaptation of secular folk tunes. The most important chorales from the present point of view are those which were adapted from secular folk songs.'

Vaughan Williams illustrated the origin and development of tunes like 'Innsbruck' and the 'Old Hundredth'. He then returned to the fray:

'In this country the old tunes, which had served our forefathers so well, lasted well into the last century. Then came a change. The village band which, with all its shortcomings, was a definite artistic nucleus in the parish, was superseded by a wheezing harmonium played by an incompetent amateur, or in more ambitious churches a new organ was set up (usually unpaid for) with all the modern devices for the propagation of vicious and mechanical sentiment. The organist had usually developed his technique at the expense of his musicianship, and his taste was formed on the sickly harmonies of Spohr, overlaid with the operatic sensationalism of Gounod; and church hymns had followed suit. Our old psalm tunes were among the best tunes in the world, and even the less excellent ones were absolutely suitable for congregational singing, but in 1861 there appeared a compilation called *Hymns Ancient and Modern* which gave the death-blow to the old system. The original intention of the compilers of these hymns was not wholly bad. Many of the old tunes were preserved, though usually in a mutilated state, and some of the new tunes, such as Wesley's 'Aurelia', were worthy companions to the old tunes. But even in the original edition there appeared a quantity of these exotic and languorous tunes which could be nothing but enervating to those who sang and heard them; and in later editions the element of maudlin sentiment has grown alarmingly until at last the bad has almost driven out the good. National music should represent the people. Will anyone dare to say that the effusions of the Barnby school represent the English people? Hard-working men and women should be given bracing and stimulating music, not the unhealthy outcome of theatrical and hysterical sentiment.'

These opinions were echoed in 1905 by Elgar, whose views did not otherwise often coincide with Vaughan Williams's, when he said in the first of his controversial lectures at Birmingham University: 'What I want to see coming into being is something that shall grow out of our own soil, something broad, noble, chivalrous, healthy and above all an out-of-door sort of spirit. To arrive at this it will be necessary to throw over all imitation.'

The Pokesdown lectures, which were repeated in Gloucester in January and February 1903, ended with 'The Importance of Folk Song'. Vaughan Williams gave four points as justification for his title, of why the folk song was of 'supreme importance' to musicians:

1. Folk songs contained the nucleus of all further development in music;
2. They invariably affected the style of great composers;
3. National music was a sure index to national temperament;
4. Folk songs were supremely beautiful.

'Great composers in all times in the history of music have not disdained to use folk tunes as a means of inspiration. We must not accuse them of stealing, for those great popular tunes are the common property of anybody who by nationality, friendship or analogous feeling finds himself in sympathy with them. . . . It is extraordinarily interesting to see the national temperament running through every form of a nation's art—the national life and the national art growing together. . . .

'I have kept my best reason for the importance of folk song to the last—namely, their own intrinsic beauty. I would not care how many sonatas could be traced to them, or how many great composers had used them if those country tunes were not in themselves superbly beautiful. It is that beauty which has preserved them, which makes them a joy for ever. . . . But there is no doubt that they are hardly sung at all by the people nowadays. They are only to be heard from some oldest inhabitant in an out-of-the-way district. That precious legacy has slipped out of the hands of those whose it was by right and passed into the hands of enthusiastic connoisseurs who collect folk tunes like old china. And just as the grandfather clocks and oak dressers have gone from the country kitchens and now decorate the drawing-room at Chelsea, so now the only place where you can hear a folk song sung is at some *soirée musicale* among the elect of Kensington. The people who originally sang folk songs now sing music-hall songs instead. I do not like music-hall songs very much, but with all their blatant vulgarity they are infinitely superior to the inane rubbish which is sung in the modern drawing-room. . . . Will the people ever come by their own again? Will they ever return to their folk songs waiting for them—as beautiful and new now as they were 60 years ago? The collectors of folk songs differ from the collectors of old china in this—the connoisseurs in china keep the china locked up in their china cupboards when they are at home and when they go away they send it in a tin box to the bank. But the collector of folk songs gives them back again to the world. . . . Will they not, perhaps, once more make their way back to the mouths of the people?'

How, one wonders, did all that affect the earnest seekers after knowledge in Bournemouth and Gloucester who, after locking their china cupboards, had gone out into the autumn night to hear this impressive young man, who had not yet collected a single folk song, speaking with such humour and erudition? Today there are still divided opinions about the effectiveness of the folk-song revival. Yet the importance of these talks by Vaughan Williams can be seen to be that they represent the embryonic composer's attitude to folk song. The vital thing to him was always the beauty of the tunes, not their sociological importance. A phrase from one of his early writings again emphasizes folk song's importance to his own art: 'How rich in suggestion the folk song may be to a well-equipped and sympathetic musician.'

There is no doubt that what moved him to undertake the arduous work of collecting was his horrified realization that these beautiful tunes were in danger of disappearing from human knowledge. He was trained as an historian, and possibly a sense of the irrecoverable quality of much that is past, added to his musical interest, drove him on. He was disturbed, as Sharp had been, to realize that people living among folk singers were oblivious of their existence. His own experience at Ingrave was a case in point. In a letter to the *Morning Post*, written on 4 October 1904, he pointed out that he was grateful to the Misses Heatley of Ingrave Rectory for arranging for singers to meet him there so that he could note down the songs, but, he added, 'it is interesting to notice that although these ladies have lived at Ingrave for several years and are intimate with the village people, they had no idea that the folk song still survived there until I suggested the possibility to them some time ago'. He had ten months previously written to the same paper urging county councils to act upon Cecil Sharp's suggestion that they should organize the collection of songs: 'Whatever is done must be done quickly. Every day some old village singer dies, and with him there probably die half a dozen beautiful melodies which are lost to the world for ever; if we would preserve what still remains we must set about it at once.' That was written on 1 December 1903. True to his precepts, at Ingrave three days later he made his first active foray into the task of collecting. On 13 December he wrote again to the *Morning Post* urging that the Folk Song Society should cease merely to theorize, and should undertake the central task of guiding folk-song collection.

This, then, was the spirit in which Vaughan Williams approached the folk-song revival. Historically it happened at exactly the right moment for his particular musical make-up. Few of his contemporaries could at any time have rivalled him in knowledge and experience of what was going on in the world of music of his day. At no time did he advocate the kind of insular prejudice against foreign influences of which the nationalist school is often accused. His concern was that English composers should be English composers and not imitation-foreign; and he held as a basic conviction that 'the composer who tries to be cosmopolitan from the outset will fail, not only with the world at large, but with his own people as well'.[1] In other words a composer must be a good citizen of his own land before he could be a citizen of the world. His intense admiration for Bach stemmed not only from the music itself but from Bach's national internationalism. . . . 'True, he studied eagerly all the music of foreign composers that came his way in order to improve his craft. [As did Vaughan Williams.] But is not the work of Bach built up on two great foundations, the organ music of his Teutonic predecessors and the popular hymn tunes of his own people?' He himself had the youthful percipience to realize that he had nowhere to turn but to his native soil if he wished to develop as a composer. Nationalism was in the air, and this was stronger for him than any general European influence. When he went to Max Bruch in Berlin it was, one imagines, with little hope that his own art would benefit more than by some extra technical gloss. In fact what, as he confessed, he did gain was confidence. Although he fell under Wagner's spell he never imagined that his own path branched from Bayreuth. He at once recognized Elgar's greatness but also that Elgar was a figure at the close of an epoch of European music as well as the herald of a

[1] *National Music and Other Essays.*

new English dawn. He was painfully conscious of the illiteracy of much of English musical life, of its sham pretensions, its worship of big names, its lack of established opera houses, its lack of permanent, fully-rehearsed professional symphony orchestras. The early 1900s were a hard and soul-destroying time for a young composer to try to find a tradition which he knew barely existed but to which he knew he was akin. In retrospect we can see that he did not 'discover' folk song, nor a tradition. He discovered himself.

He defined his aims in 1912 in his famous article 'Who Wants the English Composer?'[1] This was one of his major declarations on his own nationalist standpoint:

'Art, like charity, should begin at home. If it is to be of any value it must grow out of the very life of himself, [the artist] the community in which he lives, the nation to which he belongs.' Music ('the subtlest, most sensitive and purest means of self-expression') alone among the arts, he wrote, was detached by Englishmen from everyday life. 'The English composer is not and for many generations will not be anything like so good as the Great Masters, nor can he do such wonderful things as Strauss and Debussy. But is he for this reason of no value to the community? Is it not possible that he has something to say to his own countrymen that no one of any other age and any other country can say? . . . Have we not all about us forms of musical expression which we can purify and raise to the level of great art? For instance, the lilt of the chorus at a music-hall joining in a popular song, the children dancing to a barrel-organ, the rousing fervour of a Salvation Army hymn, St. Paul's and a great choir singing in one of its festivals, the Welshmen striking up one of their own hymns whenever they win a goal at the international football match, the cries of the street pedlars, the factory girls singing their sentimental songs. Have all these nothing to say to us? Have we not in England occasions crying out for music? . . . We must cultivate a sense of musical citizenship; why should not the musician be the servant of the State and build national monuments like the painter, the writer or the architect? . . . The composer must not shut himself up and think about art, he must live with his fellows and make his art an expression of the whole life of the community.'

One wonders what the other English musicians of the day made of this dangerously revolutionary doctrine, especially those who took the phrase 'the servant of the State' too literally. At the time he was writing, Vaughan Williams was already putting his beliefs into practice in the *London Symphony*, in *Hugh the Drover* and in short

[1] *R.C.M. Magazine*, Vol. IX, No. 1.

works like 'O Praise the Lord', written for a St. Paul's festival. He believed that a composer should reflect the life of his time from the fullness of his heart: a willing servant.

Vaughan Williams did not believe that by using folk song composers could invent a national music ready made—'we simply were fascinated by the tunes and wanted other people to be fascinated too. . . . We are now taking folk song for granted, whether we like it or not, as part of our natural surroundings.' These were the tenets of Vaughan Williams's musical faith. Paradoxically—for his whole career is one of paradox—he exemplified them yet he contradicted them. His nationalism was avowedly conscious; never was it self-conscious. There never was a less typical 'typical Englishman'. It has been suggested[1] that by consciously assuming a nationalist mantle he restricted the development of his own musical personality. There is no evidence to support this view. Through a conscious nationalism he discovered a means of self-expression. Upon a foundation of folk song and other equally important influences—Purcell, the Tudor composers, and the hymn-tunes—he erected his own personal style which was his natural voice. If his critics and those out of sympathy with his work find this a restricted, narrow expressiveness, nothing can be done to alter the fact. To others, the extreme individuality of the voice, its markedly personal idiosyncrasy, is its supreme and lasting attraction. If it is a 'limitation' to seek to be a musical servant of one's own country, then that was a limitation which Vaughan Williams not only accepted but invited; he would seek to be judged solely on whether he had succeeded in this aim in regard to his fellow-countrymen. His own words on this subject are again the most eloquent advocacy for his work:

'Every composer cannot expect to have a world-wide message, but he may reasonably expect to have a special message for his own people, and many young composers make the mistake of imagining they can be universal without at first having been local. Is it not reasonable to suppose that those who share our life, our history, our customs, our climate, even our food, should have some secret to impart to us which the foreign composer, though he be perhaps more imaginative, more powerful, more technically equipped, is not able to give us? This is the secret of the national composer. . . . But is he prepared with his secret? Must he not limit himself to a certain extent so as to give his message its full force? . . . What a composer has to do is to find out the real message he has to convey to

---

[1] *Musical Opinion*, Vol. 78, No. 932, May 1955.

the community and say it directly and without equivocation. . . . If the roots of your art are firmly planted in your own soil and that soil has anything individual to give you, you may still gain the whole world and not lose your own souls.'[1]

It is clear, then, that Vaughan Williams regarded his gift as something he should place at the disposal of his fellow countrymen, yet on his own uncompromising terms. His romantic nature was the paradox here. He regarded himself as a craftsman doing a job, but a job which could only be impelled by some undefinable impetus within himself. He wrote of artists experiencing moments 'when we want to get outside the limitations of ordinary life, when we see dimly a vision of something beyond'. He told a friend in his last years: 'I can only write music when something happens in here,' tapping his heart. But he well knew that 'the spark from heaven' fell only to those who sat, pen in hand, working for it. 'The origin of inspiration and its final fruition should be one and the same thing,' he said; in between, he knew, was where craftsmanship was essential —in the hours of what he called 'manual labour'. To a gushing fellow-composer who said that he had written his most popular work 'on his knees', he gave the devastating reply: 'I wrote *Sancta, Civitas* sitting on my bum.'

It cannot too strongly be re-emphasized that Vaughan Williams never deliberately disregarded 'influences' in the music of his time. He disingenuously admitted 'cribbing' from other composers. He did not set himself out to adventure along totally new paths, for he was one of those composers who, by using the accepted language of their own day and of the past, showed in a fresh light things one had thought to be already fully illumined. His new paths were adventures of the mind, not revolutions of technique. His interest in and use of the ecclesiastical and folk modes has led to charges of deliberate 'archaism'. This he himself contemptuously rejected as a 'trade' protest by vested interests. 'It seems to me,' he wrote in his *Musical Autobiography*, 'that so long as good music is made it matters very little how it is made or who makes it. If a composer can, by tapping the sources hidden in folk song, make beautiful music, he will be disloyal to his art if he does not make full use of such an avenue of beauty.' Again, 'Why should music be "original"? The object of art is to stretch out to the ultimate realities through the medium of beauty. The duty of the composer is to find the *mot*

[1] *National Music and Other Essays*, pp. 9 and 11.

juste. It does not matter if this word has been said a thousand times before as long as it is the right thing to say at that moment. . . .'

Humility is a word often misapplied to Vaughan Williams. In the above passage we see the true humility of an artist relating himself to the whole perspective of his art's development; but the proper word is pride, for here is a genuine pride in the intention which underlay his whole creative outlook: to speak his mind in his own way. He knew what folk song had done for him and he lived to see a whole new varied and vital group of composers writing in many styles. How fortunate that the greatest figure to emerge from our nationalist movement was a man of unpredictable, non-conforming, creative integrity, for when all is said about traditions and national styles, what matters in the end is the personality of the artist.

CHAPTER FOUR

1895–1906

Principal Works

BUCOLIC SUITE . IN THE FEN COUNTRY
HEROIC ELEGY AND TRIUMPHAL EPILOGUE
LINDEN LEA . THE HOUSE OF LIFE
WILLOW-WOOD . SONGS OF TRAVEL
NORFOLK RHAPSODIES . THE ENGLISH HYMNAL

WHEN Vaughan Williams re-entered the Royal College of Music in 1895 he was in many respects a more self-confident man as a result of his Cambridge days. He was determined to widen his training as a musician, no doubt influenced by Stanford, who never made the mistake of thinking that composers could be made by theory alone. He therefore became organist at St. Barnabas, South Lambeth—'I never could play the organ,' he wrote later, 'but this appointment gave me an insight into good and bad church music which stood me in good stead later on' (when he came to edit the *English Hymnal* and *Songs of Praise*). Not many other methods of gaining practical musical experience were open to young men in those days unless, like Elgar and Holst, they played in an orchestra. Vaughan Williams had to train the choir, give organ recitals and accompany the services. He held this post for two years, without any particular delight in the performance of his duties. He lived near his church at 2 St. Barnabas Villas, South Lambeth Road, and was paid £50 a year. When he left, in October 1897, he offered to recommend Holst for the post in 'this damned place'. Holst had helped him out with choir practice occasionally, but the organistship went to John Ireland. Vaughan Williams's letters to Holst describing the chores of taking the morning service (printed in *Heirs and Rebels*[1]) are amusing, but they also disclose a weariness of

[1] Letters of Ralph Vaughan Williams and Gustav Holst to each other and occasional writings on music, ed. Ursula Vaughan Williams and Imogen Holst (London, 1959).

spirit in what must have been an enervating task. He founded a choral society—'whenever it intermittently exists'—and an orchestral society, and they managed once to perform a Bach cantata. He certainly did not make this foray into ecclesiastical life because of any deep religious feelings. At Cambridge he had had a reputation as a 'most determined atheist', according to Bertrand Russell,[1] who was at Trinity at the same time, and he was noted for having walked into Hall one evening saying in a loud voice, 'Who believes in God nowadays, I should like to know?' It is important to realize, and it cannot be over-emphasized, that the religion of Vaughan Williams's life was music. He was that extremely English product the natural nonconformist with a conservative regard for the best tradition. In the music of the Church he recognized the only continuous musical tradition in English life. When he was at Cambridge he would go to Ely Cathedral in time for morning service and sit at the back of that beautiful church listening to the chants echoing among the lofty recesses of the roof. The marvellous prose of the Authorized Version, the fundamental simplicities of *The Pilgrim's Progress*—these were necessary food for his artistic spirit, and he himself responded to their proclamation of the ultimate mysteries as artists have done throughout the ages. There is no lack of sincerity in his religious music, almost all of which is strongly affirmative. The atheism of the undergraduate was replaced by a more mature Christian agnosticism, as Sir Steuart Wilson has brilliantly described it. He had a deep-rooted humanitarian faith: beyond that, he would not go.

Amid the organ-playing and the lessons with Stanford, composition continued. Holst left the R.C.M. in 1896 and for the next seven years earned a livelihood as a trombonist in theatre orchestras, in pantomime, at the seaside in the White Viennese Band conducted by Stanislas Wurm ('Wurming' was the nickname given by R.V.W. and Holst to this activity) and later in the Carl Rosa Opera Company and Scottish Orchestras. Vaughan Williams and he corresponded, though few letters survive. One from Vaughan Williams, written from Brighton in the summer of 1897, after he left the R.C.M., mentions that he had been 'scoring my Mass all day. I am approaching the end of the Credo'. This work was his exercise for his Cambridge doctorate. This same letter also extols *Walküre* played by a brass band. Truer Wagnerian experiences had awaited him on a visit to Bayreuth in 1896. No young musician of that day could

[1] Letter to the author.

escape the tremendous influence of Wagner, and with Parry's encouragement both Holst and Vaughan Williams were in the toils. By this time, too, Vaughan Williams was approaching the major personal step of marriage to Adeline Fisher. He felt he needed some study and experience abroad and his bride-to-be, understanding the compulsive claims of music, willingly agreed that their honeymoon should be spent in Berlin, which was the only place outside Bayreuth where *The Ring* was at that time performed without cuts.

Stanford, thinking that Vaughan Williams was already too Teutonic, wanted him to go to Italy to hear opera at La Scala, Milan. But once again his pupil defied him, and, armed with an introduction to Heinrich von Herzogenberg, who had just returned to the professorship of theory and composition at the Hochschule in Berlin, he went to Germany after his marriage on 9 October 1897, three days before his twenty-fifth birthday.

Herzogenberg looked through some of the Englishman's work, which reminded him, he said, of Mascagni. We cannot know which long-forgotten scores Vaughan Williams showed the professor, but Herzogenberg's judgement showed a striking perception of a quality in Vaughan Williams's music which was to manifest itself later by occasional similarities to Puccini. He advised him to study with Max Bruch. It cannot be said that any great success attended the results of this advice but, as Vaughan Williams said many years later, 'it is difficult to say what it is one learns from a teacher. I only know that I worked hard and enthusiastically, and that Max Bruch encouraged me, and I had never had much encouragement before.' Bruch was interested in folk song and he at once seized, like Stanford, upon Vaughan Williams's fondness for the flattened seventh. He also warned his young pupil against writing music for the eye as opposed to the ear. As far as results were concerned this warning was well heeded, but Vaughan Williams interpreted it also as a criticism of his habitual use of the pianoforte when composing. He was much relieved years later to discover that Ravel insisted upon use of a pianoforte—'otherwise you cannot invent new harmonies'.

In Berlin the Vaughan Williamses took every opportunity of hearing performances, especially at the State Opera. They heard Bach cantatas at the Singakademie, quartets played by the Joachim and Halir teams, and the Brahms Double Concerto played at the Hochschule as a pianoforte trio by Joachim, Hausmann, and Karl Barth —a strange experience which Vaughan Williams found memorable.

The Staatsoper at this time had achieved high standards of performance under the management of Count Bolke von Hochberg and with Richard Strauss and Felix Weingartner among the conductors. Lortzing's *Undine* and Meyerbeer's *Robert Le Diable* were among the works Vaughan Williams heard. He retained an admiration for Meyerbeer throughout his life. He published an arrangement of the 'Blessing of the Swords' from *Les Huguenots*, and surprised his pupil Michael Mullinar on one occasion by asking him to play through a pianoforte transcription of the opera, to which he listened with evident enjoyment.

After his marriage on his return from Berlin, Vaughan Williams lived in rooms at 16 North Street, Westminster, and in July 1898 moved to 5 Cowley Street. Early in 1899 he and Adeline bought 10 Barton Street, their home for the next seven years. Thus throughout his student days and in the early years of his married life, while he was forging his musical character, the sights and sounds of London, and especially of Westminster, formed the daily background and accompaniment to his existence.

The years from 1898 to 1902, when performances of his works began to attract notice and his writings spread his name and fame, are years not fully documented but nevertheless full and important. The number of compositions in these four years is sufficient evidence of the existence of a strong creative urge. Though little of the work has been allowed to survive, it was copious and earnest. During this period his formal musical education may be said to have ended when he passed the examination for Doctor of Music at Cambridge in 1899, although for some reason he did not 'take' the degree until 23 May 1901. He thus became Dr. Vaughan Williams, the title which he proudly carried to the end of his days and which he refused to exchange for any other.

These turn-of-the-century years were full for him in other respects than the labours in his own study. This was a time of rebirth in English music and of new ideas penetrating our musical life from abroad. There was much to hear, read, and absorb. It is true that Vaughan Williams never needed to work for his living, but his possession of personal means never deflected him from his routine of eight hours' work a day on his own compositions. It fortunately enabled him to travel about the country to hear new works wherever they were played. This was the time when the music of Richard Strauss invaded concert programmes. The names of

Debussy and Sibelius were beginning to be known. Tchaikovsky's music was in the first flush of its never-receding popularity. Most important for an Englishman was the emergence of Edward Elgar as a major figure, from 1899 onwards. Vaughan Williams attended one of the early performances of the 'Enigma' Variations, which had first been played on 19 June 1899. He had gone to the concert to hear another work in the same programme, but the Variations' masterly originality swept all else from his mind. Here, at last, was an English masterpiece. He was at the Birmingham Festival in 1900 when *The Dream of Gerontius* received on 3 October its first and nearly disastrous performance. Vaughan Williams left the performance in the company of Mrs. Stanford[1] and recalled her saying: 'Is not that a fine work?'

There was also, at this time, the absorption in folk song; but two other equally potent formative influences were at work on Vaughan Williams. The bicentenary in 1895 of Henry Purcell's death coincided with the renewed interest of scholarship in his achievements. Pupils of the Royal College of Music performed *Dido and Aeneas* at the Lyceum Theatre on 20 November 1895. Vaughan Williams sang in the chorus and Agnes Nicholls made her stage debut as Dido. Possibly he was present the next day at Westminster Abbey when seven Purcell anthems were sung, or at Queen's Hall on that same evening when the Philharmonic Society revived the *Ode on St. Cecilia's Day* of 1692. At the Birmingham Festival of 1897 *King Arthur* was performed. The Purcell Society, founded in 1876 by a committee of the most respectable names in English music, with the aim of publishing his music, had languished until 1887 when the joint enterprise of W. H. Cummings and W. Barclay Squire had revivified it and inaugurated a steady flow of volumes of his music, thus for the first time making it generally available for study. Cummings himself edited the first volume—the *Yorkshire Feast Song*—which appeared in 1878. Other editors were Gore Ouseley, J. A. Fuller Maitland, Squire, E. J. Hopkins, Stanford, Sir Frederick Bridge, and G. E. P. Arkwright. It was therefore a compliment to the young Vaughan Williams that he should have been invited by the Society to edit the Welcome Odes. This he did in two parts, the first published in 1905 and the second in 1910. That he was at work on the first volume in 1900–1 is evident from a

[1] Stanford was not knighted until 1901. Throughout this book I have referred to people by the titles they held in the year about which I am writing.

letter to Holst, undated, but—to judge from the mention of the *Bucolic Suite*—written either at the end of 1900 or the end of 1901, depending on whether by 'finished' he means the original version or the revision: 'I've finished my "Bucolic Suite" and written a song and made a rough copy of the score of the Trombone thing and finished a volume of Purcell and am starting another thing called a "Sentimental Romance".'

His work on the Purcell odes earned him respect among scholars and critics and led to Fuller Maitland's request for him to contribute articles on 'Conducting' and 'Fugue' to the 1904 edition of Grove's *Dictionary of Music and Musicians*. In this latter connection, too, the friendship of Nicholas Gatty, who assisted Fuller Maitland in the editorship of the second edition, played its part.

The other major influence upon an impressionable young English musician at this date was the parallel revival of interest in William Byrd. The Mass for five voices was published in 1899, in a new edition, by Breitkopf and Härtel. The Mass for four voices had been published in 1890 by Novello and that for three appeared from R. & T. Washbourne in 1901. Four movements from the five-part Mass were performed at the 1900 Birmingham Festival, where they would certainly have been heard by those who had travelled to hear Elgar's *The Dream of Gerontius*.

Then there was the growing friendship with Holst. The surviving letters from 1897 onwards indicate their close musical unison and their mutual encouragement. A letter of late 1897 or early 1898 from Vaughan Williams states: 'Did I tell you that I was setting "The Garden of Proserpine" to music for chorus & orchestra with lots of trombones and things—I've just finished the first sketch—a sort of 6 lined affair most of it?"

Readers of *Heirs and Rebels* will know the fascination of the exchange of letters between these twin souls who yet were so different in background, outlook and, fundamentally, in their music. There is a strong impression of the much greater innate self-confidence of Vaughan Williams, despite his occasional questionings and fears. He, one knows, felt that each man must work out his own salvation and steadily he was doing so. Holst, on the other hand, was more deeply involved with the whole problem of music, not necessarily his own alone. It is tantalizing to think that letters in which perhaps they expressed views on works they had just heard for the first time —such as the *Enigma Variations*—are lost. Nevertheless what remains is a sobering commentary on the nakedness with which the young English composer of the early twentieth century had to face the world. In 1901 both young men were operatically minded. Vaughan Williams's sketch-books of this period contain fragmentary ideas for an opera called *Belshazzar* of which a libretto was completed many years later. He also toyed with the idea of an opera founded on *The Scholar Gipsy*.

The libretti of operas was a subject which was naturally occupying a large place in Vaughan Williams's mind and he gave expression to his views in two articles on 'The Words of Wagner's Music Dramas' which he contributed to the musical magazine *The Vocalist*, founded in April 1902. These articles appeared in the June and August numbers. Once again it is stimulating to quote from them not so much for their intrinsic merit as for the light they shed on the embryonic composer and for the evidence of his whole-hearted devotion to the single ideal—Music. He rejected the then still fashionable advocacy of Wagner as both poet and musician:

'He does not dabble in two arts, but he is the exponent of a single art—and that is the Musical Drama. When we feel that it is Wagner's music which we care for—that without the music there is nothing—we have arrived at the root of the matter. . . . The grand opera is a play which should be spoken and is sung; the musical drama is a play regarded entirely through the medium of music. . . . The words are an absolutely necessary part of Wagner's scheme, nevertheless their position in that scheme is quite subordinate.

'The duty of the words is to help the music. Where the music needs no help it would be most presumptuous of the words to offer their well-meant but clumsy assistance.'

He then gave examples of the orchestra's skill in acting as a pointer, in other words the effectiveness of *leitmotif*. Here there is a significant personal detail when, in discussing music's power of calling up 'a whole train of memories, old and forgotten moods and frames of mind', he mentions particularly 'the low notes of a viola'. These were, indeed, to be a *leitmotif* throughout Vaughan Williams's own music.

'The one thing that is not wanted for a musical drama is "musical verse". A decorative scheme of artificial metres and rhymes makes the most unsuitable word-book imaginable. . . . Contemptible as nearly all librettos are, their real defect lies in their utter unsuitability for musical treatment, both in subject and in style. The reason of this failure is that librettists, good and bad, have always regarded the opera from the standpoint of the spoken play; when they found that a good play was unsuitable they merely substituted a bad one. . . . Who, then, is to write the words of a musical drama? . . . There is only one man . . . and that man is the composer of the music, for the drama must generate in the music.'

When he came to compose operas, Vaughan Williams set other men's words, although in three cases he collated them. He never altered his view that words were important only as adjuncts to the music, helping on the plot or stating a fact. But, as will be seen, there is evidence that, in *Riders to the Sea*, he had profited from Debussy's example in *Pelléas et Mélisande* where words and music are fused to a degree never approached even by Wagner.

'I rather think you know more music than I do, anyhow I am sure I don't know enough about Beethoven's sonatas or Schubert's songs and heaps of other things.' So Holst wrote to Vaughan Williams in 1903. It is clear from his *Vocalist* articles in 1902 that Vaughan Williams at twenty-nine had studied and read music with thoroughness and application, as well as having heard an immense amount. Though his own composition was still at an indeterminate stage, his attitude to the art of composition was fixed, and he deviated from it hardly at all for the rest of his life. In a pungent article called 'Good Taste' (*The Vocalist*, May 1902) he wrote that 'many a young composer has stifled his natural impulses in the desire to be musicianly'. This wise head on young shoulders instinctively knew that a musician could only be himself, and this sympathy with a creator's aims is shown in every sentence of these articles when, for a brief time, he turned critic. Their interest now is historical. It is difficult to think oneself back to the days of a Brahms clique and a Tchaikovsky clique. Yet Vaughan Williams put a finger unerringly on these composers' weaknesses:

'Never a stroke fails; every emotion which he [Tchaikovsky] feels he translates into music with the readiness of a true Russian linguist. And herein lies his weakness, that the expression is often too intense for the emotion behind it; the very fact that expression comes so easily to him is apt to make him careless as to whether his idea is worth expressing. . . . If Tchaikovsky's fault is insincerity and glibness, Brahms's is certainly a certain long-windedness and laboriousness which often verges on the dull. . . . Is not Brahms's failure (when he does fail) owing to the immense heights which he set himself to scale? Is not Tchaikovsky's success largely due to the easiness of the task which he undertakes?'

But the most significant of these early writings from a biographical viewpoint is that on Palestrina and Beethoven (*Vocalist*, May 1902). He seeks to answer the question 'Is Palestrina unemotional and if he is not emotional is Beethoven also unemotional?' and in so doing answers much about himself:

'What are the chief reasons why Palestrina and his contemporaries should be considered "unemotional"? One reason may be that they represent a calm mood; this is perfectly true, but it is not hard to find instances of music which represents the composer in a *calm mood*, and yet has a highly emotional effect on the hearer. . . . It is a great mistake to suppose, as many people do, that music is a sort of phonograph into which the composer speaks his emotions and that these are in turn reproduced in the hearer. . . . There is but one really musical emotion, and it is produced by the music composed, and not by the agency which composed the music. . . . The composer's intention can only affect the listener by the beauty of the music which is the result of such intention; the function of music is to be beautiful and nothing less—it cannot be more. . . . Therefore we see that the music of Palestrina is emotional, and that of Beethoven is also emotional; and that, to the hearer, the emotion produced by the music of each is the same, namely that which arises from pure delight in beauty; that is the only true musical emotion. The feelings which lead different people to write music may be as the stars in number, but the artist, like the alchemist, can take every feeling, calm or wild, happy or miserable, and turn it into the precious metal of music. We are not called on to peep into the mysteries of the laboratory; it is enough for us to delight in the lustre of pure gold.'

This was Vaughan Williams's artistic credo; he never recanted.

Some of the first performances of Vaughan Williams's music outside Cambridge and the R.C.M. were at Hooton Roberts, near Rotherham, Yorkshire, where he and Adeline stayed with Nicholas, Ivor, and René Gatty. A madrigal 'Rise early Sun', was included in a concert of the Hooton Roberts Choral Society in 1899, and it is very likely that the performance there on 4 September 1902, of 'Linden Lea' was the first. Vaughan Williams liked to try out his 'new tunes' among friends or in congenial surroundings.

With 1901 came his first appearances before a wider public as a composer. On 5 March of that year his *Heroic Elegy and Triumphal Epilogue* was played at a R.C.M. concert. A month later, on 4 April, the Serenade was performed at Bournemouth under Dan Godfrey. At the last of George A. Clinton's ninth series of Chamber Concerts the Quintet in D major for wind, strings, and pianoforte was played in the small hall of Queen's Hall. The *Musical Times* noted 'considerable originality of conception'.

The next year, 1902, was still more productive. The *Bucolic Suite* was played at Bournemouth, again under Godfrey, on 10 March. Godfrey also performed Holst's *Cotswold Symphony* in this year. But Vaughan Williams's major advance in 1902 was as a song-writer. One of the earliest, if not the earliest, London performances of his vocal work was on 14 May 1902, at the St. James's Hall, when his part-song 'Rest', to Christina Rossetti's words, was sung by the Magpie Madrigal Society. The 'Magpies' are mentioned in 1901 in a letter to Holst in which Vaughan Williams praises his friend's 'Ave Maria' for its beauty and mentions that he has sent it to a cousin of his who sang in the 'Magpies'. This was Diana Massingberd. The Society's membership, drawn from what we should now call the 'top people', included Mr. & Mrs. Alfred Lyttelton, R. A. Streatfeild, Lady Mary Lygon,[1] Herbert Gladstone, the Scott-Gattys, the Countess of Cavan, members of the Stuart-Wortley family, C. L. Graves, and Lady Susan Gilmour. Their programmes were admirable. Madrigals by de Wert, di Lasso, Wilbye, Sweelinck, Parry, and Stanford were varied by pianoforte solos by an artist such as Leonard Borwick and songs by J. Campbell McInnes, who was then coming to the fore. Their conductor was Lionel Benson and their accompanist was C. A. Lidgey. 'Rest' was repeated at another Magpie concert on 4 June, when *The Times* found it 'refined and musicianly'.

In April 1902 the first number of *The Vocalist* appeared. With the renewed interest in the development of English song which stemmed from Parry's and Stanford's example, the time was obviously ripe for a journal which dealt exclusively with singing and which discussed and published new songs. The principal feature of the first issue was a biography and portrait of Noel Johnson, 'the young composer whose songs have been so well received of late'. A new song, 'Roses and Lilies', by Johnson was included. There was an article on Sullivan's *The Golden Legend*, criticisms of London and provincial concerts, a treatise on Handel's 'I know that my Redeemer

---

[1] Later Lady Mary Trefusis. It was her voyage to Australia which is immortalized in the 13th of Elgar's 'Enigma' Variations. While she was in Australia she met Cecil Sharp and began her lifelong interest in folk song.

Liveth', Vaughan Williams's article, quoted in Chapter Three, 'A School of English Music', and three other songs, by Gounod, George S. Aspinall, and Vaughan Williams. It was because of the song by the last-named that the first issue of *The Vocalist* has its place in English musical history. The song was 'Linden Lea'.

'The song,' the editor wrote in his introductory message, 'came to our notice on the strong recommendation of Professor Stanford, whose pupil the composer was at the Royal College of Music.' Thus began the career of its composer's most famous song, which earned him more money than anything else he wrote and which retains its freshness even after over half a century's service as a regular test-piece in competitive festivals throughout the land. The first London performance, as far as can be discovered, was on Tuesday, 2 December 1902, at the St. James's Hall, by Frederick Keel (baritone) accompanied by C. A. Lidgey.

The second and third issues of *The Vocalist* included respectively the songs 'Blackmwore by the Stour' and 'Whither must I wander?' The latter was written before the rest of the *Songs of Travel*. Both songs were given in London for the first time on Thursday, 27 November 1902, by Campbell McInnes, accompanied by C. A. Lidgey, at St. James's Hall. Chief press interest in the recital was centred on Lidgey's song-cycle *A Lover's Moods*, which was receiving its first performance, but the *Daily Telegraph* found 'Whither must I wander?' a 'thoughtful setting' and the periodical the *Guardian* thought 'Blackmwore' was 'deliciously quaint'. McInnes, Francis Harford, and Plunket Greene were at this time bringing forward new English songs at their recitals. Stanford, William Y. Hurlstone, Alan Gray, Ernest Walker, and Richard Walthew were among the names which began to appear in these programmes. Harford, accompanied by Vaughan Williams's friend, Evlyn Howard-Jones,[1] the pianist, introduced Vaughan Williams's setting of 'Tears, Idle Tears' on 5 February 1903. The critics were in many minds about this song. *The Times* held it to be 'One of the most beautiful settings in existence of Tennyson's splendid lyric. The musical material is of the most beautiful and striking quality, and the accentuation of the words is so just as to bring out all their meaning. It were well if some of the authors of the group of seven songs that came in the

---

[1] He was a College friend of both Holst and R.V.W. A letter in 1897 quoted on p. 2 of *Heirs and Rebels* refers to 'H.J.' going abroad. This is annotated as a reference to H. J. Wood but Howard-Jones is the more likely to be correct.

later part of the programme would take example by this beautiful work of art. . . .'

The *Globe*, too, found it 'a really fine song', but other writers, notably in the *Daily News* and the *Westminster Gazette*, found no melody in the vocal part.

McInnes again sang 'Whither must I wander?' on 8 February at a Sunday afternoon Queen's Hall concert conducted by Henry J. Wood. Two other February performances were of the Quintet for pianoforte, violin, clarinet, horn, and cello, in D major, at the Oxford University Musical Club on 17 February, and two nights later at the Oxford and Cambridge Musical Club. On 10 March, at the St. James's Hall, Harford again introduced new songs by Cecil Forsyth, Nicholas Gatty, Graham Peel, H. F. Birch Reynardson and Vaughan Williams. The last-named's offering was 'Silent Noon' which he allowed to be detached from the Rossetti cycle, *The House of Life*, on which he was at work at this time. Its first performance was interrupted during the first verse by the noise of the muffin-bell outside the hall and was re-started. Despite this interruption of his concentration, *The Times*'s critic noted 'passages of sheer beauty'. This song was a prelude to more Rossetti-Vaughan Williams at a Broadwood Concert in the St. James's Hall on 12 March 1903, when Campbell McInnes and Howard-Jones gave the first performance in a pianoforte version of the cantata *Willow-Wood*. *The Times* was again impressed, but noted 'passages where the music seems almost turgid, while its complexities and its breadth of colour seem to demand an orchestral medium'—advice which had been anticipated. The *Guardian* also felt the need of an orchestra, finding that the composer 'was struggling with a somewhat intractable medium. . . . The passionate climax at the end of the second sonnet is very finely conceived, and the subdued droning chant, to which the Song of Love . . . is set, has an original and strangely weird effect'. The critic who remarked that the work 'is of a very lugubrious tendency' was right. But Vaughan Williams's early Swinburne-Rossetti phase can be attributed to something beside the natural romanticism of the age twenty-five to thirty, and that is a wish to enlarge the scope of English song by following Parry's example and evoking the atmosphere and re-composing the verbal rhythms of a poem as well as merely setting it to music. He found a metrical freedom in their verse which he eventually found fully in Whitman.

It is worth mentioning these early performances in some detail, not only as historical facts which should be recorded, but because they discount the old theory that Vaughan Williams was practically unknown until after his folk-song collecting had begun. It is also right that there should be a record of the amount of encouragement which concert organizers gave to the younger school of English composers, much more than is often suggested. The legend of a hearing being refused to them is just not true. In these early days one notices, too, Vaughan Williams's characteristic delight in providing music for all sorts of occasions. For instance, the Rossetti setting 'Boy Johnny' was sung in Oxford in Commemoration Week of 1902, before its publication in *The Vocalist* jointly with 'If I were a Queen', which appears first to have been sung by A. Foxton Ferguson at Exeter on 16 April 1903. The Rossetti part-song 'Sound Sleep', which soon won favour, was written especially for the East Lincolnshire Musical Competitions at Spilsby in April 1903. These were run by Margaret Massingberd, wife of Vaughan Williams's cousin Stephen, of Gunby Hall. Perhaps it was during his stay at Gunby on this occasion that he conceived the idea of an orchestral impression of the Fen Country, on which he worked during 1903–4.

The Exeter concert mentioned above also included his arrangements of two folk songs, 'Departure' and 'Cousin Michael', a further reminder of his practical interest in folk song before he became an active collector. His arrangement of an old German Volkslied, 'Entlaubet ist der Walde', had been sung by Campbell McInnes in November 1902, and 'Blackmwore' had already been described by *The Times* as the 'cleverest imitation of a genuine folk song'. There was awareness in all the many columns devoted to music in all journals and in newspapers, provincial as well as national, of the new spirit in English music. A writer in *The Strad* of 28 March 1903, wisely deploring proposals for a marathon festival of British music, stated his firm conviction that 'the creative germ', as he oddly phrased it, had come once more to Britain, but it needed careful nurturing.

'To put it upon a pedestal . . . while as yet it has hardly opened its eyes is to proceed on the lines best calculated to kill it. . . . Mr. Cyril Scott . . . who has the keenest sense of beauty of form and of sound I have ever met with in a young composer, is even now writing beautiful music with masterly ease; Mr. Ralph Vaughan Williams has ideas of real beauty; Mr. Percy Grainger and Mr. Cecil Forsyth the same. . . . But they would be the first to acknowledge that the hour is not yet for them to produce their greatest and most representative work.'

The *Daily News*, in the same year, called upon festival committees to look farther afield for their novelties:

'Richard Strauss is not the only foreign composer of note, and really it is time some of our younger composers should be encouraged. There are several who might write something worth hearing if they did but receive a commission. . . . The Committee [of the Leeds Festival] should have applied to Mr. W. H. Bell, Mr. Percy Pitt, Mr. R. Vaughan Williams, Mr. Ernest Blake, Mr. William Wallace, Mr. Granville Bantock, Mr. Josef Holbrooke, or Mr. Rutland Boughton—all of whom would write an orchestral work or a cantata of more than ordinary interest.'

A significant omission from this list is the name of Delius who, despite a concert of his works at St. James's Hall in 1899, was still largely unknown in his native country at this time.

W. Barclay Squire contributed an interesting survey of the English musical scene in 1903 to the 21 March number of *The Pilot*. He begins by noting a greater willingness to perform British works— 'Even Mr. Wood, whose programmes generally show more appreciation of foreigners than of Englishmen, has played a violoncello concerto by Mr. D'Albert and an orchestral piece by Dr. Elgar.' After a side glance at Donald Tovey ('from one so steeped in music old and new much creative individuality can hardly be expected'), Squire named Cyril Scott, Vaughan Williams, T. F. Dunhill, Cecil Forsyth and W. Y. Hurlstone as the most promising young composers, and of these he selected Scott, Vaughan Williams and Forsyth as the most interesting. Of Vaughan Williams he wrote:

'Good as his vocal music is, the remembrance of a very striking orchestral work, which was performed some time ago at a concert at the Royal College of Music,[1] makes me regret that the undoubted power he exhibited on that occasion has not yet resulted in the production of some instrumental composition of important dimensions. Of the little group whose names I have selected for comment, Mr. Vaughan Williams interests me the most. His work, so far as one can judge, is at present rather undecided in its tendencies, and he seems, like Richard Strauss, to be attracted by the idea of a return to the horizontal view of composition, disregarding the unpleasant effects which it entails for the sake of greater freedom of rhythmical expression. At the same time, the two songs sung

---

[1] 1901. The *Heroic Elegy and Triumphal Epilogue*.

at Miss Verne's concert[1] prove that he has command of melody and of clearness of form, when he chooses to use them, while throughout all his work there is present a strong poetical feeling. . . . Mr. Vaughan Williams's predilection for strongly-marked poetical subjects has doubtless led him to attempt the setting of Rossetti's sonnets quite regardless of the fact that the sonnet-form . . . presents almost insuperable difficulties for musical illustration. The most successful of the series . . . was the setting of "Silent Noon", but in this, as in the *Willow-Wood* series, I fancy that the composer's ideas would have found fuller expression with an orchestral accompaniment than with the necessarily monotonous tone of a pianoforte. . . . A noticeable and very promising feature [of the young composers' work] is their freedom from any strongly pronounced extraneous influences. . . . It is from such beginnings that one may hope that something really original may arise, and that the birth of a really individual school of English composers may be looked for. It is in this respect that the contrast is so marked when one compares the rising generation of the present day with that of thirty years ago.'

Edwin Evans, at this date aged twenty-nine and already foremost among champions of young English composers, also dealt with Vaughan Williams's work in a perspicacious and historically fascinating article contributed to the *Musical Standard* on 25 July 1903. It began:

'One of the names which has most frequently been mentioned to me in the course of preliminary inquiry connected with these articles is that of Mr. R. Vaughan Williams, who was described to me as a very earnest young man with more than the average allowance of what the Germans so aptly name *Fertigkeit*, and well provided with ideas, but somewhat in the unsatisfactory state of not yet having "found himself". This is the present stage of a large number of our young composers, but whereas many of them are unaware of the fact, this one is rather painfully conscious of it, and has a disposition to be less satisfied with what he does than would be desirable as an incentive to push on. . . . Mr. Vaughan Williams has little reason for this extreme diffidence as there are amongst his works many which reveal a subtle personality with individual traits none the less calculated for being presented free of the remotest suggestion of blatancy.'

Evans then singled out the *Heroic Elegy and Triumphal Epilogue*, a work which was first played in 1901, as that which had impressed him most.

---

[1] 3 March 1903, St. James's Hall. McInnes sang 'Blackmwore' and 'Whither must I wander?', and Mathilde Verne played new piano works by Hurlstone and Dunhill. Holst's 'Invocation to the Dawn' was also sung.

'It is not only that it displays the composer's craftsmanship both as re-gards actual composition and orchestration to the best advantage, but because it is also characteristic of his style. The two movements of which it is composed vary widely in importance, the first being considerably shorter than its companion. It takes the form of a dirge, and the solemn note is well sustained, the effect being principally derived from a rhythm which from the first bar creates the desired impression, and which at the end of the movement takes the form of an organ point on which the or-chestral structure gradually subsides. The second section of this work is much more important, and is indeed subdivided in a manner which would almost suggest an independent work but for the presence, in the course of the development, of much of the material of the Elegy. On the whole I consider it superior to the piece which precedes it and which, whether the composer intended it or not, I feel rather disposed to regard as intro-ductory. For one thing, the themes are more interesting, particularly that which opens the movement and plays an important part in it. This is a chant-like melody of the type which leads the practised listener to expect great things. In spite of all the chromatic tendencies of modern schools, there is nothing so majestic as a well-defined diatonic phrase, and nothing lends itself so well to symphonic treatment in the epic man-ner; the only manner consistent with the title the composer has chosen in this instance. The movement rises to a fine climax of a somewhat com-plex construction, and if its shape is on a first impression a little hard to define, it is none the less symmetrical in its main features.'

That both Barclay Squire and Evans should have picked out the *Heroic Elegy* for special comment makes its withdrawal the more aggravating. The use of the term 'Epilogue' clearly shows Vaughan Williams's mind turning to a device he made peculiarly his own. Evans also shrewdly spotted a future symphonist; and later in the article, discussing the *Bucolic Suite*, he noted that 'the principal movements are rather more genuinely reminiscent of the countryside than pastoral music is apt to be. This is not the pastoral music of silk-clad shepherds and shepherdesses, but rather of brawny clod-hoppers in corduroys . . . the key-note of the work is essentially the real country merry-making as opposed to that of ladies and gentle-men indulging a passing fancy in the country. . . .'

After praising the 'definite romance' of *Willow-Wood*, and the 'leanings towards modernity' of 'Tears, Idle Tears', Evans con-cluded:

'Mr. Vaughan Williams belongs to the more level-headed of our young writers, and I am convinced of the absolute conscientiousness of his work.

Of this I feel that the best has still to come. That sounds a little trite, as it is said of so many, but in this instance I feel persuaded that it *will* come. His future career depends rather more on his own self-confidence than on any very startling development. He has the ideas, the method and the manner, but wants to be a little more autocratic with each of them.'

This diffidence, the state of 'not yet having found himself', was of deep concern to Vaughan Williams. It is clear from Holst's replies to letters in 1903 that Vaughan Williams had been telling his friend about his feelings of inadequacy. From Berlin, where he was on holiday that summer, Holst wrote:

'Don't you think we ought to victimize Elgar? Write to him first and then bicycle to Worcester to see him *a lot.* . . . I think we are "all right" in a mild sort of way. But then mildness is the very devil. So something must happen and we must make it happen. While I remember—the voice parts of your opera [probably *Belshazzar*] are impossible. You must not do this sort of thing. Don't show them to a singer but *get singers to sing them.*'

The next letter is more personal:

'I really cannot feel concerned about your fears that all your invention has gone. I am sorry but it is impossible. You got into the same state of mind just before you wrote the Heroic Elegy so that I look on it as a good sign and quite expect to hear that you have struck oil when you write again.

'I have thought about it a good deal and these are some of my conclusions:

'(1) You have never lost your invention but it has not developed enough. Your best—your most original and beautiful style or "atmosphere"—is an indescribable sort of feeling as if one was listening to very lovely lyrical poetry. I may be wrong but I think this (what I call to myself the *real* RVW) is more original than you think.

But when you are not in this strain, you either write "second class goods" or you have a devil of a bother to write anything at all. The latter state of mind may seem bad while it lasts but it is what you want to make yourself do for however much I like your best style it must be broadened. . . . . Probably you are right about mental concentration—that is what you want more than technique. For that reason perhaps lessons would do you good but it would be a surer way to try and cultivate it "on your own".'

Holst then, in his practical way, made various suggestions for 'going into training' in composition, all of which express the total lack of a sturdy musical background which these two young men felt:

'Would it be good, do you think, for you to re-write as a matter of course *everything* you write about six months after it is finished. . . . Cannot invention be developed like other things? And would it not be developed by your trying to write so many themes every day? Three decent themes a day for instance. . . . Another thing we must guard against and that is getting old! Especially you—I am more juvenile than ever, I think, but I have my doubts about you. . . . We have so much to contend against and in England there is no one to help, so that progress is sure to be a bit erratic. For instance, I doubt whether your Rhapsody will sound half as good as the Elegy and if you feel old you will be disappointed. Whereas the real truth is the Elegy was a climax and the Rhapsody a new start—a broadening out—which will in the long run probably do you far more good. . . . I wonder if it would be possible to lock oneself up for so many hours every day. If so, it would be far easier for me than for you as you have so many friends. I feel it would be so splendid to "go into training" as it were, in order to make one's music as beautiful as possible. And I am sure that after a few months' steady grind we should have made the beginning of our own "atmospheres" and so should not feel the need of going abroad so much. For it is all that makes up an atmosphere that we lack in England. . . .'

The subject was continued in Holst's next letter. Vaughan Williams's replies have not survived.

'To begin with, what the Hell do you mean by talking about premature decay and getting fat? I meant "getting old" in the sense of "becoming mature"—that is when progress either stops or becomes slower. We must not get old for the next forty years because we have such a stiff job and you sometimes have said that you feel that "it is time you did something" after all these years—I forget your exact words, but I have felt the same myself often but it is *rot*. We are not old enough and we have not had enough training *of the right sort*. . . . There is no one in England to teach us as far as I know. Twelve years ago Parry would have been the man. . . . If you really must have lessons in London I sometimes think that Stanford is the only man now that he has learnt the elements of good manners towards you. *But I don't want you to go to him.* Could not you go to H.J.W. once every two months or so and get his opinion on all you have written? . . . But I believe that really the only good that will last will be done by struggling away on your own. Stanford is all crotchets and fads and moods although the latter have improved. And that healthy vigorous beefsteak optimism of Parry is a delusion that blinds one to the real difficulties in the way. . . . We must be more thorough when we play each other our things and we ought to play each one two or three times over at each meeting until the other one knows it thoroughly. The only drawback is that whenever we are together I have always such a lot to talk about! . . .'

The famous 'Field Days', when Vaughan Williams and Holst met to discuss, play, criticize and re-write each other's works, had begun and were to continue until Holst's death in 1934. Vaughan Williams took the advice given in these letters of 1903. He tried to compose something every day of his life, even if he tore it up afterwards. He became an inveterate re-writer, revising works years after they had been published. He wrote to Elgar, as he has recounted in his 'Chapter of Musical Autobiography',[1] asking for lessons especially in orchestration—'I received a polite reply from Lady Elgar saying that Sir Edward was too busy to give me lessons but suggesting that I should become a pupil of Professor Bantock. . . . But though Elgar would not teach me personally he could not help teaching me through his music. I spent several hours at the British Museum studying the full scores of the Variations and *Gerontius*. The results are obvious in the opening pages of the finale of my Sea Symphony. . . .' He did not return to Stanford for lessons and for the next five years he dropped the idea of taking lessons from anybody. Perhaps this was in accordance with Holst's advice; or, more probably, it was because of the turn of events in 1903 and 1904 which placed two tremendous new interests in his path. The first of these was the need to collect folk songs, of which I have written in the previous chapter. The second began when, midway through 1904, the Rev. Percy Dearmer called at Barton Street and invited Vaughan Williams to be the music editor of a proposed new hymn book.

Before this event, which was to have almost as profound an effect upon Vaughan Williams's work as the discovery of folk song, is considered in detail, it is as well to continue a survey of the early performances, nearly all of which were of works composed before his collecting of folk song began and which thus complete the formative years. The end of 1903 saw the spread of Vaughan Williams's name to the programmes of provincial towns and cities, wherever Harford and McInnes gave recitals. One can therefore date with some certainty the first performance of a work by Vaughan Williams in Manchester as 14 October 1903, when McInnes sang 'Whither must I wander?' and in York as 2 December 1903 when Harford sang 'Silent Noon'. The Broadwood Concert of 11 February

[1] Reprinted in *National Music and Other Essays*.

1904 introduced the arrangements of three French troubadour songs, 'Jean Renaud', 'L'Amour de Moy', and 'Réveillez-vous, Piccars', sung by Harford, who also brought forward new songs by Hurlstone, Tovey, and Walker, while the main attraction was Dohnányi's playing of Beethoven, Brahms, and his own cello and pianoforte sonata. On 7 March 1904 Dan Godfrey conducted the *Symphonic Rhapsody*, an orchestral commentary on a poem by Christina Rossetti, at Bournemouth. This work has been destroyed and little can be learned of its content from local press criticism. The critic of the *Bournemouth Observer* wrote of an impression of ' "chaos and black night" rather than of a clear and symmetrical composition entitled to be called really musical' and was thankful for Beethoven's 'Pastoral' Symphony after 'a tedious production when the attention of both players and hearers has been subjected to severe trial'. The three folk-song arrangements 'Adieu', 'Think of me', and 'Cousin Michael' were in a recital of vocal duets at the Steinway Hall, London, on 22 March by Beatrice Spencer and A. Foxton Ferguson, soprano and bass.

A concert by these same artists at Reading on 24 October 1904 is of some interest because it contained the first performance of settings of Whitman by Vaughan Williams. These were the vocal duets 'The Last Invocation' and 'The Birds' Love Song', with accompaniment for pianoforte and string quartet.[1] An early string quartet in C minor had been played for the first time at the Oxford and Cambridge Musical Club on 30 June. The year culminated in a recital at the Bechstein Hall on 2 December promoted by Vaughan Williams himself and consisting of his own and of Holst's music. The singers were Beatrice Spencer, Edith Clegg (contralto), Walter Creighton (baritone), and Foxton Ferguson. The violinist was Harriet Solly and the accompanists Hamilton Harty and Gustav Holst.

The programme was:

Songs   *Calm is the Morn*   } Holst
                        I will not let thee go
                        Walter Creighton

---

[1] In 1920 Vaughan Williams told Katharine Eggar that he considered one of these duets to be 'perfectly awful' and the other 'an unconscious crib'—*The Music Student*, Vol. XII, No. 9, p. 515.

Song-cycle	*The House of Life* (First performance) Edith Clegg and Hamilton Harty	Vaughan Williams
Duets with violin obbligato	*The Last Invocation* *The Birds' Love-Song* Beatrice Spencer and Foxton Ferguson Violin: Harriet Solly	}Vaughan Williams
Songs	*Soft and Gently* *Peace* *In a Wood* (First performance) Edith Clegg (accompanied by the composer)	}Holst
Song-cycle	*Songs of Travel* (First performance) Walter Creighton	Vaughan Williams
Songs	*Orpheus with his Lute* *Claribel*	}Vaughan Williams
Song	*Cradle-Song* Beatrice Spencer	Holst
Songs	*Boy Johnny* *Blackmwore by the Stour* Foxton Ferguson	}Vaughan Williams

E. A. Baughan, writing in the *Daily News*, has left the fullest account of the occasion. He found Vaughan Williams 'not at his best in expressing aloof sentiment; I should say there is but little kinship between his mind and Rossetti's. He is much more individual in verses that are informed by open-air feeling. Thus the second cycle, a setting of Stevenson's poems, is by far the more original and real of the two. Even here his lack of sentiment is noticeable.' The Whitman duets Baughan found had 'the air of experiments, and they were not well enough performed'. A writer in the *Clarion*, of all papers, found the Whitman the best things in the concert. There was general agreement that the sonnet proved intractable to musical setting and that none of the performers distinguished themselves on this occasion. One newspaper tartly complained of the 'ultra-smart audience', headed by the composer's uncle, Lord Justice Vaughan Williams (who is credited with the suggestion years before that his nephew should be provided with an organ at Leith Hill Place). The highest praise came from the London correspondent of the *Manchester Courier* who thought that Vaughan Williams had never more convincingly shown that he had in him 'the stuff of which great composers are made. . . . Mr. Vaughan Williams has an unusual gift for inventing beautiful melody and his fine musicianship enables him to put his ideas to best use.'

Five of the *Songs of Travel*, plus a setting of Heywood's 'Ye little birds' were in Plunket Greene's recital on 3 February 1905, at which Arthur Somervell's *Shropshire Lad* song-cycle had its first performance—an event which possibly directed Vaughan Williams's mind to the same source. *The Times* in particular selected 'Whither Must I Wander?', 'Silent Noon' and 'The Vagabond' as 'so full of poetry, of melodic beauty, and of picturesqueness as to deserve the best attention of the best singers.' 'Silent Noon' was 'one of the most perfect settings of the sonnet form in musical literature'. Not everybody was as lyrical. The *Manchester Guardian*, true to its perennial rôle of growing suspicious of anything remotely verging on popularity, began its notice:

'Much has been said in certain quarters of the extraordinary merit of Mr. Vaughan Williams as a writer of songs, and some of the language used might lead to the belief that another Schumann had arisen. These eulogies had doubtless something to do with the uncomfortably crowded state of the Aeolian Hall yesterday, when Mr. Plunket Greene was to sing six songs by this very earnest and gifted composer.

'In one respect Mr. Williams reminded me of "our new friend Lady Bertram", as described by Lord Beaconsfield. "We must resist conventionalism," said that lady with authority. Mr. Williams certainly aspires to follow this leading, but although, like his brilliant model, he no doubt wishes to guide and inspire, like her he finds it difficult to decide which path to follow, and his songs, instead of showing a complete and uniform aim, are not much more than clever amalgamations of variously derived phrases. Mr. Williams seems endowed with a facility which he uses with prodigality; his melodies curvet according to the most approved tenets of modernity, while his accompaniments prance about like a very Mazeppa. But after all the music strives quite worthily to avoid what is commonplace, and it is quite likely that some day Mr. Williams may produce songs of the first class, if he will be a little less flowery and ingenious.'[1]

The *Heroic Elegy and Triumphal Epilogue* was played in Leeds on 21 January 1905, its last known performance, at a concert by the Leeds Municipal Orchestra. The composer conducted. The Yorkshire correspondent of the *Musical Times* described it as 'a well-written piece, melodically interesting and sympathetic in feeling'.[2]

It is not difficult to understand why Vaughan Williams and some of his contemporaries came into prominence as song-writers. Orchestral music in England had not yet reached a standard where much pioneer work could be undertaken for the young generation of native composers. Dan Godfrey, with a small orchestra at Bournemouth, did what he could. An occasional concert of some enterprise, such as that at Leeds just mentioned, was but a drop in the ocean. At Manchester, Hans Richter championed Elgar but otherwise his activities were on behalf of well-established composers. Beecham, never a convinced champion of English music, was only coming to the fore. Henry Wood kept to well-worn paths at this date. The Crystal Palace concerts of Manns were sadly missed. Young composers, burdened by the thought of a century and a half of masterpieces just behind them, by the new harmonic adventures which were filling the air, by the mammoth orchestras of Strauss and Wagner, by the lack of permanent professional orchestras, may well have shied away from embarking upon careers as orchestral composers, still less as composers of opera. Within three years, however, by 1908, already a change had occurred and the lead given by McInnes, Plunket Greene and others had been followed, albeit cautiously, by larger groups.

Any suggestions of creative 'laziness' which Vaughan Williams confessed to Holst are hardly borne out by the facts during this period.[3] In nine months of 1904 he was collecting folk songs in Essex and Sussex, particularly the Horsham area, and Wiltshire,

---

[1] I cannot resist recording an extract from a notice in the *Manchester Guardian* of 8 March 1905 in which, discussing 'Silent Noon', the anonymous critic wrote: 'A word like "cow-parsley", however pretty the picture it conjures up, is obviously unfitted for singing.'

[2] *Musical Times*, 19 March 1905.

[3] He claimed to have a bad memory and said that at this time he found bicycling a splendid way of stimulating composition, but that when he dismounted to take out his notebook he could not remember the tunes he had invented. 'Surely,' a friend suggested at his 80th birthday dinner, 'if the good Lord sent you the tunes once, He would send them again.' R.V.W. replied: 'I think it was the good Lord's way of weeding them out.'

and in Kent. He had begun to sketch a large-scale work to poems by Whitman, which was eventually to become *A Sea Symphony*, and mention of a cantata in a letter to Holst suggests first thoughts of *Toward the Unknown Region*. He revised a quintet, and by April he had finished the first version of *In the Fen Country*. Then he began two orchestral impressions which were to be laid aside because of the *English Hymnal*.

Meanwhile 1905 contained two other significant events in Vaughan Williams's career, one deriving from his folk-song collecting and another indicative of his lifelong interest in amateur music-making as a sign of a nation's musical health. The former was his collaboration with Holst in providing the music for a masque as part of the Shakespeare Birthday Celebration at Stratford-upon-Avon in April 1905. *Pan's Anniversary, or The Shepherds' Holyday* had been 'invented' by Ben Jonson and Inigo Jones for presentation before James I, and this Stratford revival in the Bancroft Gardens was believed to be the first since the original production on New Year's Day 1625. The masque was a form which continued to fascinate Vaughan Williams to the end of his life, and *Pan's Anniversary* may be said to have been the forerunner of one great masterpiece, *Job*.

The second event was the first Leith Hill competitive festival, which was held on 10 May 1905. The festival was founded by Margaret Vaughan Williams, Ralph's sister, who was secretary, with Lady Farrer as president. Seven Surrey choirs took part in the first competition: Abinger, Albury, Capel, Coldharbour, Shalford, Shere, and Westcott, the last-named being conducted by Mrs. R. C. Trevelyan. The judge was the composer Arthur Somervell. At the evening concert, which Vaughan Williams conducted, selections from *Judas Maccabaeus* were sung, with miscellaneous instrumental, vocal, and orchestral pieces in the second half of the programme. Among the soloists was Francis Harford.

But despite work on his own compositions and the arduous task of folk-song collecting—two January days at King's Lynn in 1905 were magnificently productive—Vaughan Williams's energies from 1904 to 1906 were principally devoted to the *English Hymnal*. There had for several years been dissatisfaction with existing hymnals. In 1892, in the *Quarterly Review*, a writer had deplored the 'lack of spontaneity and fervour, their prosiness, flatness and literary baldness'. Percy Dearmer in 1901 became Vicar of St. Mary's, Primrose Hill, and soon made his church notable for the beauty of its liturgy and music. The organist was Martin Shaw, a future collaborator with Dearmer and Vaughan Williams. In 1903, with a group of friends, Dearmer began to compile a small number of hymns which could supplement *Hymns Ancient and Modern*. In November 1904 a revised edition of *Hymns Ancient and Modern* appeared and was strongly criticized. Dearmer and his colleagues therefore decided to continue their work and to publish about 150 hymns under the title *English Hymns*. The full committee had. four clergymen and three laymen as members. The Chairman was the Hon. and Rev. A. Hanbury-Tracy, with the Rev. Percy Dearmer, the Rev. W. H. H. Jervois,[1] the Rev. T. A. Lacey, Mr. W. J. Birkbeck, Mr. Athelstan Riley, and Mr. D. C. Lathbury (former editor of *The Guardian* and *The Pilot*). On the recommendation of Canon Henry Scott Holland[2] and Cecil Sharp the committee had decided in 1904 to approach Vaughan Williams to be the music editor.

'. . . I protested that I knew very little about hymns, but he [Dearmer] explained to me that Cecil Sharp had suggested my name, and I found out afterwards that Canon Scott Holland had also suggested me as a possible editor, and the final clench was given when I understood that if I did not do the job it would be offered to a well-known church musician [H. Walford Davies] with whose musical ideas I was very much out of sympathy. . . . I thought it over for 24 hours and then decided to accept, but I found that the work occupied me two years. . . .

'The truth is that I determined to do the work thoroughly, and that, besides being a compendium of all the tunes of worth which were already in use, the book should, in addition, be a thesaurus of all the finest hymn tunes in the world—at all events all such as were compatible with the metres of the words for which I had to find tunes.'[3]

By January 1905, the zeal of their musical editor and their own researches forced the committee to abandon the idea of a supplement and publish instead a totally new hymn-book. They checked all texts carefully, often restoring an author's original words where previous editors had substituted tamer or commonplace sentiments. Vaughan Williams found Dearmer and his colleague Athelstan Riley co-operative in providing words for tunes for which no

[1] Jervois died in 1905 before the Hymnal was published. It was dedicated to his memory.

[2] A lively picture of Scott Holland, Dearmer, Conrad Noel, and others of this group of clerics can be found in G. K. Chesterton's *Autobiography*.

[3] *The First Fifty Years: a brief account of The English Hymnal from 1906 to 1956* (O.U.P.).

English words were available. This was the origin of Riley's 'Ye watchers and ye holy ones'. Dearmer himself wrote 'Holy God, we offer here' to carry the chorale tune from Wagner's *Die Meistersinger*. 'While trying to include all the good tunes,' Vaughan Williams wrote,

'I did my best to eliminate the bad ones. This was difficult, because I was not entirely my own master. My committee insisted that certain very popular tunes should be retained. The climax came when my masters declared that I must myself write a fulsome letter to a prominent ecclesiastic asking for leave to print his horrible little tune. My committee and I finally settled our quarrel with a compromise by which the worst offenders were confined in an appendix at the end of the book which we nicknamed the "Chamber of Horrors".

'. . . I avoided the specially composed tune so far as I could; of course, in the case of a very peculiar metre this was impossible; I then had to have recourse to well-known contemporary composers, for choice not Church composers, and the result was some excellent tunes by W. H. Bell, Thomas Dunhill, Nicholas Gatty and Gustav Holst, among others. I also, contrary to my principles, contributed a few tunes of my own, but with becoming modesty I attributed them to my old friend, Mr. Anon.'

These tunes, which are now almost traditional, were 152, 'Come down, O Love Divine' (Down Ampney); 524, 'God be with you till we meet again'; 624, 'Hail thee, Festival day', and 641, 'For all the Saints' (Sine Nomine). Among the 16 which he adapted from folk songs were no. 15 'O Little town of Bethlehem' (Forest Green) and the Bunyan Pilgrim hymn, no. 402 'He who would valiant be' (Monk's Gate).

Other tunes specially written for the *English Hymnal* with their names, their number in the hymnal and the first line of the hymn are:

W. H. Bell ..	*Hail, harbinger of morn* (no other name); 225.
	Fling out the banner! (Cathcart); 546.
Walford Davies	*O King Enthroned on High* (Temple); 454.
T. F. Dunhill ..	*Lord, to our humble prayers attend* (Beatus); 650.
Nicholas Gatty ..	*Come rejoicing, faithful men* (Laetabundus); 22 ii.
	Sing we triumphant hymns of praise (Tugwood); 146.
A. M. Goodhart	*God of our fathers, unto thee* (Etona); 559.
Gustav Holst ..	*In the bleak mid-winter* (Cranham); 25.
	From glory to glory advancing, we praise Thee, O Lord (Sheen); 310.
	Holy Ghost, come down upon thy children (Bossinery); 571.

John Ireland	..	*Holy Father, in Thy mercy* (Eastergate); 520.
Sir Walter Parratt		*Holy Father, cheer our way* (Huddersfield); 270.
Arthur Somervell		*We give Thee but Thine own* (Windermere); 522.
		When wilt Thou save the people? (Kendal); 566.
		Every morning the red sun rises warm and bright (Langdale); 590.

Only the tunes by Holst, Vaughan Williams, and Ireland have achieved the success which might have been hoped, but possibly this did not disturb the musical editor, for he stated in the preface to the first edition (1906) that the principal aim was congregational. Where there was congregational singing it was important that 'familiar melodies should be employed, or at least those which have stood the test of time. . . . There are already many hundreds of fine tunes in existence.'

Vaughan Williams explained that the problem of discarding certain tunes which were popular but 'quite unsuitable to their purpose' and 'positively harmful to those who sing and hear them' had been solved because the owners of the copyright had not allowed their inclusion.

'The committee believe that many clergymen and organists . . . will welcome a tune-book in which enervating tunes are reduced to a minimum. The usual argument in favour of bad music is that the fine tunes are doubtless "musically correct", but that the people want "something simple". Now the expression "musically correct" has no meaning; the only "correct" music is that which is beautiful and noble. As for simplicity, what could be simpler than "St. Anne" or "The Old Hundredth", and what could be finer?'

Then follow these important words:

'It is indeed a moral rather than a musical issue. No doubt it requires a certain effort to tune oneself to the moral atmosphere implied by a fine melody; and it is far easier to dwell in the miasma of the languishing and sentimental hymn tunes which so often disfigure our services. Such poverty of heart may not be uncommon, but at least it should not be encouraged by those who direct the services of the Church; it ought no longer to be true anywhere that the most exalted moments of a church-goer's week are associated with music that would not be tolerated in any place of secular entertainment.'

Here spoke the scion of Darwin-Wedgwood, and here spoke the true national composer. Vaughan Williams undertook the task of musical editing of the hymnal not because of any strong religious opinion, but because it offended his artistic sense that such a national feature as the Established Church should propagate bad music. Throughout this preface one can perceive what offence had been given to him by his experiences of the worst kind of church music at St. Barnabas. True to the traditions of his family, when the opportunity came to *act* to right a wrong, he took it thoroughly and to the best of his ability.

Vaughan Williams took particular care that the children's hymns should be of a high standard. As he said in a broadcast fifty years later: 'Cecil Sharp had just made his epoch-making discovery of the beautiful melody hidden in the countryside: why should we not enter into our inheritance in the church as well as the concert room?' In the 'At Catechism' section of the hymnal there are twenty-seven hymns. Of these ten are set to eleven English traditional melodies, since 591, 'Gentle Jesus, meek and mild,' is given two tunes both based on folk song. Three of the arrangements in this section were by Vaughan Williams, numbers 595 ('I think when I read that sweet story of old'), 597 ('It is a thing most wonderful'), and 607 ('There's a friend for little children'). The last-named tune is called Ingrave, after the village where he collected 'Bushes and Briars'. The other tunes in this section are well-chosen, one from fifteenth-century German manuscripts, the famous 'Indian Air' for 'There is a happy land', a fourteenth-century German carol for 'Who is he, in yonder stall?' and, among modern tunes, Baring-Gould's lifelong-haunting 'Now the day is over'.

In the preface, Vaughan Williams explained that austerity had not been unduly sought (the *Standard* of 30 November 1904, commenting on his editorship, said that it was a choice 'which ensures purity of musical taste, perhaps even leaning to the side of severity'), nor had difficult and colourless music been preferred to that which was vigorous and bright. 'A tune has no more right to be dull than demoralizing.' The *English Hymnal* broke new ground by fixing the pitch of all the tunes as low as possible for the sake of mixed congregations. 'Some choirmasters may object to this on the ground that it places the hymns in the worst part of the boy-chorister's voice, and that it takes the basses and altos rather low. The obvious answer is that hymns are essentially for the congregation; the choir have their opportunity elsewhere, but in the hymn they must give way to the congregation, and it is a great mistake to suppose that the result will be inartistic. . . . And it may be added that a desire to parade a trained choir often accompanies a debased musical taste.' Vaughan Williams laid it down that the congregation must always sing the melody only, but he urged choirs to learn the rather more elaborate harmonizations, especially Bach's, instead of 'rehearsing vulgar anthems by indifferent composers'. There is no doubt that the hymnal achieved this object, and it also largely eradicated the custom of singing hymns too fast.

The case of each tune to be included was decided on its merits. 'The object has been to print the finest versions of every tune, not necessarily the earliest. Thus the later forms of 'Wachet auf', 'Nun Danket' and 'London New'[1] . . . have been preferred to the originals. . . . The original rhythms of many of the old psalter tunes have also been restored, especially the long initial on the first syllable (the gathering note) which gives such a broad and dignified effect to these tunes.'

To help him to select, arrange, and correct the tunes, Vaughan Williams relied on Gatty and Holst. W. H. Bell, Dunhill, E. W. Goldsmith, W. H. Harris, and John Ireland helped to harmonize many of the tunes. He went for advice to Hugh Allen, Arthur Reynolds, and the Rev. M. F. Bell. The Rev. J. B. Croft was his source of help in dealing with French church melodies, and the Rev. Hugh Davies and the Rev. W. L. Richards with Welsh hymn-tunes. (Despite the accident of his name and the efforts of some partisans to claim him for their own, Vaughan Williams was Welsh only by descent.) Something of the wide range of music which had to be examined and explored for the hymnal may be gathered from this list of principal sources of tunes:

1. England.
   (a) Tunes from Day's, Damon's, Este's, Ravenscroft's and Playford's psalters of the sixteenth and seventeenth century. 'I explored particularly Wither's *Hymns and Songs of the Church*, because they contained beautiful tunes by Gibbons . . . also Archbishop Parker's Psalter containing fine tunes by Tallis.'

---

[1] 'Wachet auf'. Hymn 12. Bach's harmonization of Philipp Nicolai's tune, with Nicolai's words translated by F. C. Burkitt—'Wake, O Wake! with tidings thrilling.' 'Nun danket'. Hymn 533. J. Crüger's version of the famous setting of Rinckart's hymn, translated by Catherine Winkworth as 'Now thank we all our God'. 'London New'. Hymns 394 and 542. Tune used from *Playford's Psalms* (1671), adapted from *Scottish Psalter* (1635), as settings for Cowper's 'God moves in a mysterious way' and Addison's 'How are Thy servants blest'.

(*b*) Tunes by Gibbons, Lawes, Tallis, etc., from their own collections.

(*c*) Tunes from eighteenth-century books, especially those by J. Clark and Dr. Croft. 'The eighteenth-century psalm books contain many very fine tunes which had been allowed to drop out. . . . Then there are the strong Methodist tunes of the eighteenth century.'

(*d*) Carols and other traditional melodies.

(*e*) Nineteenth- and twentieth-century composers' tunes.

2. Scotland.

(*a*) Melodies from sixteenth- and seventeenth-century psalters.

(*b*) Tune-books of the eighteenth and nineteenth centuries.

(*c*) Traditional melodies.

3. Wales.

(*a*) Archdeacon Prys's Psalter.

(*b*) Welsh traditional melodies.

(*c*) Tunes by eighteenth- and nineteenth-century Welsh composers 'which partake decidedly of the nature of their traditional melodies'.

4. Ireland. Traditional melodies and tunes by Irish composers.

5. Germany.

(*a*) Lutheran chorale tunes, sixteenth and seventeenth centuries.

(*b*) Tunes from sixteenth- and seventeenth-century Catholic song books, chiefly Leisentritt's (1567), and the 1608 *Andernach Gesangbuch*.

(*c*) Eighteenth-century tunes by Bach and Freylinghausen.

(*d*) Modern German tunes.

(*e*) Traditional melodies.

6. France and Switzerland.

(*a*) Sixteenth-century Genevan psalters.

(*b*) Ecclesiastical tunes from the paroissiens of various French uses, notably those of Rouen and Angers.

(*c*) Traditional melodies.

7. Italy, Spain, Flemish, Dutch, America. Ecclesiastical and traditional melodies.

A glance through the composers' index shows many illustrious names besides the modern Englishmen already mentioned: J. C. Bach and J. S. Bach (thirty-three tunes by the latter), Louis Bourgeois, Campion, Dowland, Dykes, Fuller Maitland, Gauntlett, Gibbons, Maurice Greene, Hadow, Handel, Lawes, Mendelssohn, Monk, Vincent Novello, Gore Ouseley, Palestrina, Parratt, Purcell (three tunes), Rockstro, Scott-Gatty, Shrubsole, Henry Smart, Sullivan, Tallis, Wagner, J. and S. S. Wesley, and Whinfield.

Gibbons (sixteen tunes) and Tallis (eight) were thus restored to general circulation instead of remaining the preserve of a few 'crack' choirs. By far the largest single contribution to the hymnal[1] was from English folk songs with thirty-five tunes for thirty-nine hymns. It is, I think, important that in a comprehensive work on Vaughan Williams these tunes should be set out, with their original collector and copyright-owner (where appropriate), name and number in the hymnal, for their part in the nationalist revival of English music has perhaps been under-estimated. I have given the name of the folk song from which the hymn tune was derived where it has been possible to establish it with some certainty:

No.	First line of hymn title	Tune Title	Owner of Copyright	Name of folk song
15.	O little town of Bethlehem	Forest Green	R.V.W.	The Ploughboy's Dream
16.	The maker of the sun and moon	Newbury	Miss Arkwright	There is six good days set in a week (carol)
23.	Hark, how all the welkin rings!	Dent Dale	R.V.W.	Tarry Woo'
89.	Soul of Jesus make me whole	Anima Christi		The Staines Morris
90.	To my humble supplication	De Profundis		
*186.	Come, let us join the Church above	Rodmell	R.V.W.	The Bailiff's Daughter of Islington
*239.	Saints of God! Lo, Jesu's people	Sussex	R.V.W.	
275.	Sweet Saviour, bless us ere we go	Lodsworth	W. P. Merrick	The Unquiet Grave
294.	The year is swiftly waning	Devonshire	L. E. Broadwood	
295.	'Tis winter now; the fallen snow	Danby	R.V.W.	Brisk Young Farmer (Died for Love)
*299.	When spring unlocks the flowers to paint the laughing soil	Gosterwood	R.V.W.	
*344.	Thine for ever! God of love	Horsham	L. E. Broadwood	Stinson the Deserter
355.	In paradise reposing	Hambridge	C. Sharp	The Unquiet Grave

* Indicates tune is used for another hymn.
The arranger, where shown, owns the copyright. Where no arranger is given it may be presumed that the musical editor chose the tune for the words.

[1] This chapter deals solely with the first edition.

No.	First line of hymn title	Tune Title	Owner of Copyright	Name of folk song
379.	'Come unto me, ye weary'	Rusper	L. E. Broadwood	The Merchant's Daughter
*385.	Father, hear the prayer we offer	Sussex	R.V.W.	
388.	Fierce was the wild billow	St. Issey		
389.	Fight the good fight with all thy might	Shepton-Beauchamp	C. Sharp	Tarry Trowsers
*390.	Firmly I believe and truly	Shipston	{ L. E. Broadwood J. A. Fuller Maitland	
402.	He who would valiant be	Monk's Gate	R.V.W.	Our captain calls
417.	Jesu, my Lord, my God, my All	Stella		
448.	O God of mercy, God of might	Fitzwilliam		
498.	There is a land of pure delight	Mendip	C. Sharp	
525.	From Thee all skill and science flow	Farnham	R.V.W.	How should I your true love know?
562.	O God of earth and altar	King's Lynn	R.V.W.	Young Henry the Poacher (Van Dieman's Land)
*572.	I could not do without Thee	Gosterwood	R.V.W.	
574.	I heard the voice of Jesus say	Kingsfold	L. E. Broadwood	Dives and Lazarus (Maria Martin)
591.	Gentle Jesus, meek and mild	{ *Farnaby Lew Trenchard	S. Baring-Gould	
*594.	I love to hear the story	Gosterwood	R.V.W.	
595.	I think when I read that sweet story of old	East Horndon	R.V.W.	The Bold Fisherman
597.	It is a thing most wonderful	Herongate	R.V.W.	In Jessie's City
*599.	Jesu, tender Shepherd, hear me	Shipston	{ J. A. Fuller Maitland L. E. Broadwood	
601.	Lord, I would own Thy tender care	Eardisley	Miss Andrews	Dives and Lazarus
606.	Sing to the Lord the children's hymn	St. Hugh	L. E. Broadwood	Little Sir William

* Indicates tune is used for another hymn.

The arranger, where shown, owns the copyright. Where no arranger is given it may be presumed that the musical editor chose the tune for the words.

No.	First line of hymn title	Tune Title	Owner of Copyright	Name of folk song
607.	There's a friend for little children	Ingrave	R.V.W.	Sheffield Apprentice (Died for Love)
*609.	Through the night Thy angels kept	Horsham	L. E. Broadwood	Stinson the Deserter
*611.	When Christ was born in Bethlehem	Rodmell	R.V.W.	The Bailiff's Daughter of Islington
638.	Jerusalem, my happy home	St. Austin	A. Foxton Ferguson	In Peascod Time
		Southill		Northill Mayers' Song
*654.	God the Father, God the Son	Farnaby		
656.	See Him in raiment rent	Bridgwater	C. Sharp	Sweet Europe
		Langport	C. Sharp	Lord Rendell

* Indicates tune is used for another hymn.
The arranger, where shown, owns the copyright. Where no arranger is given it may be presumed that the musical editor chose the tune for the words.

Also included in the hymnal were four traditional carols and one May-Day carol:

No.	First line of hymn title	Tune title	Owner of Copyright	Name of folk song
20.	Behold the great Creator makes	This Endris Nyght		
29.	The great God of Heaven is come down to earth	A Virgin Unspotted		
*221.	The winter's sleep was long and deep	King's Langley	L. E. Broadwood	The Moon shines bright
485.	Teach me my God and King	Sandys		A Child this day is born (Sandys Collection, 1833)
488.	The Church of God a Kingdom is	Capel	L. E. Broadwood	King Pharim

* May Day.

'I have been blamed for using adaptations of folk tunes for hymn purposes,' Vaughan Williams wrote in 1956,[1] 'but this is, surely, an age-old custom. Tierssot[2] has proved, to my mind conclusively, that certain church melodies of the Middle Ages were adapted from secular tunes, for example, the Tonus Peregrinus.' (See previous chapter for further views on this subject.) At all events this feature

[1] From *The English Hymnal: the First Fifty Years.*
[2] Julien Tierssot, *Histoire de la Chanson populaire en France* (Paris, 1889).

of the hymnal was popular. The tunes for 'O little town of Bethlehem', 'Thine for ever, God of Love', 'I heard the voice of Jesus say,'
'There's a friend for little children,' and 'God the Father, God the
Son' were within a generation part of an Englishman's heritage.
And the tune 'Monk's Gate', derived from the folk song 'Our captain calls' and put to the words 'He who would valiant be', has
remained the most famous of the 'new' tunes introduced in the
English Hymnal.[1] In this practical way he gave meaning to the
words he had spoken at Bournemouth and Gloucester in 1902 and
1903:

'The collector of folk songs gives them back again to the world.
. . . Will they not, perhaps, once more make their way back to the
mouths of the people?'

Of course they could never again be sung in 'villages like nests of
singing-birds' now that the sophistications of modern life were
spreading everywhere. But here, in the churches, was one method
of 'giving them back to the world'.

The *English Hymnal* was strongly criticized when it first appeared.
But by the time of its golden jubilee five million copies had been sold,
and its influence is still spreading. The Archbishop of Canterbury
of 1906, Dr. Davidson, expressed in public the hope that his clergy
would not use the new book. 'That in itself,' Sir Steuart Wilson
wrote in 1959,[2] 'might account for its quick acceptance.' Wilson
considered the *English Hymnal* Vaughan Williams's 'most enduring
work, which has raised the standard more widely than any other
single event'. When its musical editor began work on it he had
grave doubts because 'this meant two years with no "original"
work except a few hymn tunes. I wondered then if I was wasting
my time. But I know now that two years of close association with
some of the best (as well as some of the worst) tunes in the world
was a better musical education than any amount of sonatas and
fugues.'[3] It was, in fact, by coming as a tributary from, and corollary
to, his folk-song collecting, another 'liberating' influence.

Years later, in 1943, he wrote[4] movingly of what one of these

[1] Vaughan Williams regretted that he had given way to Dearmer in setting his
bowdlerization of Bunyan's 'Who would true valour see'. Dearmer's defence, based
mainly on the unsuitability of singing about 'hobgoblins' in church, can be found in
Songs of Praise Discussed (London, 1933), pp. 270-2.

[2] *Music and Letters*, Vol. XL. No. 1.

[3] 'A Musical Autobiography'.

[4] 'Shrubsole', in *National Music and Other Essays*.

great tunes—William Shrubsole's 'Miles Lane' (E.H.364: 'All hail the power of Jesu's name')—had meant to him:

'It is from the eighteenth century that some of the strongest and most characteristic of our musical invention dates, albeit on a small scale, exemplified, perhaps, by a hymn tune or a chant; but what does size matter? Who would not rather have drawn eight bars straight from the fountain-head than have compiled whole symphonies strained very thin through the medium of the best foreign models? . . . Shrubsole wrote this one superb tune and no more—at least no more of any note. He was a "one tune" man. There are many such: people who get a glimpse of the eternal glory once in a lifetime for a few moments and, like Gerontius, are blinded by it and turn their faces away for ever; but in that one moment these Shrubsolian composers may have achieved something which neither Beethoven nor Bach could have bettered. . . . The interminable oratorios and cantatas of minor composers . . . are not waste because without them the moment of inspiration could not have been caught. It is on these foundations that the music of a nation is built up, on this soil, and this only, that the great artist can come to maturity. It takes a thousand small composers to make a great one.'

But of most significance in the career of Vaughan Williams were five tunes which he included in the hymnal and which, in varying ways, were to haunt him all his life. The folk song 'Our captain calls' which Mrs. Harriet Verrall of Monk's Gate, Horsham, sang to him and which he adapted for 'He who would valiant be', was one of the small and many factors which set him thinking about *The Pilgrim's Progress*. He used the tune for a Bunyan dramatization at Reigate Priory in 1906.

'Dives and Lazarus' he had known for years. The shape of its melody determined many of his own tunes; its notes brought the very man himself before the eyes of the mourners at his funeral in Westminster Abbey as its gentle strains broke the heartfelt silence before the service began. The Scottish Psalter tune 'York' was to find its way into *Hugh the Drover* and was to open and close the Morality *The Pilgrim's Progress*. The 'Old Hundredth', with trumpet flourishes added, was to revolutionize the music of a royal coronation service by allowing the whole congregation to join in the singing, a triumph which gave Vaughan Williams immense pride and pleasure and was, in a very real sense, a consummation and symbol of his service to England's musical life. Greatest of all, in working on the hymnal, he discovered Tallis's marvellous Third Mode

Melody which appears as No. 92, set to Addison's 'When rising from the bed of death'. Within a few years Vaughan Williams's fascination by this great Phrygian tune was to result in one of English music's indisputable masterpieces, a marriage of true musical minds across the centuries. This work, the *Fantasia on a Theme by Thomas Tallis*, in itself is justification of the two years' work on the *English Hymnal* if there were no others. It also justifies one of Vaughan Williams's own beliefs. He recorded[1] Bax's sardonic remark to him: 'You know, V.W., all your best sellers are not your own.' Developing a theme he had propounded often before, Vaughan Williams said at Cornell University in 1954:[2] 'Inspiration and originality do not necessarily mean something no one has ever heard before. . . . If another composer has said the same thing before, so much the worse for the other composer. The originality, or perhaps I should say the personality, of music depends very little on the actual outline of the notes.' The notes in the *Tallis Fantasia* theme are Tallis's. The personality is Vaughan Williams's. It was in no way the worse for Tallis than Brahms's variations were for Haydn (or whoever wrote the tune in question). Perhaps a theme on which variations are written is hardly the un-originality which Vaughan Williams had in mind, but the principle is surely the same as the derived influence from a folk song.

II

The length of the list of works written during this period is enough to illustrate the struggle which Vaughan Williams made to 'discover himself'. Few composers of his stature can have had such a bewilderingly diverse and erratic apprenticeship. The R.C.M. works —such things as the *Gloria* and *Anthems* 'done for Dr. Parry'— contain not a glimpse of the Vaughan Williams we know. Later efforts, such as the Serenade and the *Bucolic Suite*, though interesting, are gauche in comparison with what was to follow a few years later. The chamber music works are slightly more promising than the orchestral, and both of these forms of music are inferior at this date to his vocal settings. Throughout his life, Vaughan Williams was enterprising in his choice of lyrics. It is ambitious to set Swinburne and still more so to set a cycle of sonnets to music. Although

[1] *Music and Letters*, XXXV, No. 1.
[2] Reprinted in *National Music and Other Essays*.

Vaughan Williams was perhaps overcome for the time being by the Rossettis' brand of romanticism, it is more likely that the poems simply appealed as vehicles for music by reason of their shape. At any rate they served to stimulate his gift of melody, and right from the start it can be seen that Vaughan Williams's principal concern was whether he had 'a good tune'. A song such as 'Claribel', probably 1896, is still characteristic and recognizably by Vaughan Williams. The harmonies of the accompaniment are more adventurous. Another famous song of about 1900, 'Whither must I wander?', to one of Stevenson's *Songs of Travel*, struck its first hearers as an Irish tune, possibly because at that time more Irish folk songs than English would be known. Like 'Linden Lea' it is a grand song to sing, and the freshness and vitality of the tune have prevented its falling into disuse. The two Barnes settings, 'The Winter's Willow' and 'Blackmwore by the Stour', are similarly engaging despite the rather dull nature of the pianoforte accompaniments.[1] The pianoforte never entered very fully into Vaughan Williams's affections.

In 'Linden Lea' and 'Blackmwore' Vaughan Williams developed a type of song midway between folk song and art song, for 'Linden Lea' owes as much to Schumann's 'Widmung' as to any folk tune. It is not easy at this remove of time to understand with what eagerness the singers at the turn of the century seized upon songs such as these, and others by Ireland, Somervell, Gatty and Holst, as a relief from the royalty-ballad, but the fact that Vaughan Williams's reputation as a song-writer was quickly established is proof of the enterprise of men like Harford, McInnes, and Plunket Greene.

Now that the score has been unearthed, it can be seen that the strongest clues to the mature Vaughan Williams may be found in the *Heroic Elegy and Triumphal Epilogue* for orchestra of 1900–1. As I have already said, both Edwin Evans and W. Barclay Squire were impressed by this work. Their memory of it was comparatively recent; for others the memory was still green after over

[1] Rupert Erlebach, a pupil of Vaughan Williams in the 1920s, recalled (*R.C.M. Magazine*, Vol. LV, No. 1, Easter 1959) that 'he had no mercy on some of his own early compositions and used to tell us that the accompaniment to "Linden Lea" was *not* a pattern to be followed. I fear I did not agree with him.'

In March 1925, J. B. McEwen made an offer to Vaughan Williams to publish *Shepherds of the Delectable Mountains*. Vaughan Williams refused, saying, 'I ought to make the effort myself only I am too lazy. . . . Also I feel that I ought to be able (if necessary) to do this myself out of the ill-gotten gains of such sins of my youth as "Linden Lea" which becomes every year more horribly popular.'

fifty years. John Ireland, writing to Vaughan Williams for his eightieth birthday in 1952, recalled that after the *Heroic Elegy* had been rehearsed at the R.C.M. Stanford said to him, 'That's better than anything you could write, me bhoy'—'a remark,' Ireland wrote, 'the truth of which is borne in upon me whenever I hear your works.' A work of Ireland's called *Tritons* was played at the same time. James Friskin, the pianist, remembered the 'power' of the *Elegy* and Dr. W. H. Harris recalled that Frank Pownall, registrar of the R.C.M., said to Parry during the performance, 'Fine strong stuff, Hubert.' 'Yes,' Parry replied, 'there's no shadow of doubt about *him*.' The work was last played at Leeds on 21 January 1905, after which the score apparently disappeared, only to re-emerge in the United States several years after the composer's death.

The first major works by Vaughan Williams belonging to these early years are three song-cycles, the first two *The House of Life* and *Willow-Wood* being settings of sonnets by D. G. Rossetti, and the third, *Songs of Travel*, by Stevenson. *The House of Life* shares a theme with *Willow-Wood*, both works being written at roughly the same time. This interest in the pre-Raphaelite poets was shared across the Channel by Debussy, whose *The Blessed Damozel* dates from 1887. Since both composers were developing towards musical impressionism it is easy to see that Rossetti offered scope for fluidity in setting the rich vocabulary of his sonnets. *The House of Life* contains plenty of scope for the clue-hunter. First and foremost is the sensitivity to words, partly inbred, partly learned from Parry, that remained a paramount feature of Vaughan Williams's work. The first song, 'Love-Sight', with its romantic if conventional melodic line, has a fine postlude for pianoforte which recapitulates and develops the vocal melody. There is a strong reminder that work on *A Sea Symphony* began in 1903 in the setting of the largamente phrase 'Death's imperishable wing':

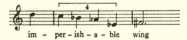

The second song, 'Silent Noon', which was performed and published ahead of the cycle, is deservedly popular for it is complete in itself and is one of the first pieces of music by Vaughan Williams which captures a moment of eternity and holds it in musical terms for perpetual contemplation. The syncopated accompaniment magically mirrors the summer's day scene; the quasi-recitative passage banishes any sense of a sonnet's strict metrical discipline.[1] 'Love's Minstrels', though unsuccessful, is full of striving to break through to a freer style, as in the characteristic recitative passage at the beginning:

ev - en where my   la –   –   dy and I

and in the plainsong-like narrative style. The sharp clash of triads at the very start of the song is also prophetic, and there is an economy of means which was to mark the best of the pre-1914 songs. 'Heart's Haven' is duller, though not without a certain *fin de siècle* charm. 'Death in Love' is on a grander scale, moving towards a more spacious style and having in its declamatory, fanfare-like beginning another seed of *A Sea Symphony*. The sixth sonnet, 'Love's Last Gift', begins with the melodic phrase which occurs throughout Vaughan Williams's music, a diatonic cadence of simplicity found in 'For All the Saints' (Sine Nomine), 'O taste and see', *The Pilgrim's Progress*, and many other works. Here it accompanies the words 'Love to his singer held a glistening leaf':

Andante con moto

p dolce

There is in this fine song an awareness of Elgar's influence; and some curious harmonic progressions to depict the moaning of the wind are another sign of the liberating process. At the end, there is the nobility of utterance which was to be repeated in greater works. *Willow-Wood* is a good deal less successful but more ambitious. The sonnets in this sequence are inferior to those in *The House of Life* and seem to have cramped the composer's style as he tried to bend them to his purpose. The work was written for singer and orchestra, but the first performance, on 12 March 1903, was given

---

[1] In a letter to Mr. Graham Steed, dated 18 November 1938, Vaughan Williams gave some advice about this passage: 'I think the rule would be that the words should be sung just as in speaking—treating the note values fairly freely. There is one point, however, where most singers go wrong. They break thus
        Deep in the sun-search'd growths the dragonfly hangs
        like a blue thread.
This to my mind spoils the phrase. I prefer the break after dragonfly.'

with piano accompaniment. The full score is marked 'finished, April 12, 1903'. Subsequently the songs were re-scored with an ad lib. chorus of women's voices who have a wordless 'ah' to articulate much of the time. This preoccupation with a slightly unusual choral force is *Willow-Wood*'s principal interest, and it might be considered as a trial for the semi-chorus effects in *A Sea Symphony*. The performance of the revised version at Liverpool in 1909 was considered by the composer as sealing the work's fate, although the *Musical Times* correspondent thought highly of it. By 1909 the composer knew better than the critics how far he had travelled in the six years since he put *Willow-Wood* on paper. A better Rossetti setting, also 1903, is the part-song 'Sound Sleep', written as a competition-piece; later an accompaniment for small orchestra was added.

The *Songs of Travel*, less prophetic than *The House of Life*, are a more successful entity although they have rarely been performed as the complete cycle of love-songs which they are—a kind of English *Winterreise* with the wanderer philosophically accepting what life brings to him. In Stevenson's virile open-air verses Vaughan Williams found a half-way stage to Whitman. He withheld the final song of the series, although it gave unity to the whole set by quoting from other songs. Because of the publisher's insistence that the songs should appear in two books Vaughan Williams lost much of the contrast of mood which is an essential part of his original conception. But despite these handicaps the songs made their way in the world because of their individual sturdiness. The most popular is undoubtedly the first, 'The Vagabond', whose striding bass accompaniment is a kind of leitmotif for the cycle. 'Let Beauty Awake', conventionally of its time, has a charm and personality not found in songs of the same type by lesser composers. There is magic in the phrase 'And the stars are bright in the west':

which can mainly be defined by what is the supreme achievement of the whole cycle: the infallible setting of the words, the gift of correct accentuation so that poem and melody fuse into one. This is particularly notable in 'The Roadside Fire', a splendid song marred by the poorest accompaniment of the nine until one comes to the

unexpectedly lengthened final verse where the poetry of the composer's nature lifts him above the commonplace. 'Youth and Love',
on the other hand, has a delicate accompaniment and looks ahead,
in its imaginative and dramatic style, to operatic developments.
Poetically embedded in the accompaniment are quotations from
'The Vagabond' and 'The Roadside Fire'. 'In Dreams' is the
weakest song of the group, poor melodically and bowed down
with the melancholy of the verse. The setting of 'The Infinite
Shining Heavens' is in a similar vein to 'Silent Noon' and is equally
successful in execution. This is the unmistakable voice of the later
Vaughan Williams, a hint of the Herbert setting of eight years later.
'Whither must I wander?', with its semi-modal cadences, was
written earlier than the rest and has defied the years because its tune
is so good, so apt to the words, that singers will not allow it to be
consigned to the shelf. The best song is 'Bright is the ring of words',
which begins with the 'Sine Nomine' phrase, although to speak of
it thus is to be anachronistic:

It begins as a strong, outdoor song and modulates midway into that
moving tenderness which is to be found throughout Vaughan
Williams's music and especially when he is setting words which
refer to music or its performers. 'After the singer is dead, and the
maker buried. . . .' One cannot now hear this phrase, so simply and
beautifully set, without emotional reference to the composer himself
and those singers, long dead, who first sang these splendid English
songs. The little epilogue, with its cross-quotations, rounds off the
cycle perfectly with the Vagabond tramping, pianissimo, off into the
blue. *Songs of Travel* is a major achievement of the early years. The
peculiarly English combination of sturdiness and melancholy
lyricism gives it a vitality which deservedly keeps it in the repertoire.
   Of other songs of this period the now forgotten 'If I were a queen'
(a 'song for children') is a tasteful *morceau*, superior to another
Rossetti setting, 'When I am dead, my dearest.' This latter song
fails like 'The Winter's Willow' because of the poor harmonic invention in the accompaniment. More significant are the first of Vaughan
Williams's settings of Whitman, the two vocal duets which he wrote
in 1904 for the folk-song enthusiast Foxton Ferguson and his wife

Beatrice Spencer. These are in the *Songs of Travel* idiom but they show Vaughan Williams's determination, under Whitman's liberating influence, to free himself from the shackles of a pianoforte accompaniment.

Walt Whitman's poetry played a major rôle in the renascence of British music in the early twentieth century.[1] Composers found in its untrammelling metres an outlet for musical settings which would seem to be at one with the words, despite the oddity of some of the similes. It also reflected the spirit of a new century, a bursting forth to new worlds of human and scientific endeavour. Although Vaughan Williams, Holst, and Delius are principally connected with the poetry of Whitman, they were by no means the only composers of their time to fall under his spell. Charles Wood, Vaughan Williams's teacher at Cambridge, had set the 'Dirge for Two Veterans' for the 1901 Leeds Festival, as well as writing a solo song to 'Ethiopia saluting the Colours'. Holst had written *A Whitman Overture* as early as 1899. Hamilton Harty, like Holst, set 'The Mystic Trumpeter'. W. H. Bell, a College contemporary of Holst and Vaughan Williams, wrote a *Whitman Symphony* which was conducted by Sir August Manns in 1900. The two duets of Vaughan Williams were performed in October and December 1904, preceding by six months the Queen's Hall performance at a Patron's Fund concert of Holst's *Mystic Trumpeter*.

The reason for Whitman's appeal to Vaughan Williams is fairly obvious, apart from the sheer technical challenge to his musical powers. In Vaughan Williams's nature there was a strong vein of mysticism veiled by a thoroughly down-to-earth commonsense approach to his art. He was a romantic; he was also an agnostic, a questioner; he believed in the strength of national roots and he looked to the past in order to venture into the future. It is possible that the Rossettis' medievalism had some appeal for him before he discovered, in folk song, a truer traditionalism. Whitman presented a love of nature plus a combination of plain statement with mystical yearnings; he drew, like the folk singers, on vivid verbal material shorn of academicism. It is, therefore, significant that Vaughan Williams's first settings of Whitman were coincident with his first folk-song collecting year. It has often been accurately remarked that Vaughan Williams's debt to folk song is that he was able to absorb it into his own idiosyncratic idiom. From 1903 to 1906 this permea-

[1] R.V.W. was introduced to Whitman's poetry by Bertrand Russell in 1892. His teacher, Stanford, set Whitman in 1884.

tion can be traced with fascination. His first published and performed arrangements were of German and French folk songs. The
latter were stimulated by acquaintance with Walter Ford, who
shared his enthusiasm for foreign collections and lectured about
them. Ford, born in 1861, had been at Cambridge with Cecil Sharp
and helped to illustrate Sharp's first talk on his discoveries, which he
gave at Hampstead in 1903.[1] Vaughan Williams's interest, though
not pursued beyond 1904, found expression twenty years later when
he introduced the French tune 'Vrai dieu d'amours, comfortez moy'
at an appropriate moment in *Sir John in Love*.[2] The setting of
'Orpheus with his lute' was clearly written in the first flush of folk-
song enthusiasm late in 1902, for it is an advance on the imitative
folk-song style of 'Blackmwore'. It was not, though, Vaughan
Williams's vocal but his orchestral style which was most deeply
stimulated by folk song. *In the Fen Country*, first completed in
April 1904, is a conscious attempt to weld the outline of folk melody
into an 'original' composition. The 1903 *Solent* and *Burley Heath*
were the first efforts in this direction, the former representing a
marked advance on the *Bucolic Suite*. It contains a theme which
haunted Vaughan Williams all his life, appearing in various guises in
A Sea Symphony, the Ninth Symphony and in some late film music.
In *In the Fen Country* there are signs of a more mature outlook. The
harmonic idiom is a curious mixture of the chromaticism of Strauss
and his imitators, the pure diatonic style in which Butterworth was
to write, and occasional glimpses of the Vaughan Williams of a
few years later:

[1] Ford died on 21 August 1938.
[2] Vaughan Williams first heard this tune sung by Théodor Byard, in Paris in 1913.

Portents of the *Fantasia on a Theme by Tallis* are in the false relations. A viola (Vaughan Williams's own instrument, with the violin) has a benedictory solo to end the work. There is a concern for effects of sound (which shows itself in all the early works and belies the legend of amateurish clumsiness in these matters); for instance, he wrote against one passage 'These three bars on the trumpet to be omitted unless they can be played quite smoothly'. The work has a spaciousness, a sense of the Fens' mysterious spell, which was a new element in English music at this date. He immediately, in *Harnham Down*, tried something of the same kind, but he laid this work aside principally because of the pressure of work on the *English Hymnal* but also because he was excited by the rich crop of tunes he collected at King's Lynn in January 1905. The need to give these tunes a wider circulation by incorporating them into orchestral rhapsodies, in the manner of Dvořák and Liszt, was pressing. So in 1906 and 1907 the three *Norfolk Rhapsodies* were composed and performed. Only the first has been allowed to survive in a revised version. The second, of which the MS. score is extant, shows a delight in the tunes but is poorly constructed, with awkward modulations. No doubt its composer anticipated the truth of Constant Lambert's much quoted saying that nothing can be done with a folk song except repeat it louder, though Lambert might have added that putting it in canon was also effective. It is easy to see why the First *Norfolk Rhapsody* was retained. For one thing, its principal theme, 'The Captain's Apprentice', is one of the most beautiful of all English folk songs. Its introduction by an improvisatory viola solo while strings and flutes evoke the Norfolk landscape is a typical and successful moment:

The transition from the romantic mood of this tune to the rollicking 'Bold Young Sailor' is well managed. It can be deduced from the programme-note for the first performance that the end was completely reshaped by the more practised hand of 1914, and instead of a 'brilliant' ending, which no doubt provoked the cheers of the Prom audience, there is the more familiar quiet fade-out by a return to the opening pages of ruminative music. In the revision, the scoring has been thinned; altogether, the surprise one feels that such a cool, poetical orchestral work should occur in 1906 when other orchestral compositions by Vaughan Williams of that date are far inferior is to be discounted, because this is really a post-*London Symphony* work, revised after the period of study with Ravel. It is not as highly organized as Delius's *Brigg Fair*, but its simple orchestration, its brevity and its fresh, moving quality give it a special place in the affections of the composer's admirers. Many writers have assumed that *In the Fen Country* was a product of the Rhapsodies, but it was completed nine months before the folk-song collecting in East Anglia.

There remain, in this period, the arrangements of folk tunes as hymn tunes, and of course, the four great original hymns which Vaughan Williams wrote for the *English Hymnal*. Of these the best-known is 'Sine Nomine' whose opening bars are a key-motive for expressing jubilation throughout Vaughan Williams's life:

And the great 'Alleluia' motif is equally significant:

The most beautiful of the tunes is that named after his birthplace at Down Ampney, to the words 'Come down, O Love Divine', a tune of simple grace that enters one's heart and, once there, stays for ever. The lesser-known 'Hail thee, festival day' is another strong tune which congregations would enjoy if they received more chances of singing it.

The end of 1906, therefore, is a critical point in Vaughan Williams's career. His 'apprenticeship' was over. Folk song and Whitman, working upon each other, had matured the composer's musical manner so that the Brahmsian influence discernible in such works as the pianoforte Fantasia and the discarded quintets was never to recur. He had as yet written no major large-scale work, but he had written at least a dozen tunes which passed at once into the treasury of English song.

CHAPTER FIVE

1907–1914

Principal Works

I

WITH the completion of work on the *English Hymnal* and the resumption of composition, Vaughan Williams searchingly re-examined his musical self. He found it difficult to study and 'learnt almost entirely what I have learnt by trying it on the dog'. One exercise of the kind Holst advocated he did employ: 'One summer [1904] I retired for a month to a Yorkshire farmhouse with several classical scores and the themes of my own "compositions". These themes I proceeded to treat and develop according to my classical models, choosing, of course, themes which more or less corresponded in structure. I found this a wonderful discipline, and I have passed it on to my pupils (I believe,Charles Wood used much the same method). . . . The model I most frequently use is the slow movement of Beethoven's Sonata op. 2, No. 2.'[1]

Holst's statement to Vaughan Williams, 'We ought to be writing now what will enable us to write well later on,' aroused no sympathy in R.V.W., who found it 'very difficult to observe'. It sheds light on the curious relationship of these two friends, who were so close and yet were, in fundamentals, poles apart. Occasionally, Vaughan Williams evaded Holst's frank criticisms—'When I had a new work in the beginning stages my first idea would always be to show it to

---

[1] 'Chapter of Musical Autobiography.'

him. But sometimes I let a work go without his advice and counsel. I probably felt that there was some lapse in it from the highest endeavour and I felt ashamed to submit it to that truthful gaze.' This is a typically modest comment, as is the next sentence—'When this has been so I have always regretted it'—but perhaps Vaughan Williams instinctively knew that some of his works would not have benefited from Holst's advice. The unbuttoned, lyrical, exuberant side of Vaughan Williams's nature expressed itself in music far removed from Holst's idiom. One of the things he valued highly in Holst was Holst's practical experience as an orchestral player, something which he found more useful than the days he himself had spent as an organist. They shared, too, an approach to music as a part of everyday life, taking part in performance as often as they could. (Vaughan Williams would often play the viola in a quartet at the Passmore Edwards Settlement, where Richard Walthew was director from 1900–4 until Holst succeeded him.)

From 1905 to 1907 was the peak period of Vaughan Williams's commitment to folk song, and one wonders how he managed to undertake so much work on the hymnal, collect songs, go to concerts and resume his own composing. This is the period when the mature Vaughan Williams emerged. He wrote the three *Norfolk Rhapsodies*, and his 'Whitmania' was first effectively channelled into a short choral work for the 1907 Leeds Festival, *Toward the Unknown Region*. This became a memorial for the historian F. W. Maitland whose death in 1906 had grieved Vaughan Williams. He dedicated it to Maitland's widow, Florence, sister of Adeline.

The Rhapsodies, light-weight works, were favourably received by the majority of critics and also by the public, for the newspapers were nearly always able to record that the composer was 'loudly cheered'. *The Times*, after the first performance of the first rhapsody at the Promenade Concerts of 1906, described it as 'a very taking and charming orchestral piece'. By treating folk tunes, the critic thought, the composer had 'shirked a great part, perhaps the greatest part, of the composer's responsibility. It is at any rate the part in which very many modern composers fail, the originating of new and beautiful themes. But the conception of the piece as a whole is quite his own . . . the result sounds like a piece of music and not a patchwork. It is unnecessary to remark on the dainty colours of the score, an art which nowadays is almost common property, but the first section, in which various instruments, like people sitting round and suggesting what song shall be sung, in turn suggest fragments of tunes used, is particularly happy'.

Thirteen months later, at the Cardiff Festival of September 1907, the composer conducted the first performances of the Second and Third Rhapsodies. Again it is *The Times* correspondent to whom one must refer for the fullest account of the event. He indicates that seven folk-tunes 'of the utmost distinction and vigour', of which he found 'Ward the Pirate' the most splendid, were used in the two works.[1] 'All are scored with remarkable skill, and the thematic development is ingenious and often most humorous. The last piece of the set is a most inspiring march and both, played under the composer's direction, fairly brought down the house.'

The second and third Rhapsodies were eventually withdrawn; the first was revised nearly twenty years later. Undoubtedly the Norfolk and other beautiful folk tunes were more effectively and lastingly 'given back to the people' in the fifteen simple and haunting arrangements which Vaughan Williams published in 1908 as *Folk Songs from the Eastern Counties*.

From one festival to another fourteen days later, at Leeds; and there *Toward the Unknown Region* had a tremendous success. 'The merit of the work lies in the way in which the composer used choral effects in the way usually referred to when speaking of modern orchestral music as the quality of colours. . . . The music moves along with a certain spiritual form. . . . The very striking work, original, and showing a homogeneity that very little of the British school reveals, met with immediate and hearty approval.' So wrote Herbert Thompson in the *Yorkshire Post*, and Plunket Greene has described it (in his life of Stanford) as 'new in its outlook, and new in its working out, and enthralling in its beautiful interpretation of the words'. *The Times* was even more positive. The 'little cantata', its critic wrote, was 'easily ahead of anything the young composer has yet given us, and here we see the perfect maturity of his genius, the art that conceals art most effectually and a nobility and earnestness of invention which mark the composer as the foremost of the younger generation.' The music 'ends in an almost hysterical outburst suggesting an apotheosis of muscular vigour. In the art of piling climax upon climax and of carrying our feelings irresistibly forward from beginning to end the composer is already a master.' Loud cheers greeted the work. Holst and Vaughan Williams each

[1] Three in No. 2 and four in No. 3.

made a setting of this text. They compared their scores and decided that Vaughan Williams's setting was the better.[1]

The two orchestral 'impressions', *Harnham Down* and *Boldre Wood* were played in Queen's Hall the next month at a concert sponsored by a friend of Carthusian days, the pianist and composer, H. Vivian Hamilton, and conducted by the Czech composer and conductor Reznicek, best known in Britain for his opera *Donna Diana*, the overture to which was played at this concert. Hamilton's *Suite de Ballet* and Ethel Smyth's *Three Songs* with accompaniment for flute, harp, strings, triangle and tambourine also received their first performances the same evening. *The Times* critic found that the Impressions' 'power and originality' were not to be denied. 'The first, *Harnham Down*, is a vivid picture of a still summer day, and *Boldre Wood* is a longer and far more beautiful study of wood-magic. . . . All the resources of the most modern harmonies, abrupt transitions and strange orchestral effects are there in plenty and nearly all of them make all their intended impression and that is a very picturesque one.' Acclaimed as the leader of his generation, with increasing performances, many a man of thirty-five might have felt a certain satisfaction. But not Vaughan Williams. Conducting his own works and hearing them under other conductors, he felt that his work was still deficient. He came to the conclusion, as he wrote in the 'Chapter of Musical Autobiography', that he was 'lumpy and stodgy, had come to a dead end and that a little French polish would be of use'. He consulted his friends and other composers about the major step of acquiring it. For instance on 24 October 1907, a few days after hearing Delius's pianoforte concerto played at a Promenade Concert by Theodor Szanto, he wrote this:

Dear Mr. Delius,

I hope you will not think I am making a very audacious request. I should so much like to show you some of my work. I have had it in my mind (and especially now that I have heard your beautiful concerto) that I should profit very much by your advice and if you saw my work you might be able to suggest ways in which I could improve myself—either by going to Paris or not. Have you ever any time to spare—and if you have would you allow me to come and see you? I don't know if I ought to ask this on so slight an acquaintance.

Yours very truly,
R. Vaughan Williams.

[1] Letter from R.V.W. to Imogen Holst.

Delius agreed, and their meeting was described by R.V.W. in his Musical Autobiography where he says that he 'burst in on the privacy of Delius . . . and insisted on playing through the whole of my *Sea Symphony* to him. Poor fellow! How he must have hated it! But he was very courteous and contented himself with saying "Vraiment, il n'est pas mesquin".' Why Delius, a Yorkshireman, should have addressed his compatriot in French is one of life's mysteries.

The critic Edwin Evans advised Vaughan Williams to go to Vincent D'Indy's Schola Cantorum. M. D. Calvocoressi suggested Maurice Ravel, not an obvious choice, for Ravel was not well known in England at that date. Calvocoressi arranged a meeting, and in January 1908 Vaughan Williams went for three months to Paris to study with a man younger than himself. Extracts from letters to Calvocoressi show what a successful piece of advice had been offered:

'Ravel is exactly the man I was looking for. As far as I know my own faults, he hit on them exactly and is telling me to do exactly what I half felt in my mind I ought to do—but it just wanted saying.'

'I am getting a lot out of Ravel. I hope it doesn't worry him too much. Only I feel that 10 years with him would not teach me all I want.'

'I must thank you for introducing me to the man who is exactly what I was looking for. I have got *Antar* and have set to work on him. It is awfully kind of you to have been present at the lessons—it was such a help.'

Vaughan Williams chiefly practised orchestration with Ravel. 'I used to score some of his own pianoforte music and bits of Rimsky and Borodin, to whom he introduced me for the first time. [Hence the reference to *Antar*.] After three months I came home with a bad attack of French fever and wrote a string quartet [the G minor] which caused a friend to say that I must have been having tea with Debussy, and a song cycle [*On Wenlock Edge*] with several atmospheric effects.'

Ravel evidently admired his pupil—'the only one who does not write my music'—and tried to advance Vaughan Williams's music in Paris.

Vaughan Williams's decision to seek lessons in France was remarkably prescient in 1907, for Germany would still have been the obvious and natural choice. How little of French music was known in certain English circles in 1906 is illustrated by the letter from the secretary of the Philharmonic Society to Debussy inviting him to conduct one of his works at a London concert, adding, 'Shall it be *Pelléas et Mélisande*? Can you tell me approximately how many minutes this work requires in performance? . . .'

The visit to Ravel restored Vaughan Williams's confidence (although throughout his life he had fears that he was 'drying up', usually when a big work was in the gestation stage). The next five years were productive: it is worth noting that of the orchestral works written before the visit to Ravel only one, the first *Norfolk Rhapsody*, was retained. *In the Fen Country* at last came to performance, in February 1909, when Beecham conducted it at one of his own ventures in Queen's Hall. 'Though the theme is fragrant of the soil it appears to be only in the style of folk-music, not an actual specimen,' *The Times* said. 'The treatment of the theme and its derivation is remarkably powerful, and all the composer's orchestral devices make their full effect. . . . If all the new school of composers knew how to use their tools as well as he does, the outlook for the future would be a good deal brighter than it is.' At the same concert Beecham conducted the first London performance of Delius's *Sea-Drift*, and *The Times*'s critic thought that Delius could well imitate Vaughan Williams's certainty of handling his orchestral resources, an opinion which comparison of the two scores hardly justifies. Despite this encouraging response to an ambitious work—and the *Musical Times* also found it 'a highly creditable product of the composer's thoughtful and imaginative attainments'—Vaughan Williams was still dissatisfied. He withdrew it and revised it again years later. Although *In the Fen Country* has had several performances and its parts are available on hire, it has not, to date, been published. Beecham retained an admiration for it.

During 1908, after returning from Paris, Vaughan Williams immediately set to work on his G minor quartet and the settings of Housman's *Shropshire Lad* poems. One of these, 'Is my team ploughing?', was first sung in public on 26 January 1909, at a concert sponsored by Gervase Elwes and James Friskin. This song, *The Times* said, was 'a miniature tragedy of the utmost force and originality'. It is not possible to say whether the whole cycle, *On Wenlock Edge*, had been completed at this time. It received its first performance at the Aeolian Hall on 15 November 1909, at a concert jointly promoted by Elwes and Vaughan Williams. This undertaking was doubly threatened by disaster. There was a last-minute rush to get Housman's permission for the printing of the words in the programme,[1] and then, a few days before the concert, Elwes was stricken with laryngitis. It was feared he would not appear, but a doctor's treatment enabled him to sing *On Wenlock Edge*, although he cancelled some other items in the programme. Elwes's wife, Lady Winefride, remembered that, afterwards, 'Vaughan Williams came up to me, his eyes shining with delight. By nature he is far from effusive and I have never seen him look so excited. All he could say to me was "If Gervase can sing like that when he has laryngitis, I hope he may always have it".'[2] It was, incidentally, Elwes's forty-third birthday.

The main preoccupation of 1908 and early 1909 was extensive revision and completion of the big Whitman choral work on which he had been working since 1903 and which now became *A Sea Symphony*. He also wrote two other works which had their first performances within a week in September 1910, and which separately indicated the two major influences on his music, folk song and the Tudor composers. Both had the title 'fantasia', itself a link with Byrd, Morley and a golden age of English music. The first, played at the Promenade Concert on 1 September, was the *Fantasia on English Folk Song* sub-titled, significantly, 'Studies for an English Ballad Opera', the first adumbration of work on *Hugh the Drover*. Rosa Newmarch, in her programme-note for the Prom performance, discussed the appeal of treating folk music by 'a process of assimilation . . . in order to give it forth in a new, individual and artistic disposition', and, 'while sympathising with the tendency', asked if there was not a risk of 'sterilisation of the highest imaginative power in carrying it too far, as the Russians have undoubtedly done. It is possible to work the national vein for a little more than it is worth.' The fantasia was founded on matter suggested by folk song but did not contain any verbatim transcriptions. *The Times* critic noted that there was 'scarcely a decent acknowledgment in applause', but this did not matter very much as 'the fault was so obviously that of the audience rather than of the work'. But, he went on, there was 'something to be said in excuse for the want of appreciation, for the composer has not made his plan as clear as he did in the *Norfolk*

---

[1] Housman disliked the many musical settings of his poems and he disliked *On Wenlock Edge* most of all.

[2] *Gervase Elwes, the Story of his Life*, by Winefride Elwes and Richard Elwes (London 1935).

Rhapsody. The treatment [of the tunes] is . . . more abstract and the composer seems purposely to have avoided letting any one of them be heard in its simple form'. The second fantasia, written for the Gloucester meeting of the Three Choirs and played on Tuesday, 6 September,[1] was the *Fantasia on a Theme by Thomas Tallis*, for strings. This masterpiece made comparatively little stir at its first performance and was not immediately seized upon by orchestras. A few people—Herbert Howells among them—who were present in Gloucester Cathedral that evening, primarily to hear *The Dream of Gerontius*, realized the beauty of the new work which preceded it, its gravity and strength reflecting the same qualities in the black-haired, handsome giant who was conducting his own music. The *Musical Times* critic complained that the *Fantasia*, in which he curiously found the quality of 'charm', was 'over-long for the subject-matter'. The composer again heeded criticism and the work was withdrawn, revised and cut before its publication in 1921. As it now stands, it is one of the sublime masterpieces of English music. It is almost impossible to dissociate the music from a cathedral such as that for which it was written. Those youthful days of listening to the choir at Ely are here transformed into music. Though Tallis is the work's inspiration, it perhaps owes something to Palestrina. Vaughan Williams conducted a small Palestrina Society of enthusiasts at this time, and no doubt he knew the *Stabat Mater*, where there is a refrain repeated with varied harmonies and a double chorus which could have suggested the contrasted string orchestras used in the *Fantasia*. Is it not possible, too, that a basic idea of the *Fantasia*— homage to the past—led Ravel in *Le Tombeau de Couperin* (1914–17) to follow his pupil's example?

Fuller Maitland, of *The Times*, was one who at once perceived the beauty and importance of the *Tallis Fantasia*. His notice of the first performance is as true and moving today as on the day it was written. After describing it in some detail he wrote:

'The work is wonderful because it seems to lift one into some unknown region of musical thought and feeling. Throughout its course one is never quite sure whether one is listening to something very old or very new. . . . The voices of the old church musicians . . . are around one, and yet there

---

[1] Several books on Vaughan Williams and many articles give the date of the first performance as 1909, under Beecham at Queen's Hall. This error originally arose, I suspect, from the simple typographical misplacement of a bracket in Grove's *Dictionary*, third edition. The work which was played by Beecham in 1909 was *In the Fen Country*.

is more besides, for their music is enriched with all that modern art has done since. Debussy, too, is somewhere in the picture and it is hard to tell how much of the complete freedom of tonality comes from the new French school and how much from the old English one. But that is just what makes this *Fantasia* so delightful to listen to; it cannot be assigned to a time or a school, but it is full of visions which have haunted the seers of all times. We can recall no piece of pure instrumental music produced at a Three Choirs Festival which has seemed to belong to its surroundings so entirely as does this *Fantasia*. It could never thrive in a modern concert-room, but in the quieter atmosphere of the cathedral the mind falls readily into the reflective attitude necessary for the enjoyment of every unexpected transition from chord to chord. . . .'

The great work, in which Vaughan Williams forged a link with the leader of the English musical renascence of nearly four centuries earlier, has, of course, thrived in the concert-hall, but it is still true that it sounds best in surroundings similar to those for which it was composed. Another, possibly more general, opinion of the *Fantasia* at its first performance was given expression by the critic of the *Gloucester Journal*, who evidently resented the interpolation of this new work between him and *Gerontius*. 'We confess,' he confided, 'that the "theme" on which the *Fantasia* is founded is not familiar to us, and the impression left on the mind by the whole composition was one of unsatisfaction (if we may use such a word). We had short phrases repeated with tiresome iteration, and at no time did the *Fantasia* rise beyond the level of an uninteresting exercise. The band played the piece as well as it could be played, and we had some nice contrasts in light and shade. But there was a feeling of relief when the *Fantasia* came to an end, and we could get to something with more colour and warmth. The piece took nineteen minutes in performance.' Samuel Langford, in the *Manchester Guardian*, also invoked Debussy's name to explain the 'exotic' harmonies and suggested that the work would have been better called 'Exaltation' than fantasy.

From 1907 there had been a distinct increase in the propagation of work by English composers and English artists, the fruit of various schemes as well as of the growth of the renascence. Many young composers had the chance of hearing their works played at concerts of the Patron's Fund of the Royal College of Music. This fund of £27,000 given in 1903 by Sir Ernest (later Lord) Palmer made possible the engagement of professional orchestras to play British works. Holst's Suite in E flat and his *Mystic Trumpeter* were first played at Patron's Fund concerts in Queen's Hall in 1904 and 1905. The latter year saw the foundation of the Society of British Composers, whose principal objective was to promote the publication of music by British composers sometimes by defraying all or part of the cost. The Society's publications were known as the Avison Edition, undertaken first by Breitkopf and Härtel and subsequently by Novello and by Cary. It also gave concerts, at one of which, in November 1909, Vaughan Williams's G minor string quartet was first played. *On Wenlock Edge* was an Avison publication. In 1918 the Society was wound up in view of the supposed healthier outlook, for British musicians. A shorter-lived venture was the Music League founded in 1909 to assist British endeavour. Elgar was president, and Delius, Bantock, Havergal Brian, Bax and Ethel Smyth were associated with it. Its main achievement was a festival at Liverpool in September 1909. Vaughan Williams's orchestral version of *Willow-Wood* received its first performance there. Three young private patrons of music, H. Balfour Gardiner, F. B. Ellis and Edward Mason, sponsored the work of their contemporaries between 1910 and 1914. Wood and Beecham had by 1907 established their reputations. Beecham's New Symphony Orchestra gave enterprising concerts. Within a fortnight, late in 1907, London heard Beecham conduct Mahler's Fourth Symphony, with Blanche Marchesi as the soloist, and Fritz Cassirer conducted the first performance of Delius's *Appalachia*. Each work was scorned by the critics and would probably still have been scorned if, as might seem more credible, the conductors had exchanged works! British soloists, too, were beginning to make their names. Myra Hess, May Harrison, Frank Merrick, Lionel Tertis and others of their calibre came rapidly to the fore to join the singers—McInnes, Plunket Greene and Elwes—who had led the way.

Vaughan Williams, in spite of his growing fame, continued to uphold his principle that a nation's musical health could not be measured by the standards set in London concert-hall and opera house. At the Leith Hill Festival he stimulated amateur endeavour by bringing it into contact with professional prowess. He published in 1908 his first arrangements of folk songs from his own collection. In the summer of that year in Herefordshire, with Mrs. E. M. Leather, and in Derbyshire, he rediscovered the beauty of old

English carols, a subject in which he had kindled Sharp's interest. Sharp published his *English Folk Carols* in 1911, and dedicated it to Vaughan Williams who said: 'It is a fine book. I've always loved carols. I remember the time when, if I said "carol", I could not get a spark out of you—now as usual you have gone ahead and left me in the lurch.' (Not too far in the lurch, though, for the compliment of dedication was returned in 1912 in the *Fantasia on Christmas Carols*.) Another event which gave much pleasure to Vaughan Williams was the invitation to write the incidental music for the Cambridge Greek Play in 1909, *The Wasps* of Aristophanes, thus enabling him to follow in the footsteps of his masters Parry, Stanford, and Charles Wood. In the chorus were two brilliant young men. One was the tenor J. S. Wilson—Steuart Wilson—who sang the solo serenade in Act I. Between him and Vaughan Williams a lifelong friendship here began. The other was Denis Browne. He was a gifted pianist and composer, organist of Clare College and a pupil, as Vaughan Williams had been, of Charles Wood and Alan Gray. Browne, who was an enthusiastic performer of Vaughan Williams's music, was to find immortality in company with another Cambridge man, Rupert Brooke. He was at the poet's bedside when Brooke died, he was present at the burial on Skyros, and in a final letter to Eddie Marsh, not received till after Browne's death in action at the Dardanelles on 7 June 1915, he described 'Rupert's island' at sunset in a phrase which epitomized a tragic chapter in English literature: 'It seemed that the island must ever be shining with his glory that we buried there.' These names; Cambridge; the heyday of the Edwardian era —it is no wonder that *The Wasps* music exerts such emotional power on those who were young when it was first played and for whom it represents part of the eternal summer of their early lives, though in fact the performances were at the end of November. Iris, Lady Wedgwood, widow of Sir Ralph Wedgwood, 'Randolph' as he was known to the family, remembered[1] Vaughan Williams telling her and her husband that at one moment a member of the orchestra was to shake a bag full of broken china. 'Will it be Wedgwood?' asked Randolph. 'Of course,' Ralph replied. 'It is the only china which would make the right sound.' Cecil Sharp and Vaughan Williams stayed with Randolph and Iris in Northumberland shortly after the Wedgwoods were married. Iris has written:[2] 'I was always

[1] *R.C.M. Magazine* 1959, Vol. LV, No. 1.
[2] Op. cit.

surprised and slightly disturbed by Ralph's utter disregard of his appearance and clothes, also by the passionate vigour with which he supported his opinions. But the warmth of his personality held a compelling charm; he was so kind, so lovable!' Passionate vigour . . . warmth. The very qualities, surely, which stand forth in *A Sea Symphony*, the major work of his early manhood, on which he had spent seven years and which received its first performance at the Leeds Festival of 1910 conducted by the composer on his thirty-eighth birthday. Rehearsals had been held at the Royal College of Music on 3 and 5 October. He liked to tell the story of his nervousness before the first performance and of how C. A. Henderson, the timpanist and a burly ex-Coldstream Guardsman, told him: 'You just give us a good square four-in-the-bar and we'll do the rest.' Many famous players were in the orchestra on that occasion: among them the Hobdays, W. H. Reed, the Carroduses, Draper the clarinettist, Aubrey Brain and F. Paersch the horn-players, Solomon the trumpeter, Harry Barlow, tuba, and the Man-chester harpist Charles Collier who, nearly fifty years later, attended the rehearsals of the eighth symphony and talked about Leeds of 1910 to his fellow octogenarian. The baritone soloist was Campbell McInnes and the soprano Cicely Gleeson-White. Vaughan Williams had written the part with Agnes Nicholls in mind. She was singing at Leeds in 1910 but he was unable to obtain her for his work. Later, when she sang in the first London performance, he was slightly disappointed with her interpretation.

The symphony was the first item in the Leeds concert and was the only choral work. It was followed by Rachmaninov's playing of his own C minor concerto and by Strauss's *Don Juan*. The Vaughan Williams work and *Songs of the Fleet* by Stanford were the only 'novelties' in 1910, a contrast to the 1907 festival when, besides *Toward the Unknown Region*, Stanford's *Stabat Mater*, Somervell's *Intimations of Immortality*, Brewer's *In Springtime*, Rutland Bough-ton's *Two Folk Songs with Variations*, and Bantock's *Sea Wanderers* were performed. 'Novelties do not pay,' the *Yorkshire Post* said of the 1910 festival, 'and in times so precarious for all artistic enter-prises it becomes doubly necessary to proceed warily, especially when a festival is linked with a charity and its mission is to make a profit, as seems to be essential in this country where a purely artistic aim is regarded with suspicion.' The *Yorkshire Post*'s critic of that day was Herbert Thompson, an early champion of Vaughan

Williams's music, as his analytical notes for the first performances of *A Sea Symphony* and of the *Five Mystical Songs* exemplify. His notice of the first performance of the symphony is still valuable:

'. . . It [V.W.'s music] is certainly more individual, [than in *Toward the Unknown Region*] bigger in conception, richer in ideas and much freer in expression. The music is difficult, unnecessarily so, one would imagine, for probably the desired effect might have been obtained with less complication and fewer awkward passages, but however this may be, it strikes one as sincere, highly poetic in feeling, and showing the power to deal with a big canvas. The ideas are never puny or finicking, and the music has breadth and grandeur. . . . The composer's method is very modern in its elusive and tortuous harmonic progressions, but they leave the conviction that they are not affected for the sake of singularity, but are the genuine expression of the composer's ideas. . . .The performance was a wonderfully good one. . . . The Scherzo, with its tricky entries and rapid changes, was a piece of virtuosity in choral singing such as one seldom witnesses. . . .'

The last sentence disposes of the allegation made by Sir Hugh Allen, and quoted in the biography of Allen by Cyril Bailey, that the Scherzo had been omitted at Leeds because the Festival Chorus found it too difficult. *The Times* critic also described the singing of the Scherzo as 'wonderful'. He was even more enthusiastic than Thompson. 'It will not be surprising,' he accurately prophesied, 'if the Festival of 1910 is remembered in the future as the "Festival of the *Sea Symphony*". . . . The opening two chords produced an almost visual effect upon the hearers as though a curtain were drawn back and the expanse of the sea revealed.' The first movement in particular impressed the writer. Whitman's 'queer use of neologisms' was more than justified by the musical setting, he wrote. The 'chant for the sailors of all nations' had 'an almost Purcellian simplicity'. It was 'a pleasure to recognize the poetical grasp with which Mr. Vaughan Williams has handled his subject, bringing forth ever richer and richer musical treasures as the words inspire him'. By the last movement 'a feeling is created that the composer's invention is so little exhausted at the end that he might well lead us on to further and further climaxes'. Poet and musician were 'marvellously akin. . . . In both there is the distaste for the old-fashioned forms, both are striving for the newer poetic life; and in the ferment there must be some refuse thrown off, some ungainliness of verbal phrase or musical progression. But there is no denying the presence of great imaginative poetry in one and the other.' Langford, in the *Manchester Guardian*, was equally emphatic that the symphony 'definitely places a new figure in the first rank of our English composers. It is unique in several ways. . . . It is the nearest approach we have to a real choral symphony, one in which the voices are used throughout just as freely as the orchestra. It is also in scope much the finest piece of sea music that we, a seafaring folk above everything, possess. It accepts right away the challenge thrown down by Wagner to all composers of sea music when he wrote *The Flying Dutchman*. . . . The last movement is by far the most chastened in its expression and it . . . reveals most certainly the fine gifts of the composer.'

The Times report specifically mentioned that the work was 'warmly received', which makes Vaughan Williams's description of the reception as 'doubtful'[1] rather puzzling. He said he owed its life to two men, Stanford, who persuaded the Leeds Committee to include it in the festival, and H. P. Allen, who campaigned for it after the performance and, according to Vaughan Williams, 'pushed it down people's throats after the Leeds performance was a complete flop'.[2] Stanford loved the work, and considered that all that came from Vaughan Williams's pen thereafter was a decline. At the orchestral rehearsals at the Royal College of Music before the Leeds performance, he noticed mistakes in the parts and in the playing, although using only a vocal score. Performers in a work are often more conscious of imperfections than listeners, so perhaps Vaughan Williams's recollections of that historic first performance were conditioned by his own constant dissatisfaction with his music and his conducting of it, and by opinions such as this, in a letter written to him after the performance by a member of the chorus: 'I *wish* we had done more justice to it. "Away, O Soul" especially rankles!'

He had consulted his friend Donald Tovey about certain points in his score. Writing years later he said:[3] 'In my original score, which is still preserved in the pianoforte score, I started the full orchestra on the first beat of the bar. I then realized this would obscure the word "sea" sung by the chorus. On the other hand, I did not wish to have nothing for the orchestra and asked Tovey's advice; he suggested the plan I have carried out—only the timpani and the organ on the first beat.' This point still occupied Tovey

[1] 'Chapter of Musical Autobiography.'
[2] Letter to Hubert Foss, 1941.
[3] *Donald Francis Tovey* by Mary Grierson (London, 1952).

after twenty-eight years for in November 1938 he wrote to Vaughan Williams:[1]

'About the drum-roll that supports the chorus on the word "sea" at the very beginning: what would you think of having the stroke of the big drum on the first beat instead of on the second? Now that I see you have the big drum on the second beat I am in two minds about it, but I had hitherto always thought that a boom on the big drum would add an oceanic solemnity to the crack of the timpani.'[2]

Both *A Sea Symphony* and the *Tallis Fantasia* had to wait two and a half years for performances in London. The former, however, was sung in the meantime at Oxford, Cambridge, and Bristol. (The university cities had already relished *Toward the Unknown Region*. The C.U.M.S. performance on 12 June 1908 was conducted by the composer, and the timpanist was E. J. Dent! Another artist for whose admired playing Vaughan Williams was to write music also appeared at that concert, the violinist Marie Hall.)

For *A Sea Symphony* its composer had a special affection. He liked to conduct it. 'I'm glad if bits of the old S.S. withstand the ravages of time,' he wrote to Maud Karpeles in the late 1920s. In the last month of his life, when I told him how much I liked it, he said, almost guiltily, 'So do I, rather.' In the same conversation he mentioned various literary enthusiasms of his lifetime which had 'gone off the boil' for him. 'And Whitman?' I asked. 'I've never got over him, I'm glad to say,' he replied.

It is truthful to say that *A Sea Symphony*, more than any other work, put him 'on the map' before the First World War. Its impact in the long run was greater than that of either *On Wenlock Edge* or the *Tallis Fantasia*, both of which are more completely successful works. For the Worcester Festival of 1911 he produced the *Five Mystical Songs*, settings of poems by George Herbert on which, according to Herbert Thompson's programme note, he had been at work spasmodically for five years, rewriting them in 1910–11. The composer again conducted the first performance, and it was at this concert that the famous incident occurred when he was amazed to see Kreisler playing at the back desk of the violins. The great violinist was to play Elgar's concerto after the Songs and was 'playing himself in' in Vaughan Williams's work. At Hereford in

---

[1] Op. cit.

[2] On the first page of the MS. full score Vaughan Williams wrote: '*Note:* a *roll* on the cymbals to be made with **two** soft timpani sticks.'

1912 the hat-trick of Three Choirs first performances was completed with the *Fantasia on Christmas Carols*. The years 1911–14 saw a growing interest in his music among musicians of all types. Several publications of his folk-song arrangements date from this period; his lecture, quoted in Chapter III, on folk song was given in 1912; his famous article 'Who Wants the English Composer?' was published in 1912 in the *R.C.M. Magazine*. During all this period he was writing his opera *Hugh the Drover* as a culmination of his folk-song enthusiasm. Early in 1912 Ravel wrote to him (January 4) explaining that his Société Musicale Indépendante had been unable to perform the G minor string quartet in the 1911 season but that the committee had decided to organize an English concert and to play Vaughan Williams's quartet or 'Les mélodies avec accompagnement du quintette [*On Wenlock Edge*] que je trouve tout-à-fait remarquable'. On 2 February he was able to announce firmer plans: 'The concert will be exceptionally brilliant. Fauré will accompany Jeanne Raünay. . . . We thought of engaging as your interpreter Plamondon, a well-known tenor and excellent musician who sings in English. The Wuillaume Quartet will accompany him. If you would consent to play the pianoforte part yourself that would be splendid. If not I offer you my services.' The songs had a striking success with the French audience at an S.M.I. concert on 29 February 1912. Vaughan Williams himself told his intimates in later years that it was the worst performance he had ever heard, 'which was probably why the French liked it'. But Ravel, on 5 August 1912, was able to write to his friend that in everyone's opinion 'vos poèmes lyriques ont été une révélation'.[1] Among those to whom they were a revelation was presumably the French critic Marcel Boulestin who, in an article in January 1914, in *La revue musicale*, acclaimed Vaughan Williams as the leader of the post-Elgar generation in England. This was too much for Ernest Newman, never a particular admirer of Vaughan Williams, who replied in the *Birmingham Post* of 16 February 1914, that it was 'strange that it should be left to a Frenchman to discover a fact of which no one in England has hitherto been conscious! . . .

[1] More English music was given at S.M.I. concerts in Paris on 22 and 29 May, 1913. At the former Théodor Byard sang unspecified songs by Cyril Scott and Vaughan Williams. An orchestral concert a week later gave Delius's *Appalachia* and Vaughan Williams's First *Norfolk Rhapsody*. At about this time, too, the English Folk Dance Society gave a display in Paris. Rodolphe Plamondon, of Canadian origin, sang in Paris between 1906 and 1918. It has not been possible to discover the identity of the pianist in *On Wenlock Edge*, but most likely it was Ravel.

strange that no one I have ever met had any intuition that Dr. Vaughan Williams was our messiah! We live and learn. The truth simply is that M. Boulestin is insensitive to the greater English music because it is not French, and he prefers some of the minor English music because it coquets with the modern French idiom'.

At least it must have been a change to be accused of French influences instead of having the label 'folky' stuck on to anything he attempted. Yet, while his enthusiasm for the beauty of the English songs was paramount, he never succumbed to the worst excesses of the folk-song revivalists and his whole connection with the movement was a plea for level-headedness. When Sharp was preparing his pamphlet on *Folk-Singing in Schools* in 1913 he sent the manuscript to Vaughan Williams, whose criticisms of it are representative of his practical approach. Even without the specific objects of his criticisms, they are still worth quoting:

'Please cut out the word "lower" before classes—if it is the usual word at present it's high time we dropped it—I have known several people who are much *put off* by references of that kind to the folk-singing class. Besides, a little more explanation is required. "Unsophisticated and unlettered" or "untravelled and unlettered" seems much better. Also I should leave out "classes" and substitute "members" or "portions".

'Folk-singers are most usually found in small *country towns*. They have doubtless migrated there from the country, but the fact remains. Indeed I think the whole distinction between "town" and "country" song is misleading. The distinction was not there, probably, in olden times, and is not now. The distinction is between spontaneous, traditional, oral music and deliberate, written conscious music.

' "The advent of the grammarian . . .", etc.—seems to me most misleading and seems to suggest that *all* art-music is pedantry—it is also probable that the folk song had its pedants also, and probably there was a sort of "etiquette" of folk-singing much more rigid than our musical grammar—which only the geniuses over-stepped—just as savages have customs and taboos more rigid than our reasoned laws.

'Leave out the words "voice production"—as this seems to me a most important part of a child's education. You seem to me to give the words "voice production" an evil connotation because so much so-called voice production is bad and unnecessary—but surely real voice production—the encouragement of a full clear pleasant sound whether in speaking or singing, and (as you yourself say) of clear enunciation, is *absolutely necessary* and a most important part of the development of the child's best nature. To take an extreme case: supposing a child tried to sing (or speak) with its mouth *tight shut* the teacher would have to tell it to open it and what wd. this be but a lesson in voice production? I heard only the other day of a teacher who told children that when they sang folk songs they must *shout* and *roar* and *discouraged* a pleasant tone—with the result that the managers of a neighbouring competition decided to have *no* folk songs. This seems to me the *direct* outcome of this talk about voice production being unnecessary.'

In the Spring of 1913 Vaughan Williams was musical director at the Stratford-upon-Avon festival from 21 April to 14 May with Sir Frank Benson's company. It was not the happiest musical experience. Benson, though polite, was obviously neither pleased nor interested by the new music, and went back to his old 'hotch-potch' as soon as the musical director departed. Vaughan Williams, on the other hand, was fascinated by this contact with the stage and he interested some of the actors, Harry Caine in particular, in the folk-dance classes which were held in Stratford at the same time by Sharp, Douglas Kennedy, Maud and Helen Karpeles, and George Butterworth. Vaughan Williams also was always willing to join in folk dances to the best of his ability, something which those who did not see it can only dimly imagine.

For *Henry IV, Part II*, and *The Merry Wives* the entr'actes were selected from Holst's 'Country Song' and 'Marching Song' (his two *Songs Without Words*, for orchestra, dedicated to Vaughan Williams and first played at the Royal College of Music on 19 July 1906), *Three English Dances* by Roger Quilter, the 'Pavane', 'Country Dance', and Suite of Ancient Dances by German, and four Elizabethan dances and a Suite of English Melodies by Vaughan Williams. For *Richard II*, Beethoven's *Coriolan*, Elgar's Serenade, Mozart's G minor symphony, Schubert's *Rosamunde* entr'actes, Mendelssohn's 'Pilgrims' March' and Holst's 'Country Song' were the motley collection from which entr'actes were devised. It is impossible to know whether Vaughan Williams's innate taste imposed some kind of artistic style on this odd selection. His own 'incidental music' was chiefly based on folk song. The local Stratford dramatic critic at any rate was not impressed. Of *Richard II* he remarked:[1]

[1] *Stratford on Avon Herald*. 25 April 1913.

'The music seemed at fault in many places. It was not conducted with that knowledge of the theatre which comes of long sympathetic experience. It was too loud in the Garden Scene, it was melodramatic at various points and frequently the actors had to talk against it. If we will have music mixed up with the literary theatre, let it be kept in its just realistic position.' He was rather more pleased with the accompaniment of Frank Benson's monologues in *Henry IV, Part II*, but even here 'the music should have stopped earlier in the scene than it did: it was lovely, but there is such a thing as drawing linked sweetness out to too great a length'.

George Hannam-Clark, one of Benson's company, recalled that 'after one Friday rehearsal Vaughan Williams worked all night orchestrating and even writing out the parts for a new setting of "Greensleeves". It was played at the matinée on the following day'. This was for *Richard II*; and if it did nothing else, the Stratford experience obviously sowed the seed for a Shakespearean opera, which became *Sir John in Love*.

A curious sidelight of the 1913 Stratford Festival deserves mention. On the afternoon of 24 April, a recital of music for harpsichord, virginals, and flute was given by Mrs. Violet Gordon Woodhouse, assisted by the great French flautist, Louis Fleury. As well as, 'by request', a group of folk dances collected by Cecil Sharp and arranged by Mrs. Woodhouse for her instrument, the programme included some 'Folk Airs for harpsichord and flute' arranged 'especially for the occasion' by Dr. Vaughan Williams. There is no other known occasion when he wrote for the instrument which he detested so much.[1]

Work on *Hugh the Drover* ran parallel with work on the largest orchestral composition Vaughan Williams had yet attempted, the *London Symphony*. Opera and symphony are a reflection of his pre-1914 nationalism at its most intense. In both works is mirrored the creed, already quoted, which he set forth in 'Who Wants the English Composer?'. 'Have not we all about us forms of musical expression which we can take and purify and raise to the level of great art . . . the children dancing to a barrel organ . . . the cries of the street pedlars. . . . Have all these nothing to say to us?' It was George Butterworth, a friend from early in the century, companion on folk-song-collecting expeditions, gruff and honest admirer, who suggested that Vaughan Williams should write a

---

[1] The manuscript of this work has not been traced.

symphony. Some sketches for a symphonic poem about London were looked out and 'thrown' into symphonic form.[1] Early in 1914, while Vaughan Williams was in Italy, the opportunity of a first performance occurred at one of two concerts of modern orchestral music given by F. Bevis Ellis in order to bring forward the young conductor Geoffrey Toye, who at this date was twenty-five. So that the work could be ready for rehearsal various of the composer's friends, Butterworth[2] among them, revised it and made a 'short score'. The performance was at Queen's Hall on 27 March, when Toye conducted the new symphony, the revised version of Delius's *In a Summer Garden* and Balakirev's *Thamar*, and Ellis conducted Arnold Bax's *Three Songs with Orchestra*, the orchestral transcription of Ravel's *Valses Nobles et Sentimentales* and—sole concession to comparative familiarity—Franck's *Pièce Héroïque*. The *London Symphony* was at once a success. All the Press reports mention the cordiality of its reception, the first movement in particular being 'tremendously applauded', according to the *Daily Mail*. The general verdict was that a notable English symphony had appeared. The *Mail*'s notice was written by a young and sympathetic critic, Richard Capell, who noted that the new work was 'almost un-heralded' and, in the solemnity of youthful responsibility, found the 'ragtime ditties' of the first movement 'perhaps unnecessarily trivial'. He found 'Stravinsky's influence . . . often perceptible, notably in the mouth-organ imitations in the amusing Hampstead Heath scherzo'—an unconscious echo, perhaps, of *Petrushka*. The slow movement Capell at twenty-nine rightly called 'one of the noblest symphonic pieces in modern English music'. *The Times* was glad that, when so many English composers were contenting themselves with short works, Vaughan Williams could take the long aim. 'His harmonic freedom is exhilarating. Where one feels a certain sameness and tendency to heaviness is in the details of the background, the accompaniments to which are apt to be more harmonic than rhythmic.'

[1] In 1912 Vaughan Williams went to Cambridge to attend the 500th concert of the University Musical Club, at which Steuart Wilson sang *On Wenlock Edge*. He stayed with Armstrong Gibbs who was then studying under Stanford and Dent. Gibbs relates (in *Composers' Gallery* by Donald Brook (London, 1946) p. 65): 'Out of his bag he produced the sketches of the first two movements of the *London Symphony*, and did his very inadequate best to beat them out on my upright piano!'

[2] Butterworth's Idyll *The Banks of Green Willow* was first performed in London at the Ellis concert on 20 March 1914.

H.A.S. of the *Westminster Gazette* was the least impressed of those first-night critics—'it is in truth not easy to perceive any intelligible connection between the music and its theme. . . . It is for the most part very dry and laboured, with plenty of clever workmanship, no doubt, skilful thematic manipulation, academic ingenuities . . . but little enough suggestion of anything approaching genuine inspiration or even felicitous invention of a humbler order . . . the first movement introduction (is) rather reminiscent, like a good many other pages of the work, of Charpentier's *Louise* . . .' *T.P.'s Weekly* produced the most favourable comment—'the birth of a great work. . . . There is a soul of London, an impulse and strength, a whirl and a sorrow, a desire to understand, even to rebel. Whatever Vaughan Williams's intentions may have been, the result is a symphony that is full of noble and unforgettable music. Its popularity was instant and will be permanent . . .'

In the next few days there was the enthusiastic response of friends, chief among them Holst, Edward Dent, Steuart Wilson and, of course, Butterworth, who had written the programme-note for the first performance. Another friendship had sprung from this work, with Arnold Bax, eleven years younger than Vaughan Williams and beginning to make a name both as pianist[1] and composer. Vaughan Williams's *Phantasy Quintet* had had a first performance four days before the *London Symphony*, also at a Bevis Ellis concert, and two Bax piano pieces had been played. The two composers discussed the older man's new symphony: 'One passage disappointed me,' Vaughan Williams wrote[2] years later, 'and I asked his advice. He suggested the addition of a counter-melody on the oboe. Indeed he sat down at the pianoforte and improvised one. This actual passage was too obviously Baxian to make its inclusion possible. But, following his advice, I made up another which, though not nearly so good as his, was more in keeping with the rest of the movement. Later on I was able to do something to return the compliment when I persuaded him to add about sixteen bars to the

---

[1] It is sometimes forgotten that Bax, even as a brilliant student at the Royal Academy of Music, could play any orchestral score on the pianoforte from sight. Strauss's *Heldenleben*, Debussy's *Nocturnes* and Scriabin's *Prometheus* were among these feats. In 1912 at a reception given to Schoenberg in London at the Music Club, Bax played the accompaniment to his songs at sight after a well-known professional pianist had withdrawn.

[2] *Music and Letters*, Vol. XXXV, No. 1, January 1954.

coda of the first movement of his Third Symphony.' A general criticism of the *London Symphony* in its original form was its length, over fifty minutes. A. H. Fox Strangways, writing in 1920,[1] said: 'We remember the composer going about when it was over, asking friends to tell him what to cut out. The modesty of asking us to look five years ahead of him who is ten years ahead of all of us!'

'Ahead of all of us.' . . . The phrase is significant at this juncture of Vaughan Williams's career, for the *London Symphony* was to mark the end of a phase in his life. He was forty-one. His first opera was completed and he had heard it played through and sung at Cheyne Walk by Steuart Wilson and Denis Browne. He had sketched a work for the brilliant English violinist, Marie Hall. This was *The Lark Ascending*. He had completed a setting of *Four Hymns* for tenor and strings or pianoforte with viola obbligato. These were due to be played at Worcester in September 1914; in July the proofs were ready and Steuart Wilson, to whom they are dedicated, had sung from them at Cheyne Walk. Since their meeting at *The Wasps* in 1909, Vaughan Williams had fostered Wilson's career. On 16 November 1910, for instance, when he gave a lecture to the Oxford Folk-Music Society, he asked Wilson to sing the musical illustrations.[2] Wilson was but one of several young men whom he helped at this time, others being Clive Carey and Arthur Bliss. But the *Four Hymns* had to wait six years for their first performance. On 4 August 1914, Britain declared war on Germany, and the young men abandoned their careers and went to fight. So did Vaughan Williams, although at forty-one he scarcely need have considered himself as immediately eligible. But throughout his life he never considered the passing of the years: he always felt young, and he did not seek to be set apart as a 'leader'. That is why he would have been unable to sympathize with Fox Strangways's remark about his being 'ahead' of everyone. He could not, however, evade the natural leadership with which the strength of his personality, for all his diffidence, endowed him. The memories of those men who were young before 1914 bear this out. John Ireland, recalling the student-days discussions in Wilkins's tea-shop, said, 'There was no question among us of which was the greatest.'[3] Adrian Boult, singing *Toward the Unknown Region* and *A Sea Symphony* under Hugh

[1] *Music and Letters*, Vol. I, No. 2.
[2] Full report of the lecture is in the *Musical Times*, February 1911.
[3] *Musical Times*, October 1958.

Allen, was to find that 'the impact of Vaughan Williams, this magnificent-looking young man, and his fresh and vital music, was unforgettable.'[1] Frank Howes, enchanted as a schoolboy by the early songs, was deeply affected as an undergraduate by Allen's Oxford performance of *A Sea Symphony*. Steuart Wilson has said that Vaughan Williams was 'the hero of young Cambridge'. After Wilson had sung 'Orpheus With His Lute' at a College Concert in Magdalene in May Week, a middle-aged don rushed to him afterwards saying, 'Where did you get that? It's the most beautiful thing I ever heard in my life.'[2] Another young Londoner who saved his pennies to attend the Elwes performances of *On Wenlock Edge* was John Barbirolli. For all these varied men, this music awoke in them the feeling that they were being personally addressed by a new, strong English voice. With his fellow-composers, younger or older, Vaughan Williams affected no sense of ivory-tower self-sufficiency. They were his colleagues; he was just another musician, doing his job. He would, as has been seen, seek advice from his juniors; he also was always ready to help those who took him their scores for discussion. Arising from this, John Ireland had a charming anecdote[3] from 1908 when he showed the slow movement of his first violin sonata to R.V.W. 'When we reached the central theme in E flat minor (in Dorian mode dress) he stopped me and was silent for a minute or two. Then he said, 'Play that theme again'. After another pause he said, 'Well, that's odd. I have used practically the same theme in a song.' I was rather taken aback and asked him what we should do about this curious coincidence of a musical idea. After a moment's thought V.W. said, "Well, we must both have cribbed it from something else, so we had better both leave it as it is—nobody will notice it." And so far as I know, nobody ever has!'

These were the reactions of friends, colleagues and a new generation of musicians. What was Vaughan Williams's true position in English musical life when he went to war in 1914? To a wider public he was little known, for it was largely a specialist public which attended Bevis Ellis's Queen's Hall concerts, and the popularity of 'Linden Lea' and the hymns was a post-war development. He had not yet, as Elgar had, 'reached the hearts of the people'. His

---

[1] *R.C.M. Magazine*, Vol. LV, No. 1.
[2] *Radio Times*, October 1952.
[3] *Musical Times*, October 1958.

music had not yet penetrated deeply into provincial musical life.[1] Up to 1914, for example, his name appeared only once in the programmes of the Hallé Orchestra of Manchester, and then only as the arranger of a piece by Purcell. What Leeds heard at its triennial festivals and what it heard in the intervening time were two very different things. The English musical scene up to 1914 was dominated by Elgar and no other. Practically every one of the first thirteen years of the twentieth century produced a new major work from his pen. An Elgar first performance was enough to draw composers and musicians from London to Worcester, Gloucester, Hereford, Leeds, Hanley, Birmingham or wherever it might take place. We know that Vaughan Williams attended most of them and listened acutely. (He often recalled how, after *The Kingdom* at Birmingham in 1906, 'a distinguished musical amateur, one of those who have not got beyond worshipping orthodox technique for its own sake, complained to me that the double choruses in that work were not really in eight parts at all. I think he somehow felt that he had been cheated and was inclined to ask for his money back. If he had known a little more he would have remembered that Bach in the *Matthew Passion* owed him just as much hard cash as Elgar.')[2] The enigmatic Delius was another whose music dawned upon English musicians from 1906, after it had had a vogue in Germany. Like Elgar's, it was in a European, post-Wagner tradition, curiously un-English English music and it is not surprising that it was in many cases foreign musicians who played and conducted it on its introduction to England—for example, Szanto in the piano concerto at a Prom in 1907, *Appalachia* by Cassirer in 1907, and the two famous short tone-poems by Mengelberg in 1914. English conductors were slower to appreciate it: Wood conducted *Sea-Drift* at

---

[1] In 1913, at a meeting in Manchester, Sydney Nicholson, the cathedral organist, declared that 'Vaughan Williams is appreciated in Germany but not in Manchester'. It is not possible to discover how much of his music was played in Germany before 1914, though it is known that the first *Norfolk Rhapsody* was played in Berlin on 5 December 1906, four months after its first performance, and conducted by Walter Meyrowitz, who was well known in England, where he conducted the Carl Rosa and other opera companies. The Continent did not entirely turn a deaf ear to English music. Several of Elgar's works were played at the Turin Exhibition of 1911. The composer conducted some of the works, and Toscanini conducted the Introduction and Allegro for strings, with which, it was stated, the orchestra was very familiar, 'having continually played it while on a tour'. This event is mentioned in Percy Young's *Elgar O.M.* where it is wrongly assigned to 1909.

[2] *Music and Letters*, Vol. XVI, No. 1.

Sheffield in 1908, and Bantock in the same year gave the first performance of *Brigg Fair*, at Liverpool, before Beecham took it up in London. Beecham became Delius's principal champion, introducing *Paris*, *A Mass of Life* and *A Village Romeo and Juliet* to England and finding in this luscious and emotional music a cosmopolitan warmth and technique which he was never able to perceive in Elgar. In an age internationally overshadowed by Richard Strauss, it is only to be expected that the grandiose works of Bantock and Holbrooke should have attracted attention. The other great foreign influences of the time found their champions, too. At Henry Wood's concerts, the music of Debussy, Ravel, Scriabin, Glazunov, Schoenberg, and Reger was performed. Beecham, with his flair for colourful, if sometimes second-rate music, played d'Indy, the Russians, Saint-Saëns, and Stravinsky. The name of Bartók was known to few, and to those mainly as a pianist, although Richter played his *Kossuth* symphonic poem in Manchester in 1904. Better known, through his advocacy of his own piano music, was Dohnányi. Sibelius was at the beginning of his powerful influence on English minds. The first performance of a Sibelius symphony in England was of the Second under Richter in Manchester on 2 March 1905. Thereafter, thanks partly to Bantock's enthusiasm, there was an increasing interest by musicians in his music, culminating in the performance of the fourth symphony at the 1912 (and last) Birmingham Festival. It was not until about 1930 that the general public became 'Sibelius-minded'. A large percentage of English music was included in the major London concerts and provincial festivals of the pre-1914 decade, apart from that by composers already mentioned. The 'senior' generation—Parry, Stanford, Cowen, Mackenzie—was still productive. Other names occur frequently—Percy Pitt, Percy Grainger, York Bowen, Cyril Scott, Norman O'Neill, Thomas Dunhill, Walford Davies, Coleridge-Taylor, Arthur Hervey, William Y. Hurlstone, William Wolstenholme, W. H. Bell, Frederic Cliffe, Edward German, Gustav Holst, J. B. McEwen, Hamilton Harty, Ethel Smyth, Benjamin Dale, and Frank Bridge. Their works were not segregated into special concerts—though a few of exclusively modern or English music were held—but were put into programmes cheek-by-jowl with established classics.

Some words by Edwin Evans, written in April 1914, disclose a contemporary view of that 'English' quality of Vaughan Williams's

music which was always apparent. Evans was acutely perceptive of
how fundamental this quality was compared with the mere adoption
of an interest in folk song: 'Music is primarily the expression of an
individual. It expresses a race only in the degree in which its
creator is typical of that race. . . . Vaughan Williams must, in some
way, be typical. It has nothing to do with externals, or his critics
would not be so eager to seize upon the unfamiliar elements of his
idiom and ascribe them conveniently to French influences. . . .
Moreover, the interpretation in music of mere English externals is
quite another matter. In his very small manner, Edward German
accomplished it fairly well. . . . The fact is that the Englishman tends
to express himself outwardly in conventions, and it is these that a
composer like German seizes upon, whilst Vaughan Williams
expresses the Englishman within him. There is no screen of convention between him and his music. That in itself, however, is not
enough. The inner personality must be in some measure typical, and
that must be revealed by his music, if the general impression is
justified. . . . I distinctly feel in Vaughan Williams's music a type of
personality which I believe to be so frequent in these islands as to
be rightly considered national. It is a personality that is intellectually aristocratic—not to say fastidious—and biologically, if that
word expresses my meaning, democratic. Using the word 'caste' in
a purely intellectual and not a social sense, it is a temperament that
without compromising caste and, above all, without conscious condescension, can be sincerely and whole-heartedly of and with the
people. Now that is a combination that I believe to be peculiarly
English. The intellectual democrat of the Continent either con-
descends or becomes a vulgarian.'[1]

By 1914 there was already enough evidence of Vaughan Williams's
profound influence upon his fellow-musicians for his future to have
been predicted in very nearly the shape it was fortunately to take.
If he had been killed in the war, we should still have had enough of
his work to accord him a special place in English music.

II

Within this period of seven years there emerged the Vaughan
Williams whose distinctive voice was heeded at once by his contemporaries. Four at least of the works written before 1914 will

[1] *The Outlook*, 4 April 1914.

continue to carry his name down the years. Later works were to have a greater depth and a longer vision, but he did not always recapture the prolific melodiousness and the rich sound of the pre-1914 decade.

The Song for chorus and orchestra, *Toward the Unknown Region*, closes a chapter in its composer's career as well as heralding the fuller development of his powers. Here, for almost the last time, he glances back to the chromaticism of his early works and then strides forward. The work made a profound impression at its first appearance for its 'newness', something not easily realizable today when, with the wisdom of hindsight, we can perceive its derivative moments. But the listeners of 1907 evidently recognized a choral style which, in its breadth and directness, was a reminder of the days of Purcell. In shape and general outline it seems to be modelled on Parry's *Blest Pair of Sirens*. Certainly it follows Parry's advice to his pupil to 'write choral music as befits an Englishman and a democrat'. Almost for the first time an English festival choir was singing aspiring, liberating words which were not specifically religious i.e. were not drawn from the Bible. In this way did Vaughan Williams commemorate the lately-dead historian F. W. Maitland whom he had dearly loved: 'Darest thou now O soul, walk out with me toward the unknown region. . . . All is a blank before us, all waits undreamed of in that region, that inaccessible land.' This early work retains its hold for a variety of reasons: first, its intrinsic musical value, which is high; secondly, its excellence as a vehicle for a good choir; thirdly, its remarkable evocation of the liberal fervour of the new age of the early twentieth century. If Elgar's music captures one aspect of the Edwardian age—sounding its hollow note as well as its confident one—Vaughan Williams's pre-1914 choral works enshrine another, the growth of a wider sense of humanity's destiny and interrelationship. In this he was typical of his Cambridge generation.

The opening of *Toward the Unknown Region* recalls 'Bright is the ring of words'; it is in the Lydian mode, its tonality A:

The music is at once gripping, as the quiet and solemn fanfare answers the opening phrase. The voices enter quietly and the truth of Plunket Greene's opinion—'Enthralling in its beautiful interpretation of the words'—is confirmed. The lift from 'soul' to 'walk' is inevitable yet never fails to thrill the hearer. As the unknown region is described—'no map there, nor guide, nor voice sounding, nor touch of human hand'—a *misterioso* phrase in the bass occurs which is practically a sign-manual of its composer, and recurs in various shapes and rhythms for the rest of his career:

It is, in outline, an early forerunner of the main theme of the sixth symphony's finale, which also describes the unknown region.

The work is built in sections based on the opening melody, the choir's first entry

and the melody at 'nor touch of human hand'

This last is worked to a fine climax in which a trace of Elgarian influence can perhaps be imagined. All the time, despite the comparatively slow tempo, one has a sense of urgency, of moving relentlessly to a goal. The 'dark inaccessible land' is a demanding moment for a choir: '*parlando* (dark tone)' is the composer's marking, rarely obeyed satisfactorily. As 'the ties loosen, all but the ties eternal' the music grows more excited until, *maestoso con moto* and *brillante*, the choir declaims 'Then we burst forth' and the orchestra has a striding bass derived from the first bars of the work and, ultimately, from the hymn-tune 'Sine Nomine', a motif which runs throughout Vaughan Williams's music at times of elation or release:

Then   we burst   forth

The 'Sine Nomine' theme

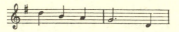

had its origin in 'Love's Last Gift', the final song of the *House of Life* cycle

Possibly there is a symbolic significance here in the similarity of musical image presenting itself in Vaughan Williams's mind when he contemplated the saints resting from their labours, love's last gift and the bursting forth to Whitman's 'Joy, O fruit of all', the fulfilment of the soul. At any rate, this great tune reminds us that *Toward the Unknown Region* is a Song, not a cantata. Vaughan Williams goes hammer-and-tongs for his final exultant blaze, in positive, confident affirmation. The abrupt key changes, the marching crotchets of the bass part—these foretell the composer's future as accurately as any historian could ever wish.

Although there are so many signposts in *Toward the Unknown Region*, it must have been the performances, close together, of the two later *Norfolk Rhapsodies*, the *Unknown Region* and the two orchestral *Impressions* which gave Vaughan Williams the idea that some lessons in orchestration might benefit him. Hence there are few works of importance in 1908, although it is notable for the publication of *Folk Songs from the Eastern Counties*. The three unpublished Whitman *Nocturnes*, written after the lessons with Ravel, show a markedly freer choral style which presumably found permanent expression in renewed revision of the proposed *Sea Symphony*. The first-fruits of the Paris visit were the G minor string

[1] Compare also this from *The Pilgrim's Progress*:

He that is down need

quartet and the Housman song-cycle *On Wenlock Edge*. Despite the revision the quartet underwent in 1921, it remains a pre-1914 work, a curious amalgam of not yet fully absorbed influences. Yet it also has more than enough of the essential Vaughan Williams to make it a pleasure to hear and to play. The best movement is the first, beginning with the viola's statement of a theme which lends itself to Vaughan Williams's method of development, a presentation of the theme in various hues and moods rather than in any convoluted form. Wonder is sometimes expressed that the *Tallis Fantasia* should have been written comparatively early in Vaughan Williams's career. The coda of the first movement of this quartet plainly shows the composer thinking in terms of the string-tone which he perfected in the *Fantasia*—the intermingling of the parts as they arch upwards until the first violin is, at D, three octaves above the next instrument. The Minuet and Trio contain flattened sixths and sevenths and show that the folk-song influence was becoming transformed into a personal style. For the slow movement he used the title 'Romance', a favourite term. This serene little movement, in ternary form, is in strong contrast to the boisterous Rondo Capriccioso with its colourful effects—*sur la touche, sul ponticello*, etc.—and its *fugato* section. An unusual feature of a charming work is the use of the word 'solo' from time to time to give melodic prominence to the instrument concerned. The sign ⊗ indicates that it 'resumes its normal place in the ensemble'. It is extraordinary that so uncomplex and blithe a work should have occasioned such bewilderment at its first performances. *The Times* critic was willing to forgive 'such an original thinker' for experiments that failed, among which he numbered this quartet: 'The first movement proposes so many subjects that development within reasonable limits of time is an impossibility, so that we get little more than the statement above harmonic progressions that often torture the ear. . . . The "Romance" is very difficult to assimilate.' The critic of the *Musical Times* was equally at sea; the quartet was 'an extreme development of modernism, so much so that not even the advanced tastes of an audience of British composers could find everything in [it] acceptable'. The work was put away for several years. Edwin Evans and Fox Strangways writing in 1920 both described it as lost, perhaps irretrievably. But it reappeared from the composer's desk drawer in 1921, was revised, and was published in 1923. It deserves to be played more often than it is.

On Wenlock Edge may have been begun before the visit to Ravel. The sketches of 'Clun' could possibly date from 1906, or earlier, and the fact that 'Is my team ploughing?' was performed ten months before the complete cycle as a song for voice and pianoforte may indicate that the more elaborate apparatus of string quartet and pianoforte suggested itself after this performance. This work is now accepted for what it is: a moving setting of moving poems. But controversy raged for the first ten or twelve years of its existence when it received many performances from its first interpreter, the great Gervase Elwes. The gist of the argument was whether the poems' spirit was faithfully reflected in the music, and the two chief arguers were Ernest Newman and Edwin Evans. Their battle-royal took place in the columns of the *Musical Times* in June and September 1918. Undoubtedly there is a fundamental divergence of outlook between Housman and Vaughan Williams. The poet's fatalistic outlook, the sense of disillusionment at the heart of the passion, is not the philosophy of Vaughan Williams, who was an optimist. What made Vaughan Williams want to set Housman's poems was, paradoxically, the very thing which made Housman dislike the thought of his poems being set to music—their innate musicality. Other composers have come nearer to the essential spirit of Housman, have more faithfully mirrored the polished, miniature element in his poetry. Butterworth's settings are probably the nearest of all, and Gurney's two cycles (using pianoforte and string quartet) are undeservedly neglected. None but Vaughan Williams has brought to Housman such symphonic—or, more properly, operatic— breadth and expansion, so that the verses and music together have a universal rather than a particular application.[1] Newman disliked *On Wenlock Edge* and did not agree that the music was an example of fine setting of words. He thought that Vaughan Williams's lyrical gift was 'a very small one' and that in his hands the poems became 'mere pictorial melodrama'. In the *Sunday Times* of 29 October 1922, he wrote that Vaughan Williams's *On Wenlock Edge* failed to do justice to its theme because the composer approached his task 'in a medium unfamiliar to his previous experience', a very odd remark. This is, perhaps, the place in which to reiterate that it is not a wholly accurate observation to say that Vaughan Williams's music is founded on a literary basis. True, the whole body of his work

---

[1] It is instructive to compare his later Housman settings, *Along The Field*, in which the atmosphere of the music is a great deal more introspective and the music itself cooler.

would seem to support this theory—the Bible, Whitman, Herbert, Housman, Blake, Skelton, Bunyan, Synge, are but a few literary sources reflected in his music—but literature was but the spark which set his imagination alight so that he could transform the literary inspiration into his own musical language. In doing so, he may sometimes have 'interpreted' the poet in a manner that seems at variance with the nature of the poetry. That did not trouble him, for it was the composer's job, as he saw it, to re-create the poem as music. His own views on the literary aspect of music were firmly stated in an article on Elgar which he contributed to *Music and Letters*, January 1935 (p. 15):

'The one question we have to ask is, has Elgar achieved beauty? This is the one thing that is vital. And this is the one question that Elgar commentators seem to shirk. They talk of his irony, his humour, his skill. There seems a general consensus of opinion among this class of critic to praise Elgar's *Falstaff* at the expense of his other works. They try to correlate music with literature. I rather suspect these people of not being very sure of their literary qualifications and therefore very anxious to parade them rather than take them for granted. The best composer is surely he who has the most beautiful melodies, the finest harmony, the most vital rhythm and the surest sense of form. There is no other criterion. I lose patience with those people who try to put up Berlioz as a great composer because he interpreted Shakespeare, because he could give literary reasons for his beliefs, and do not see that a composer like Dvořák, a reed shaken by the wind, is far the greater man of the two because the wind was the divine afflatus. Elgar has the one thing needful, and all his philosophical, literary and technical excellences fall into their proper place: they are a means to an end.'

Nevertheless, in two of the six poems which make up *On Wenlock Edge*, Vaughan Williams did 'interpret' Housman in a remarkably faithful manner. In the first, *On Wenlock Edge*, there is the simile of the gale that plies the saplings double and the gale of life, blowing through the troubled heart of man as it blew through the Roman's heart in the days of the occupation of Britain. All this is in Vaughan Williams's magnificent setting. 'The "gale" . . . has not so much the sound of actual wind as the feeling of the body being blown about while the mind is thinking,' wrote Fox Strangways [in Cobbett's *Cyclopedic Survey of Chamber Music* (London, 1930), Vol. II, p. 585.] In the closing bars, as the gale subsides, is a musical impression of continuity: the gale, we know, is blowing somewhere even though the music has stopped. In the fourth song, 'Oh when I was in love with you', is the perfect quasi-folk-tune for quasi-folk-poetry. Moreover the epigrammatic poem, with its softly ironic conclusion, is matched by the nearest that music can go towards being itself an epigram. The final comments by viola and violin rarely fail to bring a wry smile to the lips:

When the work first appeared it was natural that everyone would try to find French influences. The song-cycle was generally acclaimed. *The Times* critic (who informed his readers that the poems were 'from Laurence Housman's *A Shropshire Lad*') found each setting 'remarkable for accurate accentuation of the words and for genuinely deep expression, with an appropriate rustic flavour'. Bredon Hill was 'in the manner of Ravel's "Vallée des Cloches", but there is humanity in this which is not in the French piece. . . . The whole six songs have admirable unity of style: they are really worthy of the composer of *The House of Life*.' The last remark may cause a raised eyebrow today, but it does show critical percipience. It is tempting to wonder how different the work would have been if there had been no visit to Ravel. Certainly the atmospheric effects are slightly French, but the use of swaying consecutive fourths, the melismata of a few notes, and the consecutive triads are thorough-going Vaughan Williams, plus some chromaticism and hurried triplets from his Rossetti phase. The French, when they heard it, found it something new and certainly did not consider it as imitation-Ravel. Vaughan Williams himself has said: 'I could not have written Ravel's music even if I had wanted to.'[1] The second song, 'From far, from eve and morning', is perhaps the most beautiful Vaughan Williams wrote. The wide consecutive common chords on the pianoforte forcibly emphasize that one of Vaughan Williams's achievements from early in his life was his wonderfully imaginative reconception of uses of the common chord. As in 'The infinite shining heavens' so here, with the simplest means, is created an atmosphere in which the listener holds his breath. If anyone wants

[1] 'Musical Autobiography.' Vaughan Williams said that at least he did not 'succumb to the temptation of writing a piece about a cemetery', but he forgot the churchyard in Bredon!

to know what is meant by the perfect metamorphosis of speech-rhythm into music, he only has to consider the setting of the lines, 'The stuff of life to knit me Blew hither: here am I.' In the fourth bar of the song there is a melodic device utterly characteristic of Vaughan Williams, the falling triplet which lifts back to its starting-point:

from eve_ and morn-ing

At the second verse the strings creep in, gently to sustain the voice's more urgent and passionate questioning. In a few brief minutes has been experienced the heartbreak that can last a lifetime.

In 'Is my team ploughing?' the setting is more elaborate, and was the occasion for some cheap humour by Newman about the shouting of secrets of the heart. The ghost asks his plaintive questions over a held note in the strings and a held chord on the pianoforte. The living man replies to an accompaniment of agitated pianoforte triplets, a reminder of earlier works, while the cello slides chromatically down the scale. The *dénouement* is well and dramatically managed: a lift to the 'whose' of 'Never ask me whose', which is followed by a sudden fortissimo and diminuendo in the strings and pianoforte.

'Bredon Hill' is the most ambitious, as well as the most pictorial, setting. The string quartet and pianoforte set the lazy scene; the haze of summer is over the music and the coloured counties are at our feet. It is simple and magical, and Vaughan Williams is one of the few who can paint such a scene in musical notation. It is silent noon, still as the hourglass. The voice enters freely and softly, the melismata on 'ring' and 'happy' having a languor which is another evocation of high summer. Gradually the tolling bells—pianoforte minor thirds and open fifths on the strings—become more insistent until the return of tranquillity at 'But here my love would stay'. The transformation to the wintry scene is again simple but effective. The chords of the opening are barer: all is stark and frozen, the scented thyme a far-off memory. The funeral bell tolls an octave G on the pianoforte, and as the steeples hum the vibrations on the lower strings fill our ears with the din, until they subside at the command to be dumb and the song ends with a memory of the lovers' last summer together. Newman objected to the clangour of the bells because of over-insistence on 'the external in a line', pictorial representation being easier to accomplish than complete realization of the 'real mood of the poem'. How one can realize the mood of bells without representing them is not explained. For Housman as well as for Vaughan Williams, the bells were the leit-motif of 'Bredon Hill'. The last song, 'Clun', is a complete change of mood. The quartet's opening cadence is freed of the tension of tragedy, and 'the country for easy livers' is shown bathed in sun-shine, with 'the springs of rivers' rippling gently in the pianoforte part. The sense of fatality in the poem is not at all conveyed by the music. The Lad contemplates death, even perhaps Lethe, the river of forgetfulness, instead of Thames and Teme. The music tells us that the quieter place than Clun is the Celestial City, the haven where we would be, and there is a beautiful melody to convince us of its lure:

On Wenlock Edge has unity. Although its songs can be performed separately hardly anyone has been inartistic enough to do so. It has a power and conviction which more than outweigh some crudities and immature passages. It has been questioned whether the medium of pianoforte and string quartet is the best available; the songs certainly seem to invite the subtler and more extensive range of colours obtainable from the orchestra, and early in the 1920s the composer provided an orchestral dress. It is well done, but somehow the music still sounds better in its first form, where the obvious effort to obtain the last dram of effect from a chamber combination imparts an extra strength to the notes. The composer, it should be said, liked his orchestral version.

The publication of Vaughan Williams's folk-song arrangements began in 1908 and continued, on and off, for fifty years. There is little doubt that his most effective are those for unaccompanied voices. While he avoided the over-elaborate pianoforte accompani-ment which turns the folk song into the art song, he did not always achieve harmonic felicity. In some respects Cecil Sharp's accom-paniments show more imaginative aspects, although Sharp sought advice from Vaughan Williams about harmonization. 'Take any chord you want,' was the typically blunt reply. Vaughan Williams's words about Sharp's accompaniments bear upon his own problems:

'His creative impulse came from the tune he was setting. That is why his settings are often better than those of more technically gifted arrangers because they come to the task as composers and let the suggestions started by the tune run away with them and so forget the tune itself. . . . In all the best of Sharp's accompaniments it is the tune that counts and the arrangement falls into its proper background. In some cases his accompaniments look wrong, and sometimes even when played by themselves seem awkward, but they stand the important test that they make the tune sound right. . . .'[1]

The tune always counts in Vaughan Williams's arrangements, but the arrangement does not invariably fall into the proper background.

The most obvious results of the lessons on orchestration from Ravel are to be found in the music for *The Wasps*. This does not mean that it sounds like Ravel: very little of Vaughan Williams's music does, as Ravel himself acknowledged in his tribute to 'the only one of my pupils who does not write my music'. But the more skilful use of woodwind and strings derives from the so-called 'impressionist' French composers such as Debussy, whose music was gradually gaining a footing in programmes at this time. The use of a whole-tone scale in *The Wasps* is another sign. In the Overture especially can be discerned an interest in Borodin, to whose work Ravel had introduced Vaughan Williams (the finale of the B minor symphony, one imagines!) The tendency has been to dismiss the music to *The Wasps* as merely a *jeu d'esprit*, hardly worth serious consideration. There is more to it than high spirits alone. It is, for one thing, the first of Vaughan Williams's works in which the absorbed spirit of folk song is made wholly manifest as an original and idiosyncratic style. The tunes in the overture are original tunes, and as good as any folk tunes. The famous central tune, which represents in the play the reconciliation of Bdelycleon with his father Philocleon,

seems to spring magically from a passage for solo horn:

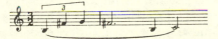

[1] *Cecil Sharp* by A. H. Fox Strangways and Maud Karpeles (London, second edition 1955), p. 120.

Which came first one cannot tell, but it is an episode representative of Vaughan Williams's ability to develop a broad melody from a mere acorn. The four subsequent movements of the suite are of the best variety of incidental music. They must have sounded well in the theatre, and they transplant to the concert-hall without drooping for an instant. The first entr'acte, derived from the chorus, (Section 6), of the original music, has a tune in counterpoint for the lower strings which is a moment of rare beauty, as are the wistful violin and oboe solos in the second entr'acte. In all Vaughan Williams's scores, no matter how transitory may have seemed their initial conception, there are always passages of depth and intensity which could have graced a symphony. He never 'wrote down' to anything. The 'March Past of the Kitchen Utensils' is a short moment of fun, hinting at parody of 'Here's a health unto His Majesty'. In the original score it was called 'March Past of the Witnesses', who were a pot, pestle, and water-jug summoned to bear testimony to the excellence of a dog accused of stealing cheese—the play is a satire on Athenians whose litigious propensities were strengthened by the money they received for sitting in judgment. The finale is the highest-spirited movement, in which the three sons of Carcinus, a rival poet of Aristophanes, are made to dance; the climax comes with the return of the overture's principal theme. As the revelry dies away, Philocleon, who has been asleep in a corner, staggers to his feet, tries to imitate the dancing and wanders off-stage, whereupon a fortissimo chord brings down the curtain and ends the suite. There is no attempt to make the music sound Greek by introducing ancient scales. Vaughan Williams's Athens is Edwardian Cambridge, with the folk songs blowing in from the fens. Sometimes the music is too hearty when it is played in the solemnity of a concert-hall and one is reminded that the 'Ward the Pirate' side of Vaughan Williams's folk music is much less adaptable than the 'Bushes and Briars' side. But the score is colourful and adept; the Frenchman it most often calls to mind is the Massenet of *Le Cid* rather than any later figure. It pleased in its day, too: the *Musical Times* report[1] of the first performance said that the composer had 'won the hearts of a section of his audience by introducing quotations from *The Merry Widow* and from Debussy. His sound scholarship and ability to weave ornamental device round a simple theme

[1] *Musical Times*, January 1910.

are shown at many points. The music, in spite of certain subtleties not always comprehensible to the uninitiated, was well received. . . .'

The person who wrote the notice which appeared in *The Times* was determined to show that he was not among the uninitiated: 'The overture starts with a tune in Debussy's septave of whole tones. . . . As far as style is concerned the overture is an epitome of the work, for the uncouth and jarring intervals preferred by the new French school contrast very oddly all the way through with the broad tunes that seem racy of the English soil.' The *Hymn to Apollo* was 'a fine plainsong melody' and 'the musical allusion to Richard Strauss at τοὺς ζητοῦντας καινόν τι λέγειν is the kind of joke that has always seemed fitting in modern musical settings of Aristophanes'. (The quotation, marked in the score (p. 61) in inverted commas, is from Debussy's *L'Après-Midi d'un faune*. Black mark for *The Times*. The English text at this point says: 'For the future, this I ask ye, O ye paragons, when a poet ventures something new and uncommon, smile on his essay, court him, flatter him and in your memory store his wisdom, in cupboards enshrine his mellow lays with the mellow fruit. And thus if ye do, your raiment through all the following year will yield you musical fragrance.' This type of humour is rare in Vaughan Williams's work, for he did not particularly like musical jokes.) *The Times*'s critic noted another quotation: 'At the entry of the tipsy Philocleon his first words are spoken (in rhythm) through a version of the famous march in *The Birds*, transformed into the whole-tone scale with ridiculous effect.' This quotation from Parry's Greek play music of 1883 is marked in the score (p. 94) with an asterisk, and his pupil has added 'with apologies to a great English composer'. A broadcast revival of the complete incidental music showed conclusively that it is too good to be wholly forgotten, notably the long *Parabasis* (section 12), in effect an operatic *scena*, the first part of which anticipates the finale of Act III of *The Pilgrim's Progress* and the *Serenade to Music*. It is also thrilling to find the great central tune of the overture in its vocal version (section 16).

Few who heard *The Wasps* music in 1909 could have imagined that the same mind was at work on the *Fantasia on a Theme by Thomas Tallis*. The revival of interest in the Elizabethan composers, in full swing in 1910, revived interest also in the 'fancy' or 'fantasia' form. For English musicians at the end of the sixteenth century, the fantasy was instrumental music which was based solely on thematic development, even though fundamentally the form was madrigalian.

A snatch of theme would be announced, developed, and abandoned for another theme related to the original. There would be no fugal treatment. Vaughan Williams did not strictly follow the Elizabethan model, but the work is sectional with related material, even though in performance it sounds unified and indivisible. Common ground between the Elizabethan composers and folk song is their modal harmony. Neo-modalism was seized upon by Vaughan Williams and Holst as their escape-route from the dilemma facing all composers at the start of the twentieth century, when chromaticism threatened to destroy ordinary major-minor tonality and people like Schoenberg devised a system of composition as a means of avoiding the possible stagnation of the art of music. Tallis's great tune (to be found as No. 92 in the *English Hymnal*) had a flattened seventh as one of its intervals; the flattened seventh is the principal distinguishing feature of the folk-song modes. So we find in the harmony of the *Tallis Fantasia* this:

and the use of parallel consecutive fifths as a firm bass line.

The *Fantasia* begins with a version of the theme which has already been encountered in 'Bright is the ring of words' and *Toward the Unknown Region*:

Under a high held note on the violins, the plucked lower strings hint at Tallis's tune, punctuated by a subject of swaying chords which recurs several times. The first full statement of the theme uses Tallis's own harmonization, in nine parts. The tune is then repeated, embellished by arpeggios. The string orchestras divide into antiphonal groups, the larger group, assisted by the string quartet, commenting on one part of the theme, to be answered by the smaller orchestra with the 'swaying' subject

Now, in correct Fantasia fashion, comes a new tune derived from Tallis's theme and played by the solo viola. Moreover this is a tune which Vaughan Williams associated in *The Pilgrim's Progress* with the idea of the celestial city:

Both orchestras comment briefly on this tune, whereupon the solo violin takes it up to be rejoined after five bars by the viola. Solo quartet and the two orchestras then weave a complex tapestry of string-sound based on parts of Ex. 3 and derivatives of Ex. 2. A short adagio section calls the music to order in preparation for the return of the main theme. Pizzicato fragments of Tallis's tune herald the ever-magical colloquy between solo violin and solo viola which brings back the full Tallis theme in both orchestras, tremolando and *sur la touche*. Ex. 2 is also recalled in a rich harmonization. There is a dramatic change from fortissimo to pianissimo, and the eight-bar coda consists of a soaring phrase on the solo violin, espressivo, above a softly held chord in the second orchestra. As the soloist descends, the full forces bring the great work to an end on a firm chord of G major which gradually fades into silence.

Much has been made, rightly, of the *Fantasia*'s grave beauty. But there is nothing austere, nothing cool, about it. Tallis's tune was originally set to the words 'Why fumeth in fight', and Vaughan Williams has re-echoed something of the same impassioned train of thought. The directions 'molto espressivo', 'espressivo' and 'appassionato' occur in the score, and there are many dramatic dynamic contrasts. The great spread string chords give the work power, massive spaciousness and a four-square solidity. In its quieter moments there is tender intimacy flowering into lyrical ardour. The violin and viola, operatically intertwined, seem almost to assume human and personal significance. There are sombre minutes, in which darkness and doom seem to be contemplated; there are others in which sunlight floods through the arches and coloured glass of the cathedrals in which this music is often played. Best of all is the strong impression that the work is as old as time itself and yet as new as though it had been written yesterday. To apply the adjective 'sublime' to this music would not be overstating its wonderful blending of spiritual strength and physical exaltation.

Physical exaltation is the first impression one receives from the beginning of *A Sea Symphony*. Where the *Tallis Fantasia* showed a taut and strict control of material, the setting of Whitman as a choral symphony produced expansiveness, rhetoric, grandiloquence and a musical poetry as unexpectedly direct as the words. The sea as a subject for music seems to have attracted composers at the turn of the century: was it, perhaps, the feeling that a new epoch for mankind had begun, and the sea and voyages symbolized the spirit of adventure which characterizes the start of a century or a new reign? Whatever the answer, we have the results in Stanford's *Sea Songs*, Vaughan Williams's *A Sea Symphony*, Debussy's *La Mer*, Elgar's *Sea Pictures*, and other works. Frank Bridge wrote a work called *The Sea*, and W. H. Bell planned in 1900 a Whitman choral work to be called *In Great Waters*, with three movements called 'Outward bound', 'The Night Watches' and 'On the Fo'c's'le'. It became an orchestral suite, *Mother Carey*. Though it is possible to accept Vaughan Williams's *A Sea Symphony* as a breezy, salty evocation of nautical emotions it was plainly not thus intended by the composer who, in the first, second, and last movements has carefully selected words which support an analogy between the voyager on the sea and the voyage of the soul into the unknown. Here again, as in the 1907 Song, is expressed in music the liberal-radical, questing, agnostic, hopeful attitude of Vaughan Williams's generation. It is worth remembering, as one listens to the moving finale of this work, that Freud described religion as 'that vast *oceanic* feeling'.

The symphony begins with a master-stroke. The fanfare from the brass on the chord of B flat minor, in D major, is a gesture of genius, bringing an almost visible picture of the swelling ocean as the choir enters with the tremendous announcement 'Behold, the sea itself', and the full orchestra, *largamente*, has a thrilling phrase which not only represents an aspect of the sea, but seems also to proclaim the composer's confidence that he has at last found the language in which he can speak to his countrymen. Major and minor triads a third apart are the means by which this startling opening is effected, and the same device recurs at various parts of the work as a binding factor. For the words 'And on its limitless heaving breast, the ships' a theme from the early tone-poem *The Solent* finds its true application. The exultation of these first six and a half pages of the score is invariably exciting and moving. It is as if the noble figure of the composer was ever-present on the platform.

As this prelude fades away, the orchestra has a brief reference to the folk song 'Tarry Trowsers' before the baritone begins his 'rude brief recitative of ships sailing the seas'. The orchestration vividly describes the 'dashing spray', and for these brilliant choral pages the tang of the sea and the shanty-ish rhythm are evoked and sustained. The baritone introduces a solemn note with his chant for the sailors of all nations; it is still a matter for wonder that Whitman's words should have found music which fits them so naturally, the speech-rhythms having an inevitable musical cadence. The whole Purcellian passage in which the baritone's phrases are first answered by the chorus and then accompanied by it, to end in a forceful declaration of 'untamed as thee', builds up a tension released by the return of the opening fanfare and the dramatic entry of the solo soprano with her 'Flaunt out O sea your separate flags of nations'. She introduces the theme of 'the soul of man' and 'a spiritual woven signal for all nations', an emblem 'elate above death', in music of growing warmth which culminates in her thrilling A flat melody 'Token of all brave captains'. This is the development section of what is in essence a symphonic sonata-form movement. The chorus's lament for 'all that went down doing their duty' sinks down as each section echoes 'young or old', and gathers new heart as the composer recalls the section of the poem 'emblem of man, elate above death'. The words 'above death' are hammered out triumphantly and fade to a whisper as the baritone launches the recapitulation: 'A pennant universal subtly waving all time o'er all brave sailors, all seas, all ships'. As this diatonic tune is developed the soloists are heard together for the first time in the work and the mighty climax, 'One flag, above all the rest', is thundered out to the tune which at first had accompanied the description of the sea's 'limitless heaving breast'. The 'Behold the sea' theme now recurs, *misterioso*, in the soprano and tenor parts and the solo soprano declaims it like a recitative. On her last note the baritone and the chorus, softly and with tranquil effect, intone 'all seas, all ships', and the soprano voice floats gently above them to close the movement pianissimo.

In the slow movement, 'On the beach at night, alone', the orchestra plays a large part. The dark-toned introduction shows the sea lapping the shore while the baritone, echoed by a contralto semi-chorus, watches the bright stars shining and thinks his thought of the clef of the universes. Brass, *dolce*, begin a new major-key melody and the full chorus join the baritone as he lists those things which are all interlocked by 'a vast similitude'. Key changes symbolize 'all distances', then 'all souls' and finally the chorus burst out, in six-part harmony. Thereafter the music returns to the soloist's initial reflective mood and an orchestral postlude of rich beauty, perhaps expressing thoughts for which the poet found no words.

The virtuoso scherzo 'The Waves' is the one movement in which no philosophical reflections occur and is the only one which could successfully be detached from the work.[1] It serves excellently, however, as a breathing-space before the immense finale—though the choir get little breathing-space! This is one of the perennial challenges to any choir's ability, requiring rhythmical precision and lusty tone. It opens with a version of the fanfare from the beginning of the symphony, a peremptory command for discipline, and the juxtaposition of minor and major thirds which runs as a binding thread through the work. Here the sensation of a stormy sea is exhilaratingly communicated—whistling winds and flying spray and 'waves, undulating waves' (a thrilling part for the chorus). Whirling chromatic scales for the orchestra, with the folk song 'The Golden Vanity' quoted in the woodwind, prepare the way for the fine, broad, Parry-ish tune of the Trio to depict the great vessel ploughing her way through the tumultuous ocean, with a snatch of 'The Bold Princess Royal' in the harmony. As she passes she leaves 'a motley procession with many a fleck of foam—and many fragments'; and the music becomes keyless, with whole-tone scales (vocal score, p. 73) until the fanfare sounds again and the recapitulation of the Scherzo, shortened, with a brief glance again at the Trio tune, takes the chorus to its final shouts of 'following'.

With the finale, 'The Explorers', the mood reverts to solemnity and the music attains its noblest shape. The choir sing 'O vast rondure, swimming in space' to a seminal Vaughan Williams tune

---

[1] The first Cambridge performance of the Symphony omitted it altogether.

(which, written in 1903, was the forerunner of the slow, augmented version in the overture to *The Wasps*):

This choral introduction is an example of that ability of Vaughan Williams to make the simplest of musical statements uplift the heart of man, to say the ancient truths in a new and evergreen way. To analyse it is pointless; suffice it to say that the quality of the choral part-writing imparts an individual stamp to the music that could have been written by nobody else and ends in an impassioned orchestral passage of seven bars. Yet, curiously, this very passage is one in which Vaughan Williams has twice admitted the influence of Elgar:

'I spent several hours at the British Museum studying the full scores of the *Enigma Variations* and *Gerontius*. The results are obvious in the opening pages of the finale of my *Sea Symphony*. . . .' ('Musical Autobiography').

'I find that the Elgar phrase which influenced me most was "Thou art calling me" in *Gerontius* . . . not so much perhaps in its original form as when it comes later on in combination with another theme (e.g. p. 19, figure 37 (v.s.)). For proof of this see *Sea Symphony* (vocal score, p. 84, nine bars before letter B) and *London Symphony* (full score, p. 16, letter H).' (*Music and Letters*, Vol. XVI, No. 1.)

In the same article from which the second quotation above is taken Vaughan Williams wrote: 'I am astonished . . . to find on looking back on my own earlier works how much I cribbed from him [Elgar], probably when I thought I was being most original. . . . Real cribbing takes place when one composer thinks with the mind of another, even when there is no mechanical similarity of phrase. When, as often happens, this vicarious thinking does lead to similarity of phrase the offence is, I think, more venial. In that case one is so impressed by a certain passage in another composer that it becomes part of oneself.'

There is nothing Elgarian about the next episode in this finale. To a tune in the Dorian mode, the creation of man is considered while a female semi-chorus, unaccompanied, sadly asks 'Wherefore, unsatisfied soul ? Whither O mocking life ?' While this 'sad, incessant refrain' continues, the music is modal, filmy and uncertain. As the poet's answer is given—'Yet soul be sure the first intent remains'—the clouds disperse and the diatonic directness of the first movement returns. The supreme climax of the symphony is reached with a thrice repeated 'Finally' and then 'shall come the poet worthy that name, the true son of God shall come singing his songs', a moment of high ecstasy with mystical melismata on the word 'singing'. Then, to a downward rushing passage on the orchestra not far distant from the opening of the Sixth Symphony of thirty-five years later, the ecstatic vision fades, to be renewed as the baritone hastens into a new tune, 'O we can wait no longer', and is joined by the soprano. A long, urgent and operatic duet follows in which the soloists sing of pleasant explorations while the orchestra impetuously scurries along, sustaining their mood. It is a signpost to *Hugh the Drover* and *Sir John in Love*. The passion relaxes as the baritone, *tranquillo*, murmurs 'O soul, thou pleasest me, I thee' and we are launched into the most beautiful part of the symphony as 'sailing these seas, or on the hills, or waking in the night' there come 'thoughts, silent thoughts, of time and space and death'. The peak of emotion is reached thus, in a tune which might have found a place in the *English Hymnal*:

This wonderful passage concludes as the baritone considers the vastnesses of space, the orchestra echoes the 'Limitless heaving breast' tune and the chorus, in block harmony unaccompanied, begins what is in effect the first of Vaughan Williams's symphonic epilogues though it is not so-called in this case:

Greater than stars or suns
Bounding O soul thou journeyest forth

with the favourite emotional device of a falling triplet on

jour - ney - est

Excitement ripples from the soloists to the orchestra and to the chorus at the cry 'Away, O soul, hoist instantly the anchor'—to a shanty rhythm—and all join in the exhortation to 'Sail forth, steer for the deep waters only', as the soloists are bound 'where mariner has not yet dared to go'. 'Sail forth' is again roared out and the orchestra, with nine giant chords, emphasizes the importance of the moment. A pause, and the soloists' 'O my brave soul! O farther sail', *molto adagio*, is echoed softly by the chorus and the vast work descends into the deeps of silence where, buried full fathom five in the orchestra, is a transformation of the initial fanfare.

Vaughan Williams was to write greater choral works than *A Sea Symphony* but none of them has become so popular with choral societies as this early work written at the zenith of English choral singing. This is partly due, no doubt, to the familiarity of its idiom, but only partly. It is a 'fine song for singing, a fine song to hear', and it creates the atmosphere of a special spiritual experience whenever it is well performed. It may be ungainly; it is a curious mixture of styles, as its long gestation made inevitable. But it is still essentially Vaughan Williams's individual voice. Some sensitive souls find Whitman's words an embarrassment—the adjurations to the 'Soul', and phrases like 'Bathe me O God in Thee' and 'old husky nurse'—but this is a hypersensitive reaction. Hubert Parry, to whose art this symphony is perhaps English music's highest tribute, found it 'big stuff, but full of impertinences as well as noble moments'. The impertinences no longer matter. The noble moments are immortal. And it passes the test of all great music: one finds more in it, not less, as the years go by.

Like another work first heard in 1910, Elgar's Violin Concerto, *A Sea Symphony* is profuse in melodic invention, having enough tunes to last some composers for three symphonies. Prodigality of melody is found in all these pre-1914 works and especially in the next important work to be performed, the 1911 *Five Mystical Songs*, the title given by Vaughan Williams to these well-known poems of George Herbert. These songs had been in the making for five years. Herbert attracted Vaughan Williams because the poet was himself a musician who, it is said, recognized in music 'not a science only but a divine voice'. The mysticism of Vaughan Williams is to be found in that self-same divinity of music through which alone he could perceive the ultimate realities. In his music this mysticism nearly always finds expression in melismata. He firmly believed that the melismata of plainsong were not ornamental flourishes but the natural outpouring of people when their 'mystical' emotions found no outlet in words alone. The first of the Herbert songs uses music as a simile for the emotions of Easter. Christ's 'stretched sinews taught all strings what key is best to celebrate this most high day'; 'Consort both heart and lute, and twist a song pleasant and long; or since all music is but three parts vied and multiplied, O let Thy Blessed Spirit bear a part, and make up our defects with his sweet art'. To an accompaniment of triplets the baritone soloist declaims 'Rise heart' in a fourth rising from B flat to E flat. It is, once again, a striking opening and if its continuation harks back to the Rossetti period it is still singularly appropriate to the poet's manner. Herbert, after all, was only forty when he died and this is young man's poetry and music. At 'Awake my lute', the key and rhythm change, and harp and woodwind impart a sensuous tone. It is a remarkable feature of this cycle that the religious sentiments are expressed in music of much romantic ardour which does not seem at odds with the text. Colles, at the very first performance, recognized that this was mystical 'not with the mystery of complexity which leads to confusion but with that deepest kind which is compatible with simplicity'. It is joyous music, serene and happy. No. 2, 'I got me flowers', again has harp and wind as principal support for the voice. There soon occurs this phrase, pregnant with the secret of Vaughan Williams's ability to make the simple notes express the most complex emotions:

I got me boughs off ma - ny a tree

For the second verse in E major the chorus hums to a short 'u' sound and the lovely song ends with the affirmation 'There is but one, and that one ever', yet another use of the 'Sine Nomine' descending phrase. Further traces of study of Elgar's orchestral scores can, I think, be detected in the orchestration of these first two songs, and there are several cross-references which show that a great deal of the music was written alongside *A Sea Symphony*. The most ambitious song is No. 3 'Love bade me welcome', the last to be written (in 1911). It is full of pointers in the musical Pilgrim's Progress towards other landmarks of his career. After two cool bars of wind introduction, the muted strings set the atmosphere of the whole song with a persistent flexible accompaniment which vividly anticipates the *Pastoral Symphony*. The dialogue in the poem is most beautifully set to music, with a strong echo of 'Bredon Hill' at 'Truth, Lord, but I have marred them':

The heights of romanticism are reached when the chorus, to a wordless 'ah', sings the chant 'O sacrum convivium', the ancient antiphon sung on the Feast of Corpus Christi, while the baritone quietly sings ' "You must sit down," says Love, "and taste my meat" '. Elgar, it will be remembered, had used the same theme, for orchestra, in the early part of *The Kingdom*.

No. 4, 'The Call', is one of those simple tunes which came naturally to Vaughan Williams—for instance, 'O taste and see' of 1953—and are entirely personal to him yet sound as if they had always existed. The modal harmony probably accounts for the feeling of antiquity, the consecutive triads for the strong personality. It is a very beautiful song; and its quietness makes even stronger the contrast as the last song, 'Antiphon', comes scurrying vigorously in with fourteen bars of orchestral *moto perpetuo* before the tenors and basses chant out 'Let all the world in every corner sing'. The exultant mood of this song was many times to be repeated in later works: the *Benedicite*, the *Festival Te Deum*, the last chorus of *Dona Nobis Pacem* and the finale of the Eighth Symphony. Its rather noisy heartiness does not always ring true if the performance is loosely conducted and raggedly sung. Nowadays we recognize this exuberant, bell-chiming, rhythmical music as V.W. in his 'open-air service' mood. When the songs first appeared, the idiom of 'Antiphon' was remarked upon as being 'strange' to most English composers. What was also truly said in *The Times*, after the first London performance, was that 'the spirit of the words is reproduced with extraordinary sympathy; and the words themselves are declaimed in a way which indicates a true musical descendant of Lawes and Purcell'. The songs are usually heard today in the arrangement for voice and pianoforte, but the version for soloist, chorus, and orchestra is much to be preferred.

One has to browse only for a while among the pages of the musical periodicals of the 1909–14 period to recapture vicariously the excitement that was felt at the re-awakening of interest in the Tudor composers, and of the belief that English music was at last stirring from its long sleep. The outward and visible sign of its effect upon Vaughan Williams is the number of works of this period which bear the word Fantasia in their titles. The year 1912 saw the completion of two of them, the Cobbett quintet and that on Christmas Carols. The Phantasy Quintet (Cobbett preferred the spelling 'Phantasy') is an attractive work, short and rather slender, with prominence given to viola tone. The viola starts the work pentatonically and anticipates by forty years the Nocturne in *Pilgrim's Progress*. The harmonies are plain—'clear to the understanding and restful to the ear' as Fox Strangways wrote[1]—and again exploit the possibilities of new uses to which the common chord can be put. The scherzo begins as an ostinato movement and subsides into a sarabande, in which the cello is silent. The *burlesca* finale is lively and rhythmical and brings back the main theme of the Prelude. As in the G minor quartet, the mark 'solo' is used to show where the tune must be most prominent, followed by a sign indicating that the instrument must fall back into the general ensemble out of the limelight. Altogether, this is one of the most endearing of the earlier works. Its opening and closing mood of rapt ecstasy and the restrained sarabande are both beautiful and gratefully written for the instruments. It is also fascinating to hear the lark begin to ascend near the end.

The *Fantasia on Christmas Carols* is a work about which the commentators on Vaughan Williams's music are curiously divided in views. It is not of major importance, but its attractiveness has kept it in favour with choral societies. Colles, in *The Times* after the Hereford performance, lamented that 'a composer who has so much that is interesting to say should refrain from saying it and should devote his efforts to the arrangement of other people's tunes, however delightful these may be'. His successor, Frank Howes, called this *Fantasia* 'this most happy and beautiful, hearty and mystical Christmas music'.[2] It is a brief work but in its short course it amply fulfils its purpose of dwelling on the beauties of several carols which

[1] *Music and Letters*, Vol. I, No. 2, p. 83.
[2] *The Music of Ralph Vaughan Williams* by Frank Howes (London, 1954), p. 128.

were probably unknown to the audiences at its earliest performances. The solo cello opens with a free eight-bar improvisation on 'This is the truth sent from above'. The baritone takes it up and is accompanied by the chorus in humming tone. Tenors and basses introduce 'Come all you worthy gentlemen' to which 'The First Nowell' is opposed as an orchestral descant after the second verse. As the refrain 'O we wish you the comfort and tidings of joy', with choral melismata on 'comfort' and 'tidings', falls to a soft whisper, the baritone, in G major, sings 'On Christmas Night', one of the great tunes Vaughan Williams collected from Mrs. Verrall at Monk's Gate, Horsham, in 1904. He is echoed line-by-line by the sopranos while the rest of the chorus sing 'Ah'. At the climax, *pochettino animato*, the orchestra quotes from the Yorkshire 'Wassail Bough' which is the appropriate cue for the baritone to sing 'God bless the ruler of this house', the last verse of 'Come all you worthy gentlemen'. The chorus replies with some lines from 'On Christmas Night', the orchestra quotes snatches of a folk-dance tune, of 'A Virgin Unspotted' and 'The First Nowell'. The bells chime as the chorus wish us a happy new year. On this time-honoured phrase of greeting, the composer makes a gradual and magical *diminuendo* as the wassailers' voices vanish into the distance, across the snow-covered fields and away into the night. This is music of a sweetness and warmth which belong to the time it celebrates in traditional words and notes.

In 1913 came the greatest and most elaborate of Vaughan Williams's folk-song settings. Hitherto he had been content to set the old tunes to pianoforte accompaniment; or it is more likely that he had not been content, but felt that in this way they would reach a wider audience. But in the *Five English Folk Songs* for unaccompanied chorus the tunes were treated with great freedom so that the whole work becomes almost another fantasia. It is well to recall some of Vaughan Williams's words on folk songs which are particularly applicable to this work: 'There is no original version of any particular tune . . . in one sense any particular tune is as old as the beginning of music; in another sense it is born afresh with the singer of today who sang it.' In these five settings Vaughan Williams became 'the singer of today', and he practically re-created the songs. 'The Lover's Ghost', for instance, is in effect variations on a canto fermo, with part-writing and polyphony which rank with Weelkes and Dowland in beauty and skill. Similarly in 'Just as the tide was flowing' there is a most testing florid passage for all the voices, yet the essential spirit of the song is preserved.

The culmination of this period of Vaughan Williams's career came with *A London Symphony*. Although he never abandoned his nationalist beliefs, never again was he to fulfil so utterly his creed, expressed in 'Who Wants the English Composer?', that the composer should take 'the forms of musical expression' which were all about him and 'purify and raise [them] to the level of great art. . . . We must cultivate a sense of musical citizenship'. Purify and *raise*, be it noted. Vaughan Williams's liberal beliefs did not admit of a lowest common denominator. 'It is not enough for music to come from the people, it must also be for the people,' he said in America in 1932.[1] 'The people must not be written down to, they must be written up to. . . . The ordinary man expects from a serious composer serious music and will not be at all frightened even at a little "uplift".' *A London Symphony* was 'written up to' the people, and its continued popularity proves the wisdom of this course. Much ink has been used in discussion of whether this is a programme-symphony or absolute music. The composer bedevilled the issue by insisting that the various London landmarks which appear in the work are 'accidentals, not essentials' and that the symphony ought to be called 'Symphony by a Londoner'. Later he relented and disclosed that the 'life of London (including possibly its sights and sounds) . . . suggested an attempt at expression'. His fears, if fears they were, were unfounded. This *is* a programme-symphony, but it is also perfectly acceptable as 'absolute' music. Since it is called *A London Symphony*, however, it is obviously going to affect more deeply those who know their London.[2] In precisely the same way, it would be foolish to sweep away all thoughts of the sea while listening to Debussy's *La Mer*, although it would still be a great 'purely musical' composition. It is always a mistake to take too rigid a view of symphonic form, and most great composers, from Beethoven to Britten, have broken the rules for our delectation.

The first movement, mainly in G minor, is in a more or less regular sonata form. An Introduction on cellos and basses, clarinets and violas, quiet but spacious (and pentatonic), begins with a motif

[1] *National Music and Other Essays*, p. 66.

[2] R. O. Morris wrote: 'There is a questioning in it and a weariness—the weariness of one who is not quite sure whether he loves London or hates her, yet knows that, loving or hating, he is for ever a victim to her evil fascination.'—*The Nation*, 15 May 1920, Vol. 27, No. 7.

of four notes based on a rising fourth. Here we find London before the break of day: 'all that mighty heart is lying still,' just as Vaughan Williams must have seen it from his home in Cheyne Walk. 'I was quite unconscious that I had cribbed from *La Mer* in the introduction to my *London Symphony* until Constant Lambert horrified me by calling my attention to it,' Vaughan Williams wrote[1] in 1949. In 1934 he had written: 'I do not consider that the opening of my *London Symphony* is a crib from the beginning of *Gerontius*, Part 2; indeed, my friends assure me that it is, as a matter of fact, a compound of Debussy's *La Mer* and Charpentier's *Louise*.'[2] Harp and clarinet intone the Westminster Chimes (the half-hour), the whole orchestra stirs, there is an expectant pause and the main *allegro risoluto* theme is stridently announced. Tune swiftly germinates tune: the melodies in this work proliferate in a manner that makes disciplining them symphonically a constant problem to the composer. All these melodies, some cheeky, others more subdued, are welded into a long exposition. 'Noise and scurry' are the composer's own words for the basic mood of the movement. A *cantabile* 'bridge passage'—at letter H in the full score; this is the passage where Vaughan Williams says he was influenced again by Gerontius's 'Thou art calling me'—leads to the declamatory second subject, on wind and brass, which generates an episode of Hampstead Heath high spirits (this is the 'American ragtime' section to which Butterworth and Capell called attention at the first performance). After a brief return to the main theme and its attendants, followed by a woodwind dialogue, the flute, *tranquillo*, has a new tune against a background of divided strings. A solo cello and solo violin then begin a magical passage of quiet reverie which seems to suggest London's green places, or the inside of a church. A string sextet, accompanied by divided strings, with harps and woodwind, takes the feverish note out of the music. The mood is changed softly, by string *tremolandi*, into the recapitulation. The principal tunes are reviewed. Grandeur sweeps into the music, driving to a climax with strings chiming like bells. Two high peaks of sound are reached, and the first subject is roared out by the brass, triple forte then quadruple. A hint of tragedy returns but the second subject, broadened in G major, and now affirmatory rather than declamatory, has the last word.

[1] 'Chapter of Musical Autobiography.' Op. cit.
[2] *Music and Letters*, Vol. XVI, No. 1, p. 16.

George Butterworth, the first 'analyst' of this symphony, also wrote about it in the *R.C.M. Magazine* (Easter Term 1914). There he said of the Lento: 'The slow movement is an idyll of grey skies and secluded byways—an aspect of London quite as familiar as any other: the feeling of the music is remote and mystical, and its very characteristic beauty is not of a kind which it is possible to describe in words.' Vaughan Williams likened it to 'Bloomsbury Square on a November afternoon'. The strings set the scene with a series of wide-spanned chilly chords against which the cor anglais, *misterioso*, has an evocative solo. There is a pause and the music is repeated, in E major, scored for harps and trombones. The strings then have the theme, more richly harmonized and with a horn pendant. Against a throbbing background of muted strings, flute and trumpet introduce another theme while the horn sounds the rising-fourth motif from the symphony's first bar. This music is developed and repeated until, after a pause, the solo viola, in a melody strongly marked by triplets, begins a conversation with the woodwind and breaks off to play a variant of the lavender-seller's street-cry. (In Vaughan Williams's notebooks is a 'Lavender Cry', noted in Chelsea on 21 July 1911.) Clarinet and other woodwind echo the cry eerily, and there is a touch of realism in the jingle of hansom-cabs. The music becomes momentarily restless and foreboding—note the strong and sinister rhythm from timpani—and then rises with passion to a *largamente* climax for full orchestra, obtained by the favourite use of widely separated treble and bass. The fervour subsides, and the themes are softly recalled. The horn sounds its note of romance and leaves the solo viola to close this very beautiful movement. Not altogether 'remote and mystical' music: the sense of human passion and warmth is not absent. But Butterworth was right in perceiving the mystical quality which stems from the peculiarly personal use of common chords throughout the symphony.

The Whistlerian Scherzo-nocturne is perhaps the finest movement of the work and represents the highest point of Vaughan Williams's orchestral art before the 1914 war. The material is deftly handled; all is assured and confident. Moreover this musical evocation of the mood of a city at night has not been excelled by any composer, of any nation. The music begins in a modal D minor, with snippets of theme tumbling over each other, and scurrying strings keeping up the pace. The scoring is delicate and apt, principally for woodwind and strings—combinations of clarinet and violas, cellos and bassoons; a flute solo; and a fragment for trombones and tuba which has an air of nocturnal mystery. This section is repeated, and eventually cellos and horns announce a more ponderous *fugato* theme, *poco animato*, which stamps its noisy way across the orchestra, barracked by some of the jig-like snippets from earlier themes. This leads to a shortened repeat of the Scherzo. A chattering bassoon introduces the Trio, in C major, a remarkably picturesque episode in which a scene of Cockney conviviality centred on a mouth-organ and accordion is vividly painted. A sinister mood then transforms the music, reminding us of the loneliness and tragedy one finds in a city at night. The movement runs down into silence on bassoons and strings. Just before the end there is a short harp solo which Frank Howes has poetically likened to the 'nocturnal striking of a distant church clock'.

A tragic cry from the full orchestra, *appassionato*, begins the finale and diminishes until nothing is left but a solo cello. Cellos then introduce a solemn march tune. This reaches a majestic G major climax for full brass and leads directly into an E minor allegro. The music becomes animated and staccato, with a portentous figure for strings and horns. Butterworth thought that this section may express discontent with the seamier side of London life and that 'fierce delight in the struggle which imperfection of any kind involves', the sounding of a challenge. Undoubtedly something grim gave rise to this turbulent music. Since its composition the Cenotaph has been built, and the music's prophetic universality now evokes memories of London in wartime. The march and the spirit of conflict alternate until the portentous theme is pressed to a gigantic climax, repeated twice and then, the third time, with a great stroke on the gong at the summit. The theme of the first movement's *allegro risoluto* returns and the music is stilled. The Westminster Chimes sound the third quarter and the Epilogue begins with a rippling figure. This is music's equivalent of 'Sweet Thames, run softly, till I end my song'. Brass and woodwind interpolate memories of old themes, but all passion is spent and the strings guide the symphony to the goal of G major. A benedictory violin solo, the music swells, and London is left behind.

The composer said in a letter:[1] 'For actual coda see end of Wells' *Tono-Bungay*.' This is the chapter called 'Night and the Open Sea' where London is marvellously described. As the narrator passes

[1] Letter to the author, 30 September 1957.

down the Thames in a destroyer he seems 'to be passing all England in review', an idea which would certainly have appealed to Vaughan Williams:

'To run down the Thames so is to run one's hand over the pages in the book of England from end to end. . . . There come first squalid stretches of mean homes right and left and then the dingy industrialism of the South side, and on the North bank the polite long front of nice houses, artistic, literary, administrative people's residences, that stretches from Cheyne Walk nearly to Westminster and hides a wilderness of slums. . . . We tear into the great spaces of the future and the turbines fall to talking in unfamiliar tongues. Out to the open we go, to windy freedom and trackless ways. Light after light goes down. England and the Kingdom, Britain and the Empire, the old prides and the old devotions, glide abeam, astern, sink down upon the horizon, pass—pass. The river passes —London passes, England passes. . . .'

The poetry of that prose became the poetry of music in the symphonic Epilogue, which was Vaughan Williams's invention of a way of unifying a symphony without following a merely mechanical cyclic form. Perhaps *A London Symphony* is diffuse, overburdened with tunes, but it is also highly concentrated and organized. It is a brilliantly successful masterpiece, unique of its kind. It is also a notable example of Vaughan Williams's sheer professionalism. The scoring in the work is nothing short of masterly; each mood is limned by instrumental 'colour' as surely as in a Monet painting. Yet the legend began hereabouts of the 'clumsiness' of this composer. Even Butterworth wrote of 'not infrequent failure' by Vaughan Williams to express his 'beautiful and original ideas' because of 'some inherent incapacity for perfecting a technique'. Fox Strangways wrote of 'hammering beauty out of ugliness' in the symphony. In the *London Symphony* Vaughan Williams said what he wanted to say exactly as he wanted to say it. It is the natural successor to Elgar's two brilliantly scored symphonies; and a certain opulence and richness of sound place it within its period. None of the subsequent symphonies is as copious in invention nor as colourful in its expression.

The time has surely come to put an end to the nonsense so often written about 'the countryman's view of London' in this symphony. Though, like many passionate lovers of London, Vaughan Williams was not born there—he was born in a Gloucestershire vicarage and he spent his childhood in a Surrey country-house—from his late teens, with short spells in Cambridge or abroad, he lived and worked in London and he was fifty-seven before he left it for Dorking, to return for the last five years of his life. This is both a London Symphony *and* a symphony by a Londoner about Londoners. In it, its composer lived up to his ideal: he took the everyday things of life and made them beautiful. Most of all he must have cherished the letter Holst wrote to him from Brook Green two days after the first performance: 'You have really done it this time. Not only have you reached the heights but you have taken your audience with you. . . . I wish I could tell you how I and everyone else was carried away on Friday.'[1]

Among Vaughan Williams's last tasks before he went to war was a commission to write four articles on English music from Elizabethan times to the mid-nineteenth century for the *Music Student* and its Home Music Study Union. 'Is music a mere set of tricks, devices, rules, or is it something inborn in human nature?' he asked. There is no need to quote his answer. It was the statement of a romantic artist, yet one who paradoxically was to be fitted by his admirers into a niche marked 'intellectual' and 'restrained'. It is clear that his reason for liking *A London Symphony* all his life was that he felt that, in its pages, he had done what he had set out to do—to reflect the life of the nation. For Holst and him, music was for people. The sinister phrase 'the people', with its ideological overtones, had not yet gained full sway. After the war, perhaps, Vaughan Williams felt that what he had to say was not to be expressed in such realistic terms. It is significant that this symphony and *Hugh the Drover* were the most frequently and drastically revised of all his works.

[1] *Heirs and Rebels*, pp. 43–4.

CHAPTER SIX

1914–1924

Principal Works

FOUR HYMNS . THE LARK ASCENDING . A PASTORAL SYMPHONY
MASS IN G MINOR . OLD KING COLE
SUITE, ENGLISH FOLK SONGS . HUGH THE DROVER
THE SHEPHERDS OF THE DELECTABLE MOUNTAINS

I

'I FEEL that perhaps after the war England will be a *better* place for music than before—largely because we shan't be able to buy expensive performers etc. like we did.' So wrote Vaughan Williams to Holst on Midsummer Day 1916, just before his ambulance unit left for France. 'We don't take music as part of our everyday life half enough—I often wish we could all migrate to some small town where there could really be a musical community—London is impossible from that point of view. Goodbye and good luck.'[1]

A more despairing tone permeated Vaughan Williams's next letter to Holst, from France:

'I've indeed longed to be home in many ways during the last month—but in other ways I should not like to come home for good till everything is over, or in some other normal way. . . . I sometimes dread coming back to normal life with so many gaps—especially of course George Butterworth —he has left most of his MS. to me—and now I hear that Ellis is killed— out of those 7 who joined up together in August 1914 only 3 are left—I sometimes think now that it is wrong to have made friends with people much younger than oneself—because soon there will only be the middle aged left—and I have got out of touch with most of my contemporary friends—but then there is always you and thank Heaven we have never got out of touch and I don't see why we ever should.'

The gaps were indeed tragic. Cecil Coles, a promising composer, had been a particular friend of Holst, who dedicated the *Ode to Death* to his memory. F. B. Ellis had promoted concerts of English music with the same unselfish zeal as Gardiner. So had Edward Mason, the cellist and for fifteen years assistant music master at Eton, who was killed at the age of thirty-six on 9 May 1915. At Edward Mason's Queen's Hall concerts of English music in 1910 and 1912 first performances had been given of Holst's *Somerset Rhapsody* and the second group of hymns from the *Rig Veda*.[1] Mason's wife was the violinist Jessie Grimson whose brother Stanley had been leader of the R.C.M. orchestra in Holst's college days and who founded the Grimson Quartet, of which Frank Bridge was the viola player. Jessie had played in the first performance of Vaughan Williams's D major quintet in 1901. Denis Browne, the first to play the score of *Hugh the Drover*, was killed in 1915, and Patrick Shaw-Stewart in 1918. Unfulfilled talent was here snuffed out in plenty; perhaps the greatest loss was George Butterworth, who was killed at Pozières on 5 August 1916, twenty-four days after his thirty-first birthday. The last music of his own which he heard played was his folk-song idyll *The Banks of Green Willow*, at an F. B. Ellis concert on 20 March 1914. In his *Shropshire Lad* Rhapsody there is all the poignancy of regret for the brilliant lost generation, as though he had foreseen in Housman's verses his own and his friends' doom. He was greatly gifted. He was a good writer; he had been a schoolmaster for a short while; and he had written criticism for *The Times*. From Vaughan Williams and Sharp he caught folk-song fever and he was an enthusiastic member of folk-dancing teams at the Stratford summer schools and on other occasions. It has been said of Butterworth, 'Few men can have been worse at making an acquaintance or better at keeping a friend'. His direct and rugged manner appealed to Vaughan Williams. It is vain to speculate on what Butterworth might have become or how their friendship would have developed. One can perhaps suspect that Vaughan Williams would not have been afraid to show the score of *The Poisoned Kiss* to Butterworth as he feared to show it to Holst 'because he would never have been able to understand how I could

---

[1] Admirers of Holst should also honour the names of Frank Duckworth and his Blackburn Ladies' Choir who sang his music when no one else would touch it. The third group of *Rig Veda* hymns is dedicated to them.

at the same time consider it trivial and yet want to write it.'[1] Butter-worth would have understood.

Others of the younger men remained, of course. Adrian Boult was coming to the fore as a conductor, having studied at Leipzig with Nikisch just before the war. In February 1918, while Vaughan Williams was in England, he conducted the *London Symphony* at Queen's Hall and repeated it, with ten minutes cut out of it by the composer, a month later. These two concerts were in effect the beginning of the career of a man who never failed to champion English music. He was chosen by Balfour Gardiner to conduct the private first performance of *The Planets* given to Holst as a present on 29 September 1918, a month before Holst sailed for Salonika: Holst had at last been accepted for war work and left England to be the Y.M.C.A.'s musical organizer among troops in the Near East. By this time Vaughan Williams had returned to France as an officer in a heavy artillery battery.

If, then, on his demobilization early in 1919, Vaughan Williams's heart was heavy, he was a man who knew that life had to be lived in the future, not in the past. His life was music and as he turned to it again, no doubt he surveyed the English scene and the international scene since 1914. Something of what he saw now follows.

During the war English musical life had been kept alive largely by Sir Thomas Beecham, who took charge of the Royal Philharmonic Society, conducted many of the Hallé Orchestra's concerts and launched a successful operatic venture. Percy Pitt, Wood, Elgar, Landon Ronald, and Parry were also to be found conducting concerts throughout the land. Under Beecham, the recent scores of Stravinsky, Delius, Ethel Smyth, Debussy, Ravel, Bantock, Holbrooke, and the Russians were fairly frequently played. Of the 'new school' of English music represented by Vaughan Williams and Holst little was heard in the concerts of the established societies. But almost as soon as the war ended the resurgence of interest in English music which had been powerfully stimulated in small groups up to 1914 mounted to a climax and was noticeable in various ways. The oldest of English musical societies, the Royal Philharmonic, began to include many more British works, largely due to the influence of Norman O'Neill, Gardiner, Boult, and Geoffrey Toye. Another who had been a foremost advocate of the nationalist revival before the war was the great choral conductor Charles

[1] 'A Musical Autobiography'.

Kennedy Scott. In 1904 he had formed his Oriana Madrigal Society and had taken part in Balfour Gardiner's series of concerts from 1912–14. Now Gardiner backed him in forming the Philharmonic Choir which made its first appearance on 26 February 1920, in Delius's *Song of the High Hills*. Kennedy Scott had also been associated with Rutland Boughton's attempt to establish an English Bayreuth at Glastonbury, a venture which Vaughan Williams encouraged and helped financially. Boughton, with Reginald Buckley as his librettist, planned a series of music-dramas on the Arthurian legends. Though the original project did not fully materialize, a start was made in 1914 under somewhat rudimentary conditions. In 1916 Purcell's *Dido and Aeneas* and Gluck's *Iphigenia in Tauris* were produced, with assistance from E. J. Dent; there was then a break until 1919 when the festival was revived. Boughton's *The Immortal Hour*, first performed in 1914, had a long run in London in 1922. This musical parallel of the literary Celtic vogue also affected Arnold Bax, whose development continued after the war when he found congenial advocates in Beecham and Hamilton Harty.

English music was assisted practically by two other factors which had developed in Vaughan Williams's absence. The Carnegie United Kingdom Trust had been established in 1914 as a kind of forerunner of the Arts Council. It gave grants to local ventures, to competition festivals and to the English Folk Dance Society. In 1917 it began to publish works which were by composers not well known to the public or which were unlikely to be a commercial proposition for an ordinary publisher.[1] The first publication of *A London Symphony* was under Carnegie auspices; so was that of Holst's *The Hymn of Jesus*, Boughton's *The Immortal Hour* and Bantock's *Hebridean Symphony*, to name but a few. The Trust also undertook the publication of ten volumes of Tudor church music.

In June 1918, Dr. Arthur Eaglefield Hull, a forty-two-year-old Yorkshireman who had edited the *Monthly Musical Record* since 1912 as well as having written a treatise on modern harmony and books on Scriabin and Cyril Scott, formed a committee of management of the British Music Society. He was honorary director; Lord Howard de Walden ('T. E. Ellis') was elected president in August. E. J. Dent and Bernard Shaw were among those who played a leading part in the establishment of the society, which was incorporated

[1] The first to be published under its auspices was Howells's Pianoforte Quartet in A minor.

in November 1919. A year later the venture was in considerable financial difficulty from which it was extricated by the generosity of its president. A wholesale reorganization took place in 1921. Eaglefield Hull resigned, and a management committee directed the society's activities. These were not primarily to give concerts but rather to co-ordinate British musical activities. It soon had branches in many parts of the country. Nor was it a purely nationalist body. Dent, who became music critic of *The Athenaeum* in 1919, dedicated himself to the re-establishment of cultural contacts between the former belligerents. He wrote about English music in Continental journals and vice versa. In the August of 1922, at a chamber music festival held by young Viennese composers at Salzburg, it was decided to form an international permanent body for the performance of new music. Dent was elected president and at a congress in London in January 1923, the International Society for Contemporary Music was constituted. The offices of the British Music Society in Berners Street were chosen as the I.S.C.M. headquarters, and the B.M.S.'s Contemporary Music Centre became the international body's British Section. In May 1920, the B.M.S.'s first annual congress was to prove a significant event in Vaughan Williams's career. The Society was disbanded in 1933 but its work lives on in the Contemporary Music Centre.

Other changes, too, even more far-reaching, affected Vaughan Williams on his return. In October 1918, his old friend and master Hubert Parry died. That he felt the loss keenly is evident from an obituary tribute which he contributed to the *Music Student* for November 1918:

'I still often go out of my way to pass his house in Kensington Square in order to experience again the thrill with which I used to approach his door on my lesson day. Walt Whitman says "Why are there men and women that while they are nigh me sunlight expands my blood?" Parry was one of these.'

The vacant directorship of the Royal College of Music went to another friend of Cambridge days, Hugh P. Allen, who, earlier in 1918, had succeeded Sir Walter Parratt as Heather Professor of Music at Oxford University, and had been conductor of the London Bach Choir since 1907. Allen was exactly the type of man the College required at this time when, after the stagnation of the war years, a huge influx of students was obviously to be expected. He had absorbed from Parry a sense of what was important in the R.C.M.'s tradition, but at the same time he brought a new energy into its curriculum, and he re-modelled the staff. He invited Holst and Vaughan Williams to become teachers of composition.[1] Very shortly afterwards Vaughan Williams became a member of the Board of Professors, and he took over the conductorship of the Bach Choir from Allen in 1920. Vaughan Williams's first concert as conductor was on 14 December 1921, at which he introduced three unfamiliar church cantatas by Bach. Allen also became a director of the Royal Philharmonic Society and Chairman of the British Music Society. His influence was used always for the betterment of English music and it was natural that he should have turned to Vaughan Williams and Holst to help him at College. He also invited Adrian Boult to teach conducting and score-reading, and eventually to take over from Stanford the conductorship of the R.C.M. Orchestra and direction of the Patron's Fund rehearsals. Herbert Howells, at the age of twenty-seven, was appointed to the teaching staff in 1920. He had been a Stanford pupil in 1912 and in November of that year, when still only twenty, had heard his Mass in the Dorian Mode sung at Westminster Cathedral under Terry. In 1913 a pianoforte concerto was conducted by Stanford at Queen's Hall. Thus, at the R.C.M. in 1919, two generations of English composers worked together as colleagues, influencing each other and their pupils.

Allen grouped not only composers and performers around him at the College. He invited H. C. Colles to join the staff as lecturer in musical history and appreciation. Colles had been twenty-seven when he joined *The Times* in 1906 as assistant music critic to J. A. Fuller Maitland, whom he succeeded in 1911.

He had always admired Vaughan Williams as composer and as man. They shared several friends on the staff of *The Times*, chief among them Bruce Richmond and Harold Child (librettist of *Hugh the Drover*) as well as Nicholas Gatty. After 1922 Colles had two younger men as assistants, Frank Howes and Dyneley Hussey. During the war his place on *The Times* had been 'kept warm' by another of Vaughan Williams's admirers, Arthur H. Fox Strangways, who was to make a major contribution to English musical criticism by founding at his own risk and under his own editorial control a

---

[1] According to A. E. F. Dickinson in his 'Vaughan Williams' in *The Music Masters No. 4* (Pelican Books, 1957, p. 385) Allen said to R.V.W., 'Come up to R.C.M. and be yourself one day a week.'

new quarterly, *Music and Letters*, in January 1920.[1] The first number did honour to Elgar and the second to Vaughan Williams, who also contributed his article, 'The Letter and the Spirit'.

In those first numbers the signature to reviews of music in London was that of Philip Heseltine, whose music, written under the pseudonym 'Peter Warlock', was known only to a very select circle at this date. His first survey criticized conventional programmes, called for more performances of Elgar's symphonies, praised the conducting of Adrian Boult and Edward Clark during the Diaghilev Ballet's London season and had many good words for the singing of Steuart Wilson. Later in 1920 Heseltine was to launch his own magazine, *The Sackbut*, and from 1921 until his suicide in 1930 at the age of thirty-six his songs were to be welcomed as an 'Elizabethan' renascence of their own. Through his name can be traced another strand of English music in the 1920s, in which other threads were Cecil Gray, Constant Lambert, Bernard van Dieren and E. J. Moeran. Vaughan Williams, to whom Warlock's Three Carols for chorus and orchestra of 1923 were dedicated, stood on the fringe of this group in whom he recognized a distinct 'English school', but not all of them were destined to fulfil their early promise.

To complete the picture of the musical life to which Vaughan Williams returned in 1919 mention must be made of some factors often overlooked. Among these was the pervasive educational influence of W. Henry Hadow. In 1919, the year after he had been knighted, he went to Sheffield University as Vice-Chancellor, where he was able to combine general educational work with his particular interest in music, an alignment still all too rare in English scholastic circles. Another significant event in 1918 was the translation from the organ-loft of Manchester Cathedral to that of Westminster Abbey of Sydney H. Nicholson. He reformed the Abbey's musical performances, founded the Special Choir for performance of church music of all ages, and, as chairman of the Church Music Society, laboured for a betterment of musical standards in parishes through-

---

[1] The contents of the first number of *Music and Letters* give a very fair sample of the musical 'atmosphere' in England at the time: a poem by Laurence Binyon, Shaw's famous Essay on Elgar, an article on English song by Harry Plunket Greene, 'Music in Country Churches' by Sydney Nicholson, 'Sailor Shanties' by R. R. Terry, 'Old Keyed Instruments' by Mrs. Violet Gordon Woodhouse, 'On Listening to Music' by A. Clutton Brock, and contributions from Harold Monro, Warde Fowler and Cecil Forsyth as well as a harpsichord piece written by Delius for Mrs. Gordon Woodhouse. The idea for *Music and Letters* was given to Fox Strangways by Cecil Sharp.

out Britain. Vaughan Williams's music had always appealed to him and he was quick to see that in this composer of the day was a focal-point for the confluence of all the several elements which were revivifying English music at this date: the folk-song revival, the madrigalists, and Tudor church music.

Thus, men sympathetic to Vaughan Williams's ambitions for the future of English music were in several influential posts, but he never sought to sway their judgement. He had the rare gift, which one finds only in the man of integrity, of being able to enjoy friendship without entering into a clique or coterie. He entered fully into musical undertakings but he stood always slightly aloof from 'schools'. He was, of course, fortunate in his friends. At Cambridge, Stanford was still professor and Charles Wood, C. B. Rootham[1] and E. J. Dent were teaching. Wood succeeded Stanford in 1924 and was himself succeeded by Dent in 1926. Among critics, besides Colles and Fox Strangways there was still Edwin Evans, his first champion. Even so he must, like many composers, have occasionally prayed to be delivered from some of his friends, especially those who cast him for the rôle of an austere intellectual composer, to which he was wholly unsuited. But the label stuck and acted as a hindering factor to ready acceptance by the public of several works. Moreover any excessive adulation was distasteful to him and he was probably glad that a corrective element existed. 'Woe unto you,' he would say, 'when all men speak well of you.' Critics nurtured in the Teutonic school, chief among them Ernest Newman and Samuel Langford, of the *Manchester Guardian*, were not wholly convinced that all was perfect in the best of all possible English musical worlds.

In what mood did Vaughan Williams resume his own creative work? The war had changed the world, and it changed in some degree the lives of all who took part in it. Vaughan Williams in 1914 had been the oldest of a group still looked upon as 'promising' composers, as the heralds of a new era. He returned to England in 1919 at the age of forty-six, with the knowledge that many of his younger colleagues were dead. They had regarded him as their leader, and he had been glad to throw in his lot with them. He was not in 1914 solely dependent on such an occasion as an F. B. Ellis concert for a hearing; yet he preferred that his *London Symphony* should appear in such conditions and under an unknown conductor

[1] At a performance of *A Sea Symphony* conducted by Rootham at the C.U.M.S. on 11 June 1920, Arthur Bliss played the triangle.

rather than in more glamorous circumstances. By 1918 he found himself a 'senior' composer and teacher although he knew in his heart that his music was still at a formative stage and that he was, in a sense, only a beginner. The war had done nothing to convince him that he should follow any path but his own, or that he should modify in any way his belief that a composer must find his roots in the music of his own country. His work for the Folk Song Society continued; Cecil Sharp and Lucy Broadwood were still alive and he re-entered wholeheartedly their sphere. This disturbed some of his admirers, particularly Edwin Evans who was perhaps afraid that nationalism would mean provincialism and who was rash enough to assert that Vaughan Williams refrained from taking any part in the 'eternal squabblings' of the folk-song movement. This was not true. If he was a member of any committee, he was a full, active member and he certainly made no attempt to evade the rough-and-tumble which is an inevitable part of any society's work. What Evans could not know in 1920 was that the folk-song idiom had by now soaked so deeply into Vaughan Williams's creative mind that his music was henceforward, and paradoxically, to be more personal, more individualistically eloquent and more deeply though less obviously 'national'. Evans did understand, however, how this could come about: 'His whole attitude towards music is a protest against leadership and an assertion of independence,' he wrote in the *Musical Times* of May 1920. 'He is at all times truly himself because he has not enough artifice to be anybody else.'

It is a curious fact that the music written after the war by English composers who had served in the forces contains no parallel to the poetry of Siegfried Sassoon. It was as if their experiences had deepened in them a love of eternal and natural things rather than impelled them to express their disillusionment with mankind. Vaughan Williams's immediate post-war period yielded some of his quietest, most meditative music: the *Pastoral Symphony*, *The Shepherds of the Delectable Mountains*, *The Lark Ascending*. Ivor Gurney returned to the lyrical poets and the Gloucestershire scene which had been his first inspiration. Arthur Bliss, who had been a Guards officer, wrote a rhapsody, a pianoforte quintet and a 'witchery' none of which reflects his experiences at Cambrai and on the Somme. Holst, who had seen the war from the sidelines, had written *The Hymn of Jesus* while it was in progress and the *Ode to Death* when it was over. If we seek for a musical expression of the embittering effect of war it can be found in the First Symphony of Arnold Bax and the A minor Sonata (No. 2) for violin and pianoforte by John Ireland, neither of whom fought, and in the Cello Concerto of Elgar, who was too old to fight.

There was no flood of new music from Vaughan Williams's pen. He 'ran himself in', as it were, with his revisions of pre-war works, such as the *Tallis Fantasia*, the *London* and *Sea* Symphonies, *Toward the Unknown Region* and *Hugh the Drover*. He completed *The Lark Ascending* and looked over the Four Hymns. Dr. E. H. Fellowes has given us a glimpse of work in progress on *The Lark Ascending* at King's Weston, the beautiful home of Philip Napier Miles, which was built by Vanbrugh and overlooked the Bristol Channel, so that one could sit in the library and watch the sun setting over the sea. Miles was a benefactor of Boughton's Glastonbury festivals where, in 1919, Shaw, Dent, Fellowes, Vaughan Williams, Hadow, Steuart Wilson and Clive Carey were among the visitors and participants. His house parties at King's Weston were occasions to which the guests looked forward; it was at one of these in December 1920, that Marie Hall and Vaughan Williams made final revisions of *The Lark Ascending* together before it received its first performance in an arrangement for violin and pianoforte at an Avonmouth and Shirehampton Choral Society concert.

Several arrangements of folk songs and of traditional tunes date from the immediate post-war period, although it is not possible to discover how many had been started before 1914. Not all of them saw print easily, as this letter from Henry R. Clayton of Novellos to Cecil Sharp discloses.

160 Wardour Street, W.1.
April 24, 1919.

Private.

Dear Mr. Sharp,

Thanks for your letter of the 23rd inst. I have made enquiries as to the reason why the Somerset tunes arranged by Dr. Vaughan Williams for male voices were rejected by us. They came before three of our experts all of whom were unanimous in condemning them as too badly arranged to admit of being published by our Firm. In fact they could hardly believe that they were the work of so eminent a musician as Dr. Vaughan Williams. I of course tell you this in strict confidence. I have no doubt that Dr. Vaughan Williams will be able, as you say, to get them published without difficulty: but we are sure that their publication by us would not reflect any credit upon our Firm. Yours sincerely,

Henry R. Clayton.

To which settings this letter referred we do not know. Possibly they were rewritten. Many arrangements made at this time were the outcome of the formation by Steuart Wilson of the English Singers. When Wilson returned from the war, the Vaughan Williamses offered him a room at 13 Cheyne Walk. The Four Hymns, written for Wilson, were sung at Cardiff and Worcester in 1920, and the young tenor's career was the impetus for a renewed burst of song-writing between 1920 and 1925 which produced the Chaucer rondels 'Merciless Beauty', some more Whitman settings and a group to words by Fredegond Shove, wife of G. F. Shove, the Cambridge economist, and daughter of F. W. Maitland. The Five English Folk Songs of 1913 had attained the dignity of performance at a Royal Philharmonic Society concert by Kennedy Scott's choir on 16 December 1920, and they had already become the *pièce de résistance* of the English Singers, whose first concert had been given in London on 28 February 1920. The original members were Flora Mann, Winifred Whelen, Lillian Berger, Steuart Wilson, Clive Carey and Cuthbert Kelly. The group's foundation was probably prompted by the republication in Dr. Fellowes's great edition of the English madrigalists whose music was the basis of their concerts. They acted as devoted propagandists for British music, visiting Prague in January 1922, for a concert series conducted by Adrian Boult, Berlin, Prague and Vienna in April 1922, Berlin and Czechoslovakia again a year later and Holland in September 1923. In October 1924 the group was re-formed when pressure of solo engagements compelled Wilson and Carey to drop out. Their places were taken by Norman Stone and Norman Notley, and Nellie Carson replaced Winifred Whelen. This new team visited America, on the invitation of Mrs. Coolidge, in 1925. Steuart Wilson became the foremost exponent of Vaughan Williams's vocal music at this time partly because of his identification with it from his undergraduate days and partly because of the tragic death at the age of fifty-four of Gervase Elwes at Boston, Massachusetts, on 12 January 1921, while on a tour of the United States. In the memorial volume by Elwes's widow, Lady Winefride, and son, Richard, Vaughan Williams paid tribute to the first interpreter of *On Wenlock Edge*:

'His nature was that of the "perfect gentle knight" and it was those qualities in him which were at once the strength and the limitation of his art. He had not the wide gamut·of musical expression at his command, and it was due to the very fineness of his nature that this was so. The grosser aspects of passion and feeling were repugnant to him. . . . To those who heard it, his singing of the Narrator's part in the *St. Matthew Passion* will be a lasting memory. . . . Those who have heard Elwes know now that it is possible for a tenor to be a great musician and a true man. Surely Bach must have imagined such a singer as this when he wrote the Narrator's part.'[1]

Something of this quality can be heard in Elwes's historic records of *On Wenlock Edge*. It is singing of a nobility that has all but vanished.

Vaughan Williams conducted the Handel Society from 1919 until 1921 when Eugène Goossens succeeded him. As well as the lesser-known works of Handel, this amateur chorus and orchestra performed modern music including, under Vaughan Williams, music by Nicholas Gatty and Holst's 'This have I done for my true love'. He gave lectures and he played a leading part in the first Congress of the British Music Society in London from 3 to 6 May 1920. (Among the subjects discussed were the municipalization of music and a world standard pitch.) There was an address on British Music by Sir Henry Hadow after a reception at the Mansion House by the Lord Mayor; and the principal item of the concert by the L.S.O. under Albert Coates in Queen's Hall on the evening of 4 May was *A London Symphony*. In after years, Richard Capell said of this performance that it turned Vaughan Williams overnight into a national figure. As Colles wrote,[2] 'a great deal of the advocacy of British music consists in describing it as just as good as some other music, but it is not what is "just as good" but what is different which counts, and the *London Symphony* is very different from any contemporary music produced either in this country or elsewhere.' It was, he decided, 'one of the substantial facts which show that music in this country is still a cause worth fighting for'. *A London Symphony* was soon taken up by conductors in the provinces,[3] first among them being Julian Clifford who, it is interesting to note, had conducted the second performance of the work, on 12 August 1914

[1] *Gervase Elwes, The Story of His Life*, op. cit., pp. 294–6.
[2] *The Times*, 8 May 1920.
[3] The first performance in Germany was given in Berlin by the Berlin Philharmonic Orchestra under Ignaz Waghalter in either January or February 1923. It was politely received, one critic noting that 'one of the popular tunes employed in it seemed to be identically the same as a German melody of acknowledged vulgarity'.

at Harrogate. *A Sea Symphony* was already moving into the repertoire of the provincial choral societies. Its post-war success probably
dated from Allen's performance with the Oxford Bach Choir on 19
June 1919, on the evening of the conferment of the honorary degree
of Doctor of Music on Vaughan Williams. It is unlikely that any of
these personal successes gave to Vaughan Williams as much pleasure
as the sensational acclamation of Holst's *Hymn of Jesus* at its first
performance on 25 March 1920, when the composer conducted it
at a Royal Philharmonic Society concert. With this work and *The
Planets*, Holst at last became a celebrity and there was a short boom
in his music. Holst himself was disconcerted by success and he too
quoted 'Woe unto you when all men speak well of you'.

The Hymn of Jesus was dedicated to Vaughan Williams. His
reaction after the first performance, so he told Holst in a letter five
years later, was a wish to 'get up and embrace everyone and then get
drunk'. In this *annus mirabilis* for them both he wrote of his friend,
in *Music and Letters*,[1] 'He is a visionary but he never allows dreams
to inhibit action'. There were some, perhaps, in the post-war decade
who thought that the dreamer in Vaughan Williams had swamped
the man of action. With the musical world's eyes on Stravinsky,
with the development of Schoenberg's art, with the experiments of
Bliss and the bare textures of Holst, what could be made of the
composer of *The Lark Ascending*, first played in London in 1921 at
the second B.M.S. congress? In a long programme it was the only
work, as *The Times* remarked, 'which showed serene disregard of the
fashions of today or yesterday. It dreams its way along.' It was, as
we now know, a pre-war work, but this mood of rapt meditation, a
distillation of the melismatic mysticism of folk song, deepened after
the war. It shows itself again in the three Chaucer settings, 'Merciless
Beauty', which baffled contemporary critics[2] and have been under-
rated by commentators. It was a plainly marked signpost to the
three major works of 1921–2, the pastoral episode *The Shepherds
of the Delectable Mountains*, the *Pastoral Symphony* and the Mass in

---

[1] 'Gustav Holst' in *Music and Letters*, Vol. I, No. 3. Reprinted in *National Music
and Other Essays* (1963).

[2] A notice in *The Times* of the first performance said: 'The rambling strings provide
the atmosphere in which a melody would flourish if there were one, but at a first hearing
we were unable to discover it; and the difficulty of the words and, in the second stanza,
of the thought, is a drawback. Something very woebegone was happening, though it was
not clear what. However it enhanced the comedy which came with the last stanza and
this was most successful, as it generally is with Englishmen.'

G minor. The mixture of diatonic tunes and triadic harmony, the texture of the music—not bare, like Holst's, nor rich, but luminous and soft—and the instrumental use of the human voice were an essential part of the mood in which Vaughan Williams expressed his reaction to the war: not by anger nor upheaval but by a profounder look into the recesses of the human spirit. In Bunyan, as well as the challenge to his operatic powers, he found stimulation in the simple strength of the prose as he did in the majesty of the Authorized Version. He did not seek solace in religion after the war, as might be inferred from a glance at the titles of his works. He found strength in the identification of his music with the imperishable glories of English prose. Thus nationalism had for him a visionary, mystical quality far removed from jingoism or John Bullishness. As an English musician he was excited by the deep roots of our language and its connection with the very core of English history. He liked to quote G. M. Trevelyan's passage[1] in which the historian tells how the Anglo-Saxon tongue was for three centuries a peasants' dialect during which 'it lost its clumsy inflections and elaborate genders, and acquired the grace, suppleness and adaptability which are among its chief merits'. It can be seen that the love of folk song was bound up in Vaughan Williams, who was himself a trained historian, with a deep sense of nationality which became for him 'the divine afflatus' and produced the ecstasy of the *Pastoral Symphony*. It is superficial to find in this music only a kind of Cotswold landscape in sound. The scenery which inspired it was, in any case, that of France; beneath the symphony's tranquillity lies sadness: it is Vaughan Williams's war requiem. A writer in the *Musical Times* after the first performance came near to finding the key to what has always been an enigmatic work when he called it 'a dream of sad happiness—a requiem for Pan with no word of grief'. Colles, in *The Times*,[2] found the work a big advance on its predecessors: 'There is nothing in the *Pastoral Symphony* but music. He is not concerned to find "a way of speaking about life" which shall satisfy anyone else even for a moment. . . . He is just living his own life simply, unaffectedly . . . it is just another stanza in the "chant of pleasant exploration".' From the very start the symphony aroused utterly divergent opinions. Bruce Richmond said it made him fall in love with music all over again; Hugh Allen said, with affection,

[1] *History of England* (London, 1926), pp. 131–2.
[2] 4 February 1922.

that it 'suggested V.W. rolling over and over in a ploughed field on a wet day'; Heseltine passed the notorious remark that it was 'like a cow looking over a gate'; Howells,[1] in a penetrating article, described it as 'a frame of mind (not consciously promoted). . . . You may not like the symphony's frame of mind; but there it is, strong and courageous; it is the truth of the work, and out of it would naturally arise whatever risk it has run of being cold-shouldered'. Cecil Sharp we know admired it because there survives Vaughan Williams's reply to a letter which had obviously been favourable: 'I am v. glad you liked the symph.—you know I value your opinion v. much—you are one of the few people who possess technical knowledge and yet do not let it bias your judgement.'[2] Holst preferred it to others of Vaughan Williams's orchestral works—'It's the very essence of you. Which is one of the two reasons (the other being that it is a beautiful work of art) why it is such an important event in my life.' So he wrote[3] on 1 September 1933, after what must have been the last time he was to hear the symphony.

Holst had been associated with the work from its early days. It was typical of Vaughan Williams that some time before the first performance he allowed the new work to be run through by the R.C.M. orchestra. Sir Adrian Boult has recalled that the composer's report that 'it is in four movements, all of them slow' did not pre-dispose people in its favour. The cantilena for soprano soloist in the last movement is cued in for clarinet and was played at the R.C.M. rehearsals by Frederick Thurston. The last run-through took place on the Friday before the first performance and Vaughan Williams asked Holst to help him to revise the orchestration before the Royal Philharmonic concert. Holst refused, saying that no one could successfully intrude upon such an individual style. Vaughan Williams did not believe that once he had committed the notes to paper, his music was unalterable. After hearing a work a few times he would nearly always make adjustments in the scoring, for he never wavered from his belief that music lived only when it was played. As he wrote in 1920 in 'The Letter and the Spirit',[4] 'the pleasure and profit of reading a score silently is at the best purely intellectual. . . . It is not the pleasure of music. This can be achieved

---

[1] *Music and Letters*, April 1922, Vol. III, No. 2.
[2] Letter from R.V.W. dated 2.2.22.
[3] Quoted in *Heirs and Rebels*, pp. 83–4.
[4] *Music and Letters*, April 1920, Vol. I, No. 2; reprinted (revised) in *National Music and Other Essays*.

through the ear only'. With some of his works he 'tinkered about', as Elgar would have put it, several times. The *Pastoral Symphony* was left alone until some slight revisions were made in the early 1950s. Like *The Lark Ascending*, it owed nothing to any fashion, except that its extreme modality links it with the peak of the madrigal and Tudor revivals. There was, said Herbert Howells in the article already quoted, an air of 'damn-the-consequences' about the first performance. 'Take it or leave it' was usually Vaughan Williams's attitude to acceptance of his music. He was never given, as other composers have been, to probing into himself and his thoughts or his own music in letters and diaries. What he felt he put into the music, and hoped by that means to communicate with those in sympathy with his thought. Even at rehearsal and in performance his concern was always with technical matters—the notes, the tempo, the balance—and never with the emotional content of the music. It was almost as if his works, once delivered into life, were detached from the emotions by which they were conceived. He went through periods of dissatisfaction with his compositions after he had heard them several times, but that in no respect altered his conviction that they were, for him, the *mot juste* at the time.

The appearance of the *Pastoral Symphony*, followed seven months later by the pastoral episode from Bunyan, gave rise to several misconceptions about their composer which dogged him afterwards. The first was that he was an aesthete, bloodless and aloof. It was perhaps easy, after Scriabin, to miss the authentic passion and warmth in the Englishman's music. A corollary to this faulty diagnosis was that these works, the symphony especially, were in some way misty and vague. They are undemonstrative but positive; by its single mood of meditative quiet the *Pastoral* is as emphatic a symphony as its successor in F minor. The modality predictably led to charges of a self-consciously assumed archaism. It was Langford, a critic not numbered among the faithful, who scotched this snake after he had heard a performance in June 1922: 'The melody in the symphony is modal, but the man is free, and the emotions he expresses are such as require no archaic sympathies to feel and understand. . . . There is no doubt that in its relation to English music it must remain among the masterpieces of the time.' The *Shepherds* episode, produced at the Royal College of Music, inevitably—because of its static action and religious theme—led to conclusions that the piece was misconceived for the stage and was merely oratorio in costume. Vaughan Williams's conception of his Bunyan setting was essentially as a dramatic spectacle and he fought all his life against the people who wanted to consign his Pilgrim to the cathedral nave. 'The *Shepherds* is not and never was a cantata but a stage piece and has had several performances as such—it was once done (and I do not think successfully) at the 3 choirs in concert form.'[1]

The appearance in 1922 of the Mass in G minor gave further ammunition to the critics who thought, as one of them actually wrote à propos *The Shepherds*, that Vaughan Williams's music was 'mock medieval' and 'pi'. The Mass had been preceded earlier in the year by the motet 'O vos omnes'. Throughout Vaughan Williams's career one finds a major work surrounded, like Jupiter, by a number of 'moons' which are separate entities but are linked eternally with the planet. Sometimes, perhaps, the 'moon' engendered the larger body. Thus the *Tallis Fantasia*, the G minor quartet and the *Five Mystical Songs* are a small constellation; *The Lark Ascending*, the Four Hymns, 'Merciless Beauty' and *The Shepherds* are the 'moons' of the *Pastoral Symphony*. The Mass circles in space surrounded by 'O vos omnes', the Preludes on Welsh hymn tunes of 1920—'Rhosymedre' in particular—the ambitious 'Lord Thou hast been our refuge', and, on the outer fringe, the unaccompanied folk-song settings. Very often, too, a work was designed for individual performers. In the case of the Mass, Gustav Holst's Whitsuntide Singers were the primary cause, together with the revelations of the glories of English church music in Tudor times by Dr. R. R. Terry's choir at Westminster Cathedral for which 'O vos omnes' was written.

Terry's work is largely unknown to present generations except by repute.[2] In 1896, at the age of thirty-one, he was appointed music master at Downside School by Prior (later Abbot) H. E. Ford, of the Benedictine Monastery. Ford and Terry recognized the worth of the English polyphonic school which scholarly research was bringing back into light. Byrd's Mass for four voices was revived by Thomas Wingham at Brompton Oratory in 1890, those for five[3] and three voices by Terry at Downside. At Downside, too, after three

---

[1] Letter to Ernest Irving dated 27 February 1947.
[2] Those who seek a fuller account should consult *Westminster Retrospect, A Memoir of Sir Richard Terry*, by Hilda Andrews (London, 1948).
[3] On 21 March 1899, a great day in English music.

centuries of neglect Taverner's 'Western Wynde' Mass and motets by Tallis, Byrd, Tye and Shepherd were sung. Earlier scholars had known of these works, but their discoveries were regarded as mere curiosities and their scholarship was suspect—for example, E. F. Rimbault's deplorable edition of Byrd's Mass for five voices in the 1840s, with organ accompaniment by Macfarren. Terry's work at Downside began to attract critical attention and there was a large audience at the opening of the Benedictine church in Ealing on 25 November 1899, when he took the Downside choir to sing Byrd's five-part Mass. Cardinal Vaughan, archbishop-designate of the Westminster diocese, was present and said, '*This* is the music I want for my Cathedral.' And in 1901 Terry left Downside to begin training the choir for the still uncompleted cathedral.

The choir became a supple and perfect instrument. Terry burrowed deep in the British Museum and elsewhere to discover and transcribe forgotten masterpieces. Westminster's performance of Palestrina's *Missa Papae Marcelli* surpassed that by the Vatican choir in the view of good judges. Although Terry revered Palestrina above all, he felt that the English School must receive preference and, as the years passed, the music of Fayrfax, Taverner, Tye, Tallis, Byrd, and Philips gained prominence in regular performance. Terry also kept in touch with modern trends. Under his baton, in the Chapter Hall of Westminster Cathedral on 3 June 1903, Elgar's *Dream of Gerontius* was first performed in London. Howells and Denis Browne wrote works specially for the choir; Stanford[1] wrote a Mass for eight voices, sung in Holy Week, 1920; also there were works by Anthony Bernard, Dunstan, Holst, Rootham, Buck, Charles Wood, Edgar Ford, and Bax ('Mater Ora Filium'). Vaughan Williams and Terry thought alike about the folk-song ancestry of much church music, about the need for good hymn-tunes, about carols, and about the preciosity of some of the folk-song collectors. In Vaughan Williams, Terry recognized the man of rock-like integrity, impervious to cliques, generous to all, practical and idealist. He regarded V.W.'s Mass in G minor as setting the seal on his own work for modern English music at Westminster. Vaughan Williams had sent the Mass to Terry for comment and Terry replied:

[1] Stanford sent his R.C.M. pupils to hear the Westminster music. 'Palestrina for twopence' (the bus fare from Prince Consort Road to the Cathedral) was his constant slogan.

'I'm quite sincere when I say that it is the work one has all along been waiting for. In your individual and modern idiom you have really captured the old liturgical spirit and atmosphere. I shall spare no pains to give the work an adequate performance. I shall try to get into touch with all the deputies that the war has scattered, and if possible do the music this term.'

Later Terry wrote again:

'I do very much appreciate the honour you do us in allowing us to give the first performance of this work. For this event the attenuated state of my choir will not matter, as I have on hand a number of educated amateurs (first-rate sight-singers) who are only too delighted to come and sing in it.'

In fact the first performance was given on 6 December 1922 by the City of Birmingham Choir, conducted by Joseph Lewis. Colles, in the *Musical Times* of January 1923, divined that 'one of the composer's lesser impulses' in writing the Mass was 'an intimation to his generation of what he held to be a true unaccompanied vocal style. The texture is intensely personal. . . . Have there since Hucbald been so many consecutive fifths in a Mass?' Thus, in semi-raillery, began the 'back to Hucbald' label which in the 1920s was pinned firmly on to Vaughan Williams and his imitators.[1] The first liturgical performance was given by Terry on 12 March 1923. He conducted the Mass again a week later and at High Mass on Easter Sunday and Monday. London's concert audience heard it first from Joseph Lewis's Wolverhampton Musical Society at Queen's Hall on 7 April 1923, when there was much diversity among critics about the quality of the performance. Of more value is Terry's comment in the *Cathedral Chronicle*:

'The London Press, almost without exception, acclaimed the Mass as a great work; some critics going so far as to call it one of the greatest choral works of the century. But the most significant thing was their practical unanimity in noting its devotional spirit and strictly liturgical character, and their attitude of mind which described the Queen's Hall rendering as a "performance" and which did not apply that term to the rendering in the cathedral. This differentiation . . . would not have been made 15 years ago.'

The work was soon taken up. Holst was sent copies as soon as

---

[1] Hucbald 840 (?)–930. A monk of St. Armand, known today only by his musical treatise *De harmonica institutione*.

they were available in the spring of 1922. 'How on earth Morleyites are ever going to learn the Mass I don't know,' he wrote to the composer. 'It is quite beyond us, but still further beyond us is the idea that we are not going to do it.' The printer had played an interesting part in saving the work from an unfortunate error. Not even Terry, when he looked it over for liturgical propriety, had noticed that the words 'et apostolicam' were missing from the line 'Et unam sanctam et apostolicam Ecclesiam', but Curwen's printer did, and Vaughan Williams was able only to fit them into the bass part (p. 27 of score). When the dedicatees did at last perform it, Holst wrote to his pupil and amanuensis, Jane Joseph: 'I am writing to R.V.W. to tell him that I have heard his Mass *sung* for the first time. I've heard * * * *perform* it or sing the notes, but now the dedicatees have sung the Mass itself with a fiery intensity that made the music glow.' Holst, at any rate, did not find the music 'austere' or 'forbidding', adjectives for long automatically and most inappropriately applied to it.

It should also be remembered that both the *Pastoral Symphony* and the Mass were performed abroad very shortly after their first performances. Vaughan Williams went to America at the invitation of Carl Stoeckel to conduct the Symphony at a concert of the Litch-field County Choral Union in the Music Shed, Norfolk, Con-necticut, on 7 June 1922. The Mass was sung in Bach's Church, St. Thomas's, Leipzig, on 16 November 1923, conducted by Karl Straube, a friend and admirer of Holst and Vaughan Williams. 'If this work represents the average of the English unaccompanied church music of the present day,' a German critic wrote, 'then we must confess that we do not possess in Germany at present any works which are so sure in form and so expressive.'

These were great years for Vaughan Williams's and Holst's friendship. Illness had not yet begun to sap Holst's vitality. They taught together and shared the pleasure of finding promising pupils. On 19 December 1923 Vaughan Williams conducted, twice in one programme by the Bach Choir, the first London performance of Holst's *Ode to Death*. Holst was overjoyed—'It's what I've been waiting for for 47½ years. The performance was so full of You—even apart from the places I cribbed from you years ago'—and Vaughan Williams, who loved this the best of all Holst's works, wrote to him of 'the wonderful experience it was for me and all of us learning your wonderful music'.

Holst did not fully share Vaughan Williams's folk-song activity, not because he was any less enthusiastic but because he had not the time or opportunity: he made his Morleyites sing folk tunes as well as di Lasso and Byrd. But Vaughan Williams's work for the Folk Song and Folk Dance Societies was the equivalent of Holst's at Morley and St. Paul's Girls' School. With work on the *Pastoral Symphony*, the Mass, revision of *Hugh the Drover* and his conducting activities, Vaughan Williams still found time for folk-song arranging. In 1921 he arranged a Christmas fantasia which in five years was to be the ballet *On Christmas Night*, and, as first president of the English Folk Dance Society's branch at Cambridge, where folk dancing was enjoying a vogue, he welcomed the invitation to write a folk-ballet for the 1923 Festival of British Music. Festival of Cambridge Music would have been an apter title, for every performer was Cantabrigian either by town or gown and many of the composers were Cambridge-trained. The university even had a music-loving Chancellor at this date in Mr. Balfour: at his installation in 1920 the Chancellor's Music had been revived and Gervase Elwes had sung in the Senate House the 'Antiphon' from the *Five Mystical Songs*. At the festival the English Singers sang what were described by the *Manchester Guardian*'s special correspondent as 'Dr. Vaughan Williams's familiar but ever-welcome arrangements' of folk songs. They also sang Weelkes, Wilbye, Tomkins, Bennet, Gibbons, and Morley. In King's the choir sang Byrd, Blow, and Purcell. In the perfect setting of the hall of Trinity two eighteenth-century English operas—Eccles's *Judgment of Paris* and Kane O'Hara's *Midas*—were performed on a high stage at the lower end of the hall, with the musicians' gallery available for the Olympian deities who appear in such works. Vaughan Williams's ballet *Old King Cole* was performed out of doors on the grass of Nevile's Court on 5 and 7 June. The weather was fine and, the *Manchester Guardian* said, the ballet 'evoked great enthusiasm. . . .'

There were no hitches, which is astonishing because Vaughan Williams was still scoring the work at the dress rehearsal. He had written to Bernhard Ord, as Boris Ord was known at this time, when, at the age of twenty-six, he had been appointed Fellow of King's, on 15 April 1923:

Dear Ord,

(*a*) I don't dare to undertake anything more—how I shall find time to score the old Ballet passes my comprehension. (By the way, I shall score it for ordinary orch. fairly thick and let it take its chance out of doors.)

(b) As regards Wassail Song—I meant ♩ = 168 or so, *vivace* refers to style (this is a good lot quicker than the man sang it to me)—and I also like the quick pace when the E.S. [English Singers] do it—with the chorus it sounds a bit too tricky quick.

(c) Congratulations on your fellowship.

Yours sincerely,

R. Vaughan Williams.

The music of the ballet is not a major work but it is fun, and from the solo violin music it is more than likely that the Concerto Accademico stirred in Vaughan Williams's mind. Once again a Cambridge event had produced gay light music. Old friends and new friends gathered there in that summer long ago. R.V.W.'s teacher, Charles Wood, was fifty-six, almost his pupil's contemporary now; as the years pass, the gaps that seem so wide in youth shrink to nothing. Cyril Rootham conducted the C.U.M.S. in Wood's *Dirge for Two Veterans* and Vaughan Williams's *A London Symphony*. Did Wood know that his pupil had set the same words in 1911—a setting which was to lie in a drawer until it was incorporated into *Dona Nobis Pacem* in 1936? Vaughan Williams has related with pride[1] how Parry withheld his own setting of *The Pied Piper* after a pupil, Richard Walthew, had shown him his setting. Parry said nothing and helped Walthew's setting to performance. (Vaughan Williams said he thought it was twenty years before Parry allowed his own setting to be sung, but twelve or thirteen is more likely, as Walthew was with Parry 1890–4, and Parry's setting was done at the 1905 Norwich Festival.) It is likely, although he would never have admitted it, that Vaughan Williams suppressed his own setting in deference to Wood and to Holst.

The summer of 1923 was eventful for R.V.W. After *Old King Cole*, the Mass was sung by the Oxford Bach Choir on 17 June, and there was more fun on 4 July at Kneller Hall, Twickenham, where the Commandant of the Royal Military School of Music, Colonel John Somerville, had asked for a work for military band. He was rewarded with the *English Folk Songs* Suite which H. E. Adkins conducted at its first performance. The now-popular suite

[1] Talk to Composers' Concourse, 1955, reprinted in *Heirs and Rebels*, p. 96.

showed, Colles wrote at the time, that its composer was 'game to write something for the pier'. It led to a commission for a military band work for the 1924 British Empire Exhibition, the *Toccata Marziale*. True to his creed of helping young musicians, Vaughan Williams put what work he could in their way. The transcription of the suite from band to full orchestra he entrusted in 1924 to Gordon Jacob who at this time was twenty-nine. Jacob, Vaughan Williams said many years later,[1] 'was, at one time, nominally my pupil though there was nothing I could teach him, at all events in the matter of technique, which he did not know better than I'. Jacob had asked to change from Stanford to Vaughan Williams as his first study professor at the R.C.M. because he wanted 'someone with progressive ideas'.[2] He did not find Vaughan Williams as good a teacher as he had hoped: 'He was an instinctive poet in music and at that time had a horror of professional skill and technical ability. As he grew older he came to realize that these qualities did not necessarily add up to superficial slickness and his later pupils were put through the mill.' R.V.W. knew that once his pupils had left College they were often hard up for money, especially if they had a wife and young family. Copying band parts was one way of earning a small living and he not only sent Jacob and others his own scores but saw that other composers did the same. He had allowed Maurice Jacobson, a Holst pupil, to adapt the Mass for use as an Anglican communion service. This was in 1923 when Jacobson was twenty-eight. A year later Jacobson was asked to arrange *Old King Cole* for pianoforte. Another ex-R.C.M. pupil, Michael Mullinar, had gone to Birmingham in 1922 and R.V.W. saw that commissions for folksong work, as pianist or arranger, went his way. It was not only he and Holst who 'shared' their pupils; there were those, too, of R. O. Morris, who had married Adeline's sister Emmie and lived for a time at 13 Cheyne Walk. ('Funny chap, R.O.,' Vaughan Williams had said to Rupert Erlebach after they had spent an afternoon correcting orchestral parts of the *Pastoral Symphony*, 'he always works by candlelight even when there's broad daylight outside.'[3]) Morris had a young private pupil named Gerald Finzi. Thus another link was forged with the future.

'A horror of professional skill and technical ability.' This attitude,

---

[1] 'Musical Autobiography.'
[2] *R.C.M. Magazine*, Vol. 55, No. 1, p. 31.
[3] Op. cit., p. 30.

as well as references to his own 'amateurishness', was probably a basic cause of much suspicion of Vaughan Williams by musicians who attached more importance than he did to virtuosity. There was something peculiar and 'provincial', they thought, about a composer who preferred to attend a meeting of Chelsea enthusiasts than to hear a German orchestra play his own *Tallis Fantasia* at Queen's Hall; who worked each spring with Surrey village choirs; who would spend as much time and trouble over a *jeu d'esprit* for a Cambridge college as on his latest major work. But he was only being true to the principle he had enunciated years before: that a country's musical life could not be judged by its 'star' events but by its unpublicized local activities. His youth had coincided with the emergence of a breed of professional virtuosi who, however brilliant their performances, were not always notable for fidelity to the letter, let alone the spirit, of the music they played. He distrusted them; and though in later years, as standards improved, he overcame this distrust, a trace always lingered. That is why he wrote no large-scale virtuoso concerto, and it is why the four concertos he did write, though challenging enough to the player, have never attained frequent performance. The soloist is required to be a good team-man as well as a star. It was the same with singers. He sought from them an understanding of the text rather than a big golden tone and he never believed that he could get both at once. He set forth his views on this subject very clearly in a letter to Holst written in December 1930, after he had heard a group of amateurs sing through Holst's opera *The Wandering Scholar* at St. Paul's Girls' School on 12 December of that year:

'It was interesting to note that the most obvious amateur of your lot (the schoolmaster) was far the most successful because he was thinking of his *words* and his *part* all the time and not worrying about his damned tone. I know the answer to this is that in a larger place he would not be heard. But is there no way of preserving that *natural* singing and yet getting the voice big enough? One thing is that it is *impossible* to get a big tone on English words—and the sooner singing masters recognize this the better—either sing English with a small tone (Plunket Greene) or don't sing English at all (Caruso).[1]

These were (and are) highly contentious views, although the experience of Benjamin Britten seems to support them. Samuel

[1] *Heirs and Rebels*, p. 75.

Langford, writing in the *Musical Times* in November 1920 about the Three Choirs Festival performance of the Four Hymns, said: 'We are breeding a school of singers who contemn everything beyond the most naturalistic aspects of vocal style. Dr. Vaughan Williams may perhaps be regarded as the leader of this new virility, and his Four Hymns . . . eschew on two accounts the professional amenities of vocalism.' The 'exemplary scholar' of this school, Langford said, was Steuart Wilson whom he thought to be the best young English tenor, although he added: 'We do not need to grow so artless or so English that we cannot face the problems of sustained tone and harmonized vowel sounds as these problems are understood by singers in general.'

No doubt the 'naturalistic' as well as the nationalist aspects of *Hugh the Drover* worried some critics when at last it attained production in the summer of 1924. It received two performances at R.C.M. 'private dress rehearsals' on 9 and 11 July, conducted by S. P. Waddington, before being publicly staged at His Majesty's on 14 July by the British National Opera Company and conducted by Malcolm Sargent, then in his twenties and beginning to catch the ear of knowledgeable musicians. The College had had the opera privately printed and had put it in rehearsal before the B.N.O.C. decided to give it. The B.N.O.C. had evolved from Sir Thomas Beecham's opera seasons towards the end of the war and came into being under the artistic direction of Percy Pitt at Bradford on 6 February 1923. Holst's *The Perfect Fool*, Mackenzie's *Eve of St. John* and Boughton's *Alkestis* were the English works performed before the company tackled *Hugh the Drover*. Colles thought that the English professional singers were least at home with their fellow-countryman's work. 'At the Royal College of Music,' he wrote in the *Musical Times* of September 1924, 'it was clearer, more finely drawn.' For the B.N.O.C. performances the composer excised Hugh's final harangue to the villagers in which the virtues of the wanderer's life were extolled. The long process of 'tinkering' with this opera had begun. On the whole, Colles's verdict was favourable. There were tunes for everyone. The music had 'body', though it demanded a particularly nice performance. It was sound and sweet and fetching and might be expected to go on being fetching for a long time to come. He, at any rate, met the work on its own terms and did not judge it as though it was grand opera. 'The outstanding thing,' he wrote, 'is its spontaneous charm.' For him the charm never diminished. Fifteen years later Colles wrote to Vaughan Williams: 'If I could write an opera, that is the opera I would write.'

II

On his return from the war, Vaughan Williams resumed his normal life where it had been interrupted. Sensitive, thoughtful and profound, he was also psychologically well balanced and adjusted. A lover of peace, he was not a pacifist. A hatred of suffering and a compassion for humanity were part of his nature, but he was able to withstand the shocks and buffets of life without being over-whelmed by their enormity. His principal desire on his return from France seems to have been to render into musical terms the craving for quietness which is paramount among those who have lived for several years not only close to the noise of battle but also amid the unremittingly communal activities of their fellow-beings. Thus, in 'playing himself in', as it were, after the four-year interval in his creative work, this thankfulness for quiet found expression in the *Pastoral Symphony*, 'Merciless Beauty', *The Shepherds of the Delectable Mountains* and the Mass in G minor.

To write these works he did not, as has been suggested, put on a new style rather as one might put on a new shirt. There were sufficient indications in the pre-1914 works that he had the vocabu-lary with which to express a meditative calm, in the *Five Mystical Songs*, the *Tallis Fantasia* and in sections of the *London Symphony*. It is present in an even more marked form in the Four Hymns for tenor with viola obbligato which were written some time between 1912 and 1914 and might well have been called a second set of Mystical Songs. The fine first song, 'Lord, come away', is fully mature Vaughan Williams, with its free declamation and, in the pianoforte accompaniment, consecutive chords of the sixth. 'Who is this fair one?' has a viola tune of a modal character.

This is developed excitedly as the ecstasy grows, pointing the way to *Flos Campi*. The modality is still, perhaps, a little self-consciously assumed, but the development which took place between the writing of the *Five Mystical Songs* and the Four Hymns is a remarkable symptom of the composer's growing freedom of expression. Another work left almost complete at the outbreak of war, *The Lark Ascending*, is equally indicative of things to come. This Romance, a unique work as it happens, is often under-rated, possibly because its very simplicity is deceptive. Much abuse has been hurled at the 'English pastoral school' for its rhapsodical style; and it is true that some lesser exponents meander and ruminate to excess and to little purpose. But Vaughan Williams's contemplative works are emphatic in utterance and strict in style. *The Lark Ascending* begins magically. The orchestra softly holds a chord of the ninth while the violin tries out the cadenza-like bird-song phrases which are to develop into its main subject:

The Lark's tune proliferates, its four-note phrase capable, so it sounds, of endless new variants. There is an agitated middle section —'as though someone had disturbed a whole bushful of birds' is Frank Howes's graphic phrase[1]—and a square folk-song-like melody for full orchestra before the violinist catches everyone up into his careless rapture and flies out of sight and sound. The little work is not a bar too long. It has been written many times that the Lark flies into other works by Vaughan Williams—the *Pastoral Symphony*, *Job*, *Sinfonia Antartica* and the Fifth Symphony—but it seems to me that the writing for the violin in *The Lark Ascending* is of a totally different character and melodic shape from the violin solos in those other works. Hence, the sound is quite different too. The bird-like trilling and the quality of cool, even rather aloof objectivity are far removed from the more emotional interludes for violin in larger works. Vaughan Williams is often praised for not repeating himself, but he has received less than his due from his admirers for that virtue in this remarkable work.

The Four Hymns and *The Lark Ascending* were revised while real work began on *the Pastoral Symphony*, which the composer had first contemplated in 1916. This symphony, again a unique work which no one has ventured to try to imitate in the risky daring of its con-

[1] *The Music of Ralph Vaughan Williams*, by Frank Howes (London, 1954), p. 99.

ception, is a major landmark in Vaughan Williams's career. Here it might be as well to put forward the view that much harm has been done to this symphony by sympathetic commentators who have given the impression, unwittingly, that it is a dull, grey, uneventful work, thirty-five minutes of dreamy rhapsodizing on folk song. In fact the scoring is anything but impressionistic, being extraordinarily translucent in texture and sharply defined. And is the symphony to be explained only as a distillation of the composer's love for English folk song? Undoubtedly this is an oak tree which grew from that acorn, but the modal pentatonic themes and the harmony of parallel major and minor triads are not exclusive to English composers. Debussy and Puccini, to name dissimilar examples, used the same methods as a means of stopping excessive chromaticism. It is a great disservice to this masterpiece of English music to suggest that it can be understood only by English ears. No doubt, by some unexplained alchemy, it 'means' more to Englishmen, but it is impossible to define what qualities in music are distinctively national. Elgar, Britten, and Vaughan Williams are 'English' in style, but how to isolate the virus which causes that Englishness is inexplicable in verbal or musical terms of any precision. Some have seen an outline derived from an actual folk tune in the opening solo violin theme of the *Pastoral Symphony*, but most of the themes in the symphony share their origins with Western European art, owing this and their apparent inter-relationship to pentatonic sources. In fact, few of the tunes in the *Pastoral* resemble folk songs. It is the achievement of Vaughan Williams that he developed for himself a symphonic style based not on tonic-and-dominant sonata-form but on his hard-won flexibility in the handling of melody itself. It is not over-simplifying the matter to say that for Vaughan Williams tune was everything. It is apparent that he responded in an extremely sensitive and extraordinarily definite way to the expressive quality of melody. As he wrote in the preface to the *English Hymnal*, 'No doubt it requires a certain effort to tune oneself to the moral atmosphere implied by a fine melody'—and he himself, all his life, was finely tuned so that even a slight variation in the notes of a melody gave it a new and separate existence or meaning. When we refer to Vaughan Williams's 'directness' of musical speech, it is merely a rather imprecise way of acknowledging that we understand his achievement in erecting large-scale musical structures without what he once described as 'the common stock of musical device', in other words formal

development sections, bridge passages and the like. His emergence
into full freedom of use of this style can be seen in the best parts of
the *London Symphony*, but it is in the *Pastoral Symphony* that it is
the whole man, as if the war had given him breathing-space to
overhaul and replenish his technical equipment. The clue to all this
is in his essay on Holst, written in 1920: 'Idiom is a part of inspiration.' It is no coincidence that in the twenty-five years from 1918
to 1943, when his idiom was expanding, he wrote the most varied
and powerful works of his career. The tunes of the *Pastoral Symphony* are not 'developed' as the classical symphonist understands
the term. There are few examples of sequences or diminutions;
instead there is a free evolution of one tune from another, a process
of regeneration, like streams flowing into each other, coalescing and
going on their way. There is much ingenious use of rhythm to bind
these elements together, and marvellous diatonic counterpoint
which has proved to be inimitable, though many have tried to
imitate it.

Only an insensitive listener might describe the *Pastoral Symphony*
as uneventful. It is indeed a *tour de force*, for to write three slow
movements with the variety of colour, harmony and melodic
resource shown here is something to be achieved only by a composer
of high genius. For all its tranquillity, and despite the scherzo in
which Falstaff's fairies make their appearance, the predominant
mood of the symphony is one of sadness and compassionate melancholy. What passes for the 'development' section of the first
movement—a violin solo version of the opening theme—is in

reality no more than a melodic variant, of greater emotional depth.
So fluid is the music that we hardly notice examples of clashing
semitones no less striking than those which were to dominate the
F minor symphony. The opening of the second movement—an
anticipation by twenty-five years of the atmosphere of the epilogue
of the Sixth Symphony—has a notable example, where an F minor
chord on the muted strings supports the solo horn's A natural,
G and E. This movement contains the famous cadenza for the
natural trumpet which enshrines an episode during the war when
Vaughan Williams heard the bugler sound the seventh instead of the

octave. The introduction of this rudimentary and haunting sound into the stillness of the music—for surely this is dusk turned into notes—is a master-stroke. It agitates the orchestra into a short impassioned reply before the music sinks back into the gathering darkness and the trumpet cadenza returns on a natural horn; the clarinet weaves the movement's first theme round it in counterpoint; and the strings play a wonderful whole-tone scale progression of common chords until the horn is left exposed on a high C natural. If this has been Rossetti's 'visible silence, still as the hourglass', the third movement breaks the mood with its emphatic brass and its heavy dance-measures. For the first time in the work the whole orchestra is employed together. Though not called a scherzo, this movement follows scherzo form, with its Falstaffian first section, its folk-song-parody trio, and its fleet-of-foot coda, vanishing into silence with a few bars of the movement's opening theme now deflated of pomposity.

The impression is strong throughout the work of Vaughan Williams's 'vocal' use of instruments, but in his finale he calls in the human voice for the startling effect he achieves when, over a drum-roll, this cantilena is sung off-stage:

The result is unbearably poignant, like a lament for the flowers of the forest cut down in the 1914–18 war; yet the grief is somehow transcended and becomes more cosmic than personal without losing intensity. As the voice dies away, the orchestra quietly enters: a passage of a beauty that seizes the imagination. All the restrained and tenderly passionate feeling of the music breaks forth in this finale, notably in a dramatic and urgent dialogue between strings and woodwind which bears a resemblance to the climax of Butterworth's *A Shropshire Lad* Rhapsody and might almost be his memorial. For the first time in the symphony the texture thickens and the soprano's theme is declaimed in unison in a fortissimo outburst to which the whole work, we now realize, has been leading. Once more the strings ascend into their high register and sustain an A while the human voice returns. As the voice recedes, the strings' held octave shimmers into nothingness. It is perhaps not surprising that this symphony is almost the least often performed of Vaughan

Williams's nine. It requires superb playing and enlightened conducting if it is to create its special atmosphere. Only proper rehearsal-
time can ensure that the rich array of thematic material is played
fluently and inevitably to give the right effect of tunes flowing from
one instrument to another, always slightly varied, like the cloud-
shadows moving over a summer landscape. Also, it never seems to
be at home in a concert-hall; and the sensitive listener is bound to
resent the presence of an audience intruding into what is an intimate
and personal communication. Of all symphonies, this is the one
which seems to have been created for the special kind of private
listening made possible by the gramophone. It will never be a popular
work; but there will always be admirers of Vaughan Williams who
find the *Pastoral* the most moving and personal of his works. In its
pages, the emotions of war are recollected in tranquillity free from
complacency.

A similar fragrance of mood and sureness of style inhabit the
pastoral episode *The Shepherds of the Delectable Mountains*, the
first-fruit of the preoccupation with Bunyan's *Pilgrim's Progress*
which had been implanted by work on the *English Hymnal* and the
Reigate Priory incidental music of 1906. It is clear that the *Pastoral*
soprano's cantilena and the viola theme which opens the opera are
flowerings from a common stem:

The *materia musica* of *The Shepherds* has been described as 'thin',[1]
but one can hardly allow that such a criticism comes from an atten-
tive listener. The capacity for handling English words which in the
early songs was more than promising is here shown by Vaughan
Williams to be as natural to him as speech. The psalm-singing of the
Three Shepherds sounds timeless, but could have been written only
by a twentieth-century composer. As the themes of the *Pastoral
Symphony* develop off-shoots, so in this pastoral episode does
Vaughan Williams set the Shepherds' greeting to Pilgrim, their
dialogue about the ownership of the mountains and the nature of
Pilgrim's journey, to music derived from the opening theme quoted
above. As they talk of the Celestial City and the Second Shepherd

[1] The *Daily Telegraph*, 10 December 1962.

says 'See, the whole region is full of chariots and horses, of trumpeters and pipers', the accompaniment hints, thematically as well as
in its general sound, at the Babylon section of the oratorio *Sancta
Civitas* which was stirring in the composer's mind:

If the mountain air is generally rarefied, this passage is a reminder,
all the more effective for its sudden robust outburst, of a world other
than that which is to come, and skilfully obtaining a contrast before
the most exquisite pastoral music of the opera when, to a flute
obbligato, the First Shepherd tells of the delights of the Mountains,
their bird-song and flowers; and a voice off-stage—again a soprano
—sings the 23rd Psalm. This is a section of superbly sustained
lyrical fervour. Its emotional power is due to Vaughan Williams's
masterly use of counterpoint. For him counterpoint was never an
academic exercise; like Bach, he used it as the means of giving
powerful expression to the profoundest spiritual parts of his music.
As the duets which Pilgrim sings, first with the soprano and then
with a Shepherd, develop into a quartet for the soprano and the
Three Shepherds we may well wonder how Vaughan Williams ever
came to describe himself as 'amateurish', so sure is the method, so
controlled the means. When a Celestial Messenger arrives to sum-
mon Pilgrim he does so to the accompaniment of chords which are
similar to those which later were to open the Fifth Symphony and
which have already been heard as the accompaniment to the Westminster Chimes in the *London Symphony*:

This phrase evidently had a strong emotional connotation for
Vaughan Williams. His sense of drama, often questioned and not

always infallible, does not desert him as the Messenger tells Pilgrim
of the arrow 'sharpened with love, let easily into thy heart' which
will tell him that his hour is come. The music's tension is heightened
despite the *senza misura* passages; and there is another foretaste of a
work yet to be born, *Riders to the Sea*, in the messenger's phrase

or you can-not come at the   gate.

which might almost come from Maurya's final aria. Pilgrim
approaches the River of Death while the Shepherds pray for the
Lord to be near him in a tune as old as the Delectable Mountains.

Be   not   thou   far___   from___   him,   O   Lord,___

There is a held chord while Pilgrim sinks in the deep waters and,
with a switch to E minor, alleluias are sung in triplets and the bells
peal. While much of the counterpoint throughout this brief work is
in strands of triads, the modal inflection of the harmony brings about
a chromaticism which to all intents and purposes is bitonal.

In the third great work of 1922, the Mass in G minor, there is a
very strict use of the modes applied to consecutive triads, with the
consequent occurrence of numerous false relations. This use of
false relation has always been regarded as a characteristic of pre-
Victorian English composers and would have been considered by
Vaughan Williams an essential part of a work which ostensibly pays
tribute to Byrd and the composers resurrected by Terry's labours at
Westminster Cathedral. But its use is also chiefly contrapuntal, and
again it gave Vaughan Williams an opportunity for the efflorescence
of his themes. The setting of the Mass is the vocal equivalent of the
Tallis Fantasia—double choir (double string orchestra), four soloists
(string quartet)—and the methods of the Elizabethan fantasy are
employed, for instance the use of a motif, always slightly varied, in
the different voice parts, thereby giving a unity to the whole colloquy. Strangely, though its mastery is indisputable and its authorship
undeniable, the Mass is in some respects the most anonymous of
Vaughan Williams's works. This is as it should be. He wrote it for
liturgical use, the music being subservient to religious ceremony.

There is none of the elaborate augmentation of the great Masses of Bach, Beethoven and Berlioz, nor indeed is there the intellectual power of Byrd. Most of Vaughan Williams's religious music is of an emotional power which would have been out of place in a setting of the Ordinary. It should not be thought, however, that there is anything austere about this Mass. Its richness is a by-product of the glowing counterpoint as well as being a fundamental of Vaughan Williams's approach to such a task. Despite an archaism which seems to be deliberately adopted, its harmonic language is essentially twentieth century and quintessentially Vaughan Williams. Yet the personal idiom is unobtrusive. The Kyrie, for instance, in its second section, has the Dorian mode illuminated, as it were, by sharpened thirds and sevenths. Various similar procedures, not bound by any restrictions of modal counterpoint or of tonality, are the composer's way of breathing new life into old styles. A tenor intones the opening of the Gloria, to be followed by eight-part harmony by the double choir and later by antiphonal use of the choirs. How could anyone ever have found this music 'cold'? Perhaps they were so excited or enraged by the consecutive fifths in the part-writing that they missed the music. The Credo is set forth swiftly and without rhetoric. Unity of music with religious dogma is obtained through use of the same theme for 'patrem omnipotentem' as for 'Et resurrexit'. The central part of this movement contains the most personal music, when the Incarnation is reached with a beautiful chord of A flat major which cloaks the music in mystery. In the Sanctus, a Holstian air of intensity pervades the simple yet resourceful diatonic notes which introduce the movement, like the gentle swaying of censers:

Here again it is the imaginative use by Vaughan Williams of simple chords that gives the music its power; first a major chord of D, then of G, then of A and eventually, in 'Pleni sunt caeli', of E, like a burst of sunlight. The Osannas are dissimilar, the first building up by antiphony and rhythmical elision to an exultant climax. In the

Agnus Dei the authentic voice of Vaughan Williams calls through the old text, as the soloists announce their prayer:

A - gnus De-i   qui   tol-lis pec-ca-ta   mun-di,

The theme of the Kyrie returns at 'Miserere nobis' and the choirs divide until, with the soloists, they unite in the coda for the final noble chords.

The influences of Debussy, and therefore of Mussorgsky, can still be discerned in these three works, for there is something of *Pelléas et Mélisande* in the melodic-recitative of the opera and of the Mass. The anonymous *bon mot* about 'L'Après-Midi d'un Vaughan' was perceptive as well as witty. The works are also indicative of the subtle and deep change which had been wrought by his experiences since 1914 in Vaughan Williams's nationalism. His beliefs were, and remained, as strong as ever: that the roots of one's art were in one's native soil. But by now his nationalism had fully become a part of his creative thinking, a projection of his fundamental nature. 'What shall it profit a man if he gain the whole world and lose his own soul?' he quoted. In the Mass, as in its shorter and magnificent companion motet 'O vos omnes', he says with Verdi: 'Let us return to the past. That will be progress.' And, like Verdi, he achieved this without losing individuality or producing pastiche. The Mass, when it first appeared, baffled many sympathetic listeners. The young Frank Howes[1] recalled his first hearing of it in the Sheldonian Theatre, Oxford, performed by the Oxford Bach Choir on 17 June 1923, with Vivienne Chatterton, Constance Taylor, Trefor Jones, and Keith Falkner as soloists. 'An eminent musician, whom I will not betray, said to me when it was over, in distressed tones: "O play me 'O Rest in the Lord'; play it as a cornet solo; play it anyhow; but play me 'O rest in the Lord' after that!" ' Mr. Howes shared his companion's view but was finally converted by Sydney Nicholson's Westminster Abbey performance in December 1924, and by a student performance at Aberystwyth. What emerges from this anecdote, besides Mr. Howes's honesty and modesty, is that, despite the work's difficulties, choirs and young singers liked to sing the Mass, for Vaughan Williams never wrote music that was impossible

---

[1] *The Later Works of R. Vaughan Williams* (London, 1937), pp. 29–30.

to perform. Tough it might be, but there were enjoyment and illumination to be gained from cracking the nut. It is also significant that Mr. Howes first heard the Mass in the dry acoustics of the Sheldonian. Like the *Tallis Fantasia*, the Mass was conceived in terms of the acoustics of a cathedral or church, and, unlike the *Fantasia*, it does not transplant well to a concert-hall. Its dedicatees, Holst and his Whitsuntide Singers, performed it whenever possible in church or cathedral, Thaxted, Chichester, and once at Canterbury whence Holst wrote to Adeline Vaughan Williams that he had discovered that it might have been 'written for this cathedral'. The best recording of the Mass so far issued was made in Canterbury Cathedral.

The tendency after the war was for Vaughan Williams to divide his work into two streams, each feeding the other, but none the less separate: on the one hand the major works involving deep personal issues and on the other groups of works, not necessarily minor, written for special occasions or for special people. These latter works were Vaughan Williams's equivalent of Hindemith's *Gebrauchsmusik*, in which Hindemith attempted to bridge the widening gulf between composers and their public by writing works which were within the capabilities of non-professional musicians yet were not 'written down' to them. It did not need Hindemith to show Vaughan Williams the need for this. At the Leith Hill Festival, in the *English Hymnal*, in *The Wasps*, all before 1914, he had shown that this ideal was part of his creed (as it is of Britten's). Perhaps the most obvious and numerous of this group of works are the arrangements of folk songs, of which there is a steady flow throughout his career because his rule was that the only way to arrange a folk song was 'with love' and his love for the tunes never failed. The odd thing was that the more like one of his original compositions he made a tune, the more it seemed to bring out the tune's indigenous quality. Many of his best and most beautiful arrangements, such as those of 'The Turtle Dove' and 'The Springtime of the Year', not to mention 'Greensleeves', are practically recompositions. This is in accordance with his own belief that each singer—and as composer he was in the role of singer—brought to the songs something of his own personality and that each generation must harmonize its folk songs afresh. That was the strength of folk song and its power of renewal. How far its idiom had become absorbed into his own is evident from the Chaucer rondels, 'Merciless Beauty', which are not in the least like folk song yet have the same wild-flower freshness. It is strange that these beautiful settings, which are a secular appendage to *The Shepherds of the Delectable Mountains* and were sung by Steuart Wilson at an I.S.C.M. festival at Venice in 1925, are now so rarely performed.

As Vaughan Williams settled back to London life, entered into R.C.M. activities, became absorbed by his work with the Bach Choir and widened his contacts with musicians of many kinds, so the withdrawn, *Pastoral Symphony* mood left him and he entered a new phase in which he drew fully on his technical prowess. Invitations to write music for Col. Somerville's military bands at the Royal Military School of Music at Kneller Hall, Twickenham, and a ballet for the Cambridge folk dancers called forth some notable *jeux d'esprit*. The Suite of *English Folk Songs* makes no attempt to develop the tunes or to rhapsodize upon them; it is merely a series of good tunes, strung together with art and artifice. The *Old King Cole* ballet music is a considerably more elaborate concoction which cannot entirely be dismissed as a light-weight 'folky' work of no great significance. The humour is more subtly handled than in *The Wasps*, although the consecutive fifths as bass harmony to the 'King Cole' tune probably upset the Cambridge professors more than they worried anybody else. The folk tunes are set in common time or in 6/8 jig rhythms, but there is nothing commonplace about the methods. Moreover the scoring has a 'bite' to it which struck home with E. J. Dent who, writing in *The Nation and the Athenaeum* of 30 June 1923, called the ballet 'a new composition by Vaughan Williams in his most ruthlessly modern style'. Since the days of *The Wasps*, Dent remarked, 'we have heard the *Sacre du Printemps*, and apparently Dr. Vaughan Williams has heard it, too.' It is not easy to deduce from the score how Dent arrived at this conclusion, but there is no doubt that *Old King Cole* has some importance in the genesis of *Job*, for the effectiveness of the old dances must have set Vaughan Williams thinking of more ambitious ventures of this kind. Dent's article continued: 'Whether traditional English steps and figures could be made the foundation of a highly elaborated ballet is a question which I must leave to the specialists in choreography. . . . There were some English dancers who startled the crowd at the Frankfort fair some three centuries ago; were they frightened of turning their native folk-dances into a ballet?' Apart from its charm and vivacity, two points from *Old King Cole* should be noted. First, the way in which the composer demonstrated a kinship between the nursery tune and 'Dives and Lazarus':

and, secondly, the beautiful episode of the Second Fiddler, with his romantic violin solo based on 'Bold Young Farmer', one of many such rapturous passages throughout Vaughan Williams's output.

Thirteen months after the production of *Old King Cole*, Vaughan Williams's pre-war opera *Hugh the Drover* at last took the stage. This simple, attractive and unpretentious work is a problem-opera, about which no two critics seem able to agree. But all join, and one joins with them, in condemning the libretto. Its construction is fascinatingly revealed in the letters which form an appendix of Mrs. Vaughan Williams's volume. It is apparent that Harold Child was the wrong man for the job. What Vaughan Williams wanted was to write a 'musical' (his own word) about English country life, 'real as far as possible—not sham'. He knew something about country life and country dwellers. He knew that it, and they, could be rough, unsentimental, harshly practical, even savage, as well as picturesque. He knew from the words of the folk songs he had collected that country folk were realists, and he admired and respected them. Child, a leader-writer on *The Times*, started the rot with his first scenario, which laughed at the English peasantry and gave the characters names like Blogg and Annis, a mayor's daughter. Later she was changed to a Ruskin-type May Queen until Vaughan Williams pointed out that the May Queen was usually the village prostitute. It is clear from then onwards that most of the libretto was worked out to Vaughan Williams's suggestions. He certainly freed it from a patronizing attitude, but an initial flaw could not be wholly eradicated. It is clear, too, that the music for a ballad opera was bubbling over in Vaughan Williams's head and could not be contained. He was busy inventing *musical* situations to which Child and

he contrived to fit *dramatic* situations. Thus the plot remains unconvincing, the characters, except for Hugh and Mary, are not developed but are merely types, and the audience is rarely caught up
into the events it is watching. From the number of times he wrote
and re-wrote the synopsis of the plot for scores and programmes, it
can be deduced that Vaughan Williams himself was never completely
comfortable about the libretto. His final revisions of the score, in
1956, tidied up a good deal of the stage action, removed some
archaic-sounding lines and attempted to remedy some defects of
plot.

Yet, with all these drawbacks, the opera has entranced thousands
who have seen it and are prepared to overlook its faults for the sheer
beauty and nobility of the music it contains. Vaughan Williams
wanted the opera to be 'full of tunes, and lively, and one tune that
will really *come off*.' He had his wish, for *Hugh* is an anthology of
good tunes, sometimes rather roughly stitched into the framework
of the opera, but still good, singable tunes. The opening scene at the
fair into which ballad-cries and folk songs are introduced is splendidly bustling and alive. The Showman's tune 'Cold blows the
wind' is not a folk tune but is original and an almost perfect representation of the real thing:

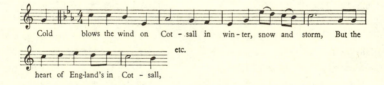

One of several effective musical and dramatic moments is the
entrance, singing off-stage, of Mary, the heroine, to the tune of the
lovely folk song 'Tuesday morning', an idea perhaps borrowed from
Madam Butterfly, which Vaughan Williams greatly admired. Hugh
the Drover's entry is almost as good, when he overhears and challenges Mary's resolve to marry John the Butcher because it is her
duty. Hugh's impetuous character is defined by his 'Song of the
Road'

which is in the vein of 'The Roadside Fire' and shares with it a bustling, tramping motif ('at a trotting tempo' is the indication in the score) such as we find whenever Vaughan Williams is handling the 'wanderer' theme. Mary replies with her seductive and yielding 'In the night time', music of haunting freshness, unsophisticated yet worldly-wise:

The love duets of Hugh and Mary achieve a Puccinian passion which is in no way mock-Italian, but has a genuine lyrical warmth. There is skill, too, in the music for the fight between Hugh and John. It keeps the action going without becoming mere background music. The early-morning-dew quality of the folk song is sustained by colourful and delicate scoring; there is a reversion to the manner, and even the notes, of 'Linden Lea' in Aunt Jane's song 'Life must be full of care'.

Act II, Scene I, was added in 1933 but is rarely performed, which is a pity because the opera is short as it stood originally and the extra scene contains some fine music.[1] It is, of course, apparent that the hand and head which wrote it were 20 years more experienced than those which wrote the rest of the work. The result, on a smaller scale and lesser plane, is not unlike Verdi's *Don Carlos*, which is middle-period Verdi revised by the Verdi of *Otello*. Hugh, who has been arrested as a spy, is brought to the village stocks by John and four of his companions. John is an ill-defined character. Presumably Mary's father liked him because of his money and position—'earning his £300 a year'—but the general feeling towards him is likely to be the deadly one of indifference. But Vaughan Williams knew that even dull dogs and rogues sang beautiful tunes, and John gets his share. He gets three more in this extra scene, but its principal claim

[1] The composer himself thought the scene was 'poor, musically and dramatically' and that it spoilt 'the dramatic effect of the sudden hush at the old beginning of Act II coming sharpest after the noisy finish of Act I. So I never want to hear it or see it again'. This he wrote in his last years to Herbert Byard, but he did not delete the scene when he made final revisions in 1956.

to be performed lies in Mary's song in which she asks her father's pardon while the orchestra tells us the true state of her affections:

There is a very beautiful orchestral postlude to this scene, based on the accompaniment to a new duet between Hugh and Mary, while Hugh sits alone in the stocks and the day changes into night. A solo violin reflects Hugh's musings and the bassoon hints very softly at a fragment of the Maying Song which is to be the big moment of Act II, Scene II. This begins magically, to the quick chiming of 'York' on the church bells; the ballad seller crosses the stage calling the hour and knocks at the inn, from which sounds of late carousal can be heard. Hugh, reconciled to his fate because at least he has met Mary, has another splendid song:

Points of repose such as this occur throughout the opera. This one is interrupted several times by John's drunken abuse of Hugh, broken off only when the May Horn sounds and the Mayers depart to find their may branches. Mary, who has taken the Constable's keys, sets Hugh free and covers the stocks with Hugh's cloak. The Turnkey enters, also drunk, sees the cloak, which he takes for Hugh, and falls asleep. As Hugh and Mary begin to creep away they hear the Mayers' horns announcing their return. Mary bids Hugh get back into the stocks and sits beside him with her feet also in them.[1] But she drops a shoe. They cover themselves with Hugh's cloak and Mary sings of their happiness:

---

[1] A revision whereby they hide behind the stocks was tried at some performances and then abandoned.

There follows the wonderful passage when John, off-stage, sings the
May Day Carol with women's chorus accompanying. He calls to
Mary's window. By now the whole village is awake and Mary's bed
is empty. John finds the shoe, four feet are noticed in the stocks and
the lovers are discovered. Mary's Aunt Jane pleads with her to come
away and this leads to Mary's great song:

Here, queen un - crown'd   in this most   roy –   –   – al   place,—

This is the musical climax of the opera. Mary's song soars above the
chattering of the lesser characters until Hugh joins in and there is
another use of the Alleluia theme from 'Sine Nomine':

Ex. – cept   my   love,——   ex – cept   my   love.

which in this case is almost identical with that other impassioned
emotional high-point, the climax of the Romanza of the Fifth
Symphony. *Hugh*, indeed, is as full of pointers to the future as is *A
Sea Symphony*.

This duet precipitates the almost symphonic episodes which now
close the opera.[1] As Hugh and Mary go off into the unknown, a
violin solo has a last caressing cadenza and the work ends pianissimo.
The opera has suffered from admirers who claim for it more than its
composer intended. It is not grand opera, it is ballad opera, and an
entertainment. On the other hand, I cannot agree with those who
find the 'Englishness' assumed in dutiful and enforced obedience to
the libretto's demands. The libretto has its faults of character and
plot, but it is clear from the letters that the composer took the lead in
shaping matters as he wanted them. Hubert Foss wrote: 'Hugh
himself is a Siegfried . . . a liberator as the free-thinker among the
ordinary people. He is to set free English music (and English
thought, perhaps, too) from the fire-ringed conventions of Mrs.
Grundy.'[2] Really, this will not do. No such intention was in the

---

[1] In revisions of the last scene carried out as late as 1956, the composer inserted a new
aria for Aunt Jane.

[2] *Ralph Vaughan Williams*, by Hubert Foss (London, 1950), p. 177.

minds of composer or librettist. 'I want to set a prize fight to music' was Vaughan Williams's first idea. 'I have an idea for an opera written to *real* English words, with a certain amount of *real* English music and also a real English subject.' It was a part of his ambition to 'reflect the life of the whole community', but somewhere along the way the fervid nationalism was lost in the sheer delight of enjoying himself.

CHAPTER SEVEN

1925–1930

Principal Works

FLOS CAMPI . SANCTA CIVITAS
VIOLIN CONCERTO (CONCERTO ACCADEMICO)
SONGS OF PRAISE . ON CHRISTMAS NIGHT
ALONG THE FIELD . THE OXFORD BOOK OF CAROLS
SIR JOHN IN LOVE . BENEDICITE
THREE CHORAL HYMNS . JOB

I

IF we consider Vaughan Williams's output between 1924 and 1930 and add to it the amount of teaching, conducting, lecturing and studying which was his lot, we can but marvel again at his energy and his powers of concentration. In these seven years, apart from minor works such as songs and arrangements, he began work on three operas—*Sir John in Love*, *Riders to the Sea* and *The Poisoned Kiss*—he sketched the first two movements of a pianoforte concerto and put them aside for six years, he wrote *Flos Campi*, *Sancta Civitas*, the Violin Concerto and *Job*. And he was joint editor of another hymn-book and a book of carols. In the mid-twenties he fully 'found himself'; and all the seminal force of folk song sprang out in a series of personal, idiosyncratic works which leave the world of Norfolk Rhapsodies far behind. Between 1925 and 1935 Vaughan Williams wrote some of his most powerful work. Yet this is the time when English musicians seem, to a later generation, to have been in a kind of vacuum, ignoring the eruptions of musical harmony and language taking place in Europe, suffering what has been termed a 'psychological blockage' and looking to Sibelius as a father-figure rather than to Stravinsky and Schoenberg. Insularity and a blinkered outlook are the charges frequently laid at the door of English music of this period; and Holst and Vaughan Williams are misrepresented as though they spent their whole life writing variations on 'Gathering Peascods'. As an earlier chapter has shown, Vaughan Williams never advocated a chauvinistic nationalism. He merely urged composers to write the music that they felt was in them, and he thought that the best way for them to do that was to examine their own native art first and then to turn their eyes abroad if they wished. He would not have sought to deny that English art had often been stimulated by foreign influences grafted on to the native stem. Purcell, for example, Elgar, Britten, and Vaughan Williams himself all owe something to Continental influences. In the case of the last-named it was the French school of Debussy, notably in *Pelléas et Mélisande*, whose echoes in his mind awoke an individual response. The result was imaginative, personal music: and this was all that he sought through his nationalism. He rejected atonality because it meant fetters and because he thought it ugly. He knew Stravinsky's inter-war music and admired some of it, but he recognized that it was also inimitable. In *Flos Campi* and even more in *Sancta Civitas*, he ploughed a lonely furrow, leaving many of his admirers behind and puzzling even such a sympathetic friend as Holst. The year 1925 brought them mutual puzzlement. Vaughan Williams had to confess that he felt only 'cold admiration' for Holst's *Choral Symphony* to words by Keats, performed at the Leeds Festival on 7 October and in London on 29 October. He attributed much to a poor performance by the Leeds chorus and added: 'I couldn't bear to think that I was going to "drift apart" from you musically speaking . . . so I shall live in faith till I have heard it again several times and then I shall find out what a bloody fool I was not to see it all first time.'[1] Holst, in reply, confessed to a similar feeling about *Flos Campi* which he 'couldn't get hold of' at all—'and was therefore disappointed with it and me. But I'm not disappointed in *Flos's* composer, because he has not repeated himself. Therefore it is probably either an improvement or something that will lead to one.'[2] They shared a muse, Vaughan Williams used to say, but not being identical twins they were really no more alike musically than were Mahler and Bruckner. Despite the 'cribbing' and the field days, they were, in fact, drifting apart musically. Holst, with his neuritis, his growing ill-health, his concern for the paring-down of unnecessary ornament, was hardly likely to

---

[1] *Heirs and Rebels*, pp. 60–1.
[2] Ibid., pp. 61–2.

respond to the wild passion surging beneath the surface of *Flos Campi* and often breaking forth in a strange Oriental exotic ecstasy which sweeps away the religious mysticism found by disturbed critics as consolatory evidence that this work was really by the composer of the *Tallis Fantasia*.[1] Here, surely, were the warmth and emotion craved by Holst as he entered what his daughter in her biography[2] has called 'that cold region of utter despair'.

In more than one way 1924 had been a year of severance with the past. *Hugh the Drover* was the last of the pre-war major works to appear; *On Wenlock Edge* was orchestrated and sung at a Royal Philharmonic concert which was also the occasion of Wilhelm Furtwängler's first appearance in England (he did not conduct the English work); and the revised First *Norfolk Rhapsody* was published at last. In March Stanford died; and two months later Cecil Sharp.

Songs of Praise was published in 1925 by the Oxford University Press, as the *English Hymnal* had also been. Again, as in 1906, the general editor was the Rev. Percy Dearmer and he and Vaughan Williams brought in Martin Shaw to assist R.V.W. as joint music editor. The new book went even further than the *English Hymnal* in its endeavour to be a national collection, drawing on poets and musicians of whatever faith so that the appeal could be not to one denomination alone but to 'the forward-looking people of every communion'. It was hoped also that education authorities might use the book. This hope was amply fulfilled, to such an extent that an enlarged edition, called for in 1929, appeared in 1931. Several hymn service-books were based on *Songs of Praise* and the B.B.C.'s religious broadcasts, when they began, used it regularly. The net was cast wide among composers and arrangers. Folk songs were again drawn upon; the music editors wrote or arranged 136 tunes. Tunes or arrangements by many living composers were included.

To the four original tunes written for the *English Hymnal*, Vaughan Williams added two more, 'Magda' ('Saviour, again to Thy dear name we raise') and 'King's Weston' ('At the name of Jesus'). Thirty of his arrangements were included, of which eighteen had previously appeared in the *English Hymnal*. In the enlarged *Songs of Praise* he withdrew two arrangements ('East Horndon' and

---

[1] A friend wrote to the composer after the first performance of *Flos Campi* that it left her 'feeling quite hopeless. There were such terrible questions and no answers.'

[2] *Gustav Holst*, by Imogen Holst (London, 1938).

'Regina') and added five original tunes—'Abinger' ('I vow to thee, my country'), 'Famous Men' ('Let us now praise famous men'), 'Mantegna' ('Into the woods my Master went'), 'Marathon' ('Servants of the great adventure'), 'White Gates' ('Fierce raged the tempest o'er the deep'), and a descant to his beloved 'Helmsley', the eighteenth-century English tune to which Wesley's 'Lo! He comes with clouds descending' is set.

As in the *English Hymnal*, there is significance in the names of the hymns. Often the place-name is a clue to the original folk song from which the hymn-tune is adapted. Sometimes the association is sentimental—'Thaxted' for Holst's 'Jupiter' tune for 'I vow to thee, my country'; 'White Gates', the name of Vaughan Williams's home at Dorking; 'King's Weston', the home of Philip Napier Miles where R.V.W. spent many happy week-ends; 'Mantegna' to denote inspiration from Mantegna's painting of the Agony in the Garden. It was *Songs of Praise* with which Vaughan Williams was really pleased, Frances Cornford recalled.[1] 'There's not a single tune in it that I'm ashamed of.' No compromises. No 'chamber of horrors'.

It was in 1925, also, that Vaughan Williams went to Prague where the *Pastoral Symphony* was conducted by Boult on 17 May at the festival of the International Society for Contemporary Music. At one of the rehearsals the composer told Boult that everything was too fast. Boult replied by reminding Vaughan Williams that at the first rehearsals in 1922 he had tried to do it all slower but had been forbidden to do so by the composer. R.V.W.'s reply was as disarming as it was unanswerable: 'Yes, but I have conducted it a good deal myself since then and I know that people are not so bored with it as I thought they would be, so I think it will go all right at the slower pace.'

While in Prague Vaughan Williams heard Janáček's opera *The Cunning Little Vixen*, performed there on 18 May, which he loved. We do not know if the composers met. Of his contemporaries in other lands, besides Ravel, Vaughan Williams knew best Kodály, though this was only an acquaintanceship. Bartók he never met, so far as is known. An unflattering estimation of Vaughan Williams at this time was expressed in a book published in 1925 by one of his contemporaries, Joseph Holbrooke.[2] In a short essay he wrote:

[1] *R.C.M. Magazine*, Vol. LV, No. 1, Easter Term 1959.
[2] *Contemporary British Composers* (London, 1925).

'He has had a fairly smooth path made for him and his music spells this fact. There is no overwhelming horror ever felt in the music of this composer. . . . There is no splendid, uncontrollable passion in him or his music to be discerned or felt. . . . The only misgiving one may have with the dreamer like Vaughan Williams is whether he can hold his own with the men who feel savagely, who feel enormously, who feel very very deeply on all things and willy-nilly put it into their music. There is a heavy suspicion to many when any artist meets favour from the academics in power. Vaughan Williams has had this huge misfortune. His art pleases the dull ones of our profession.'

This bland passage tells us more about the chip on Holbrooke's shoulder than about Vaughan Williams. He barely disguises professional jealousy and social envy. One may question whether uncontrollable passion is splendid and whether to feel deeply is to feel 'savagely'. His Byronic conception of composers would leave us with Mahlers but no Brahmses, with Liszts but no Bachs. Holbrooke, writing in 1924, could not foresee the later symphonies nor even *Flos Campi*. One would think he might have discerned the deep feeling in the *Pastoral* and *London* symphonies. The suspicion is that, to Holbrooke, to be disciplined was to be dull; and who shall say whether it is 'duller' to be pleased by *A Sea Symphony* or by Holbrooke's *Apollo and the Seaman*? Vaughan Williams himself had already answered the inference behind Holbrooke's view:

'To "live" is an expression which has had much harm done it by second-rate writers who seem to think "life" is limited to pretending you like absinthe and keeping a mistress in Montmartre.'[1]

One event in 1925 which was to have the value of rarity was Vaughan Williams's first appearance as conductor of his own music on a gramophone record. He recorded the overture to *The Wasps* and the music to *Old King Cole* on pre-electric Vocalion with what is described on the label as 'The Aeolian Orchestra'. Although he took a close interest in recordings of his music, attending the long and sometimes tedious sessions, ready with advice if it was sought, only once more did he perpetuate his own conducting. This was in 1937 with the B.B.C. Symphony Orchestra when he made what in most respects is still the most exciting recording of the Fourth Symphony, as it certainly is the best interpretation.

[1] 'Gustav Holst: An Essay and a Note' (1920), reprinted in *National Music and Other Essays*.

First performances in 1925 began with a remarkable concert on 27 March at which Steuart Wilson sang the Four Hymns, with accompaniment newly arranged for pianoforte quintet, and three groups of new songs. These were the Two Poems by Seumas O'Sullivan, Four Poems by Fredegond Shove and Three Songs from Shakespeare. All were too subtle for immediate appreciation, though one would have imagined that the Schubertian blitheness of 'The Water Mill' would have won it popularity from the start. These songs, some Whitman settings and some more Housman settings, sung by Joan Elwes in 1927 and not published until 1954, were the last songs Vaughan Williams wrote for several years.

On 10 October 1925, Lionel Tertis gave the first performance of *Flos Campi*. 'What music is intimate in the way of Vaughan Williams in this "wild flower" mood?'[1] Colles asked in the *Musical Times*. 'It seems to shrink from public light. . . . In such a self-communing not the shadow of a pretence can subsist.' This crucial work was the rock on which several admirers of its composer, besides Holst, were to founder. Here was something quite different from the bluff straight-forwardness of *A Sea Symphony*. What were they to make of the quotations, in Latin, (without, at first, an English translation) from the *Song of Solomon* and the composer's almost flippant programme-note? Colles perhaps understood, though clearly he was disturbed. In his notice of the first performance (*The Times*, 12 October 1925) he wrote:

'The composer has wilfully surrounded the flowers of his musical thought with a thorny hedge of riddles. We need not unriddle him to get at his music, in which there is nothing sphinx-like. . . . One may be a little irritated by the surface eccentricities of a very sane mind, but one cannot listen for long without being assured of the sanity.'

Five days later he discussed *Flos Campi* and Holst's *Choral Symphony* in one article. Vaughan Williams's use of voices purely as instrumental timbre—a device he had used in *Willow-Wood*, in the *Five Mystical Songs* and in folk-song arrangements—was assailed:

'The ear, which will be content to take a melody simply as a melody from Mr. Tertis's viola, feels that the same melody sung to "Ah" or with

---

[1] This drew the sharp retort from the composer, in a programme note for the Royal Philharmonic Society's concert on 3 November 1927: 'The title *Flos Campi* was taken by some to connote an atmosphere of "buttercups and daisies". . . .'

closed lips by voices has not the same eloquence, because the voices could do something more with it. There is, then, in all these modern works of vocal-instrumental music a hint of trifling with common-sense which *Flos Campi* does not escape. Its composer has made matters worse by his references to the *Song of Solomon* which, whether given seriously or not, are certainly not explanatory. He has, rather, wilfully raised barriers in the minds of his hearers which the music itself may not be strong enough to sweep away.'

Colles deserves our sympathy, for he probably would not have expected such a sensuous work from this composer's pen, the product of a new interest in sonorities combined with a mood expressive of the mingled sexual-mystical ecstasy, derived from physical passion, which the *Song of Solomon* also exemplifies. He sought an explanation in the inwardness of Vaughan Williams compared with the extrovert Holst (a strange judgement) and suggested that perhaps the work had not found its final form:

'Vaughan Williams has none of Holst's stylistic virtues. . . . He is the genuine mystic whose thought struggles to find the right terms for its expression and is never sure of finding them at once. No composer is more given to second thoughts than he.' *Flos Campi* was 'music which is essentially a process of "thinking in sound" and the thoughts may go on after the first stage of putting it on paper. . . . He is not really as oblivious of his hearers' share in the thinking as those elusive programme notes might lead one to suppose. He allows them to be elusive because he is really fearful of distracting attention from the musical thought which, though not dissociated from verbal thought in his mind, is the ground on which he wants his hearers to meet him. So we have to seize the music and not expect it to come and capture us.'

That, I suppose, represented an 'establishment' view of Vaughan Williams in 1925. Another view, expressed by Cecil Gray[1] was equally sympathetic though more querulous. He, too, recognized the importance of *Flos Campi*, which he found to be

'music of a very intimate and subjective order, devoid of any programmatic implications. . . . In this work Vaughan Williams seems to have acquired a sureness of touch and a concision which had hitherto been lacking in his art without thereby impairing the apparent spontaneity and effortless simplicity which have always characterized it. . . . The peculiar and subtle appeal . . . is due not so much to any virtues of musicianship as to a quality of mind which informs the whole.'

[1] In *The Nation and the Athenaeum* of 21 November 1925 (Vol. 38, No. 8, p. 290).

Gray rightly rejected the attribution to Vaughan Williams of a 'sincerity' which overrode all other considerations.

'Sincerity is not the right word, as it is a negative virtue, possessed more often by mediocrities. . . . Vaughan Williams is more than that, something more positive. Almost alone to-day, he is entirely without self-consciousness and has the courage to write simply as he feels, without misgivings. He is not afraid to write the kind of music that anybody could have written, with the paradoxical result that he has evolved a more personal idiom than almost any other composer in this country. In this he reminds one of George Borrow. . . . It is true that Vaughan Williams does not possess the same rich palette as [Delius] and generally speaking his talent is a more restricted and less robust one. It may not be great art, but still it is art, and that is much to be thankful for.'

Only in the last two sentences does Gray betray that Van Dieren had him in thrall. Anyone who could believe that Vaughan Williams's art was more restricted than Delius's could believe anything. But it is manifest from these two contemporary criticisms that Vaughan Williams was beginning to move into regions where not everyone was able to follow him. 'No map there, nor guide,' they might quote, but this was hardly true. The map and the guide were both in the *Pastoral Symphony* and even in such a deceptively simple piece as *The Lark Ascending*. The puzzle was intensified by the appearance, a month later, on 6 November 1925, of the Concerto Accademico, as it was then called. *The Times* critic (not, one suspects, Colles) found an escape-route in the very word Gray condemned: 'An essay in style demands that the composer should be an instinctive stylist. Neither Vaughan Williams's best friends nor his worst enemies would so describe him. What makes the bulk of his work lovable is the sincerity which surmounts every defect of style.' The work was played by Jelly d'Aranyi, to whom Vaughan Williams had dedicated it. Colles, in the *Musical Times*, struck a happy phrase: 'The play of part-writing and harmony are pure V.W. of the 1920s, strong and steady, with the face of noble melancholy which we may well describe as the Cotswold look.' It is certainly difficult, in considering these works, to fit them into the time-scheme of the 1920s, which were anything but strong and steady in certain aspects. The antics of 'Les Six' in Paris, of Walton in *Façade*, of Stravinsky in *Mavra*, and of early Hindemith cannot belong to the same decade, it seems, as Holst's *Ode to Death* and Vaughan Williams's Mass and concerto. In literature and painting the same mood of superficial flippancy predominated. The danger here is the old one of labels. There was plenty of seriousness, of un-flapperish-ness, in the 1920s which has not given rise to such amusing writing as the post-war mood of reaction and relaxation and escape. Vaughan Williams, mature as man and artist, was ready, like Stravinsky and Bartók, for adventure and experiment along neo-classic paths but they were to be within the scope of his own idiom and not into ways alien to his nature and temperament. Philip Heseltine, writing in 1920 in the second issue of *Music and Letters*, had deplored the extravagant praise bestowed on *Petrushka*, on Scriabin and on Malipiero and had craved the advent of the 'still small voice of genius who will "take homely and familiar things and make them fresh and beautiful" at his touch'. Though hardly a still small voice, Vaughan Williams's music answers this call, though perhaps people, including Heseltine, failed to recognize familiar things in the indeter-minate tonality of the opening of *Flos Campi*. At any rate, this work was not played again until 3 November 1927. On 9 April 1929 Ernest Ansermet conducted it at the I.S.C.M. Festival in Geneva.

A comparatively minor event in the world of publishing in 1925 was to mark the beginning of a famous and fruitful association between Vaughan Williams and the Oxford University Press. A Music Department had been established in the summer of 1924 under the direction and editorship of Hubert Foss. On 8 October 1925 the O.U.P. imprint appeared on an arrangement of Bach's 'Giant' Fugue made by Vaughan Williams in collaboration with his pupil Arnold Foster. On 12 November the O.U.P. published its first original R.V.W. composition, the Three Whitman Songs. Within a year or two an understanding was reached whereby the O.U.P. agreed to publish anything that he cared to offer them, and this informal contract held good for thirty-two years. It is symbolic that the first offering should have been a transcription of his revered Bach, and typical, too, that he published it in association with a younger man who had studied with him.[1]

By the end of 1925 Vaughan Williams had published his only oratorio, the comparatively brief *Sancta Civitas*, so-called because the English title *The Holy City* had already been used. Of his choral works this was the one he liked most, although it has been among the least performed because it is both difficult and expensive. On the

---

[1] Foster succeeded Holst as director of music at Morley College in 1928. He died in 1963.

fly-leaf, printed only in the original Greek, is a quotation from the *Phaedo* of Plato which was the nearest Vaughan Williams was ever to come to an explicit avowal of his agnosticism. Socrates, awaiting execution, wishes to prove the immortality of the soul and gives the geography of the regions in which spirits must move before they can enter the Elysian Fields. He continues:

'Now to assert that these things are exactly as I have described would not be reasonable. But that these things, or something like them, are true concerning the souls of men and their habitations after death, especially since the soul is shown to be immortal, this seems to me fitting and worth risking to believe. For the risk is honourable, and a man should sing such things in the manner of an incantation to himself.'

Here is the composer's answer to those who would ask how he could set a text in which he did not have literal belief. It explains why Herbert, Bunyan, Whitman, and even John Bright set his musical mind alight. Moreover it is illuminated still further by a crucial quotation from Vaughan Williams's writings:

'There is no form of insincerity more subtle than that which is coupled with great earnestness of purpose and determination to do only the best and the highest—this unconscious insincerity which leads us to build up great designs which we cannot fill and to simulate emotions which we can only feel vicariously.'[1]

In *Sancta Civitas*, Vaughan Williams was writing only of that which he knew—the value of these 'incantations'. It was performed for the first time on the fourth day of the General Strike, 7 May 1926, at the Oxford Festival celebrating the 300th anniversary of William Heather's proposal (on 5 May 1626) that a chair of music should be established at the University. True to his readiness always to give young artists a chance, Vaughan Williams had agreed that Keith Falkner should sing the baritone solos. But laryngitis intervened and Arthur Cranmer took his place. A month later the work was given in London during the jubilee of the Bach Choir. If *Flos Campi* had troubled Colles, this oratorio baffled him, as he freely confessed in *The Times* of 10 June 1926:

'The disturbance that one feels in listening to the work for the first time is partly the consciousness that his vision is greater than ours, partly a

[1] 'Who wants the English Composer?' *R.C.M. Magazine*, Vol. IX, No. 1, Christmas Term 1912. Also, in slightly different form, in *National Music and Other Essays*.

doubt whether he has really found the right notes to convey it to our ears. Certain things are so obvious; the scales and chords and parallel fifths which have become the clichés of so much 20th century music. One wonders how the vision will appear when these juxtapositions have become as familiar to the ear as the sequences of Parry and the diminished thirds[1] of Brahms.'

In a further article on 12 June Colles quoted the remark of a friend that perhaps the words had hampered Vaughan Williams. 'The problem of the oratorio composer is not to let himself be hampered by his words; he takes them to aid him. . . . The new oratorio leaves the impression that after all the composer has been afraid of oratory.'

Admittedly a thirty-five-minute oratorio was something new to the English musical scene; and admittedly the 'fire and ice' of Vaughan Williams's incandescent work is an approach to a vision of the after-life quite different from the expansiveness of Elgar. One wonders, too, how good the early performances were, at a time when English orchestral standards were low and rehearsals limited. (A letter to Maud Karpeles about *Sancta Civitas* says: 'If you care to come to hear my new tune tomorrow do come—but it will be rather bad as the chorus have not had it for a fortnight and they forget so quickly.') Nevertheless the criticisms of *Sancta Civitas*, of which Colles's is typical, labelled it as 'austere' and created a fog of words between composer and listener. Its conciseness, concentration, and complexities of texture are the very reasons why it is a masterpiece. If critics missed this point, musicians did not, least of all Edward Elgar, as Vaughan Williams himself recalled in a broadcast during the Elgar centenary celebrations in 1957:

'He came to hear a performance of my *Sancta Civitas* and gave it generous praise. He told me that he had once thought of setting the words himself, "but I shall never do that now", to which I could only answer that this made me sorry that I had ever attempted to make a setting myself.'

With becoming modesty, Vaughan Williams omitted in this broadcast to quote Elgar's complete remark which was, 'I once thought of setting those words, but I shall never do that now, and I am glad I didn't because you have done it for me.' The planned third part of Elgar's trilogy of oratorios never materialized and he finally abandoned it in 1927. The performance of *Sancta Civitas*

[1] This is how the word appears, but it may be a misprint for triads.

which he heard was probably at Hereford on 9 September 1930, when Roy Henderson and Steuart Wilson were the soloists.

Sancta Civitas was a long way from folk song; but if any of his contemporaries thought that the composer had 'outgrown' that phase then they failed to understand its importance to him. Once again we are back at his phrase about the importance of finding the musical *mot juste*. He had found it in *Flos Campi* and in the oratorio, and if it was a more remote and difficult word, that could not be helped. It did not make folk song the less valid. Side by side with *Sancta Civitas* he had been sketching a Shakespearean opera tentatively called *The Fat Knight* in which traditional tunes had their special place. A set of 'studies' of folk song, written for his friend, the cellist May Mukle, started him thinking about a larger work for cello and orchestra based on folk tunes, and this became the *Fantasia on Sussex Folk Songs*, dedicated to Casals. Moreover he was engaged with Maud Karpeles on settings of some of the tunes she and Cecil Sharp had brought from the Appalachian Mountains of America—and there was the usual work for the English Folk Dance Society and especially for the Cecil Sharp Memorial Fund, and for any event organized by the E.F.D.S. He was also responsible for the Folk Song Journal.

There was no major first performance of a Vaughan Williams work in 1927; seven of the Housman songs (nine were composed) were sung by Joan Elwes and described in the *Musical Times* of 1 December 1927, as 'of poetic interest. The composer has aimed at giving the poet the first place, obscuring the verbal effect as little as possible. Unless one is a poetry lover these songs may appear rather bare. There are the fewest possible notes. Those who are fit to appreciate them will regard them as a precious gift. Of course the severeness of this style makes for great difficulty in performance.' There had been no clash with Housman over these settings, but the poet, in an undated letter from 'Lower House', Tardebigge, Bromsgrove, managed a dead-pan thrust on behalf of the verse which Vaughan Williams had omitted from 'Is my team ploughing?':

Dear Sir,

If my consent is necessary I willingly give it to Miss Elwes to sing your settings of my poems with the following proviso. I am told that some composers in setting some of my poems have omitted portions of them;[1]

---

[1] R.V.W. cut the verse about the keeper standing up to keep the goal.

and I would not give my consent (again supposing it to be necessary) to the singing of any poem so treated.

Yours faithfully,

A. E. Housman.

In 1927 the tune 'Greensleeves', which Vaughan Williams had known first from William Ballet's *Lute Book* of 1584, attained canonization, as it were, by appearing as a tune to the words 'The old year now away is fled' in the *Oxford Book of Carols*, published in 1928 and edited by the *Songs of Praise* team—Percy Dearmer, Martin Shaw, and Vaughan Williams. Anyone who wishes to study the history of the carol and the folk carol in England should read Dearmer's fine preface to this popular collection. Once again great care was taken with words and music. Chesterton, R. C. Trevelyan, Walter de la Mare, Robert Graves, A. A. Milne, A. H. Fox Strangways, and Steuart Wilson were among those asked to translate or write carol verses; the musical editors arranged many tunes; Röntgen helped with Dutch and Flemish carols; English carols collected by Sharp, Vaughan Williams, Percy Merrick and Mrs. Leather were included; and new tunes were contributed by Boughton, Armstrong Gibbs, Holst, R. O. Morris, Ireland, Peter Warlock, Sydney Nicholson and (as the Acknowledgements oddly described him) E. Duncan Rubbra. Harmonizations by J. H. Arnold, Elizabeth Maconchy, the Abbot of Downside, Charles Kennedy Scott and Geoffrey Shaw ensured a catholic approach. The modern revival of carols is in great measure due to this excellent book.

After the trilogy of the Mass, *Sancta Civitas* and *Flos Campi* and the editorial labour involved in *Songs of Praise* and the *Oxford Book of Carols*, it is understandable that the 'unbuttoned' side of Vaughan Williams's temperament should have spurred him to start thinking about a comic opera and that the outburst of lyrical ardour which was predominant in his Shakespeare opera should have sought outlet. Some time at the beginning of 1927, he agreed to collaborate with Cecil Sharp's sister Evelyn, who was to become in 1933 the wife of H. W. Nevinson. She began a libretto based on incidents taken from 'The Poison Maid', the last story in Richard Garnett's *Twilight of the Gods*, and 'Rapaccini's Daughter' from Nathaniel Hawthorne's *Mosses from the Old Manse*. The opera was originally entitled *The Poison Kiss*, and its fantastical plot concerns a magician, Dipsacus, (all the characters have botanical names), who has been jilted in his youth by the Empress Persicaria and plans as his revenge the death of her son Amaryllus. He has brought up his daughter Tormentilla on a diet of poison so that when the two meet and, as Dipsacus intends, fall in love her first kiss will unwittingly destroy him. All comes to naught because the Empress makes the kiss harmless by nourishing Amaryllus on antidotes. But love proves to be the greatest antidote of all and the opera ends with Dipsacus and the Empress pairing off, and Dipsacus's hobgoblins marrying the Empress's mediums. The sub-principal characters Gallanthus and Angelica, servants of the hero and heroine, also find that 'Love has conquered, hearts united'. Frothy stuff; and one wonders why, remembering *The Perfect Fool*, Vaughan Williams feared to show it to Holst.

It was evidently what Vaughan Williams wanted for he began to set it act by act before the libretto was completed in detail. By August 1927 he had made 'more or less complete sketches' for six numbers, Gallanthus's 'It's really time', the duet 'It's true' for Angelica and Gallanthus, the duet 'Blue Larkspur' for Tormentilla and Amaryllus, the latter's song 'I thought I loved', Dipsacus's ballad 'The sun it shone', and Tormentilla's 'O who would be unhappy me?' The complete correspondence between Vaughan Williams and his librettist is preserved and, although it is too long and detailed to be printed in full, it provides more examples of the influence the composer exerted upon his libretti, re-shaping them and often altering the plot. All the best dramatic moments of the work were, in fact, instigated by him. Whenever the work has been performed, its libretto has been strongly criticized. This criticism is not unjustified but it is wrong to extend sympathy to the composer for being, as it were, 'saddled' with it. He wanted this kind of work and he could have refused the libretto. But he did not. What is more he spent much time and ink pulling it into shape. One of the first letters gave Miss Sharp due warning:

'I am going to ask for one or two alterations in the text of these [songs in Act I] . . . Dialogue Am. and Gall. I suggest that he did not kill the cobra which introduces rather too tragic an element but that he hit it over the head and that afterwards (as we shall see) it recovered . . . I suggest after Tormentilla's song "Father where are you?" Angelica should say "The cobra's not dead, only he's a bad headache". Tor. "Let me cure it". Sham lullaby by Tormentilla "Dear little cobra asleep in my arms"—that sort of thing and metre. . . . I'm hoping for some second act soon. I like to pick about

and not go straight ahead—I'm getting v. fond of the libretto—But there
are one or two points which worry me. Have we got enough variety of
metre? e.g. Gall's song p. 7 and Tormentilla's p. 22 are the same metre
also the duet for Am. and Gall. "What is this you tell me," "I refuse to
adopt", are all more or less in the limerick metre. I only point this out for
future guidance. Occasional short lines and mid-rhymes are useful to a
composer—also 5 & 7 lines occasionally (not always 4 or 6). Then we
want occasionally some pure lyric & romantic moments, I think, to give
the poor sentimental old composer a chance. A few suggestions for useful
ensembles are (1) a quiet lyrical 4tet or 5tet with solo lines (e.g. Sullivan
"Brightly dawns" or "Tower Tomb" in *Yeomen of the Guard*) (2) An
ensemble consisting of a *slow* tune for bne singer or group followed by a
quick 'patter' verse for another singer or group & then both together
(*vide* Sullivan *passim*) and finally—avoid closed vowel sounds (e.g. me,
be, see, thin etc) where I am likely to want a high note . . . and to conclude
I hope you will pay *no* attention to any of my suggestions—Every one
works better with a *free* hand . . . P.S. I think we might have one moment
of passion with a big scena even in a comic opera.'

By 18 August 1927 the words of Act II were sent to Vaughan
Williams who at once warned his collaborator against having too
many principal characters and advised her to study *Polly* for some
good metres. 'I believe the best method is for me to make hay of
your words *after* you have written them. (You'll have a fit when you
see all the alterations I want you to make in Act I) . . . We've really
got to make up our minds whether this is to be a musical comedy or
a real comic opera. In musical comedy (or ballad opera) the music is
purely incidental . . . in comic opera at certain points (usually the
finale) the drama is carried on through the music. . . . In our 1st Act
the music is more or less incidental & we may have to strengthen
the ensemble places.'

In September 1927, as will be seen, the first sketches of *Job* were
occupying Vaughan Williams, but a year later, on 12 September
1938, he wrote to Miss Sharp to tell her that he had finished the
music of Act II as far as he could. 'I like the lyrics v. much & have
set them all—but dramatically I can't see it.' Then, hoping that this
will not be 'the last straw', he covered twenty-three pages of large
notepaper in giving a detailed re-shaping of Act II into almost its
final form, keeping most of the lyrics but himself writing much of
the spoken dialogue. 'I feel it is rather too serious and grand opera-
ish,' he wrote, 'but perhaps this won't matter if we keep all the rest
quite light. Now as to Act III. I don't feel happy about this yet . . .'

and six more pages of re-written plot followed. The letter ends:

'Please *could* I have some spondaic or trochaic songs—yours are almost all Iambic or anapaestic—even when you start trochaically (e.g. "Wearily I go to rest") extra syllables creep in very soon which make it very difficult for the tune. The good old "choric" metre always "carries" a good tune— Lo He comes with clouds descending, Once for favoured sinners slain—. I am now setting to work on the songs in Act I which I had not done and revising the others. I expect on receipt of this you will chuck the whole thing—and I should not be surprised—but I hope not as I've managed to nab one or two rather nice tunes.'

The librettist did not 'chuck' it, beyond mildly remonstrating that she did not call his letter the last straw—'it seems to me more to resemble a whole stack! However . . . I am sure it will work out all right in the end'. Further changes to Act III were made between February and July 1929. Act II underwent further revision, at the composer's suggestion, in December of that year. He ended this particular letter with the words, 'The only other alteration I propose is the first number of Act I where we might cut one verse. When we have done this I think the thing will be ready to take its luck'. On 3 January 1930, he wrote again:

'I think the opera is ready for sending round now. But who to I've no idea. As I warned you I'm quite incapable and much too lazy to do anything myself. If I sent you the score would you care to try hawking it round?'

Evelyn Sharp promptly sent the opera to Sir Nigel Playfair who as promptly returned it. It was suggested to her by the Society of Authors that either Sir Barry Jackson at Birmingham or A. B. Horne of the Cambridge Festival Theatre might be interested and she sought Vaughan Williams's advice. 'I rather doubt about Barry Jackson,' he correctly surmised. 'It would certainly be not half precious enough for the Festival Theatre. I think on the whole the best thing to do would be to see if the O. U. Press would publish it.' And there, for eighteen months, the matter rested.

It is clear that Vaughan Williams's imagination was stimulated from the first by this strange farrago. A stimulus of a very different kind had also begun to take effect in 1927. This year was the hundredth anniversary of the death of William Blake, and the eminent Blake scholar, Dr. (later Sir) Geoffrey Keynes, was impelled to put into action a scheme which had long been simmering in his mind: a ballet 'of a kind which would be new to the English stage'[1] based on Blake's *Illustrations of the Book of Job*. He felt that despite their 'elaborate grandeur', these wonderful illustrations 'possessed a fundamental simplicity' and that if this could be successfully extracted, a remarkable stage work might result. 'Blake had, moreover, unconsciously provided in his designs settings which could easily be adapted for stage scenes, and innumerable suggestions in his figures for attitudes and groupings which cried out for their conversion by a choreographer into actuality and movement.' Keynes wrote a scenario based on the main events of Job's life. Then, with the aid of his wife's sister, Mrs. Gwendolen Raverat, he reduced Blake's twenty-one engravings to eight scenes. Mrs. Raverat provided the stage settings. She used two stage levels, setting God's throne on a platform with a flight of steps. The earthly characters move only on the stage level. At first it was feared that the Lord Chamberlain might object to the representation of the Deity on the stage, even though the scenario was careful to refer to 'the Godhead'. However, since there were no spoken words, no licence had to be obtained, and the only risk was of police prosecution under the blasphemy laws! Keynes and Mrs. Raverat found it impossible to transfer to the stage Blake's design of Job tormented by evil dreams. They therefore devised a dance of Sata n and Job's 'Trinity of Accusers', called 'War, Pestilence and Famine'. During this dance Satan reproduces the positions shown in Blake's 'Satan smiting Job with boils' (Tate Gallery). It was at this point of the scheme, in 1927, that Keynes and Mrs. Raverat decided to approach Vaughan Williams about music for their ballet (thereby completing a Cambridge triumvirate and also making *Job* a family affair, for Mrs. Keynes and Mrs. Raverat, being daughters of Charles Darwin's second son, George, were cousins of Vaughan Williams). He was 'immediately fired with an enthusiasm for the task', but he made two stipulations: that there should be no dancing *sur les pointes*, which he detested, and that the performance should be called a masque, not a ballet. No doubt he felt that ballet, through its modern associations with artificiality, smartness and impresarios, was foreign to his conception of an English work of art in which the glory of the seventeenth-century masque (without songs and poetry) could be revived in modern form. The idea could not have been broached at a more

[1] This and subsequent quotations are from Keynes's introduction to the Pierpont Morgan Library edition of Blake's *Illustrations of the Book of Job*.

apposite time, for he was, musically, in the state of mind to grapple with a theme still within the orbit of *Flos Campi* and *Sancta Civitas*; moreover, his mind was much occupied with the stage. Three operas were in his sketch-books at this time. The next step was to bring the project nearer to the possibility of performance. Serge Diaghilev was in London with the Ballet Russe de Monte Carlo, so a French version of the scenario, together with full-sized reproductions of Blake's engravings, was laid before him. He rejected the idea as 'too English', in which he was quite right, and 'too old-fashioned', where he was quite wrong. Keynes noted drily: 'The book of engravings was, however, not returned, and it was interesting to see traces of Blake's influence appearing in another Biblical ballet, *The Prodigal Son*, produced by Diaghilev in his following London seasons.' Diaghilev's refusal was not unexpected by one member of the collaboration, as this letter to Mrs. Raverat in 1927 shows:

My dear Gwen,

I amused myself with making a sketch of *Job*—I never expected Djag [*sic*] wd. look at it—and I'm glad on the whole—the 'réclame' wd. have been rather amusing—but it really wdnt. have suited the sham serious really decadent and frivolous attitude of the R.B. [Russian Ballet] toward everything—can you imagine *Job* sandwiched between *Les Biches* and *Cimarosiana*—and that dreadful pseudo-cultured audience saying to each other 'My dear, have you seen God at the Russian Ballet'. No—I think we are well out of it.—I don't think this is sour grapes—for I admit that it wd. have been great fun to have had a production by the R.B.—though I feel myself that they wd. have made an unholy mess of it with their over-developed calves.

Yours affectionately,
R. Vaughan Williams.

By the summer of 1928 the music was taking hold of Vaughan Williams's imagination, and he wrote again to Mrs. Raverat from the house in Surrey where he and Adeline were staying. Adeline's arthritis was worse and she found it increasingly difficult to manage the stairs at Cheyne Walk. The summer in Surrey, therefore, was a preliminary house-hunt.

The Rew Cottage,
Abinger Common,
Dorking.

Dear Gwen,

I am anxiously awaiting your *scenario*—otherwise the music will push

on by itself which may cause trouble later. I've got the Wicksteed book[1]—
but I'm not going to worry about the left foot and the right foot.

Yours sincerely,

R. Vaughan Williams.

And push on it did. Vaughan Williams's impetus was now so great
that the remoteness of a stage presentation does not seem to have
worried him. Blake's drawings and the magnificent prose of the
Authorized Version of the Bible were his inspirations, and he noted
on his score the number of the engraving which was transmuted
into music. He added stage directions, but devised his own scenario,
rather different from Keynes's, in which he incorporated the scrip-
tural texts. By 1929 it would not have mattered if there was never to
be a chance of *Job*'s reaching the stage: we should still have had the
music. He showed his score to Holst—'I should be alarmed to say
how many "Field Days" we spent over it,' he wrote years later.[2]
'Then he came to all the orchestral rehearsals, including a special
journey to Norwich, and finally he insisted on the Camargo Society's
performing it. Thus I owe the life of *Job* to Holst. . . .' The *Job*
rehearsals took place in the Duke's Hall of the Royal Academy of
Music on 17 and 18 October in preparation for the first performance,
which the composer conducted at the Norwich Festival on 23 October 1930. It is not likely that it was a very good performance, for the
orchestra was an *ad hoc* body formed from the nucleus of the old
Queen's Hall Orchestra or, as Richard Capell bluntly put it, 'a band
of London players euphemistically called The Queen's Hall
Orchestra.'[3]

The London orchestras at this time were undergoing a much-
needed process of reorganization precipitated by the formation of the
new B.B.C. Symphony Orchestra, which gave its first concert in the
week following the Norwich Festival, and by the successes of the
Hallé Orchestra under Sir Hamilton Harty. In later years Vaughan
Williams made a joke out of the memory and said he hadn't treated
Norwich fairly—'I told them I'd give them a suite and they thought
it was something for *thé dansant* and put it in at the end of a long
programme without possibility of much rehearsal—and they got
Job!' It was certainly an adventurous festival, because Janáček's

[1] Joseph Wicksteed's *Blake's Vision of the Book of Job*, published in 1910, in which
the symbolism of Blake's art is expounded.
[2] 'Chapter of Musical Autobiography.'
[3] *Monthly Musical Record*, December 1930.

Glagolitic Mass and Bliss's *Morning Heroes* were given their first English performances in the same week. Capell, in the article already quoted, conveys best the surprise with which *Job* was heard:

'Practically nothing had been heard about this work beforehand and from the place allotted to it on the programme something quite slight was expected. What we heard was one of Vaughan Williams's major compositions, a work of great spaciousness and rich in characteristic beauties, of the length of a symphony.'

Capell said he was not himself concerned whether it reached the stage because it was 'a noble piece of concert music', but most of his colleagues conventionally regarded *Job* as stage music without the stage and urged its complete realization as soon as possible. 'The music in its acceptance of form and its rejection of formalism is of a piece with Blake,' Colles wrote. 'It contains tunes of such a simple beauty that one seems to have known them always, but their lines lead on into a realm of musical thought that one enters for the first time.' Here, at any rate, was percipience, for in *Job* are the seeds of Vaughan Williams's final period as well as of the violence of the Fourth Symphony which lay just round the next corner. For the first time since the *London Symphony* he called on the full resources of the modern orchestra, sometimes to the horror of Holst who, after the first rehearsal, almost went down on his knees 'to beg me to cut out some of the percussion with which my inferiority complex had led me to overload the score'.[1] Holst was not entirely successful, as Vaughan Williams, in a letter thanking him for 'holding my hand all those days', confessed:

'I don't think you know Duncan (percussion)—I know him because he plays timps for me at Dorking. After rehearsal he came up and begged me to put back one of the cymbal smashes which he thought it had been a great mistake of me to leave out. I was so much touched that I said yes—regardless of the result.'[2]

This, then, was the beginning of *Job*. Its future as a ballet is best described in the next chapter when the 1930s are considered in fuller detail. It is not without interest that Vaughan Williams conducted Parry's *Job* at the 1929 Leith Hill Festival: what would his master have thought of the 'impertinences' in his pupil's latest score? He would have found it 'characteristic' to be sure, though he might have preferred the Shakespeare opera on Falstaff which was first

[1] 'Chapter of Musical Autobiography.'
[2] *Heirs and Rebels*, p. 76.

produced at the Royal College of Music on 21 March 1929, under the title *Sir John in Love*, which the composer had substituted for *The Fat Knight*. This opera, as has been seen, had been germinating for many years. Writing music for *The Merry Wives of Windsor* at Stratford in 1913 was probably the chief impetus of a lifelong ambition to compose an opera from this play which Vaughan Williams, contrary to the general run of opinion, liked immensely. In 1913, too, he had heard Théodor Byard sing the French chanson 'Vrai dieu d'amours' and this, too, played its part. Serious work on the opera began, probably, in 1924. Falstaff had been behind the scenes even in the *Pastoral Symphony*: Tovey, in his analytical note, disclosed that the composer had told him that the scherzo was 'sketched for a ballet of oafs and fairies', but he had a word wrong, for the quotation is from *The Merry Wives of Windsor*, Act IV, Sc. 4 . . . 'and three or four more of their growth we'll dress like urchins, ouphes and fairies, green and white'. To Mistress Page, planning the undoing of Falstaff, as to other Elizabethans, an ouphe was an elf, and an urchin a goblin. Vaughan Williams was in no way discouraged by the shadow of Verdi's masterpiece looming behind him as he wrote, for he was not a whole-hearted admirer of that particular work, and he did not sympathize with Holst's attempt (in *At the Boar's Head*) to fit Shakespeare's words to folk songs. His passion for Elizabethan drama and his deep knowledge of folk song encouraged him to believe that he could make a peculiarly English opera out of a peculiarly English play and he constructed his own libretto, interpolating lyrics apposite to the dialogue from other plays and other dramatists. He dedicated the completed work to his friend and adviser, S. P. Waddington.

Vaughan Williams consulted Miss Karpeles about the folk dance 'Half Hannikin' with which the opera ends. (It is found in the first edition (1650) of Playford's *The Dancing Master* but was danced in Henry VIII's reign.) She sent, on 10 March 1929, a detailed schedule adding 'Imogen will probably think of something better'. (Imogen Holst was one of the imps and fairies in the R.C.M. production.) The opera received four 'private' performances (made possible by the Palmer Fund for Opera Study) conducted by Malcolm Sargent. They were evidently good performances, for Colles wrote[1] that 'for once we were able to feel that a new opera had come

---

[1] *The Times*, 23 March 1929.

to birth, and not merely been tried through, at its first presentation'. Vaughan Williams in his *Sir John in Love* vein, was Colles's preference. Ten years later, on 8 July 1939, he wrote of it:

'What some people do say, and not without justification, is that they find the actual sound of the music, particularly the orchestration, harsh and ungrateful to the ear. . . . If the complaint is that Vaughan Williams has eschewed the mellifluousness of the late 19th century his answer will probably be "Certainly, because there was something else to be done with this particular play". It is not meant to compete with Continental masterpieces by stealing their thunder. It is meant to be enjoyed by English people who know their Shakespeare and are also at home with the music of their own country from *Sumer is icumen in* to Purcell's *Fairy Queen*. Such people may be inclined to think of it as the perfect opera ("a story sung with proper action") which Purcell dreamed of on the English stage.'

That was well said, even if it is surprising to find this most mellifluous and sweet of Vaughan Williams's operatic scores described as 'harsh'. Possibly, in the amateur performances to which it was condemned until 1946 by the inadequacy of British operatic life, the vigour of much of the last act sounded harsh. Perhaps Maud Karpeles, in a letter after the first performance to which only the reply survives, had said something of the same sort, for the composer wrote: 'I'm glad you liked most of it—I shall think seriously over Act IV—at present I *like* all the dance tunes except one. I want them to be a bit rough and grotesque—they are village boys *playing* at fairies—not real fairies.'

In July 1929 the Vaughan Williamses moved to their new home, The White Gates, at Dorking. Although he would miss London, at least Vaughan Williams would be in the thick of the Leith Hill Festival. For its jubilee in 1930 he was writing a new work for each 'division' of the choirs, the division being graded according to capacity. Thus the Towns got the *Benedicite*, Div. I the *Three Choral Hymns*, Div. II *The Hundredth Psalm*, and the Children Three Songs to words by Lady Farrer's daughter Frances (later Dame Frances Farrer). Characteristically, Vaughan Williams shared the works among the three firms which had published most of his works hitherto.

But before this important Dorking occasion, the cello work dedicated to Casals, the *Fantasia on Sussex Folk Tunes*, was played in March 1930, at a concert of the Royal Philharmonic Society, with

Casals as soloist and a former cellist, John Barbirolli, as conductor. The work, which the composer later withdrew, received a sympathetic notice from Colles in *The Times* of 14 March 1930:

'Most of his later and greater works do not quote folk song at all; they have no more to do with the folk song of England than the symphonic works of Brahms have to do with the folk song of Germany, though that is something. This Fantasia, however, is practically all folk song. One's appreciation of it must depend on how far one cares for the tunes. The composer picks the flowers and arranges them in a vase. He does not pull them to pieces, petal from petal, or invite us to examine them under a microscope or dye them in unnatural colours with aniline harmonies. They remain themselves from first to last; and Señor Casals's violoncello and the orchestra merely provide the vase in which one is tempted to imagine that the tunes have found their own places, as flowers do. Of course the composer must have done something with them, but what one hardly knows at the end of it all; they seem to be growing. . . . Señor Casals was the leader of the folk singers, but all the instruments became vocal as they could hardly fail to do in playing this spontaneous music.'

Few other critics responded as wholeheartedly to what was felt to be a disappointing work. But the concert had another significance, for it was the occasion of the presentation of the Gold Medal of the Royal Philharmonic Society to Vaughan Williams. The presentation was made by Arthur Bliss who told his fellow composer that the Society considered itself honoured in his acceptance of the medal and that younger composers regarded him as their leader. The recipient's undisguised embarrassment might have misled some of the audience into thinking that he under-valued the distinction, but they would have been wrong. He well knew that since the medal had been instituted in 1871 only three English composers had received it— Sterndale Bennett in 1871, and Elgar and Delius in 1925. By a neat turn of time's wheel, the young conductor at this concert in 1930 was to receive the medal from Vaughan Williams's hands twenty years later.

We may be sure that Vaughan Williams derived more satisfaction from the Philharmonic concert a month later, on 3 April, when the Gold Medal was presented to Holst by Frederic Austin. Next day a letter was sent from The White Gates:

Dear Gustav,
   I was distressed not to see you last night. I know you hate it all—but we had to tell you in public that we know you are a great man.

The Lament and Ground [of the Concerto for two violins, first performed at the concert by Jelly d'Aranyi and Adila Fachiri] are splendid—I'm not *quite* so sure about the Scherzo—and even that boils down to not being *quite* sure about the 6/8 tune.

Yrs, R.V.W.

Their friendship was as candid and firm as ever; it had survived undiminished through the critical years from 1925–30 when Holst's music, after its brief spell of popularity, was almost universally denigrated except by Ernest Newman. The *Choral Symphony* had been the object of critical scorn, the cruellest criticism coming from Cecil Gray who wrote that 'Holst presents the melancholy spectacle of a continuous and unrelieved decline'. *At the Boar's Head* had been similarly assaulted.[1] His neuritis got worse and his friends worried about his increasing solitariness and the ordered shelter of his existence.

But in 1927 he was happier and at work on *Egdon Heath*. R.V.W. must have been one of the few who perceived in 1928, as we so easily perceive now, that *Egdon Heath* had clear melodic outlines. The first London performance took place on 23 February 1928, just over a month after Hardy's death. Few people liked it. But Holst knew it was his best work. And on 25 February came the letter that made everything all right:

Dear Gustav,
    I've come to the conclusión that E.H. is beautiful—bless you therefore.

Yours, R.V.W.

So, with *Job* and *Egdon Heath*, the two friends entered the 1930s. If either had been in the habit of looking back they must have seen what a change ten years had wrought in the English musical scene. Although it still existed, there was less need for a British Music Society. A large number of British composers was writing and having works performed. Some of the older generation were not as fortunate and were seldom heard: Holbrooke, Cyril Scott, York Bowen, Bantock to some extent. Delius, a blind invalid in France, had a doughty champion in Beecham and in 1929 he had received the homage of

---

[1] Vaughan Williams once told the author that he blamed 'the Lambert clique' for the neglect of Holst's music. 'They had a lot of power, but I should have thought he had everything to please them.'

the musical world in London and had been admitted to the Companionship of Honour. Elgar was still the acknowledged head of the English musical profession, Master of the King's Musick since 1924 but almost silent now, living out his life in Worcestershire with his dogs, bitterly hurt by the swing of the fashion-pendulum away from him and by the half-empty Queen's Hall on his seventieth birthday, but still the revered and beloved principal figure at each September meeting of the Three Choirs. Bax, Ireland, Bliss, Howells were in their prime; Walton, Lambert, Moeran, van Dieren, and Warlock, all of a younger generation, had their following and their adherents; the names Finzi and Tippett were known to the cognoscenti. The brave venture of the British National Opera Company still attracted high hopes. Among international composers, Sibelius was at the height of his vogue; Hindemith and Bartók were played occasionally; Kodály and Szymanowski, Bloch, Honegger and Milhaud; Casella and Pizzetti—all were attended to; the Henry Wood Promenade Concerts were still the home of enterprise: Mahler, Falla, and Ravel could be heard there and at the Hallé Concerts in Manchester and occasionally at the Royal Philharmonic. Schoenberg, Webern and Berg were largely unknown; Stravinsky was regarded as in an eccentric phase. Great soloists like Schnabel, Backhaus, Heifetz, Kreisler, Gerhardt, Gieseking, Casals, Lehmann, Schumann, Rachmaninov, bestrode the concert-halls of the world. English artists, singers especially, were of fine calibre. Because the works of the atonalists were ignored, the English musical life of that day has been scorned by a later generation. The causes are many and need not be examined here: in any case it was not the business of other composers. A composer's duty is to compose the music that is in him.

But a far greater change was slowly transforming the musical life of the country: the invention of wireless. Since 1922 the broadcasting service had grown and developed. (Vaughan Williams conducted the L.S.O. in his *Pastoral Symphony* during the orchestra's first broadcast, from Southwark Cathedral, on 9 February 1924.) By 1930 the B.B.C. was able to form its own symphony orchestra, which did not need to rely on public support for its existence. For too long the standard of orchestral playing in London had been regrettably low; this was partly because players were still allowed to send deputies to perform at concerts, even after they had themselves been present at all the rehearsals. But the visits by German orchestras, notably the Berlin Philharmonic Orchestra with Furtwängler, and the example of what a provincial orchestra, the Hallé, could achieve under a permanent conductor, added to the fear that the B.B.C. would put them all out of business, at length galvanized other people into action. The post-war boom had petered out by 1928 and box-office receipts everywhere were falling. Beecham's ambitious scheme, called the Imperial League of Opera, for a permanent opera company and orchestra in London failed to attract enough backing but, undeterred, he persevered and by 1932 had formed the new London Philharmonic Orchestra which effectively disproved that the B.B.C. had taken all the best players. Elsewhere municipal support for music was rudimentary. The battle was not yet half-won. Of all the factors which were eventually to bring music into everyone's life, only the invention of the gramophone could compare with the immeasurable possibilities of radio. Much was to be gained and much lost. No one, however, would again be foolish enough to imagine that English music could remain insular and separate. It had to stand against the masters of all ages; and it could now be heard by people the world over through a miraculous scientific device.

II

The appearance of *Hugh the Drover* in mid-1924 must have made even stranger the contrast of style shown in the next group of works to be published and performed. The marked difference between the 1922 major works and the three big compositions which appeared in 1925—*Flos Campi, Sancta Civitas* and the violin concerto—can partly be explained by the natural development of a freer use of harmonic and contrapuntal skill. It is also in some degree connected with Vaughan Williams's spell as conductor of the Bach Choir, for all these works can be regarded as modern commentaries on Bach's idiom, far removed from it as they might seem on first acquaintance. This is one reason for the neo-classical framework of the Concerto Accademico. Another is that both Vaughan Williams and Holst found the contemporary foreign scene more to their liking than they had done before the war. The chromaticism and neo-classicism to be noticed in Stravinsky's works of this period, and also in the works of Bartók, have a parallel in the works of the two Englishmen. By this time, Vaughan Williams's personal idiom was so strongly developed that he could bend to his will anything which nourished and renewed it. And though Holst was possibly the more adventurous-minded and could lead his friend into new paths, Vaughan Williams was the more successful in applying the results to his work, because his richer melodic invention gave it a continuity and firm basis which Holst's to some extent lacked. *Flos Campi* is sometimes included among Vaughan Williams's choral music—and that is reasonable, because it needs a choir for its performance—but its musical place is really amid the instrumental works, for the voices, wordless, are used as instrumental colouring. This was the first of his works to show, foremost of its qualities, a preoccupation with sonorities. It is also a classic illustration of idiom breeding inspiration, because the style of the music seems to have dictated the extra-musical quotations from the *Song of Solomon* which have mystified successive commentators on this extraordinary work. These quotations were ignored by the composer in his programme-note and are another example of his habit of providing clues and then denying their existence. 'If my music doesn't make itself understood as music without any tributary explanation—well, it's a failure as music and there's nothing more to be said. It matters, of course, enormously to the composer what he was thinking about when he was writing a particular work; but to no one else in this world does it matter one jot.' That was his lifelong belief.[1] That there is a definite connection between the text and the music in *Flos Campi* is undeniable: the Oriental flavour of the sound is sufficient proof of that. In his programme-note for the second performance the composer denied that the music had any ecclesiastical basis, though he would have been the last to deny the validity of personal reactions, however varied, to his music. It seems likely that the music was generated by human passion and love, and it certainly sounds gloriously pagan. It is strange that Holst should have been puzzled by its combination of passion and tranquillity.

Flos Campi is not a concerto,[2] and the composer's title of suite is non-committal. 'Six Images' might have been nearer the mark. The solo instrument, while given a virtuoso part calling for musicianship as well as technique, is but one voice among the instrumentalists, and his part is equalled in importance by that of the chorus. Of all the works by Vaughan Williams I think this is the most beautiful

---

[1] Quoted in *The Music Student*, Vol. XII, No. 9, June 1920, p. 515.

[2] It was not, as has been said, written for Lionel Tertis. In a letter to Hubert Foss, dated 7 February 1951, giving details of errors of fact in Foss's book about Vaughan Williams, R.V.W. wrote: '*Flos Campi* was not written for Tertis, though it was first performed by him. The Viola Suite was composed for him.'

considered in terms only of sound. The juxtaposition of viola and
oboe, the delicate use of the percussion and the poetic and imaginative use of the chorus give to *Flos Campi* the quality of a mosaic.
One hopes that Ravel heard and liked it. It is significant that one of
its early interpreters, in Britain and overseas, was Ernest Ansermet.
The famous bitonal opening for oboe and viola

is the first of several masterstrokes. Another is the combination of
voices and strings at the beginning of II

which foreshadows what later becomes a glorious viola *cantabile*
melody:

This great movement is headed by the words about the coming of
spring, and its pastoral character is limned with skill and evocative
power. This rapturous mood tells us how far Vaughan Williams had
travelled from the *Norfolk Rhapsodies*. The fourth movement gives
the viola its chance for virtuoso display. The orchestra begins with
a march theme in consecutive fourths (a variant of the march in the
finale of the *London Symphony*) and the viola enters with a vigorous
contrasting theme:

which later provides a counterpoint to the march theme. The movement grows in intensity, the voices being added in the last four bars,
reaching its climax as it flows without a break into the next movement. At this climax the full orchestra and chorus are marked *ff*
(for the only time in the entire work), appassionato and largamente;
this quickly dies down to a murmur of chorus (with closed lips) and
strings, over which the viola, its voice husky with passion, as
Simona Pakenham has brilliantly remarked, sings its ecstatic rhapsody. This is surely the musical apotheosis of longing! Over beating
drums the passion dies and the viola plays the melody of fulfilment,
fragments of which have bound the movements together into a
musical unity:

This is the 'seal upon thine heart'. It spreads throughout the
orchestra, putting forth tendrils of counterpoint and entwining
among voices and instruments. The last climax of all is yet another
variation of the Alleluia theme, Vaughan Williams's instinctive
formula for his biggest emotional crises:

The opening dialogue recurs. The instruments cease to play, one
by one. Only a flute is left, then the voices, singing quietly with
closed lips (a device Vaughan Williams had tried out in several folk-
song settings), and last of all the viola, playing a phrase of its great
tune. Although the last movement has pre-echoes of later works,
never again did Vaughan Williams attempt a work similar in scope
and design to *Flos Campi*. It is truly inimitable, a masterpiece.

Flos Campi was an intimate vision. The short but massive oratorio
Sancta Civitas is a gigantic fresco. The word 'mystic' is often applied
to Vaughan Williams. *Sancta Civitas* is its justification. In it, by
means of words which excited him and in pursuit of a faith which he
held but did not define, he reached out to 'the ultimate realities' in
music. Music was for him not simply a substitute for ordinary day-
to-day religion, but the only way by which he could grope for the
meaning of spiritual activity. 'The media that artists use,' he wrote,

'are symbols of what lies beyond sense and knowledge.' Schoenberg once remarked that 'of course a soul you have to have', and here he shared the English composer's instinctive search for beauty. The 'simplicity and directness' of Vaughan Williams are real enough, but they were the outcome of his lifelong struggle to master his highly complex musical personality. No one work epitomizes complexity and simplicity with more completeness than *Sancta Civitas*. In the deployment of its huge forces, as much care for correct balance is necessary as in *Flos Campi*. The whole work has the character of a vision. It emerges from silence, cellos and basses having a simple rising progression answered by a chordal dissonance on flutes such as Holst employed in *The Hymn of Jesus*. Into this air of stillness and mystery the baritone's declamation of his vision comes like a murmured prayer, followed by choral alleluias. These are at once echoed, on another level of sound and idiom, by the distant choir and its attendant trumpet. With immense speed—for an outstanding quality of the work is its swiftness, despite the often slow tempi, as though it had all been conceived in one vivid flash— the vision of St. John is recounted, with subtle and effective use of bitonality (as at the first entry of the distant choir). When Heaven opens and the brass is unleashed, diatonic triads take over for the Vision of the White Horse. The music sweeps on, *f* rising to *fff*, until the *largamente* paean at 'King of Kings and Lord of Lords':

Just before this climax there has been an equally great one depicting the 'wine-press of the fierceness and wrath of Almighty God'. On the word 'fierceness' there is a triple forte chord of G minor which, in the accompaniment, is snapped off leaving the chorus with only the timpani beating like some supernatural pulse. The tension of the music is such that one marvels how the composer can sustain the narrative invention demanded by the text; but sustain and intensify it he does, with a ferocity and brutality of sound which anticipate the F minor symphony and are achieved by a chromatic progression of triads. At the word 'slain', there is a mighty howl of savagery down five notes. Now the ear craves contrast, and the middle section, lento, is a sorrowful lament for Babylon by a semi-chorus of sopranos and altos in antiphony with the full chorus, masterly pages of choral writing like a vast symphonic sigh. But the distant choir, in a bright remorseless A flat, calls for rejoicing, and the baritone tells of the millstone cast into the sea. The lament returns, with this ornamentation for sopranos at 'the voice of the bridegroom and the bride shall be heard no more, no more at all in thee' that might be weeping for the lovers in *Flos Campi*:

For the first time for many bars the voices stop singing. Over a deep pedal, the cor anglais changes the mood—and the harmony—from bitterness to hope and a solo violin, soaring in arabesques, accompanies the choir's hushed description of the new heaven and the new earth and the holy city coming down from heaven, set to the phrase from the unpublished Whitman *Nocturne* of 1908 which had been waiting in Vaughan Williams's mind for its proper consummation:

Violin and oboe weave in and out of the voices as they grow in fervour, chiefly in E major. The warmth of the harmony is in astonishing, almost voluptuous, contrast to that of the earlier sections, and the music imperceptibly speeds as the light brightens and the vision of immortality is revealed. As the vision fades, the violin sinks back into the orchestra and the distant choir chant the words of the Sanctus. This builds up an emphatic climax on the words 'God Almighty':

Finally comes a stroke of genius. The chorus's contrapuntal praise of God, not joyful in the Bachian sense so much as awestricken, ceases. The opening bars of the oratorio return and a tenor soloist reserved for this one moment intones, 'quasi recitativo', 'Behold, I come quickly, I am the bright and the morning star. Surely I come quickly,' to which the chorus mutters 'Amen, even so come Lord' and the music withdraws into the shades.

If, as seems likely, this great work was in the form of a homage to Bach from the twentieth century, so also was the little violin concerto which was first played a few days after *Sancta Civitas* was published. Originally called Concerto Accademico (possibly in acknowledgement of its eighteenth-century manner), it is an engaging work, a tightly-wrought synthesis of neo-classicism, folk-dance rhythms and triadic harmony. The sound has none of the richness of the *Tallis Fantasia*; it is airier, more athletic and without the lyrical sweetness of Vaughan Williams's customary writing for strings. There is more development of material than is usual, mainly rhythmical. Yet we should beware of dismissing the concerto as a blithe trifling with matters of little moment. There is a disturbing and mysterious passage of counter-melody for the soloist in the first movement, and the adagio inhabits a timeless, aloof world for all the controlled passion of the cello's opening phrase. The finale is a romp among the cross-rhythms coming unexpectedly—or, rather, running down—to what Tovey called the 'most poetically fantastic and convincing end imaginable'. It is a measure of the bursting vitality of Vaughan Williams's mind at this time that in 1926, a year after the violin concerto, he should have sketched two movements of the pianoforte concerto which is so very different a work. But both concertos are unmistakably from the same pen.

The central section of *Sancta Civitas* is a clue that, in 1925, work had begun on a setting of *Riders to the Sea*. The marvellous arioso writing for Maurya's long aria is there in genesis. Other clues are in the songs written between 1924 and 1927 where Vaughan Williams seems to be experimenting even further with setting the inflections of speech to music. He certainly chose some intractable material. Fredegond Shove's poetry, one feels, cannot really have attracted him, except possibly 'The Water Mill' which, significantly, produced a song one can justly call Schubertian. 'The New Ghost', well sung, can create a splendid effect, more than partly due to the excellence of the accompaniment. 'Motion and Stillness' is a dreary affair of fourths and fifths in the accompaniment to phrases like 'wasted wreath' and 'evanescent hopes'. For one who in his youth had tackled Rossetti's imagery, perhaps a young relative's poems presented a similar, if less rewarding, challenge. Much better are the three Whitman settings, especially 'Nocturne' with its dark accompaniment, and the Seumas O'Sullivan songs, notably 'The Twilight People'. From this time, too, come the eight Housman settings known as *Along the Field*, itself a beautiful song. Here Vaughan Williams followed Holst's successful example of a solo violin accompaniment, always more congenial to him than the pianoforte. 'Fancy's Knell' is the most ambitious setting, in which the violin provides a dance-tune commentary on the poem; possibly the most haunting is 'The sigh that heaves the grasses'. On the whole, though, these songs have not the melodic interest of the *On Wenlock Edge* cycle; and Vaughan Williams's greatest work for voice and violin remains his unequalled, unforgettable and almost unbearably poignant version of 'The Unquiet Grave'.

The *Te Deum*, composed in 1928, is one of several short occasional religious pieces written in the decade after the war. The most popular is the canticle 'Let us Now Praise Famous Men', a typically strong tune equally suitable for solo or unison singing. 'O Clap Your Hands' is an exultant motet in the composer's church-going 'Ward the Pirate' mood, not always his most convincing style, but in this case apt to its purpose of filling a great cathedral with joyous sounds. More ambitious is 'Lord, Thou Hast Been Our Refuge' in which a psalm setting is combined with 'St. Anne' as a descant. The effect, though undeniably exciting and impressive when well performed, is not wholly convincing because the two tunes seem in uneasily contrived juxtaposition. I say 'seem' because this work is rarely performed with the correct attention to the composer's markings of dynamics. When it is, it is splendid. The *Te Deum*, in G, is sturdy, chiefly in unison but with passages of antiphony. All these works are within the capacity of smaller choral societies; all are enjoyable to perform and each is well written. On a similar level are the *Songs of Praise* hymn-tunes, of which 'At the name of Jesus', in three-part harmony, is nearest in spirit to the *English Hymnal* contributions of twenty years earlier. A small but non-religious work of this period which is a jewel is the *Six Studies in English Folk Song* composed for cello and piano but available in other forms. Five are of the slower tempo of folk tune, the last is a rum-ti-tum

affair. The touching lyricism of this short and beautiful work, so
fresh and loving, is perhaps an off-shoot of the preoccupation with
some of the best of folk songs in the Shakespeare opera which was
first performed in 1929.

Sir John in Love is a big advance on *Hugh the Drover*. It has, of
course, the immeasurable advantage of a Shakespearean libretto
skilfully adapted by the composer and sprinkled with some of the
loveliest, as well as most appropriate, Elizabethan lyrics. Vaughan
Williams was not afraid of tackling the same subject as Verdi,
probably because he instinctively knew that there was ample room
for each composer to bring his own viewpoint to bear on an inexhaustible subject. Comparisons in music between one composer and
another are futile. That Verdi's work is an international masterpiece
should not blind us to the virtues of a great Englishman's setting of
our greatest poet. The one point that can be made is that where
Verdi has concentrated on the swift-moving comedy, Vaughan
Williams has expanded the love music, thus making a much sweeter
work—too sweet for one of its early critics who complained that not
enough of the seamy side of Elizabethan life was displayed in the
opera, this apparently being Vaughan Williams's fault, not the
play's! It must be obvious to anyone who hears the opera that the
romantic music is in the composer's happiest vein. That he changed
the title from his first idea, *The Fat Knight*, to *Sir John in Love* and
interpolated love-poems is sufficient proof of where his own fancy
was engaged. Not that he fails to rise to the comedy. The scene at
the start of Act II when Mrs. Ford and Mrs. Page read aloud their
letters from Falstaff is brilliant in every respect. The characters
are more fully developed than in *Hugh the Drover*, especially the
minor ones: Dr. Caius, for example, who has his moment with
'Vrai dieu d'amours', and Sir Hugh Evans whose mixture of psalm
and Marlowe in Act III is a delicious device. Falstaff is allowed to
have dignity; he is not merely a buffoon and he can laugh at himself.
His love-song in Act II, 'O that joy so soon should waste', is
dramatically funny and musically splendid. Anne Page is followed
through the opera by ravishing harmonies, and melodies as virginally
fresh as she herself. What is outstanding about the whole work—and
what makes its failure to hold a place in the repertory artistically
inexplicable[1]—is its high spirits. Its composer's delight in writing it

[1] One practical explanation in a country where there is no opera repertory company is
that there are too many singing parts.

is apparent from first to last. He has embedded several of his favourite folk songs in the score, but the tunes he has invented himself have all the spontaneity of the best folk song. Anne's 'Weep eyes, break heart', which contains this:

is one of the most beautiful original tunes in the opera, with an oboe accompaniment of delicacy and mellifluous sentiment. The drinking song 'Back and side go bare'

is in the Elizabethan spirit, a remarkable example of a composer 'thinking himself back' into a vanished epoch. 'Sigh no more ladies' is set to a waltz accompaniment for Mrs. Quickly, but it is Mrs. Ford who is given the deservedly famous and miraculously beautiful setting of 'Greensleeves' which opens Act III. But even this is challenged by the wedding chorus for Fenton and Anne in the last act. After the episode in Windsor Forest, the pinching of Falstaff by the fairies and the discovery that Caius has 'married' the page Robin, there is a soft E flat arpeggio and the chorus off-stage is heard singing

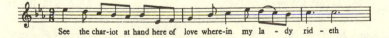

This is one of Vaughan Williams's greatest tunes, anticipated in Act I, and it fills the theatre with its richness and tenderness. Melodically, its climax derives from a theme in the finale of *A Sea Symphony*. Almost anything would then come as an anti-climax, and there is a good example of Vaughan Williams's sense of the theatre as he gradually allows the rapture to recede while Falstaff effects a reconciliation and the opera ends to the chorus 'Whether men do laugh or weep . . . there is underneath the sun nothing in true earnest done', to one of his sturdiest tunes. The additions to the opera which Vaughan Williams made in 1933 are principally worthy of a producer's notice for an extra love-song for Fenton, 'Beauty clear and fair'. Throughout the opera the use of folk songs to delineate character is skilfully justified. In particular 'John come kiss me now' is used as a *leitmotif* for Falstaff's amatory moods in a variety of guises. It is still fair to say, though, that knowledge of these subtleties—such as the introduction of the bawdy 'Lovely Joan' for Mrs. Quickly—is unnecessary for enjoyment of the music. Lastly, the orchestration is done with a light hand; the texture is lucid, the balance between voices and orchestra well judged. In the month of his death I went to a performance of this opera with the composer. As we rode back to Hanover Terrace in a taxi he was deep in thought. Eventually he said he had been 'thinking over' whether he ought to re-score *Sir John* but had decided that it 'would do'. Indeed it will.

Vaughan Williams's enjoyment of private means meant that he could indulge his fancy in writing operas without having to worry if they brought in no return. This had disadvantages too. He was only too glad to authorize performances by students and amateurs, with the result that possibly the operas were underrated from the first. Would they have fared better if England had had a full operatic life? They would almost certainly have done so. The lack of professional performances also meant that he had to teach himself stage techniques in theory, something he was happy and skilful in doing. No doubt he was delighted at the prospect of any kind of performance, for he was under no illusions about the state of operatic affairs in England, as he had confided to Harold Child when they began work on *Hugh the Drover*: 'I see hardly any chance of an opera by an English composer ever being produced, at all events in *our* life-time.' Some good judges had faith in Vaughan Williams's operas from the start. E. J. Dent, writing an eightieth birthday tribute in the *Musical Times* of October 1952, said: 'Future generations may possibly prefer them to his symphonies and choral works.' However that may be, R.V.W. was reconciled to neglect and took the practical course of extracting 'plums' from the operas and issuing them as cantatas. *In Windsor Forest* was the first of these, intended for chorus without soloists which explains the otherwise inexplicable exclusion of 'Greensleeves'.

At one point in its composition it seemed, too, that *Job* might never see stage production as a ballet, but the music had taken such a hold of the composer that he was able—happily for us—to forget the limitations of a theatre pit and score it for full modern orchestra. It was, however, conceived as a stage work and there are sympathetic commentators who think that it achieves full life only in the theatre. Others, among whom I include myself, regard it as equally splendid in the concert-room where it has the stature and cohesion of a symphony. The reasons for the existence of *Job* on two levels may be found in the various sources of its origin: first, the ballet scenario by Keynes; second, Blake's engravings; third, the Biblical text; and fourth, the opportunity to treat the dances of the Elizabethan and Jacobean periods in a symphonic manner. It is clear that Blake and the Bible were the strongest factors in Vaughan Williams's approach. His scenario contains many more quotations from *The Book of Job* than Keynes's, and there are more references in the score to the Blake drawings. Vaughan Williams's mind was always fertile ground for suggestion from literature; less attention has been paid to the impetus he gained from great paintings. The pianoforte score of *Job* includes hints to the choreographer about pictures by Rubens and Botticelli; the hymn-tune 'Mantegna's is so-called because it is a musical representation of Mantegna's painting of the Agony in the Garden; and the setting of the *Magnificat* for mezzo-soprano in 1932 suggested to Vaughan Williams's brother Hervey "a picture by Fra Angelico". In *Job* Vaughan Williams found satisfaction in translating Blake's drawings into sound; he was not at all concerned with their symbolism. In his scenario God is God, not Job's Spiritual Self or Blake's Spiritual Self or anybody else's. The drama and the pictures begat this vivid music. Certain verbal discrepancies between the Keynes and Vaughan Williams scenarios are significant. Job's visions are 'terrifying' in Keynes: in R.V.W. they are 'terrible'; Job and his friends 'shrink in terror' in Keynes; they 'cower' in R.V.W. It is no wonder that the music is itself pictorial enough not to need the stage. Job's pastoral life, Satan's machinations, and Heaven are clearly defined in music. Blake's pictures combine eloquence with simplicity. So does the music. The masque opens serenely, with no hint of the wrath to come. Flute and viola set the pastoral scene, Job's family dance the country dances of a kind they might have known, the sound of distant flocks comes to us as if borne by a gentle breeze. Job's blessing on his children is the first of the impassioned outbursts in which the work abounds:

Satan's appearance is a masterstroke. Once one has heard those two descending octaves on plucked strings and bassoons, pregnant with foreboding, they stay in the mind for ever. They are a true *coup de théâtre*:

Syncopation and sudden clashes of major and minor are Satan's hallmark. Heaven and the throne of God are majestically diatonic, as Vaughan Williams introduces the first of the ancient dances, a Saraband:

Majestic is the only word, too, for the great descending phrase which illustrates God's 'All that he hath is in thy power':

It must be clear from these few examples that this is Vaughan Williams at the height of his power and authority. Even those who had perceived the power and ferocity in the orchestral part of *Sancta Civitas* must in 1930 have been astonished by Satan's Dance of Triumph, which begins after a preliminary snarl and an augmentation of Satan's theme, in spiky single notes, the xylophone prominent, and the mood almost jocular as well as menacing.[1]

[1] This theme, the composer wrote in his 'Chapter of Musical Autobiography', was 'deliberately cribbed' from the scherzo of Beethoven's F major string quartet op. 135.

Gradually the sense of triumphant evil spreads, until a magnificent 'alla marcia' is reached at which the trombones thunder out this phrase  which combines, out of step, with a version of itself on horns and trumpets followed by great leaps for the strings as they take it up. As Satan kneels mockingly before the empty throne, a mock *Gloria in excelsis Deo* is blared by the brass, except for the horns, for nothing so mellow as a horn is allowed to soften this brazen moment. As Satan seats himself on the throne, the full orchestra, triple forte, plays part of the 'All that he hath is in thy power' theme, snapping it short with Satan's motto theme. This dance is comparable in shape and substance with the scherzos of Symphonies No. 4 and 6. The 'Minuet for the Sons of Job and their Wives' might have been by Ravel. Its antique formality is enhanced by the weaving counterpoint of strings and woodwind. This halts as a chord on horns and trumpets above a cymbal roll suddenly swells up like a whirlwind and explodes into Satan's triads, and the shrill strings again tell us that Satan indeed has Job in his power. The minuet becomes a funereal elegy. Scene IV opens with twenty-five bars of tranquil music which could be by no other composer in the world. 'I saw eternity the other night.' Such is one's thought as the violas gently twine their patterns of melody, and past and future are suspended in a timeless present. But with plodding pizzicati in the bass the visions of the night come upon Job, and the holocaust of the modern orchestra blazes in martial sounds for battle, famine, plague, and pestilence. When the messengers tell Job of his bereavement, the cortège is depicted by throbbing drum and bass, lamenting flutes and a beautiful muted *cantabile* tune for the first violins which perhaps owes something to the opening of the work and therefore may represent Job's faith in God despite his afflictions:

Hitherto the orchestral sound, though rich, harsh, frenzied or sonorous as required, has been comparatively conventional. For the three wily hypocrites (Blake's invention; in the Bible the

Comforters, although tiresome, seem sympathetic enough) a new sound is introduced, that of the E flat saxophone, whose glutinous tone, 'andante doloroso', playing the cringing theme of clashing major and minor thirds which Vaughan Williams has composed for it here, is a perfect representation of simulated grief. The dance, slow at first, grows wilder and faster and louder, and ends leaving the saxophone exposed on a high B sharp. The cringing is resumed and understandably drives Job to his cursing of God in a harshly harmonized theme which is another variant of Job's original subject. Heaven opens, the hosts of Hell are seen displayed round Satan parodying the Saraband from Scene I and the full organ lends its power to the terrible vision. Musically and dramatically a contrast is again needed, and this is forthcoming in a rhapsodical violin solo, representing the beautiful Elihu. The accompaniment to this seraphic passage is light and cool, but the violin's notes are warm and vital, quite unlike the remoteness of *The Lark Ascending* with which this passage is often misleadingly compared. The quality of string tone is quite different. As Elihu's solo ascends to its quiet close, the opening strains of the 'Pavane of the Sons of the Morning' sound reassuringly. The first bar is enough to tell us that the night is past, evil has been conquered and the music is moving to its close. The whole orchestra rises to high C, pauses, and Satan enters fortissimo, the opposite of his first, furtive pianissimo entry, to claim victory. But God, with commanding dignity, banishes him, and the earthy steps of a galliard, 'allegro pesante', surely represent a triumph for level-headedness. It is a noble tune:

and it stems from the short *Toccata Marziale* which Vaughan Williams wrote for military band in 1924 and which contains a 'try-out' of the marvellous hieratic writing for brass that dominates the works from 1926 onwards. The jubilation gives way to the allegretto Altar Dance and finally, after a wonderful passage of nine bars in which the orchestra plays clashing diatonic chords and the dynamics ebb and surge from *f* to *pp* to *ff* to *pp* to *fff* to *pp* to *ff* and lastly to *p*, the music of the opening returns and fades away slowly and peacefully in B flat major.

So ends one of Vaughan Williams's mightiest achievements

Musically, it is a perfect reconciliation of the various elements in his style: the lyrical ('pastoral') side, the folk-dance rhythms, the aggressive twentieth-century harmonies, the Purcellian diatonic splendour of a great tune. Historically, it marks the emergence of English ballet, allowing it at a crucial moment to free itself from imitative influence. *Job* is not a virtuoso ballet—indeed, the composer deliberately called it a masque for dancing. Only Satan has much chance to display his technique, but it demands wholehearted participation by every member of the company. Artistically, it represents a successful fusion of painting, literature, music and the dance; moreover, by this one stage work, Vaughan Williams restored to dancing its religious significance as Holst had done in a choral work, *The Hymn of Jesus*, with 'Divine Grace is dancing'. Richard Capell, writing of *Job*, said that Vaughan Williams was 'the one man in the musical world of today with the character, the vision and the strength of style fit to grapple with this drama of heaven and hell'. The vision included the ability, shown on a smaller scale in the *Tallis Fantasia* and the Mass, to bridge the centuries, to re-fertilize the art-forms of the past with a contemporary technique, so that time is in a sense cancelled. There is, however, an enigma. *Job* is regarded as a wholly English work. The Continental musicians who saw the ballet performed at Oxford during the I.S.C.M. festival in late July of 1931 cavilled at the music's lack of novelty because it accepted its methods from the past (as Stravinsky did, in *Oedipus Rex*) and bolstered its ideas in bold harmonies and orchestral 'colour'. They pigeon-holed it as 'nationalist' and confused originality with mere novelty. They failed to see that Vaughan Williams must be viewed, not against nineteenth-century romanticism and the reaction to it in twentieth-century experiment, but against a much broader tradition where he can be seen as a unique figure drawing together the threads of many centuries. To describe a work like *Job* in purely nationalist terms is to do its composer a disservice. Its picturesque qualities are secondary to its spiritual light, a light that is universal as well as particular.

As with other major works, *Job* produced its satellites from its composer's pen. One, the Prelude and Fugue in C minor, played in 1930 at Hereford six weeks before *Job* was played at Norwich, is an orchestration of two organ pieces, laid aside since 1921. The scoring has the power of *Job*, but the material has not. The *Benedicite*, of 1929, combines lusty choral jubilation with a gentler hymn for soprano in pastoral style, and rather harsh, unrelenting orchestration—the pianoforte is used as a percussive instrument—with 'a cappella' choral passages. Diatonic chords and modal scales alternate, and the consecutive fifths for the men's voices verge here on mannerism. The work is essentially for wholehearted admirers of the composer, who relish its vigorous style. Like all he did, it is never workaday and it is grand to sing. Its best moments are unfailingly moving. On the whole, however, it seems to be a study for works then unwritten rather than a completely achieved unity. It was chosen for the I.S.C.M.'s London concerts in 1931 where it was magnificently performed under Boult and was acclaimed as a 'masterpiece' by critics as percipient as Eric Blom. Aaron Copland was present and wrote afterwards of the work's 'bourgeois grandeur' and 'inherent banality'. It led him to write Vaughan Williams off as 'the kind of local composer who stands for something great in the musical development of his own country but whose actual musical contribution cannot bear exportation. Besides, he is essentially not modern at all. . . . His is the music of a gentleman farmer, noble in inspiration but dull.' Mr. Copland was young then, and he had the grace to eat his words in the light of later works.[1] However, one can see his point of view. The distinction between the works of wide vision, such as *Job*, and those of more modest intent, written with as much integrity but at less exalted a level, was not sufficiently understood by some of the composer's admirers. If it had been, intelligent people like Mr. Copland could have saved themselves from half-digested judgements.

Eleven days before conducting the first performance of *Job*, Vaughan Williams was fifty-eight. That he was at the height of his powers was evident. But a critic would have needed to be clairvoyant to foretell then the intensification to follow in the next twenty-seven years, for there are few examples in the history of mankind of a creative artist doing his richest work between the ages of sixty and eighty-five.

---

[1] *Copland on Music*, by Aaron Copland (London, 1961), p. 197.

CHAPTER EIGHT

1931–1943

Principal Works

PIANOFORTE CONCERTO . MAGNIFICAT
SYMPHONY (NO. 4) IN F MINOR . FIVE TUDOR PORTRAITS
THE POISONED KISS . DONA NOBIS PACEM
RIDERS TO THE SEA . SERENADE TO MUSIC
THE BRIDAL DAY . SYMPHONY (NO. 5) IN D MAJOR

I

THE music of *Job* was played for the second time, conducted by the composer, in a broadcast performance from the London Regional station at Savoy Hill on 13 February 1931. By now British ballet had been born, with the foundation, early in 1930, of the Camargo Society. Geoffrey Keynes and his brother Maynard (whose wife was Lydia Lopokova) were among the leaders of this brave venture, and it was decided—on the insistence of Gustav Holst—that *Job* should be produced in the Society's fourth season. The Keynes brothers and T. F. Dunhill bore the expense and Ninette de Valois was invited to be the choreographer. She and Lilian Baylis, of the Old Vic, had already seen and approved the Raverat settings on a model stage which Dr. Keynes and Mrs. Raverat had made in 1927. Miss de Valois studied the whole range of Blake's drawings in order to gain suggestions for attitudes and gestures. Eventually, on Sunday, 5 July 1931, the ballet was performed at the Cambridge Theatre, London, with Anton Dolin as Satan and Stanley Judson as Elihu. It was repeated the next day and again on 24 July at Oxford as part of the ninth festival of the International Society for Contemporary Music which in this year was held in London and Oxford. Vaughan Williams had not been completely happy with some aspects of the production—the '*Job* tyranny' he called it in a letter to Maud Karpeles—and there was

227

consideration among the three originators of the ballet about the order of Scenes IV and V. R.V.W. wrote from Dorking to Gwen Raverat some time between the Oxford performance and the first Old Vic performance on 22 September 1931:

'I've been carefully thinking over the *Job* situation and I don't mind trying the alteration of the order of the scenes (say at the Old Vic) *as an experiment*. It will only involve (again if we consider it experimentally) a little alteration in the opening and closing bars of the music. But in this case (indeed in any case) the *dancing* must be radically changed. It must be danced *at* Job and not at the audience and it must be *terrifying* and not comic and I think should have a *fuller* stage and Satan should not I think dance in it. But he should *start* it with a realization of the "Satan with his torch"* illustration which was absolutely not realized at all by Ninette. But this does not solve the difficulty of the messenger scene. It is quite impossible for those 3 dancers to fill out all that music—so either it must be drastically cut or my procession idea must come off. I can't see why it should be absurd if kept vague enough—figures carrying burdens moving slowly in procession across the back of the stage (after all you see the countryside all in flames and all the refugees must have been hurrying away from the "devastated area"). I've seen such processions on the stage and I know they "come off".

'Another problem will be this: The scenes at present are Job asleep—Boils—Job wakes up—Messengers—Shall we still start with Job asleep and woken up by the messengers? But then before the "boils" he must also be asleep (or at all events lying down) (see illustration) and he can't go to sleep *twice*. Perhaps the opening music might be taken to suggest just calm and not sleep—but it all requires some thought. Would you mind sending this letter (or the substance of it) to Geoffrey Keynes who has written me a kind but reproving letter on the subject (more in sorrow than in anger, I think).'

* 'I agree that this illustration is probably the finest but it doesn't follow that it makes a good *stage* climax. Also I don't feel inclined necessarily to read into it all that Wicksteed and others say that it means. I am only interested in the *picture itself* and the texts with which *Blake* surrounds it.'

The results of this discussion are to be seen in the full score of *Job* where the producer is given leave to include Scene V immediately after Job's twenty-five bars of sleep. In practice this is hardly ever done. The ballet soon established itself. An independent version was danced in New York at the Lewisohn Stadium on 25 and 26 August 1931, by the Denishawn Dancers conducted by

Hans Lange. The choreography was by Ted Shawn, who also danced the part of Satan. The Camargo revived it in the summer of 1932 and took it to Copenhagen in September of that year. From 1932 onwards it remained in the Vic-Wells (later Sadler's Wells) Ballet repertoire and was first presented on the large stage of the Royal Opera House, Covent Garden, in May 1948. It was in this production that the use of a mask (originally designed by Hedley Briggs and later by Doria Paston) for God was abandoned, since any risk of police prosecution was by then thought to be remote. The concert version of the music made its way slowly at first. It was played at the Gloucester Festival on 10 September 1931, and at a Royal Philharmonic concert under Basil Cameron on 3 December of that year when a 'miserably small audience' gave it a cold reception.[1] Its career began in earnest when its dedicatee, Adrian Boult, took it up with the B.B.C. Symphony Orchestra and, by thorough rehearsal, enabled its full stature to be appreciated. Boult conducted it first in a B.B.C. studio concert on 19 February 1933, and in public for the first time at the Canterbury Festival on 8 June 1933.[2] Between 1935 and 1939 he conducted it in Salzburg, Geneva, Monte Carlo, Chicago, and Brussels.

After *Job* and the business of settling down in a new home, creative work began again. The Pianoforte Concerto of which Vaughan Williams had written two movements in 1926 was looked over, a third movement was added, and by the end of May 1931 the work was sufficiently complete to be played through at St. Paul's Girls' School by three of Holst's helpers, Vally Lasker, Nora Day and Helen Bidder. It was sent to Harriet Cohen, for whom it was written, in the last week of October 1931. *Songs of Praise* was enlarged. Then he was revising the opera *Riders to the Sea* which he had begun in 1925. A letter to Holst[3] in December 1930 asking for 'a lesson on "Riders" soon' states that he has been 'revising and

---

[1] *Musical Times*, January 1932.

[2] The next day Boult wrote to Humphrey Milford of the O.U.P. pleading for the full score to be printed because there was only one score and one set of MS. parts. He said: 'I feel so strongly about it that if you feel it could only be done through some scheme of private subscription I would do what I have not done for ages and that is offer to help in collecting subscriptions. . . .' Milford had already received a similar suggestion from Miss Leslie Wanklyn of the Bach Choir, whom Boult had previously approached. The Bach Choir eventually collected £100 towards the cost of engraving and the O.U.P. undertook to pay this to the Musicians' Benevolent Fund as profits came in.

[3] *Heirs and Rebels*, op. cit., p. 75.

rough scoring' it. In the Spring of 1932, as we can also deduce from a letter to Holst (who was visiting America) dated 20 March, he was at work on his *Magnificat* for Astra Desmond to sing at the Worcester Festival. He was trying, he said, 'to lift the words out of the smug atmosphere which had settled down on it from being sung at evening service for so long. (I've tried hard to get the smugness out; I don't know if I have succeeded—I find it awfully hard to eradicate it.)'[1] The work was started after a conversation at Gloucester in 1931 when Steuart Wilson had remarked that it was 'not quite nice' for young unmarried women like Elsie Suddaby always to be singing Magnificats, and Astra Desmond had said to R.V.W.: 'I'm a married woman with four children. Why don't you write one for me?' Holst's comment on this was that 'Steuart's theology sounds a little unorthodox but his common sense is unquestionable'. Most important of all, and occupying Vaughan Williams's mind most, was the new symphony, to be No. 4 in F minor, on which he had started work in 1931, two years before Hitler came to full power in Germany. Who can tell when a great work begins to grow in its creator's mind? An accident can begin the process of writing it down—in this case, reading a critic's description of a typical 'modern' European symphony—but the F minor symphony had been germinating for years before that, in the *Toccata Marziale* of 1924, in *Sancta Civitas*, in the Pianoforte Concerto and, most obviously, in *Job* when Job curses the day in which he was born. The music had progressed some way by early 1932, for on 6 January Vally Lasker and Helen Bidder played it through at St. Paul's Girls' School. Alterations must have been suggested, for Holst, writing from America, on 15 April 1932, asked: 'How's the New Sym.? When I get home in July I want a 2 piano field day of both old and new versions.' The two friends were never closer than in these last years of Holst's life. 'I miss you very much when I want to know how to compose—in fact I didn't realize how much you write of my music,' R.V.W. in Dorking wrote to Holst at Harvard; and Holst in reply recounted an experience he had had while ill in Washington and 'was sinking so low that I couldn't go much further and remain on earth. . . . As soon as I reached the bottom I had one clear, intense and calm feeling—that of overwhelming gratitude. And the four chief reasons for gratitude were

[1] Ibid., p. 79.

Music, the Cotswolds, R.V.W. and having known the impersonality of orchestral playing.'[1]

To his closest friends Vaughan Williams's warm and excitable nature was well known. To the world at large at this time less was known about him. An article by Basil Maine in the *Morning Post* of 8 August 1930, gives a revealing contemporary view. The self-effacing quality of this musician, Maine wrote, 'does not always appear as such when one meets him.

As likely as not, it takes on some other form and leads to a misunderstanding of the man. To some he may appear curt, to others gruff, to others clumsy, and to others an angry man. . . . Whenever he makes public appearances there is always the danger that he will be misunderstood. If he has been called to acknowledge the successful performance of one of his works . . . you would never guess from his flurried entry, awkward bow and anxious retreat that he is grateful. If you are watching him conduct the Bach B minor Mass you will not perhaps believe that he is an extremely sensitive man, one whose conceptions are the result of the mingling of great strength and beautiful imagination. . . . The truth is that Vaughan Williams is essentially a man of solitude. Whenever he has been called upon to be a public servant in the cause of music, he has succeeded only too well in veiling his characteristics. . . . This is less true of his work as composition professor at the Royal College of Music and of his direction of the music of the English Folk Dance Society; for in each of these connections his duties are only semi-public and there is, therefore, a greater opportunity for him to reveal the essential qualities of his personality. . . . It is in the solitary places that Vaughan Williams is most himself. Is he therefore unknowable? Yes, unknowable to all save musicians in tune with his musical manner of thinking.'

Articles such as this, sympathetic and well-meant but sprinkled with half-truths, did much to create a public image of an 'aloof figure' which must have raised psychological barriers to proper appreciation of some of his works. There is a confusion of meaning between 'solitude' and 'loneliness'. Both R.V.W. and Holst were anything but men of solitude. They enjoyed the company of vast numbers of friends from all stations in life. But both knew the loneliness which is at the heart of all artistic creation—and neither could suffer fools gladly. They were at their happiest making music either with professionals or amateurs. When Vaughan Williams was conducting the Bach Mass in B minor with the Leith Hill Festival

[1] *Heirs and Rebels*, pp. 79–81.

choirs in the 1920s, there came an awkward moment in the final
rehearsal when, after several barks of annoyance, his anger exploded
in one of his sudden, swift and terrible spasms of fury: 'You will
never be able to sing Bach! Never.' A silence, but no resentment,
because the Surrey choirs knew that this was merely an outward
and visible sign of his passionate enthusiasm. 'Bar 42,' They sang
on to the end. 'Why couldn't you sing like that at first?' was the
final comment from the rostrum. Living at Dorking made his contacts with the Leith Hill Festival even fuller, although he had stayed
each year before that at Leith Hill Place for all the rehearsals and
concerts. There was never any question of 'the great man' arriving
for the last day to take over somebody else's prepared performance.
In the summer he helped make the schedule for the next spring,
attended the conductors' conferences of the three choral divisions,
held in December and January, at which a few from each choir sang
through the festival music under his direction. He attached great
importance to understanding by the choirs of the story of the main
choral work and would explain the synopsis, pointing out which
passages emphasized the work's drama and atmosphere. 'Having
run through the music he would put down his baton and say: "This
is how I want the work sung at the concert; at the competition you
will sing it as your conductor directs—I cannot promise you that
the adjudicator will approve of my interpretation." '[1] Later in the
season he took combined rehearsals of the choirs and on the days of
the festivals there were rehearsals each afternoon with orchestra and
soloists. Promising singers were always given an engagement at the
festival, and there was a succession of gifted pianists as its 'official'
accompanist, the first of them Henry Bird, followed by Leslie
Heward, Arnold Goldsbrough, Michael Mullinar, Eric Harrison,
and Eric Gritton. The orchestra was a mixture of gifted amateurs
and professionals. Vaughan Williams paid his tribute to the Leith
Hill kind of music-making in the preface he wrote for Sir Henry
Hadow's book *English Music*[2] published in 1931:

'If we want to find the groundwork of our English culture we must look
below the surface—not to the grand events chronicled in the newspapers
but to the unobtrusive quartet parties which meet week after week to play

[1] Miss Margery Cullen, hon. secretary of Leith Hill Festival, in *R.C.M. Magazine*,
Vol. LV, No. 1, Easter Term 1959.
[2] *English Music*, by Sir W. H. Hadow (London, 1931).

or sing in their own houses, to the village choral societies whose members trudge miles through rain and snow to work steadily for a concert or competition in some ghastly parish room with a cracked piano and a smelly oil lamp where one week there is no tenor because at the best there are only two, and one has a cold and the other being the village doctor is always called out at the critical moment; and there they sit setting their teeth so as to wrench the heart out of this mysterious piece of music which they are starting to learn for the coming competition.'

A picture drawn from life.

The introduction to Hadow's book is the most pungent of Vaughan Williams's statements of his beliefs. It has a vitality which still makes it stand out on the printed page. It is in an angry, even slightly embittered, vein, for in 1930 he perhaps realized that the English musical life he had hoped might emerge from the war was still dominated by influences he himself had fought to shed, even though there was no doubt of the existence of a new and talented group of composers. His principal target was artistic snobbery.

Despite the amount of work on his study desk, he still went up to London to teach at the R.C.M., still took a most active part in all the activities of the English Folk Dance Society and was always ready to help a friend.

Perhaps his pupils knew his worth as much as anyone did. He believed profoundly in a solid foundation—'Knowing your stodge', he called it, meaning strict counterpoint and fugue—but thereafter he was guide rather than autocrat. 'We can't teach these young people anything except what has been done already,' he said. 'If they want to write original music they've got to make their own technique for themselves.' Those pupils were perhaps most fortunate, as Gordon Jacob suggests, who went to him after about 1925 when 'he came to realize that [technical ability] did not necessarily add up to superficial slickness'.[1] Many went for lessons at 13 Cheyne Walk, just as he had gone to Parry at 17 Kensington Square. Fiona Mc-Cleary, for instance, daughter of his old Cambridge friend George, remembers[2] nervously ringing the bell on her first visit. 'The door opened and there he was. Tall, large, dressed in a heavy, loose-tweed suit, with a shock of grey hair and a kind smile of welcome. "Upstairs," he said. "I'm afraid it's quite a climb." There were three steep flights of stairs in that narrow, old house, leading to his

[1] *R.C.M. Magazine*, Vol. LV, No. 1, Easter Term 1959, p. 31.
[2] In a private letter.

workroom on the top floor. Manuscripts, books and papers were scattered all over the room. Against the wall stood a small upright piano. "I'm afraid it's very much out of tune," he said, rather apologetically.' Then would come the disarming and encouraging compliment. 'I wish I could write like that for the piano.' Michael Mullinar[1] remembered the ceremony of 'clearing the table of tobacco tins, pipes, pipe cleaners and match boxes galore before we could find room for our music. He was hardly ever without a pipe in his mouth.' The teaching, Mullinar said, was 'not orthodox and possibly it would not even be of great help for an examination. He never used textbooks and always stressed his point with examples from live music. He always said "Go to the music itself and not the textbooks". . . . In looking over a pupil's composition he would put his finger on the weak spot and say "I don't think you are writing what you really want here. Think it over carefully for a few days though, before you alter it".' Sometimes, in Grace Williams's[2] experience, he despaired because he couldn't find the weak spot right away. 'In order to encourage us to take criticism from each other he got us to form a composers' club. . . . He was all for our having our works played over by fellow-students and he did all he could to get them tried over by one or other of the college orchestras.' Elizabeth Maconchy[3] perhaps understood him best: 'Many people have said he was "humble", but I think of him as above both pride and humility; he was simply himself. . . . He was always on the side of the young [and] somehow imparted to his pupils his own attitude to composition, a complete and uncalculating devotion to music.' Miss Maconchy, like Dr. Jacob, was a pupil during the period when Vaughan Williams 'distrusted' brilliance in any form: 'He had no use for ready-made solutions.' As he grew older and took a few private pupils at Dorking, he would surprise some of them with outspoken comments and frank admissions such as they hardly expected to hear from England's senior composer. 'Variety within the scope of unity' was a watchword he gave to Gerald Cockshott.[4] 'If you keep doing a thing ask yourself "Is this a strength or a weakness?" and do something else. It may be a strength, but in any case you'll come back to it with extra strength.' He could not under-

---

[1] *R.C.M. Magazine*, Vol. LV, No. 1, Easter Term 1959, pp. 32-3.
[2] Op. cit., pp. 36-7.
[3] Op. cit., pp. 33-4.
[4] Information supplied by Mr. Cockshott.

stand pupils who took him unfinished works and said they did not
know how the music would go on. How couldn't they know? He
told them to improvise. 'You either think of a tune or you don't:
it's the getting from one to another that's the difficulty in composition.' He would cite the slow movement of Schubert's Great
C major symphony as an example of how to get from one tune to
another—'but there are too many of them'. Pupils knew that they
could always go back to him, and many of them did, to the end of his
life, to seek advice. He would travel miles to rehearsals of their
works or, if they were chamber works, would invite the composers to
bring players to his house. He was not the inspired teacher that
Holst was, but by sheer force of character he gave to dozens of
young people the vital things he had gained from Max Bruch: confidence and encouragement; and his friendship.

By leading a busy life he found that he worked best. 'I am sure
that one must take care of the pence in life and let the pounds take
care of themselves,' he wrote to Maud Karpeles, 'i.e. that if you hold
your head in the air and think great thoughts when you should be
doing the obvious chores of life the great thoughts won't come.'

Holst returned to England in June 1932, and Vaughan Williams
sailed in September for his second visit to the United States, where
he was to give the Mary Flexner Lectures on the Humanities at
Bryn Mawr College, Pennsylvania. These were published in 1934
under the title *National Music*. Several extracts from this statement of his artistic beliefs have already been given in Chapter III.

A fortnight before he sailed he had conducted the first performance of his *Magnificat* in Worcester Cathedral. Colles found the
orchestral opening 'rather more like Holst than himself'—a similarity
emphasized because *The Hymn of Jesus* had preceded the new work.
But 'the general plan of the *Magnificat* is entirely individual. . . .
Its beauty was emphasized in Miss Astra Desmond's intelligent
interpretation.' On his return, his first concern was the first performance of the Pianoforte Concerto, given at a B.B.C. Symphony
Concert on 1 February 1933, conducted by Boult, with Harriet
Cohen, to whom it was dedicated, as soloist. Schubert's *Unfinished
Symphony* was the only concession to popular favour in the pro-
gramme, for in the second half Bax's *Garden of Fand* and Delius's
Sea Drift were played.

Writing to Harriet Cohen four days before the first performance
he said:

'I have written to Adrian and told him that if you both feel that it is overscored anywhere he has *carte blanche* to thin out the orchestration all he thinks fit. Gustav will, I hope, be there to advise. I do hope you are better—and I know that well or ill you are going to play BEAUTIFULLY. One small point—the 2 bars of Arnold—I like them *slower* (I know Wood takes it quicker)—quite slow and very far off like a dream.'

This referred to a quotation from the Epilogue of Bax's Third Symphony which originally occurred in the finale of the concerto. R.V.W. was a great admirer of this beautiful symphony, and the inclusion of this quotation was a symbol of the friendship between Bax, Miss Cohen and himself.

The concerto had a divided reception and one malcontent in the Queen's Hall hissed it. Its percussive nature and the harsh harmonic idiom militated against its appreciation in a country which knew hardly anything of Bartók's and Hindemith's similar works. Colles even suggested that the work might not have become a piano concerto if the composer had not promised one to Miss Cohen. 'To those who still retain a preconceived notion of what a piano concerto should be, Vaughan Williams's work could not be very acceptable,' he wrote in *The Times* of 2 February. To others it was 'more surprising to find to what extent he had made the combination of piano and orchestra amenable to the expression of his own ideas'. Colles found the end of the finale unconvincing. 'Perhaps the composer shared with the pianist some personal secret about it. . . . Otherwise why did he bring in a quotation from Bax's Third Symphony just before the end?' This quotation puzzled other people, and it was removed from the score. The concerto found immediate champions in Frank Howes and Hubert Foss, but it found few among pianists, and still has not found many, even in its revised, two-piano version. Afterwards R.V.W. wrote to Maud Karpeles: 'I am so glad you like it because I rather do myself (when I don't hate it, as I do all my tunes in turn). I'm making one or two improvements before it is done again (if ever).'

It was done again, but its career was chequered. Leopold Stokowski had hoped for the first performance but it had already been promised to the B.B.C. A projected New York performance in 1933 failed to materialize. Vaughan Williams wrote to Miss Cohen:

'. . . I'm so sorry N.Y. doesn't want the concerto—but no one ever likes my stuff the first time—so we must put up with that. Also I *can't* push

my own stuff. I'm not made that way. . . . By the way before you play it
again (if you do) let me have good notice as I want to make some alterations. The fugue wants lengthening and the cadenzas want altering. . . .'

In July 1933 there was talk of a performance under Hermann
Scherchen. R.V.W. wrote to Miss Cohen on 22 July:

'It is v. exciting about the concerto but rather upsetting. I meant to have
rewritten the last movement to make it better for you—I kept putting it
off and off till I could approach it with a calm mind. Now it's got to go
once again in its old form. One slight alteration I think we can make. The
"quotation" at the end of the work does not "come off"—*we* understand
it, but the audience does not. So I will in the next few days think out a
new ending, only about 4 new bars for you to learn.'

He wrote again on 2 August:

'I trust you entirely—please do what you like with the pfte. part. Now
about the *end*—as I said in a former letter, the quotation from Arnold is
a mistake for public performance. But thinking it over I *cannot* substitute
anything. So please *omit* it and go straight from the end of the cadenza
to the final bars.'

After hearing Miss Cohen rehearse the concerto at the end of
August, Vaughan Williams decided to make a big alteration in the
cadenza which leads into the waltz in the finale. This was done by
25 October, but there were still doubts about the Scherchen
performance, as this undated letter shows:

'I'm so sorry about all this—my unhappy concerto seems born to
trouble as the sparks fly upward. As far as I am concerned my compositions are done when I hear the first performance and I leave the rest to
others (you among others!)—very selfish of me, I know, but I *must* have
peace to think of the next piece. . . . I sometimes feel inclined to tear up
all my music and have nothing to do with public performance, it's all
dead sea fruit. . . .'

In the event, Scherchen conducted the concerto, with Miss
Cohen as soloist, at Strasbourg where Bartók heard and much
admired it.

One other important letter, dated 10 June 1934, refers tactfully
to the suitable length of time for a soloist to have exclusive performance of a work:

'How long do you think you ought to have the concerto before it is
thrown open by publication or otherwise? I don't know in the least what

is right to do. I gave Jelly a 6 months run of my violin concerto (not that she made much use of it). How long did Kreisler keep the Elgar concerto? Personally I don't think anyone else will ever *want* to play it because you and Arnold (and possibly myself) are the only 3 people who like it, and as to students I know you are far too generous to mind some student from Birmingham Midland Institute (such as wrote to me the other day) having it to *study*. I don't think there was any question of public performance.'

To return to 1933, the rest of the year was taken up with revision of the new symphony, enlarging and revising the *English Hymnal*, various conducting engagements, writing the accompaniments to Maud Karpeles's Newfoundland folk songs[1] and with giving helpful advice on the biography of Cecil Sharp being written by Fox Strangways and Miss Karpeles to which he contributed a note on the accompaniments, written partly 'as an answer to Foxy's statement that Sharp was not a creative artist'.

In September Vaughan Williams conducted *The Shepherds of the Delectable Mountains* at Hereford, and disliked its performance as a cantata. On this subject it is interesting to have the comments of Sir Percy Hull, organist at Hereford from 1918 to 1950, who wrote to me: 'In 1926 I heard a performance of *The Shepherds* staged in Bristol and I returned to Hereford convinced that it was most suitable for the cathedral. I wrote to V.W. that I proposed to perform it there the following year and asked whether he would conduct "the first performance otherwise than on the stage". A somewhat furious letter arrived *by return* refusing to have anything to do with it! He said it would be entirely out of place, most unsuitable and would most certainly get me into trouble. My answer was "Right, then I'll do it without you". A week or so before the festival, another letter came asking the time of final rehearsal of soloists and orchestra in London and whether I still wanted him to conduct. My reply was "Do as you like". He turned up at the R.C.M. and went through the work and asked whether he should do it at the festival. Of course I consented but "not if it goes against the grain". He afterwards confessed that his judgement as to the suitability of the work in the cathedral, etc., was entirely wrong and that he really

---

[1] In a letter to Miss Karpeles about one of these songs he wrote: 'Why do you call it Lord Bateman in the title? If she sang Lord Akeman it ought to be so called and, if you like, Lord Bateman added as a sub-title underneath. I can't bear this habit of calling "The Water is Wide" "Waly Waly" and so on.'

enjoyed the performance. . . . I put the work in the Hereford programme again in 1933 and this gave him great pleasure and he again completely revised his judgement about its suitability in the cathedral.'

As has been seen from R.V.W.'s letter to Ernest Irving quoted in Chapter Six, he nevertheless remained opposed to non-stage performance.

By December 1933 he was able to write to Holst: 'The "nice" tunes in the finale [of the F minor symphony] have already been replaced by better ones (at all events they are *real* ones). What I mean is that I *knew* the others were made-up stuff and these are not. So there we are.'

He had been working over a previous symphony, the *London*, which Beecham conducted in a revised version[1] at the Royal Philharmonic on 22 February 1934, the eve of Edward Elgar's death at Worcester. The personal relationship between Vaughan Williams and Elgar had been closer in recent years although they were never intimates. The history of their friendship is not easy to trace. Among their first meetings was that at the Cardiff Festival in 1907 when both were after-dinner speakers, but Vaughan Williams, in a broadcast on the occasion of the Elgar centenary in 1957, said: 'The first time, I think, when I had a conversation with Elgar was on the occasion of a performance of his Violoncello Concerto, when he approached me rather truculently and said "I am surprised, Dr. Vaughan Williams, that you care to listen to this vulgar stuff!" The truth was, I think, that he was feeling sore over an accusation of vulgarity made against him by a well-known musicologist who Elgar probably knew was a friend of mine.'

This must refer to E. J. Dent, but the meeting must have long preceded Dent's article in 1931 in Adler's *Handbuch der Musikgeschichte*, in which he called Elgar's music 'too emotional and not quite free from vulgarity'. Vaughan Williams disapproved of the attitude to Elgar instilled into students by Dent. Approval was withheld from composers who had not been taught by Stanford, were not knowledgeable about the sixteenth century or were not influenced by folk

---

[1] Colles, in *The Times* of 23 February, put it well, describing the symphony as 'like London itself, in that the builders will not let it alone. Dr. Vaughan Williams had knocked down one or two of his smaller buildings before this performance—nothing very considerable but enough to make those who have known and loved the work for 20 years a little anxious. . . . We do not want a shorter *London Symphony*. . . . Part of the charm of the work is that, like the city which inspired it, it is not too logically planned.'

song. On all these counts Vaughan Williams was 'in' and Elgar 'out', but such a narrow view was anathema to Vaughan Williams. Sir Hugh Allen always referred to *Gerontius* as 'the Nightmare' and his friendship with R.V.W. may also have been an inhibiting factor to Elgar. It is sometimes difficult for sensitive and complex people, such as Elgar was, to appreciate that friends do not necessarily share each other's opinions wholeheartedly. Elgar and Vaughan Williams met many times at Three Choirs Festivals. In 1922, at a rehearsal of Parry's *Symphonic Variations*, R.V.W. was especially struck by the music's 'curious, spiky sound. I said "I suppose this ought to be considered bad orchestration, but I like it". Elgar turned on me almost fiercely and said "Of course it's not bad orchestration, this music could be scored in no other way".'[1] When Elgar was rehearsing his Second Symphony at its first Three Choirs performance in 1912, Vaughan Williams was sitting next to Lady Elgar who, he told me, 'kept nudging my elbow in the slow movement and saying "Isn't it lovely?" It was lovely, of course, but it wasn't her business to say so.' From the mid-1920s, Elgar was 'always gracious and friendly' to Vaughan Williams. 'He wished us to be on Christian name terms, and even invited me to call him Teddy. This I could not do. He was at least ten years [actually fifteen] older than me and was already famous, so I compromised, agreeing to drop Sir and Dr.'[2] At the end it was less formal. There exists a postcard sent from the nursing home in Worcester where Elgar lay ill, dated 27 December 1933. It was dictated, but Elgar signed it, the signature of a dying man. It reads:

My dear Ralph,
    Many thanks for your card. I send you all good wishes for the New Year. My love to you. Yours ever,
                                        Edward Elgar.

A greater personal blow was to fall on 25 May when Gustav Holst died after an operation. His health had given increasing concern to his family and friends for the two years since his return from America. If Ralph and Gustav had seemed to grow apart musically in the mid-1920s, the 1930s had brought them together again. *Job*, the fourth symphony, *Riders to the Sea* and the Pianoforte Concerto all met with Holst's approval though he was to hear only two of

---

[1] 'Chapter of Musical Autobiography.'
[2] B.B.C. broadcast, 1957.

them as completed works. Of Holst's last works, R.V.W. was especially enthusiastic about the Choral Fantasia of 1930 which he declared was 'IT all right' and after the first performance at Gloucester on 8 September 1931, at which the work was severely mauled by the critics, he wrote: 'It is *most* beautiful—I know you don't care, but I just want to tell the press (and especially * * * *) that they are misbegotten abortions.' Six weeks before Holst's death, R.V.W. was able to write to him enthusiastically about his *Choral Symphony*, that work for which, nine years before, he had had to profess only cold admiration. The Grecian Urn slow movement, he wrote, is '*you*, which is all I know and all I need to know'. He felt poignantly that Holst's life-work was incomplete. Now there would be no more letters, no more 'Field Days'. The candid friend who had shared the early struggles was no longer there for consultation. Vaughan Williams was stricken. He conducted the music at the funeral service; he wrote about him in the *R.C.M. Magazine* saying, 'He may have now found in new regions that which his music ever seemed to be seeking.' He wrote no music *in memoriam*. That was not his way. But in the next twenty-five years he wrote several works, the Sixth Symphony chief among them, in which his old friend's influence still seems to be discernible. He missed Holst's criticism and encouragement till the end of his life. During the time in which he worked with him, Roy Douglas felt that the man Vaughan Williams wanted to consult more than any other was not there. When in 1958 R.V.W. died there were only two photographs in his bedroom: of F. W. Maitland and of Gustav Holst.

Vaughan Williams composed music for the English Folk Dance and Song Society's Masque in 1934 and he also contributed some to the Pageant of Abinger held on 14 and 18 July in aid of Abinger Church's Preservation Fund. Abinger was the centre of a lively artistic community. R. C. Trevelyan and his wife lived there, as well as E. M. Forster, who wrote the pageant, and, later, Cecil and Sylvia Sprigge. Lord and Lady Farrer were at Abinger Hall, old friends of the Vaughan Williamses, and John Evelyn's descendants were still at Wotton. The music for the pageant was principally folk songs and dances, metrical psalm tunes and plainsong, and was played by the Band of the 2nd Bn. West Yorkshire Regiment (Prince of Wales's Own). Such affairs are often the butt of sophisticated humour, but how many villages have had a pageant written by E. M. Forster with music by Vaughan Williams and produced by Tom Harrison? In this year, too, the *Magnificat* received its first London perform-ance and the Viola Suite, written for Lionel Tertis, was played at a Courtauld-Sargent concert in November. Now that Holst had gone, R.V.W. asked Gordon Jacob to look over his scores. He took him the 'Moto Perpetuo' from the Suite and represented the solo part 'by a continuous buzzing through his teeth whilst he played the irregularly rhythmed chords of the accompaniment not always with complete accuracy'.[1] A Promenade Concert on 27 September was devoted entirely to his music, which he conducted, and introduced the famous arrangement of 'Greensleeves' as a fantasia and a quod-libet on dance tunes, *The Running Set*, which he had made for a Folk Dance Festival. Herbert Hughes, in the *Saturday Review* of 6 October 1934, called the latter 'a gorgeous little work' and pro-phesied for it a future comparable with Ravel's *Bolero*. 'There was in it,' he wrote, 'a gaiety, a gusty exhilaration of which I had never suspected V.W. . . . not until now had he shown such mastery of sheer liveliness, such brilliance of orchestration. The bringing in of "The Cock o' the North" as the climax of excitement was the final, unexpected and incredible Dionysian touch.' Hughes regarded the critical appraisal of the Mass, the *Tallis Fantasia* and the *London Symphony* as 'mumbling' and 'purblind'. . . . 'In the end, of course, it is the amateur not the professional music-taster who decides. And it is the amateur who will discover the real Vaughan Williams and take this jolly Quodlibet to his heart and keep it there.' But he hasn't. A writer in the *Sunday Referee* alleged that the climax of the *Running Set* was 'that well-known ditty "Chase me Charlie, Chase me Charlie, I've lost a leg of my drawers" '. This drew a letter from The White Gates protesting against the accusation of using 'a tune with an offensive and disgusting title. I have no knowledge of a tune with this name. The "well-known air" which I introduced into the *Running Set* was "The Cock o' the North", a tune which I hoped would be recognized even by critics.'

The year 1935 was to prove momentous in Vaughan Williams's life. The English musical scene in the mid-1930s was lively enough compared with only five years before. Boult and Wood and the B.B.C. Symphony Orchestra were performing rare and expensive works in the studios and in the Queen's Hall—Schoenberg conducted his *Variations*, three extracts from Berg's *Wozzeck* were performed,

[1] *R.C.M. Magazine*, Vol. LV, No. 1, p. 31.

and a Hindemith oratorio. Ravel conducted the first performance of his G major Piano Concerto. Italian composers such as Pizzetti were performed. Stravinsky was well represented. Was this really so 'blinkered' an outlook? Bax's symphonies were appearing now, and Walton's *Belshazzar's Feast*, at Leeds in 1931, had justified faith confirmed in 1934 when three movements of his First Symphony were performed by the London Symphony Orchestra under Sir Hamilton Harty. The names of Ireland and Frank Bridge were not rarities in concert programmes: a work, *A Boy Was Born*, by a young pupil of theirs was published in 1934. The composer's name was Benjamin Britten. It was Elgar who was comparatively neglected by the swing of fashion, and others of his generation such as Bantock. The contemporary composer in highest favour was the Finnish symphonist, Sibelius. He and Elgar found a champion in another brilliant ex-pupil of Vaughan Williams, Constant Lambert, composer, conductor and critic, who published his classic *Music, Ho!* in 1934 when he was twenty-nine. This 'Study of Music in Decline' made a devastating attack on Schoenberg and Stravinsky, made fun of folk song (the 'bogus' aspects), and hailed Sibelius as the one composer of the time who thought naturally in terms of symphonic form. It is a perceptive as well as witty book. Lambert realized, too, that Vaughan Williams could not be satisfactorily explained merely in terms of the folk-song revival. Even he, though, was probably surprised by the Symphony in F minor which Adrian Boult conducted for the first time on 10 April 1935, when its composer was sixty-two years old.

No work by Vaughan Williams has caused such a stir, nor evoked so many words, as the Fourth Symphony. Reaction from critics and friends was spontaneous, for no one could remain indifferent to this particular violent utterance. Bax, to whom the symphony is dedicated, Walton, Lambert, Cyril Scott, Albert Coates and Sir Hamilton Harty were but a few of the musicians present in Queen's Hall on that historic evening. One newspaper said that the 'vociferous applause' became 'almost hysterical when the composer took his bow', another that the symphony was 'greeted with thunderous applause and the composer was repeatedly called to the platform', and yet another described the ovations for conductor and composer as 'almost without parallel at Queen's Hall'. It is worth remarking that the notices of the concert, not merely in the national press but in the provincial, were of a length rarely seen today and of a high standard of writing. Colles, in *The Times*,[1] reserved judgement. He thought that perhaps Bax's third symphony had roused Vaughan Williams 'to venture into a larger and freer-spoken world than he had sought before . . .

'The slow movement is a lovely texture of wandering counterpoints in his more accustomed manner, and the scherzo is easily enjoyed by all and sundry at a first hearing because it has humour. . . . The finale goes further in the new freedom of mood which the composer claims . . . but is its daring and its gaiety really new, or does it hark back to something which Vaughan Williams left on one side with the works of pre-war days, an old impulse newly revived?'

Edwin Evans found it 'a work that has come to stay. . . . It is a vigorous, uncompromising work, with no superfluous matter about, only downright assertions. . . . He has definitely bid adieu to the folk-song influence. His material includes no corduroy tunes.' Eric Blom, in the *Birmingham Post*, noted that the new vein had been slowly approached in *Sancta Civitas*, *Job* and the concerto, and described Vaughan Williams as 'one of the most venturesome composers in Europe.

His latest work is as harshly and grimly uncompromising in its clashing, dissonant polyphony as anything the youngest adventurer would dare to fling down on music paper. That the symphony is a tremendously strong, convincing and wonderfully devised work cannot be questioned.'

In the *Musical Times*, William McNaught developed a theory he had expressed in the London *Evening News* the day after the performance, that the composer had 'abandoned the humanities'. ('The message of the symphony is a dreadful one,' he asserted in the *Evening News*, 'it says that music shall have neither flesh nor blood.') But if this was granted, the work was 'masterly. Very rarely do we feel this sense of the inevitable—so familiar in the classics—when we listen to modern music'.

Those were the 'pros'. The 'cons' were fewer, led by Ernest Newman who found it less original than Walton's symphony but revised his opinion seven months later, praising its 'combination of ardour and concentration . . . and the profoundly reflective beauty that is often attained'. 'Crescendo' in the *News Chronicle* complained of 'still the old lack of inspiration and still more lack of melody. . . . It is just clever academic music'. 'If the aim of modern music is to

[1] Which at this date still headed all its music notices "Entertainments."

stir its audiences to the depths of pessimism and humanity, Vaughan Williams has realized it to perfection,' said the *Jewish Daily Post*. Stephen Williams, in the *Evening Standard*, found in Schnabel's performance of Mozart's A major concerto later in the concert 'everything that Vaughan Williams lacked'. The most thoughtful of the 'anti' notices came from Neville Cardus in the *Manchester Guardian*.

'A man might as well hang himself as look in the work for a great tune or theme. I decline to believe that a symphony can be made out of a method, plus gusto. . . . I could not, for all my admiration of its parts, believe that it is likely to be listened to twenty years from to-day or that it will take its place in the works that go beyond national boundaries. . . . The music fails to warm the senses or to enter the mind as an utterance of conviction. The Continental listener this evening would wonder why the composer, having discarded the idioms and general emotional tones of pre-war English music, has stopped short of a post-war freedom of rhythm and a post-war harshness of dissonance. . . . The content of Vaughan Williams's music—considered in the abstract, apart from the technique—is respectably middle-class English, and the technique, as I have suggested, is old-fashioned, looked at from standards unashamedly modern. . . . There is a big nature behind every note. The trouble is that it does not immediately realize itself in expression.'

Three things emerge from all the writings after this concert—and there were many more, not quoted here: first, that the performance of the work was exceptionally fine;[1] second, that all seemed to assume that Vaughan Williams had renounced his former works: it did not occur to anyone that this symphony might, as it has proved, be a divergence from his path; third, and most important, nobody related the symphony to the state of the world in 1935. Colles, indeed, talked of its 'gaiety'; others, though finding it grim, did not look to Fascism for an explanation. This myth developed later, and some of his friends propagated it. Their letters descended on the composer in dozens. Perhaps the most percipient was from R. C. Trevelyan's wife Elizabeth, who noticed the music's strongly personal associations: 'I found your poisonous temper in the Scherzo, contrasted with that rollicking lovable opening of the Trio, *most* exciting.' She added: 'It struck me as having a vastly wider and profounder emotional range than your other work. . . . It is such a

---

[1] Nevertheless, a conductor who tackled the symphony some years later told me that he corrected dozens of mistakes in the orchestral parts.

relief to have it all expressed in *Music* and not merely noises that are meant to be musical.' Vaughan Williams's brother-in-law, R. O. Morris, wrote to him after one of the early performances, for Boult gave the work again soon, 'I still think that the question of reinforcing your second subject (is that the right term?) at its first appearance is worth considering before you set about having the score published. It comes through clearly enough in a way, but somehow doesn't tell in quite the way it should do.'

'The symphony is tremendous,' wrote Maud Karpeles to him, 'but alas I missed the clue. . . . Someone said it should have been called "Europe 1935" and that is rather what it conveyed to me—the feeling of some huge force at work, driving us to fight and struggle, which may eventually shatter us to pieces, and yet we know in our heart of hearts that there is something in life which withstands destruction and brings order out of disorder. The secret of it is to be found in music and above all in your music—but this time I missed it. Do please forgive me for preaching this sort of Easter sermon. . . .'

R.V.W. replied: 'I loved your Easter sermon—write me an Ascension, Whitsun and Trinity sermon also. I like you to like my music—and when you don't I think you are probably right.' His own attitude to this work was ambivalent—he was slightly surprised by it, yet he knew it was what he had intended. While he was writing it, he said in a letter to Maud Karpeles: 'I wish I didn't dislike my own stuff so much when I hear it—it all sounds so *incompetent*,' and he told Bernard Naylor shortly after the first performance, 'I feel that I have at last become master of my material, but it now seems too late to make any use of it.' This was a more disturbed reaction than, for instance, his comment after the 1930 Oxford performance of *Sir John in Love*—'It's bad Stanford'—and indeed his comments on this symphony rapidly became a legend. The first time he rehearsed it himself, probably for the recording, a player queried a doubtful note. He peered at the score and remarked 'Well—it's B flat. I know it *looks* wrong and *sounds* wrong. But it's right.' It was on such an occasion, too, when he said, 'I don't know whether I like it, but it's what I meant.'[1] But his fullest comment on the work was written in December 1937 to his close friend R. G. Longman who had told

---

[1] I have been unable to discover to whom this famous remark was made, but Mr. Bernard Shore tells me it dates from rehearsals for the first performance, and he and Sir Adrian Boult say there is no questioning its authenticity.

him that he found no beauty in the work and supposed it was because R.V.W. was thinking of things and situations which were not beautiful:

'I spent yesterday in bed—nursing a cold—so I decided to try to answer your long and splendid letter of a long time ago. . . .

(1) I agree with you that all music must have *beauty*—the problem being what *is* beauty—so when you say you do not think my F mi. symph. beautiful my answer *must* be that *I do* think it beautiful—not that I did not *mean* it to be beautiful because it reflects unbeautiful times—because we know that beauty can come from unbeautiful things (e.g. King Lear, Rembrandt's School of Anatomy, Wagner's Niebelungs etc.)

As a matter of fact

(1) I am not at all sure that I like it myself *now*. All I know is that it is what I wanted to do *at the time*.

(2) I wrote it not as a definite picture of anything external—e.g. the state of Europe—but simply because it occurred to me like this—I can't explain why—I don't think that sitting down and thinking about great things ever produces a great work of art (at least I hope not—because I never do so—and when you state your belief in me, dear Bobby, I feel the completest of frauds)—a thing just comes—or it doesn't—usually doesn't—I always live in hope, as all writers must, that one day I shall "ring the bell"—in younger days when one thought one was going to do the *real thing* each time and each time discovered one hadn't done it, one said hopefully "next time"—but when one touches on 65 one begins to wonder.

I sometimes think I ought to train my mind or my soul or whatever it is by exercises as the Yogis do—but I can never make up my mind to do it. On the other hand I think sometimes that I ought not to try to do the greatest thing on earth, which no fellow will understand, but to use my skill, such as I have, for doing useful work e.g. things for Div. 2 kind of people[1] to sing and enjoy. (By the way do you know of any good poem which would make into a cantata on the lines of "The Revenge"—I mean of course not in span but in form and design.)

'I think that is all for the present.'

The manuscript full score was sent as a Christmas present to Arnold Bax in 1935 The dedicatee wrote to the composer:

My dear Ralph,

Coming back from a few days in Devon to-night I found your ever-to-be-honoured present awaiting me. This is the finest tribute of affection

---

[1] Division 2 of the Leith Hill Musical Competition is the grade for village choral societies.

and comradeship that has ever been paid me and I shall value it all my life. I need say no more than this.

I see you have produced yet another new work in the shape of a ballet. [This would refer to a performance of *On Christmas Night* at Cecil Sharp House on 29 December 1935. It was not a new work.] I must say that I envy you, for I am derelict in the doldrums just now and cannot get down to anything. I hope this may be only temporary but you once said 'One is wretched when one is in artistic labour, and still more so when one isn't'. So *you* know how I feel.

Yours most gratefully,
Arnold.

The symphony was played abroad, where it was enthusiastically received. Boult conducted it in Vienna. In Bochum in January 1937 it was conducted by Leopold Reichwein.

Whatever people's reactions to the music, no work by Vaughan Williams had been more discussed. His position in England's musical life was unique, and acclaimed by those who welcomed the acerbity of the new symphony or loved the easier choral works or knew him by his hymns and songs. Like Elgar, he had reached the hearts of the people and it was felt to be right when, in the Silver Jubilee Honours List of 1935, he was made a member of the Order of Merit. He had accepted after much heart-searching and he wrote to Maud Karpeles: 'The affection of one's friends is the best part of all this business.'

With 1936 came two operas, both works on which he had been at work intermittently since the 1920s. Ethel Smyth and Ivor Gurney, before the 1914 war, had each toyed with the idea of making an opera out of J. M. Synge's play *Riders to the Sea*. Neither had got very far. Fritz Hart made a setting, and Henri Rabaud's *L'Appel de la Mer* is another. Vaughan Williams set it almost as it stood, omitting only a few lines of dialogue, and published it in 1936 although it waited more than another year for performance. Meanwhile the comic opera had undergone more vicissitudes since the Oxford University Press had agreed, in December 1931, to publish it. Hubert Foss's brother William revised the libretto, rather to the chagrin of Evelyn Sharp, in 1932. He objected to the title *The Poison Kiss* and it was altered to *The Magic Kiss*. Vaughan Williams wrote to his collaborator saying that 'I can't get over my surprise that our original title is not approved of—But if we have to think of a new one I feel it ought to be something which suggests the nature of the story. [Miss Sharp had suggested 'Merry Hearts'.] Would "The Empress & the Necromancer" do? I suppose that "Dangerous Lips" would be too filmy?' In 1934 Hubert Foss showed the revised opera to the manager of the Theatre Royal, Drury Lane ('for a smaller theatre', he explained), but with no result. But in August 1935 he was able to report that the Cambridge University Musical Society would give a week of performances in the following February. This had to be altered to May so that the new Arts Theatre built by Maynard Keynes would be available. On 24 December 1935 Vaughan Williams wrote to Mrs. Nevinson, as she now was:

'The Cambridge people sent an ultimatum that the evening's entertainment must not start before 8.30 so that the dons may digest their dinner and must finish by 11 in order that the undergraduates may be in bed by 11.30—that is to say 2 hours and 25 minutes including intervals. This will mean cutting to the bone . . . I am prepared to cut 20 minutes of music. Could you see your way to cut 20 minutes of dialogue? I had better tell you my proposed musical cuts as you may have something to say to them on dramatic grounds.'

She did, and there followed from Vaughan Williams more pages of suggested new dialogue and fresh manipulation of entries and exits. A postcard from Foss dated 7 January 1936 gave his 'reluctant' agreement to the new title, *The Poisoned Kiss*, under which it was first staged at the Cambridge Arts Theatre on 12 May 1936, produced by Mrs. Camille Prior and with settings by Gwen Raverat. Although apparently popular with the audience it left the critics in a quandary. Most of them took exception to the libretto and liked the music. The critic of the *Manchester Guardian* remarked that few operetta books had so many ingenious rhymes 'but, these apart, it has a strong flavour of an end-of-term charade'. More to the point were Richard Capell's words in the *Daily Telegraph* of 17 May:

'Verbal witticisms have a way of wearing thin, especially when they are merely verbal and do not arise from the expression of character. The libretto . . . gives evidence of a pretty talent for the writing of *vers de société*, and the composer probably thanks Miss Sharp for incitements afforded by her spritely rhythms. The question remains whether we can bear to witness the action of this fairy-tale—which is not a significant fable, nor a play of character, nor yet a satire—and enter into its gentle fun as often as we should gladly hear the music.'

Outside the Arts Theatre the posters announced: 'The world première of the light music event of the year.' It is significant that once again Vaughan Williams gave to Cambridge a work in the light-hearted spirit of *The Wasps* and *Old King Cole*, but it was pointed out that Germany would not have left it to the students of Heidelberg to give the first performance of an opera by Strauss or Hindemith. The aim of the work, it was suggested, was to bridge the gap between grand opera and musical comedy, between high-brow and lowbrow,[1] but the *Guardian* critic doubted whether, versatile though he was, Vaughan Williams had in him 'the seeds of the type of popularity that leads to the love of the lowbrows, a long run and a box-office success. The roots of his musical being are modal, folk-songish and neo-medieval and, try as he may, he cannot for long conceal his musical nature.' By far the truest estimate of this neglected, delightful but flawed work remains that by Capell which has already been quoted. Commending it to Londoners (for the composer conducted it at Sadler's Wells the week after the Cambridge production) Capell wrote:

'English operetta, after falling into a slough, has had the luck to attract a new rescuer, and him the most distinguished that could possibly have been thought of. . . . The songs and ensembles, all as charming as they are skilful, seem to formulate the right of music still to be what it naturally was of old—namely, good and at the same time popular.'

Capell's article deserves extensive quotation:

'He had but to shake his sleeve, so it seems, and out tumbled all the right material for an English comic opera, material somehow traditional and yet wholly his own. . . . What sort of footing "The Poisoned Kiss" itself can maintain is a different question; but at Cambridge on Tuesday the songs arrived with very much the effect that Purcell's must have had in the old Dorset Garden Theatre, the effect of creatures born to remain ever delightful and ever young.

'To enumerate the good things in the score would be to speak of every piece. Even the trio of the hobgoblins disguised as newspaper inter-viewers—a piece, so far as the text goes, of not very fresh satire in quasi-Gilbertian vein—turns out a capital piece of music. . . . No more lovely song is in the work than the third-act "Love breaks all rules". A mezzo-

---

[1] R.V.W. put it plainly in a letter to Maud Karpeles: 'I certainly *did* mean that opera to be "escapist" in so far as it is not meant to be more than good fun and good enter-tainment—which I think is definitely needed in these days of "purge our souls" as much as "pity and terror".'

soprano voice sings the first stanza, a soprano then takes up the noble strain. The listener thinks that it is perfect, but still the composer has something up his sleeve—one voice extends the final phrase while the other enriches it with a counterpoint. The simplicity of it remains within the frame of the comic-opera style, but the beauty renders the piece worthy of any company.'

Then, after his remarks on the libretto, Capell added:

'The deduction drawn is not that the composer of *The Poisoned Kiss* is absolutely not a man for opera at all: but it is this—that, not being a born musician of the theatre, he must depend more than one of that sort with only a fraction of his gifts would do upon the sheer luck of the right kind of text-book falling into his hands. The choice of this "Poisoned Kiss" theme—a theme of which we ask in vain what it is essentially "about"—was all too uncritical.

'Can the most enchanting music altogether make up for the want of sense and a motive in a stage action? It may be said that Mozart's does so in the "Entführung". But there the case is different in that Mozart's music is not only enchanting but also—as Vaughan Williams's operas are not—delineatory of character. Osmin is a person, Vaughan Williams's Dipsacus only a puppet.

'Our admired—and, let the word be said, beloved—musician has, it is clear, not the active dramatic aptitude that made such a composer as Puccini lend a drastically constructive hand to the work of his text-writers. But out of that fount of music will come a masterpiece when luck sends the right dramatic collaborator.'

When the work was produced for one night in London, before a full and enthusiastic house, there was high praise for Margaret Field-Hyde, Geoffrey Dunn, Meriel St. Clair, Mabel Ritchie, and others of the principals. But the dichotomy remained; Vaughan Williams and 'a romantic extravaganza' could not be reconciled. One does not go to *Vogue* for music criticism, but in this case an anonymous writer in that journal said bluntly that for which others found oblique and verbose means of expression: 'Never would we have thought that our austere and revered master composer could write such lilting and fascinating tunes.' Oxford congratulated itself on its decision to stage van Dieren's *The Tailor*. But perhaps the most remarkable journalistic outcome of the opera was Colles's column of angry sarcasm in *The Times* of 16 May. He had learned that the B.B.C. had rejected the opera and cited this as 'a striking instance' of lack of musical direction in the B.B.C.'s affairs.

'So long as it is left to minor officials to decide for or against a work after a glance at a score these ineptitudes will occur. . . . The B.B.C. will broadcast a foreign work, even a hideous and repulsive one, on the strength of its composer's name, but the name of Vaughan Williams still goes for nothing. Or perhaps he is held to have forfeited any claim to preferential treatment by leaving the track marked out for him and writing comic opera, the old snobbery of which Sullivan was so long the victim. . . . How can he demean himself with these ballads and dance tunes, patter songs and set pieces? One can imagine the score of *The Poisoned Kiss* being passed to and fro between the "serious" and the "light" music departments of Broadcasting House for information and necessary action and both deciding against taking any action at all!'

The composer was not worried by the critics' general response—'the fact remains that people enjoyed our joint effort very much,' he wrote to Mrs. Nevinson—but he at once began to suggest improvements, including the omission of a 'skit' on journalists and of the quartet 'Love in a hut' (which he later restored), and revision of the 'low comedy' lines in the dialogue. But his attitude generally was similar to the view he had taken of his Pianoforte Concerto. 'I don't want to shove it down people's throats,' he wrote, 'it's really not the business of the authors to act as commercial travellers.' The librettist delicately put her defence in a letter to R.V.W. on 27 May 1936: 'I should like, next time, not to work at it so much alone. An opera is not like anything else in which two people collaborate, and there would be much more continuity if we could go through it together before altering it any more.' More productions followed, in Liverpool, Bristol, Bridport, and at the Juilliard School of Music, New York, for which a cut version was devised, with further transpositions and alterations. In the late 1950s much of its dialogue was rewritten and schools and amateurs have performed it, some making their own topical adjustments to the libretto, but it still has not had a professional producer, still not had a 'real comic opera conductor', as Colles, in a long letter to Vaughan Williams, giving detailed comments on the score and the staging, said it ought to have. Moreover, by reason of its plot and dialogue, it was impossible to make a short concert work from it on the lines of *In Windsor Forest* although the overture and a short aria were conducted by the composer at a Three Choirs secular concert in 1937. So some of Vaughan Williams's most tuneful music remains little known.

But in the next new work of his to be heard in 1936 he had found words perfectly suited to his needs in the Tudor poet John Skelton. At the Three Choirs Festival in 1932 R.V.W. had been talking to Elgar and a friend of Elgar's, Colonel Isaac, and they had asked him if he had read any Skelton. He confessed he only knew the anthology pieces. Isaac suggested that he should set what R.V.W. later described in a letter to me as 'a very fine poem, rather more like Donne than Skelton, which I have since set',[1] but Elgar said: 'No, don't do that, you make an oratorio out of Elinor Rumming.' He then pointed out that the metre of Skelton was often pure jazz. Thus was born the idea of the *Five Tudor Portraits*, originally six but a setting of *Margery Wentworth* was omitted. It is his happiest, raciest, most poetical choral work. He gave the first performance to the Norwich Festival whose organizers had asked him for a new work. 'I think they thought they'd get "O Praise the Lord",' he said, 'but I sent the Five T.P.s.' Another English work received its first performance after the interval of ninety minutes, Britten's *Our Hunting Fathers*, conducted by the twenty-two-year-old composer.[2] Here poems about animals and birds and their relationship to humans had been chosen by the poet referred to in the programme as either W. H. Ander or Anden, but never as Auden!

Vaughan Williams's work captivated the critics. Astra Desmond gave 'the most delicate picture of a drunken old hag at the famous brewing', writes Colles in *The Times*. 'Everyone concerned had caught the spirit of the thing, and the composer conducted a brilliant first performance.' Edwin Evans in the *Musical Times* of November 1936, wrote that he had rarely seen an English audience 'so relieved of concert-room inhibitions'. All critics agreed that the fourth movement, 'Jane Scroop', was the gem. 'One is inclined to claim that "Jane Scroop" is the loveliest piece of music that Vaughan

---

[1] *Prayer to the Father of Heaven*, 1948.

[2] The soprano soloist in *Our Hunting Fathers* was Sophie Wyss who wrote the following to Mrs. Vaughan Williams in late August, 1958: 'I will remember him not only as the great composer he was but as the champion of fair play. . . . In 1936 I was giving the first performance of *Our Hunting Fathers* by Benjamin Britten and the orchestra behaved like naughty schoolboys, not understanding Britten's musical idiom. Dr. Vaughan Williams was at the rehearsal and reproved them and they pulled themselves together and gave a fair performance.'

Dr. Heathcote Statham, who prepared the choir, tells me that Vaughan Williams was most concerned that his work preceded Britten's, thinking that this might be unfair to the younger man. When it was pointed out that there was a 90-minute interval he agreed that this made a difference.

Williams has ever written,' wrote Colles after the first London performance, given by the B.B.C. Symphony Orchestra under Boult, in January 1937.

An interesting postscript to the B.B.C. performance was a letter dated 21 January 1937 from Philip Henderson, whose edition of Skelton Vaughan Williams had used. He regarded 'My Proper Bess' as 'one of the loveliest songs I have ever heard', thought that the extension of 'Jolly Rutterkin' with the lines from 'Magnificence' was 'extraordinarily effective' and that the atmosphere of 'Elinor Rumming' had been skilfully caught. To this R.V.W. replied on 31 January:

'Your very kind and appreciative letter makes me feel guilty of discourtesy in not having sent you a copy of my musical setting. My reasons were two (1) I had no idea you would be interested (2) I thought and still think that you may be horrified at all I have done. As perhaps you know we composers are an unconscientious crowd and are much too apt to use the great poets as mere pegs on which to hang our silly little tunes—so I expect you will think I have made horrible hay of Skelton—My only excuses are the ones which I have given in my preface. It may interest you to know that I was first introduced to Skelton by Elgar. Previously I had only known the one or two lyrics which appear in the anthologies and a scrap out of Jane Scroop from the Week-end Book.

'Elgar said to me "I think I must make an Oratorio out of Elinor Rumming". Alas he never did so. He also said that the Skelton metres were "pure jazz".

'Having now read your preface I imagine he got that idea from you.'

It is important to note that this version of what Elgar said (suggesting that he himself wanted to set 'Elinor Rumming') differs from the account quoted earlier from a letter to me. I suspect, in view of the dates, that the version told to Mr. Henderson is correct.

Although the F minor symphony had no conscious direct connection with the turbulent days of the 1930s, there was no question about the cantata which he composed for the Huddersfield Choral Society's centenary on 2 October 1936. This was *Dona Nobis Pacem*, and it is clear from the text that it was directly related to the growing danger of war. Vaughan Williams anticipated by twenty-five years Britten's method in the *War Requiem* of interpolating English poems into the Latin Mass, in his case Whitman. He also set, in recitative style, John Bright's 'Angel of Death' speech, and he claimed he was the only man ever to have set to music words spoken in the House of Commons.

The next few years brought forth no major work except a ten-year-old opera. 'My imagination is now permanently sluggish,' he told a friend, but this was merely a disguise. Already the first sketches for what was to be the Fifth Symphony were being made. Meanwhile, in 1937, there was a great national occasion to celebrate, the Coronation of George VI. For this he composed two works, the Flourish and the *Te Deum* based on traditional tunes. When Elgar died he had been offered the post of Master of the King's Musick but had refused it. Nevertheless he was an unofficial laureate by virtue of his artistic creed, and when George V died in 1936 Sir Walford Davies, Elgar's successor, at once rang up 'The White Gates' and was rewarded forty-eight hours later with the setting of 'Nothing is here for tears', written in one day.[1]

An age was drawing to its end, but there were still glimmers of hope, such as the award to Vaughan Williams on 20 October 1937 by Hamburg University of its first Shakespeare Prize, a move to strengthen cultural ties between Britain and Germany. R.V.W. went to Hamburg to receive it on 15 June 1938, pointed out that England had other composers besides himself, and heard Eugen Jochum conduct the *Tallis Fantasia*[2] and the *London Symphony*. He welcomed the influx of foreign musicians to Britain—refugees from Nazi oppression—and some of them, Robert Müller-Hartmann, for instance, became his friends. But he was more than a little concerned about their influence on English musical life as can be seen from this extract from a letter to Mr. Jani Strasser about opera in England:

'It seems to me that foreign artists whom we welcome here, if they are to become good citizens to our musical policy, must not try to impose their culture *en bloc* on us . . . but join in *our* musical life and fertilize it by their own incomparable experience and tradition—not try to destroy *our* small and weak tradition, which can easily be destroyed like a weak flame, if we are not careful. . . .

'Your task, it seems to me, is to become musically an Englishman and to see music as we see it and then add to it your own unique experience and knowledge.'

[1] At the Royal Philharmonic Society concert on 30 January, 'Sine Nomine' was sung 'in memoriam'. No one apparently remembered that in 1917 the King had commented adversely on the substitution of this tune for Barnby's at a ceremonial service!

[2] It was during the second half of the 1930s that this work attained its popularity. Until then it had been relatively neglected.

He had had precious little encouragement from the paladins of British operatic life for his own ventures. *Hugh* was revived at Sadler's Wells in the Coronation season, and on 30 November 1937, the one-act *Riders to the Sea* was produced at the Royal College of Music. That such a work should have been left to students to present for the first time is itself an indictment of operatic policy, for the originality and power of the work must have been obvious from the published score. Moreover the principal part of Maurya requires not merely an experienced singer, such as even the most gifted student could hardly expect to be, but an actress of considerable ability. However, Colles in *The Times*, considered that the performance 'revealed the extraordinary qualities of an exquisite opera'. He had found the work 'powerful; it is interesting; but above all it is purely beautiful'. None of the London opera companies showed any interest in the work. Its next performance was by the Cambridge University Musical Society in 1938. It should be made clear that Vaughan Williams never sought any special consideration for the English composer. When on 24 March 1936, he had spoken at a dinner given in his honour by the Musicians' Club, he was annoyed when *The Times* reported him as having said that 'English music was not appreciated by the average Englishman as it should be'. In a letter published on 31 March he wrote:

'I hope that I have never been and shall never be guilty of making in public this time-dishonoured complaint. What I did say was that the average Englishman hated English music; that this fact pointed to something wrong, either with the average Englishman or with the music or with the general situation.'

He seems to have found delight in 'occasional' works during 1938. Ursula Wood, a young woman unknown to him but later to become his second wife, sent him a scenario based on Spenser's *Epithalamion* from which they devised a masque for the E.F.D.S.S. called *The Bridal Day*. This was played through in the spring of 1939 but was postponed by the war. The music had the same sweetness and lyricism as characterized the Serenade to Music, written in 1938 for Sir Henry Wood on his golden jubilee as a conductor and performed at the Royal Albert Hall on 5 October. The Serenade was a truly virtuoso composition, for it contained parts for sixteen solo singers who had been associated with Wood. How well Vaughan

Williams knew and understood those voices: each one was given a phrase typical of his or her style. Fortunately for posterity, opportunity was taken to record the work a few days later while its all-star cast was still assembled, and the result was an historic document in our musical history. The singers were: Isobel Baillie, Stiles Allen, Elsie Suddaby, Eva Turner (sopranos); Margaret Balfour, Muriel Brunskill, Astra Desmond, Mary Jarred (contraltos); Parry Jones, Heddle Nash, Frank Titterton, Walter Widdop (tenors); Norman Allin, Robert Easton, Roy Henderson and Harold Williams (basses). Wood himself was delighted by such a gift.

The holding of another pageant written by E. M. Forster, this time in aid of the Dorking and Leith Hill District Preservation Society, was an opportunity for Vaughan Williams to try out some of the music which was taking shape as the Fifth Symphony and had originally formed part of an opera on *The Pilgrim's Progress*, an opera he then thought it unlikely he would complete. So visitors to *England's Pleasant Land* at Milton Court, Westcott, on 9, 14 and 16 July 1938, hearing Vaughan Williams's 'Exit of the Ghosts of the Past' and 'Funeral March for the Old Order', were receiving a 'preview' of parts of the scherzo and preludio of the D major Symphony of five years thence. The music, which also included arrangements and original compositions by William Cole, Mary Couper, David Moule Evans, Julian Gardiner and John Ticehurst, Holst's 'I vow to thee my country' and Parry's 'Jerusalem', was played by the Band of the 2nd Bn., the Duke of Cornwall's Light Infantry. Tom Harrison again was the producer.

More than the Surrey countryside was in need of preservation, for in September came the Munich crisis and the realization that England was again on the brink of an abyss. In that week of international tension, Vaughan Williams conducted his *Pastoral Symphony* at the Promenade Concert on 29 September. A writer in *Truth* (5 October 1938) perceived its appositeness to the hour: 'This great symphony, performed as it was in a week of crisis, brought together in its ample folds the emotions of all that was best in Britain in those dreadful days.'

Not far from Dorking, at Horsham, was Christ's Hospital where the school director of music, C. S. Lang, had made many arrangements for massed unison voices and the usual four-part chorus. In this way all the five hundred boys were able to take part in the canticles. This was an idea to appeal to Vaughan Williams, who wrote them a complete set of canticles for morning and evening services. In January 1939 his *Double Trio* was played for the first time, but he was dissatisfied with it. He went to Manchester in February 1939 to conduct the B.B.C. Northern Orchestra in a studio performance of the *Pastoral Symphony*. He produced two other new works in 1938–9. One was for Sir Adrian Boult, as he now was, to conduct at the New York World Fair in June 1939. This was in the tranquil style of the *Serenade*, being Five Variants of the folk song 'Dives and Lazarus' which he had loved all his life. It seemed as if the fury of the F minor, the rumbustiousness of the *Tudor Portraits* and the vigour of *Dona Nobis Pacem* had left him temporarily content to recall an earlier and simpler style, matured by years of experience. The first performance, Sir Adrian recalls, took place during a heat-wave. There was no air-conditioning in the hall, the thermometer registered eighty-nine degrees (F.) and the audience fanned themselves continuously with their programmes. The second work was a Suite for Pipes, first played at a Chichester Summer School in 1939.

The outbreak of war found Vaughan Williams in a strangely intense mood, less phlegmatic than was his usual outward appearance, his mind numbed by the possibilities of world catastrophe.

He had by now given up his teaching at the R.C.M. When war reduced the College's numbers by half, he at once offered his private pupils to colleagues whose work was most seriously depleted. He was ever ready to aid those down on their luck, and went to St. Paul's Cathedral on 19 March 1940, to conduct a choir of solo performers from the Incorporated Society of Musicians who sang his Mass, in aid of distressed musicians.

In June 1940 his old friend Dorothy Longman, wife of Bobby, died, and five months later he made his setting of Mr. Valiant-for-Truth's great speech in *The Pilgrim's Progress*. Though he never said it in so many words, this was R.V.W.'s memorial to one he had known from the far-off days before 1914, and who had shared many happy times with him. These were dark days, and he needed some new stimulus to set his restless imagination alight. He had mentioned to Arthur Benjamin that he would like to 'have a shot' at film music. Benjamin had passed this on to Muir Mathieson, director of London Films, who telephoned one Saturday evening in 1940 and asked Vaughan Williams to write the music for *49th Parallel*. On asking how long he could have to prepare it, he was told 'Till

Wednesday'. As he wrote in his essay 'Composing for the Films',[1] the time limit could be a stimulus—'when the hand is lazy, the mind often gets lazy as well'—and he found film music a splendid discipline. 'A film producer would make short work of Mahler's interminable codas or Dvořák's five endings to each movement.' Naturally he had his own approach to this new art—'ignore the details and intensify the spirit of the whole situation by a continuous stream of music'—and he recognized great possibilities if the author, director, photographer and composer worked together from the beginning. 'It is only when this is achieved that the film will come into its own as one of the finest of the fine arts.' In my research into Vaughan Williams's associations with the film companies I have collected much evidence of his enjoyment of the work and of his friendliness to all connected with it. While working on *Flemish Farm* with Muir Mathieson and Jeffrey Dell, the director, he coined the phrase 'plug-tune' for his *leitmotif*, and arrived one day full of excitement over his idea for coping with the $\frac{1}{3}$ second that appears on all film-music timing sheets. 'He had added an occasional $\frac{1}{8}$ bar to get rid of the $\frac{1}{3}$ sec.', Mr. Mathieson wrote to me. 'It had the effect of "God Save Our ($\frac{1}{8}$) G-Gracious Queen". However, he was thrilled.' Mr. Dell, who says that he blushes 'at the memory of our effrontery', was only one of several directors who found that Vaughan Williams invited criticism at the recording sessions and was ready and willing to alter his score on the spot to meet their ideas. He did this from his first film, 49*th Parallel*, to the last on which he was actively engaged, *The England of Elizabeth*, in 1956. Mathieson, Ernest Irving, Anthony Asquith and Michael Balcon became his friends; and Ian Dalrymple, who made *Coastal Command*, was deeply touched when, just after the war, he and his wife organized a fête at Bourton-on-the-Water to start a fund for a new church organ and R.V.W. travelled from Dorking to attend the gathering and to make a short speech.

Film music was one way, he found, in which he could serve his country at war. In a broadcast on 'The Composer in Wartime' in 1940[2] he suggested other ways, for he still had his vision of the musician as a vital part of the community and could not believe that artists could be immune from what was happening around them.

---

[1] First appeared in 1945 in *R.C.M. Magazine*. Reprinted in *National Music and Other Essays*.

[2] Reprinted in *Heirs and Rebels*, op. cit., pp. 90–93.

'I have known young composers refer with annoyance to this "boring war",' he said. 'Such a phrase as this, I confess, shocks me.' Times were not normal; the composer must condition his inspiration by the nature of his material. He then challenged his own theory that music was useless. 'Are there not ways,' he asked, 'in which the composer without derogating from his art, without being untrue to himself, but still without that entire disregard for his fellows which characterizes the artist in his supreme moments, [can] use his skill, his knowledge, his sense of beauty in the service of his fellow men?' He suggested works for voices and combinations of all manner of instruments which might be played by people whiling away the waiting-hours of war. He, at any rate, followed his own advice and wrote the charming Household Music to be played on whatever instruments were handy. Through the anxious years of 1941 and 1942 he composed mainly film music—*Coastal Command*, *The People's Land* and *Flemish Farm*—and the new symphony was sufficiently ready to be played through to close friends. On Monday, 12 October 1942, came his seventieth birthday when perhaps he was astonished and pleasantly surprised by the warmth and number of the tributes. His position, unsought, as leader of English music had been apparent before the war but it had perhaps needed that upheaval to bring home fully to the mass of people the strength and nobility of his work.

On his birthday he went to London for a National Gallery concert by the Menges Sextet, which gave the first performance of the revised version of the *Double Trio* and played his *Phantasy Quintet*. Robert Irwin sang and Howard Ferguson played for the first time a set of *Five Shakespeare Songs* 'for Ralph Vaughan Williams on his birthday' by his friend Gerald Finzi. This was the kind of intimate, friendly music-making he liked, but the whole week was devoted to his major works on the B.B.C. and on the evening of his birthday music written for the occasion by Alan Bush, Patrick Hadley, Gordon Jacob, Constant Lambert, Elizabeth Maconchy, Robin Milford and Edmund Rubbra was broadcast. The Royal Philharmonic Society opened its 131st season on 7 November with *A Sea Symphony* and *Dona Nobis Pacem*, both of which the composer conducted. It all left him rather depressed. He wrote to Jean Stewart, one of the Menges Sextet's viola players:

'The piece [the *Double Trio*] sounded dull and muddy—you know, I've tried all my life for *clarity* and never achieved it—I always put too many ingredients into the pudding. But I suppose at my advanced years it's too late now—perhaps I ought to scrap the work—I don't think I can re-write it a second time.[1] This sounds ungrateful but it is not—you all played it beautifully and it is entirely the fault of the work. . . . There, my dear, I have written a doleful letter but the more I hear my own tunes the more I dislike them—and I haven't the courage *not* to listen all this week.'[2]

Despite his dissatisfaction with this chamber work (which received one more performance in this form, on 18 February 1947), he began a new string quartet during the winter of 1942–3. The first two movements were delivered by Ursula Wood to Jean Stewart as a birthday present in February 1943 with a note from the composer: 'Alas the scherzo refuses to materialize and will have to wait for next birthday.' On the score was written the dedication 'For Jean on her birthday'.

While doubts assailed him Vaughan Williams wrote to his old friend and adviser S. P. Waddington, now seventy-three and living in retirement at Lyme Regis.

Waddington replied (6 January 1943) refuting

'your quite misguided idea that you have been running ahead of your technical powers. Nothing, I am convinced, could be further from the facts. You have been a monument to patience, perseverance and pertinacity. When you were young I know you found it difficult to pin down your ideas, but any biographer of yours will say that you attained by sheer determination a sureness of touch and a mastery of your own individual style which is completely satisfying. I almost fear you have been envying the merely slick—those who can write faultless acres of unimaginative and entirely soulless music.'

At the Promenade Concert in the Royal Albert Hall on 24 June 1943, the Fifth Symphony in D major was played for the first time. The composer conducted the London Philharmonic Orchestra and let it be known that some of the themes were 'taken from an unfinished opera *The Pilgrim's Progress*—but except in the slow movement the symphony has no dramatic connection with Bunyan's allegory'. Above the slow movement, on the manuscript, was a quotation from Bunyan, since removed: 'Upon this place stood a cross, and a little below a sepulchre. Then he said: "He hath given

---

[1] He did, as the Partita for Strings (1948).
[2] *R.C.M. Magazine*, Vol. LV, No. 1, op. cit., p. 42.

me rest by his sorrow, and life by his death".' The original dedication, shortened in the printed score to 'To Jean Sibelius, without
permission', read 'Without permission and with the sincerest
flattery to Jean Sibelius, whose great example is worthy of imitation'. The great music—a testament of beauty, Neville Cardus[1]
has called it—came like a benediction to English music-lovers at this
time of the war. Surely the violence of the F minor was here finally
renounced? Had not the Delectable Mountains been reached and
the Blessing given? So it was argued, how wrongly the next fifteen
years were to show with a vengeance.

<h1 style="text-align:center">II</h1>

After *Job*, Vaughan Williams began work on his Fourth Symphony,
but he found time to complete the Pianoforte Concerto, of which
two movements had been written in 1926. This contains some of
Vaughan Williams's best music though it is not one of his best works
in a complete sense. Like Bartók and Hindemith at the same period,
he treated the pianoforte, an instrument for which he had little love,
percussively. It is employed in its eighteenth and twentieth-century
rôles, but not in its discursive, arpeggio-bound nineteenth-century
part. The harmonic style of the music is in some respects harsher
than that of the F minor Symphony, and the texture is at times
impenetrably thick. A very remarkable solo pianist is needed to
establish the instrument's predominance; the composer's jocular
reference to the work as his 'orchestra and pianoforte concerto' is not
without point. It is unfortunate that these undeniable difficulties in
'presentation' stand in the way of appreciation of some extraordinarily powerful and beautiful music. Yet of all Vaughan
Williams's works, it is this concerto which has been played, and

[1] A letter from Cardus to Vaughan Williams on 2 February 1953, is of much interest.
It was in reply to one in which R.V.W. had said he supposed that Cardus was 'allergic'
to his music. Cardus wrote: 'Let me give you an example. When I was in Australia
[during the war] records of your fifth symphony arrived, with no notes about the work,
no information: just the title, the number, the key. I played the records over the air
in one of my weekly broadcasts on music for the Australian National Radio. And I said:
"The music seems to me as though inspired by the faith and gentle austerity of Bunyan
... in the closing pages of the Finale the Alleluia strains create an elevation of mind and
sense of a shining light coming from a distance—ideas and emotions familiar to anybody
who has read Bunyan at all. 'Who would true valour see, let him come hither. . . .'"
I did not know, as I wrote and spoke all this, that you had ever thought of Bunyan. . . .
Isn't this a remarkable proof of how perfectly the symphony enshrines a spiritual
essence? And it's proof, I hope, that I am far from "allergic" to your music.'

appreciated, more overseas than at home. Structurally, in its use of comparatively short phrases, welded together by gigantic blocks of chords, it is a key work in the composer's development. The theme in the first movement, 'Toccata', based on rising fourths, is a far cry from pre-1914 works.

The slow movement is called 'Romanza', a title which Vaughan Williams gave to movements into which it appears that he poured himself heart and soul. The writing for the pianoforte is more conventional, but it is of Ravel and Fauré that we think rather than of Schumann or Brahms. Flute, oboe and horn bear the weight of the accompaniment against which the soloist muses and dreams on a theme skilfully centred on one note. There occurs a tender passage worlds away from the prevailing mood of the work which few people, alas, may know.

At the end of the movement the oboe has a descending chromatic phrase which is the link with, as well as the progenitor of the finale. This is in two sections, 'Chromatic Fugue' and 'Finale alla tedesca', each separated by a virtuoso passage for the soloist, a plan followed years later by Walton in his cello concerto. The fugue is brazen and harsh (and exciting), culminating in a massive stretto with the organ as foundation-stone. After the display cadenza, the waltz finale, based on the fugue, is perhaps the most vital and invigorating music in the concerto. It, too, is cut short by a cadenza in which themes from the first two movements are recalled in summary and the work ends with ten bars of tutti, curt, definite, and uncompromisingly in G major. Sir Adrian Boult was among those who suggested to Vaughan Williams that a better balance could perhaps be obtained if the solo part were to be arranged for two pianos, and this was done in collaboration with Joseph Cooper in 1946. Certainly the impression of power and vigour is intensified by this arrangement. The ending of the one-piano version is changed so that instead of the blaze of angry sound there is a quiet and serene disintegration of the fugue subject in the strings, pizzicato, against a chord in the pianos: a beautiful but less convincing finale. One must hope that a pianist of the right calibre will one day reveal the full originality and power of this concerto in its original form. It suffered, perhaps, from the determination of English critics always to cast Vaughan Williams in the rôle of prophet, or mystic, or metaphysician instead of just composer. It is very much to be doubted whether the Piano Concerto, however 'tough' its language, was intended as a sermon in sound. Its successor, the Fourth Symphony, was not, but it soon became so fettered with 'meanings' that it became difficult to hear the notes for the words.

It is often said that the F minor Symphony was a new departure, that with it the composer set off upon a new path in his development. In fact it was the culmination of a ten-year period, the final summary rather than the preface. It is the logical conclusion of the vigorous and adventurous decade which had begun with *Flos Campi* and *Sancta Civitas*, continued in the then unfinished *Riders to the Sea* and developed fully in the Piano Concerto and the satanic moments of *Job*. The increased tautness of his style and the starker harmonic idiom are evident in these other works, which were programmatic and descriptive or, in the case of the concerto, a vehicle for a virtuoso of a special kind. In the classical form of the symphony, still the greatest challenge to a composer, they would be 'naked and unashamed' as 'pure' music. So, at first, the work was accepted; but as the consciousness of growing international tension grew, this symphony, coming from one who was regarded with awe as a remote seer, was interpreted as a commentary on the times in which it was first heard. Very sincere people held this view, among them Frank Howes and Adrian Boult. The latter wrote in 1958[1] that Vaughan Williams 'foresaw the whole thing [i.e. war] and surely there is no more magnificent gesture of disgust in all music than that final open fifth when the composer seems to rid himself of the whole hideous idea'. All great art is capable of many interpretations; and in that disturbed time it was understandable that this view of the symphony should seem perfectly valid. Let the historical record be set straight, though. The bulk of the work was written before the average Englishman was conscious of the gathering storm. After it had been played, when Fascism's danger was more apparent, what

[1] *Musical Times*, October 1958, p. 536.

did Vaughan Williams produce? The riotous and relaxed *Five Tudor Portraits*, the comic opera *The Poisoned Kiss*, the colourful and ornate Coronation works, the moonlit Serenade to Music, the lyrical and amatory *The Bridal Day*, the first sketches of the Fifth Symphony. Only one work in the period 1936-9 can be directly related to the contemporary scene and in that, *Dona Nobis Pacem*, there is throughout a note of optimism, a faith held by most of Britain at that time that the clouds would pass away. In the finale, before its hushed last prayer, the bells ring and the chorus sings of a vision of peace.

When Vaughan Williams said of the F minor Symphony that 'I don't know whether I like it, but it's what I meant', he was not uttering a political warning but merely stressing his view that a composer must write what comes to him in the way in which the ideas occur. The F minor Symphony occurred to him as it stands. He could have written it in no other way. To some it will remain his greatest achievement because of its sheer musical logic, its compression of a heady new wine into the old bottle of a more or less regular sonata-form design, its rhythmical elasticity and its remarkably effective orchestration; from others it will command respect rather than love. It is possible, too, that some will find that its thematic unity has not resulted in emotional unity. It may be that generations yet unborn will find that Vaughan Williams's originality lies more truly in his unique manipulation of his natural musical language in a work such as the *Pastoral Symphony* than in his magnificent affray on a style of music which was basically foreign to his nature and which he never sought to repeat. The difficulties of the Fourth Symphony have perhaps been exaggerated in the cause of profundity. Angry, violent, and discordant it certainly is. It is not, however, a tragic work. It has humour. There is an unholy joy in its ribaldry. The composer, one feels, had a gleam in his eye as he put down on paper the comminatory opening[1] which he said he 'cribbed' from the finale of Beethoven's Ninth Symphony.[2]

For an analysis of the work nothing is finer or more terse than the composer's, for he effectively demonstrates that the work has a multiplicity of themes, each growing from the other—the same formula as in the *Pastoral Symphony* but here telescoped to suit the pace of the music—and the whole growing from two four-note phrases.

[1] See music example on page 266
[2] 'Musical Autobiography', reprinted in *National Music and Other Essays*.

All that is necessary here is to point out the pulsating splendour of the appassionato second subject which gives the movement a richness not always mentioned by commentators. After it has subsided, the grinding against each other of semitones recurs with added force, but the movement sinks into a quiet passage for strings, a soliloquy based on what had been one of the 'angriest' opening phrases. These bars contain the tenderness and loneliness which remain when passion has cooled and they prepare the way for the slow movement. This is probably the most impressive of Vaughan Williams's symphonic slow movements; others are more heart-easing, none is more compact, more pregnant with inner tension, more economically yet aptly scored. Again, rising and falling fourths are the germane material. A cantabile melody for strings over a pizzicato bass sets off a train of tunes, for oboe with strings and clarinet, then bassoon, then full orchestra. The music is angular, yet not everyone will regard it as cold or inhuman. Despite the dissonant counterpoint, the sound is often rich enough to merit the adjective Brahmsian, and the movement can be seen as a typical Vaughan Williams rhapsody contained within the strict and disciplined framework of this particular symphony. There is no heaven-scaling violin solo, no consolatory viola, but there is a tender cadence for the flute of great compassion and calm:

and, a few bars later, a vivid anticipation of the D major symphony:

Having brought the music to an incandescent climax, Vaughan Williams gradually unwinds it all, almost in a Sibelian manner, presenting the fragments as isolated phrases. At the end, over a remarkable accompaniment of muted trombones, the flute sings its mournful lament, coming to rest on E natural. The irruption of the Scherzo into the reverie induced by this music is almost indecent. Scherzo means joke, and this is a truly Beethovenian scherzo, full of brusque, noisy jests, dashing along helter-skelter and owing a debt to Holst. Some of the sudden and eccentric alterations of rhythm have the effect of erratic gear-changing: successfully accomplished, the music drives on its hectic course, carrying all before it in boisterous high spirits. The Trio, much slower, seems to be the thematic godfather of 'Jolly Rutterkin' in the *Five Tudor Portraits*.

When the scherzo returns there is one curious and notable moment of thoughtful repose. The music is pulled to an emphatic stop and a throbbing link-passage to the finale, in the manner of Beethoven's fifth and Sibelius's second symphonies, ends with a convulsive leap into a theme which is almost note-for-note a transformation of the slow movement's flute cadence:

Tagged on to it is the 'oompah' bass and a march tune on woodwind which has variously been described as 'a march for a brave new world' or 'sarcastic', but which sounds like an ordinary R.V.W. march very apt for symphonic development. Of all the movements this finale, though perhaps rather too long, is the richest in subject-matter. It also seems to me to be the one in which the composer's spirits are highest, as far away from prophecies of war as it is possible to get. He revels in his themes and in his new-found ability to produce exciting clashes of brass and string tone. The music is full of sheer exhilaration, as waves of sound pound against each other;

there is one wonderful passage where woodwind and strings swirl and shrill, chasing one another up the scale until the 'oompah' bass ends the game by stamping off to start up another row. For a few moments the din ceases while the composer reminds us in a meditative passage for strings that this is, after all, a Vaughan Williams symphony. But his energy is soon restored and all forces are mustered for the fugal epilogue. The first of the two four-note themes is combined with other tunes of the finale, swiftly generating higher tension. Just as this section reaches boiling-point, the grinding opening bars of the symphony return with reinforced deliberation and the great work ends with the musical equivalent of a shake of a fist and a slammed door.

At any level the F minor is a masterpiece. The efforts to increase its acceptability by giving it a meretricious programme are a poor compliment to its musical vitality and self-sufficiency. It is a work which triumphantly proves that dissonance and stark orchestration, handled by a poet, can lead to a thing of beauty. It is also a triumphant assertion of Vaughan Williams's stubborn independence of mind. A 'satellite' of this symphony is the 1932 *Magnificat* for contralto, women's chorus and orchestra, a setting which is one of the few to treat these words as what they are: a hymn of praise by a young woman chosen for perhaps the strangest moment in history. The setting is characteristic of Vaughan Williams's practical and undogmatic approach to a religious subject. The music is again Holstian in example: high swaying chords, strings and celesta, bare fifths on brass with percussion. The Virgin's melismatic and ornate vocal part illustrates her wonderment and joy; the flute cadenzas represent the Holy Spirit. As in *Flos Campi*, the final orchestral climax has an oriental fervour. From nearly the same period comes the *Viola Suite*, notable for its curious design (which skilfully avoids monotony) of eight short movements divided into three groups. The orchestra is small, and its use colourful and subtle. Those who think that Vaughan Williams had no use for an orchestral palette should hear this work and note its carefully varied use of the instruments: flute, clarinet and bassoon without violins in the Prelude; brass in the Polka; and a happy use throughout of the harp. Even in such a relaxed work as this—for it has no pretension to be other than enjoyable, light music—there is a movement of deep beauty: the Carol. The Suite is also interesting as an example of the kind of sophisticated 'original' music which Vaughan Williams could derive from his folk-song interests. A more obvious case is the short *The Running Set*, an orchestral *jeu d'esprit* of infectious humour.

The year 1936 was marked by two major choral works by Vaughan Williams. The first of them, the *Five Tudor Portraits*, is among his finest achievements, yet it has not attained the popularity which one would think was its due and has not ousted *A Sea Symphony* as first choice among choral societies anxious to sing a Vaughan Williams work. Some reasons may be suggested. First, it is difficult and, being a choral suite of portraits, requires powers of character-study not always readily found. When it first appeared various 'crack' choirs, such as those of Croydon and Newcastle upon Tyne, seized upon it, but the growing ascendancy of purely orchestral music has not encouraged them to maintain it in their repertoires. Skelton's words, also, are possibly a drawback where audiences are concerned. Their archaic humour is perhaps a special taste, too rarefied for all its earthiness; and in spite of the brilliance of the musical setting they are a stumbling-block, especially the dog-Latin mock requiem for John Jayberd. Remarkable as it may seem, too, members of choirs have been known as recently as 1954 to object to some of Skelton's verbal imagery in 'Elinor Rumming'. The design of the suite is also perhaps to blame: the three short movements, each a gem, can seem to be outweighed by the two long movements, the latter of which, 'Jane Scroop', is so good that it is inclined to overshadow the whole work. In a really superb performance—such as I once heard the composer conduct—the total effect is cohesive and satisfying. Anything less is all too often episodic. That said, I must declare myself a passionate devotee of almost every bar of this racy, ribald and poetical suite. 'Elinor Rumming' bursts into life with a splendid motto-theme

which recurs throughout the movement whenever the composer wishes to restore order. Its first bar determines the shape and rhythm of much that follows, and it is clear that Elgar's suggestion of a setting of Skelton's verse had delighted Vaughan Williams, for the music sweeps and blusters along, sometimes in waltz time, at others in brisk 9/8. It is all uninhibited, virtuoso stuff, brought to a halt by 'Drunken Alice' whose hiccups and slurs are accompanied by a persistent nattering on piccolo, trumpet and horn as she retails her scandal. As she sinks to sleep, like Elgar's *Falstaff*, 'in cometh another rabble' who are not quite so spontaneous as the first arrivals. Their music is rather self-consciously 'folk', and they outstay their welcome by several bars. The Intermezzo, 'My proper Bess', is one of Vaughan Williams's charming love-songs, with the male chorus echoing the baritone's affirmations. It is simple, but most carefully wrought. The *Epitaph for John Jayberd of Diss*, whom Skelton had known and, evidently, detested, is for male chorus. They make no bones, if that is the phrase in this instance, about their pleasure at the unfortunate man's demise. The music rattles along, bursting out uncouthly every so often and breaking into 6/8 for a drinking-song. Eventually, after some brilliant choral writing, there is a heavily enunciated parody of the sacred office for the dead. The 'Romanza' which follows could hardly be in greater contrast. This too is a requiem, but not a parody. Instead of men celebrating the hoped-for departure of a dissembler, this is a convent child bemoaning the slaying of her pet sparrow by a cat. Skelton's delicacy is matched by the music, which has a tenderness and innocence wholly in keeping with the subject. The opening bars for solo cello, with woodwind plaintively crying overhead, evoke the picture of Jane (mezzo-soprano) and her companions (women's chorus) carrying their pathetic little coffin to its resting-place and chanting words from the Requiem. The *Dies Irae* is plucked out, and Jane describes her Philip's death in a remarkable melody which twists and turns on itself in grief:

Vengeance on the whole race of cats is cried; and Jane describes Philip's ways—'how he would leap and skip and take me by the lip'—in a G major passage, harmonized in sevenths and ninths, and accompanied by a vivid piece of bird portraiture in the orchestra.

The delicacy and brilliance of the orchestration throughout this movement have not had enough praise. The summons to all the birds to attend the funeral is followed by a marvellous orchestral passage as the air is filled with their flutterings and chirrupings: music of remarkable audacity and effectiveness. No less fine are the imaginative use of the *Dies Irae* and the chorus's assignation of funeral rôles to the birds accompanied by vivid portraiture and subtle changes of rhythm which gradually increase the tempo and avoid any tendency to monotony. At the height of the climax Jane's voice intones the Miserere, and the chorus, in a passage of superb beauty, sing of the oncoming of night and pray for rest for Philip Sparrow's soul. Jane sings her farewell, which is gently echoed by the choir. These last pages blaze with genius. The whole wonderful movement avoids parody, mawkishness and sentimentality. God marketh even the fall of a sparrow; and this music unerringly conveys how the smallest tragedy can mirror the greater cataclysms. The only way to follow this movement was by music of opposite mood; so Vaughan Williams closed the suite with a scherzo, 'Jolly Rutterkin', about a Tudor spiv, which brings the work to a satisfying end. Of great harmonic simplicity, its exciting and varied use of cross-rhythms is masterly.

Something of the bubbling energy of 'Elinor Rumming' spilled over into *Dona Nobis Pacem* where it was put to quite different use. As has been said often before, this cantata is avowedly propagandist and its design has been said to lack unity. Possibly on paper it does, but it is undeniably effective in performance. The opening prayer is strongly atmospheric: the orchestration is dark and rich, and the first two bars for orchestra generate the impassioned, almost frantic, choral supplication for peace which is in marked contrast to the soprano's more ethereal pleas. The frenzy of 'Beat, beat, drums!' is soon unleashed, Whitman's description of war's total impact upon the community. Drums and trumpets predominate, the music describing the bustle as well as the clangour of war. The storm subsides into E major, and the baritone sings the compassionate 'Reconciliation'—

Word over all, beautiful as the sky—

with its picture of the soldier and his dead enemy—'a man divine as myself'—which is surely a progenitor of Owen's *Strange Meeting*. The pathos of the poem is reflected in the following passage for unaccompanied chorus:

after which the soprano's 'Dona Nobis Pacem' is touching in its poignancy. The central movement, the 'Dirge for Two Veterans', was written before 1914. Nevertheless it fits into the cantata, for its simpler style is suited to this particular poem. The music abounds in beauties—the cool moonlight, for instance, evoked by women's voices, and the gradual domination by the bugles, leading into a noble C major dead march, proud and uplifting. The final pages are exquisite: the graveside, the bugles, the moonlight and the poet whose heart goes out to the father and son killed together:

The baritone declaims John Bright's famous words, and once again soprano and chorus make their frantic plea for peace. The baritone answers them with words of reassurance and a mood of optimism floods the music as the words 'Nation shall not lift up a sword against nation' and 'Peace on earth, goodwill towards men' are sung to an accompaniment of bells and other emanations of rejoicing in the manner of 'Let all the world in every corner sing' and of the finale, twenty years hence, of the eighth symphony. The jubilation dies away and the soprano has the last word, *niente*, but this does not obliterate the impression of happiness that the whole work, curiously, leaves. With the advantage of hindsight, we know that the optimism and faith were unjustified. The tract was too much of its times, but its splendid choral writing, its broad tunes, and the inspired quality of its finest moments give it vitality. And, taking the widest view, who shall say that its optimism will not finally be justified?

Two other vocal works appeared in 1936 which had been in progress for a decade. These were the setting of Synge's *Riders to the*

Sea and the romantic extravaganza *The Poisoned Kiss*. Neither is correctly described as an opera; the title-page of the former merely states '*Riders to the Sea* by J. M. Synge, set to music by R. Vaughan Williams', and the latter has set numbers and spoken dialogue. *Riders to the Sea* has its place among the half-dozen finest achievements of its composer. It has been called 'the English *Pelléas*', with some justification (if rather superficially) because, though on a much smaller scale, it is based on the same principle of subordination of the music to the inflections and rhythms of the characters' speech. Yet, as with Debussy, and even more positively, the music insidiously takes control, so that one leaves the theatre with the realization that one has heard one long unending melody. Vaughan Williams loved and understood *Pelléas*; Holst hated it. This is perhaps why *Riders to the Sea* is so much more effective than *Savitri*, which it resembles. The Synge setting is, in fact, the ultimate expression of Vaughan Williams's fascination by the Skye preacher whose excited words broke spontaneously into musical rhythms. The orchestra is treated as subtly and delicately as the singers, acting as a kind of emotional overtone to the events on the stage and to provide the incessant background of the sea. The music is constructed from closely linked thematic material, much of it deriving from the short orchestral prelude which represents the sea, the mighty element which shapes the destinies of the fisherfolk about whom Synge was writing:

The opening dialogue between Cathleen and Nora as they discuss in hushed tones whether some clothes from a drowned man in Donegal could have belonged to their brother Michael, who has been missing for a week, is typical of the mastery of the setting: natural speech supported by an occasional chord or by fragments of wood-wind phrases. The music takes command only at references to God and when the state of the sea is discussed: whether it will allow their only surviving brother, Bartley, to take the horses across to Galway Fair. It becomes even more positive on the appearance of Maurya, their mother, who has her own *leitmotif* based on rising intervals of a third

From this moment it is this old woman, a figure from Greek tragedy, who dominates the action. She has lost a husband and four sons to the sea. She knows she will lose Bartley and she quarrels with him when he insists on taking the horses to the mainland. Vaughan Williams, with infinite skill, allows the music gradually to expand as her rôle grows. When the girls persuade her to go after Bartley and take him a loaf of bread as a peace-offering she stands in the doorway and says: 'In the big world, the old people do be leaving things after them for their sons and children, but in this place it is the young men do be leaving things behind for them that do be old' and the music prophesies the Sixth Symphony of 1944-7:

It is strange that Vaughan Williams should have weakened the dramatic force of these lines by omitting what the play makes clear: that she picks up Michael's stick. On her return she rivets attention with her quiet monotone

one of the starkest, most compelling moments in opera. She
describes her vision of Bartley riding to the sea 'on the red mare'
followed on the grey pony by Michael, in fine clothes. This, she
knows, means that both sons are dead. She begins the long arioso
passage which is the *raison d'être* of the whole work and gives it very
nearly the character of a scena for contralto and orchestra. She
describes the deaths of her husband and sons to a 'keening' accompaniment of (off-stage) women's chorus: the same musical forces as
are used for the lament for Philip Sparrow but with what different
effect! As she sings, the villagers bring in Bartley's body: the grey
pony had knocked him into the waves. The body is laid on the table
and there is a long pause. The expectation is that Maurya will lose
her mind or act hysterically, but this is to be Synge's psychological
masterstroke, equalled by the music. A remarkable sense of relaxation and relief enters the music as Maurya sings 'They are all gone
now, and there isn't anything more the sea can do to[1] me'. Her
struggle against nature is over, and she is glad: 'But it's a great rest
I'll have now.'

The music hovers between C sharp minor and E major. Cathleen
and Nora, unable to understand the resignation of age, think
Maurya's mind is broken, but she does not hear their comments.
In a passage of plainsong she blesses the departed, and the music
radiantly enters E major as she prays God's blessing on the living,
a remarkable example of a dramatic switch from minor to major
and a notable musical affirmation of life's triumph over death.
'No man at all can be living for ever, and we must be satisfied' are
the last words of this thirty-minute masterpiece.

Apart from the symphonic logic and economy of the music, what
are the reasons for the superiority of *Riders to the Sea* over Vaughan
Williams's other vocal stage works? Part of genius is the power to
do the unexpected and to perceive where, in the unlikeliest

---

[1] In the vocal score the phrase is printed as 'do for me' and this is usually sung,
although it is plainly nonsense. The autograph vocal score shows that the error arose
from Adeline's copying of the text, although R.V.W. corrected the 'for' to 'to' in pencil.

surroundings, poetry lies. No one could have expected that Synge's gloomy play would appeal to Vaughan Williams, yet he clearly saw its musical potentiality at a glance. Its theme of man's fortitude in the face of implacable nature is the same as later evoked powerful music from him to illustrate Scott's journey to the Pole. Moreover it gave him his best libretto. Maurya is a wonderfully developed character. She interests us from her first appearance. We care about her, more perhaps than we care about Falstaff, certainly much more than we care about Hugh and Mary or any of the cardboard characters of *The Poisoned Kiss*. As she acts out her hour upon the stage, she develops and grows, which Pilgrim in *The Pilgrim's Progress* does not. Nor has Vaughan Williams had to deal here with the conventional villainy of opera or with more sinister human evil, depiction of neither of which came easily to him. The 'villain' in *Riders* is the sea. This extraordinary work has been consistently underrated while other works of a similar kind not by Englishmen have been over-praised.

There could be no greater contrast to the Synge opera than *The Poisoned Kiss*, one of Vaughan Williams's tantalizing problemworks. This charming work suffers from one fatal flaw: despite all appearances to the contrary the libretto and the music are at odds, and the libretto, to make matters worse, is at odds with itself. Much of Evelyn Sharp's book is genuinely witty; other parts have a rather obvious, schoolboyish humour which is peculiarly English—the type of humour to be found in some of Elgar's letters and Vaughan Williams's writings. This humour is amusing enough in the private circle at which it is aimed, but it does not happily translate into the more public medium of stage dialogue. Thus *The Poisoned Kiss* is in a way too sophisticated for amateur societies and not sophisticated enough for the West End. It is both smart revue and pantomime, and its characters are emblems of situations, not really living creations. The music, often witty too, is basically too simple and too heartfelt to fit comfortably into the artificial background. Try as he might, Vaughan Williams could not be brittle. He could be as melodious as Sullivan but not as detached. So we have the unhappy result that *The Poisoned Kiss* seems to be doomed to performance by schools and amateurs who can vary the dialogue to include their own private allusions and topicalities but who rarely have the voices and the instrumental forces to give the music its proper due in strength and full-bloodedness. Such tunes as 'Blue larkspur in a garden', 'O who would be unhappy me', 'Wearily I go to rest', 'Long have I waited', 'Love breaks all rules' and 'When I was young' do not deserve to be consigned to a dusty shelf. The music accompanying the vision of the young lovers which the Empress conjures up for Dipsacus is of heart-breaking beauty. The mediums' tango is typical of the enjoyment the composer obviously had in writing the work. One day, perhaps, English operatic life will not be governed wholly and solely by box-office returns. When that day comes, *Riders to the Sea* should receive the acclaim it has not yet fully achieved, and *The Poisoned Kiss* may have a chance to show that its virtues—its grand tunes—outweigh its defects. It will not be the first opera to survive such a situation.

For the next few years, Vaughan Williams was content with smaller works, several of them commissions, while he prepared the Fifth Symphony and for what was to prove to be his remarkable last fifteen-year creative period. The two Coronation works of 1937 were effective enough. The *Te Deum* in F is founded on traditional tunes, but the words and the music do not 'go' well together, and one feels that the exultant blustering from the brass is needed to sustain the impulse. Only when 'Dives and Lazarus' makes a late appearance at 'Thou sittest at the right hand of God' does the work really touch the heart. It is, in any case, a thoroughly extrovert ceremonial piece, right for the right occasion.[1] The *Flourish for a Coronation* is a much better work, particularly in its first half where the florid ornamental writing is in the true Purcellian manner, and at 8 there is a spikiness reminiscent of Walton's *Portsmouth Point*. Neither is in the class of the exquisite Serenade to Music of 1938. This, as I suggested earlier, is a virtuoso piece, but the quality of the music is so high that one is never conscious of artifice because art predominates. Vaughan Williams could always find the apt lyrical mood in which to hymn music—as in the *Five Mystical Songs*

[1] R.V.W. had a 'soft spot' for this work. He wrote to Graham Steed in November 1938: 'I'm so glad your boys like my *Te Deum*. Most people don't.' I received also the following reminiscence from Sir William McKie of a conversation with R.V.W. about the 1953 Coronation music: 'We discussed the question of a Te Deum for some time. I think he would have liked me to offer to repeat his 1937 *Coronation Te Deum* for he obviously cared for it very much and talked a good deal about it; the high point of the afternoon came when he looked at me with a mischievous gleam in his eye and said: "One of the folk songs I used in it was ——, and no one has ever noticed!" This story is spoilt because unfortunately I simply cannot remember the name of the folk song; it was something like "Tarry Trowsers" but far more frivolous.' It may have been 'Lovely Joan', from which the brass fanfare-motif could conceivably have been derived.

and the 'music in the house' passage from *The Pilgrim's Progress*—
and in the Serenade he deepens the mood by its nocturnal associations. The work is all silver and moonlight. Harp, clarinet, violin
solo and strings create an atmosphere of calm and peace into which
the voices enter as mellifluously as in any music there is. Fanfares—
later borrowed for *The Pilgrim's Progress*—punctuate the music,
there is a touch of humour at 'the man who has no music in himself',
but the enchanted mood of the opening returns in D major. What
a work it is, unique and original. Music is often described as
'glowing'. This Serenade shines, as strongly and clearly as the full
moon. There is no doubt that its original form, for its sixteen
special singers, was undoubtedly its best. The orchestral version has
beauty, but this is essentially music for voices, not even music for a
choir, and to subtract voices from its texture is to damage it almost
irreparably.

Another labour of love is the Five Variants of 'Dives and Lazarus',
a musing upon shapes and aspects of the great folk song he had
known from his childhood, written for strings and harp with that
superb technical skill which enabled Vaughan Williams to extract
the utmost in nuances and sonorities from the instruments. The tune
goes back to the sixteenth century, being mentioned in Fletcher's
comedy *Monsieur Thomas*. It was usually sung as a carol, 'Come all
ye faithful Christians', and was known in Ireland as 'The Star of
the County Down' and in Scotland as 'Gilderoy'. Other variants are
'The Thresher' and 'Cold blows the wind'. The tune as it appears
in *English County Songs* was noted by A. J. Hipkins in Westminster,
of all places, without words. Vaughan Williams collected many
variants, one of them, in Norfolk in 1905, to the words 'The Murder
of Maria Martin in the Red Barn'. In the work for strings, the tune
is announced in the rich harmonies it craves. Variant I is in triple
time, with the harps giving an antiphonal commentary; Variant II
is faster, an outline in three-bar phrases; III has a new modal
version of the tune in D minor, followed by a variation in F minor,
and a solo violin; IV is a lively 2/4 and V is 'Maria Martin' slightly
changed. This is driven to a great climax which diminishes to a
cello solo and a rising arpeggio and brings the tune full circle.

The *Six Choral Songs to be sung in time of war*, to words by
Shelley, have been rarely heard, but are far from negligible. Their
style is perhaps severe, although the *Serenade to Music* sent an
echo into the closing bars of the third song

Household Music subjects three famous hymn-tunes to affectionate familiarity. The best movement is the second, where 'St. Denio' is treated rhythmically, as Holst treated it in his 'Festival Chime', and the tune is presented in its familiar form only at the end. No work more aptly illustrates Vaughan Williams's belief that music should be a part of everyday life and that the humblest music should have distinctiveness. In none of these small works does one feel that a great mind was stooping to trivial tasks; a great musician was giving of his best to whatever he undertook. On a larger scale this is true of the film music. Writing for the films, whatever its mental discipline, seems to have rekindled the opulent orchestral style of *A London Symphony* matured by experience. Warmth and freedom characterize *49th Parallel* and *Coastal Command*, but their claim to attention is as a sign of a mind moving towards the E minor symphony.

The culmination of this period in Vaughan Williams's career was the Fifth Symphony in D major written between 1938 and 1943. No supreme work of art—for such it is—has seemed to be the product of so many varied constituent elements as this noble symphony. Parts of it were first heard as music for a pageant about preservation of the countryside from 'bungaloid growth'; it shares several themes with the morality *The Pilgrim's Progress*; its original dedication to Sibelius talked about flattery and imitation, although a passage for strings in the first movement, the similarity of the opening to the opening of Sibelius's fifth symphony, and the use of germinal *motifs* are the only possible justification for such terms. Then, it was subjected to as much verbal commentary of an irrelevant nature as its predecessor had been. Naturally, for those who thought that the Prophet Vaughan had foretold World War II in the F minor Symphony, the D major was heaven-sent. Now, in the midst of war, he had seen the vision of Peace Eternal. Unfortunately, they did not know that the vision had first taken shape in 1938. Then, even more laughable as it now seems, there were those who announced that this was a symphonist's farewell, a musician's Nunc Dimittis. They, too, were soon confounded. It really is safer to regard Vaughan Williams's un-named symphonies as absolute music. Other delvers discovered that the opening of the Fifth Symphony could be derived from the quiet episode in the finale of the F minor. It can also be derived from *A London Symphony* and *The Shepherds of the Delectable Mountains*. That the symphonies are linked is indisputable, but the link seems to be that both begin with uncertain key centres and proceed to demonstrate, one forcibly, the other tranquilly, how the uncertainty can be resolved. Nor can one scoff at those who retain wartime emotional associations with this work.

The composer was uncertain what key-title to give the symphony. It begins with an octave C held by the cellos and basses above which two horns play the call in D major which haunts the movement:

Two other fragments are the plain material out of which this glorious movement is made. This for cellos and basses:

and this for the violins:

a characteristic ascending theme. These tunes are expanded and the music's uncertainty turns to assurance and to the famous moment when it soars out of C minor into E major, a dramatic and moving passage of exultation which is a musical parallel with the sun breaking through the clouds. The short development section makes much play with a three-note figure containing a flattened second:

which passes from one instrument to another like some sinister

warning and flares up the strings to a Sibelian climax. The horn call
reappears and there is a mighty affirmation—for the full orchestra
dominated by the brass—of the second subject which can now be
heard to be yet a further use of the 'Sine Nomine' tune, this time
the 'Alleluia', identical in melodic outline for twelve notes, except
for the omission of a passing-note:

The Scherzo comes second for the first time in Vaughan Williams's
symphonies. It is the swiftest moving, most Arielesque of his
scherzos, but its orchestration has a curious tartness which justifies
some commentators' references to Bunyan's 'hobgoblin and foul
fiend'. There are at least five themes, one cantabile, one (for oboe and
cor anglais) with a spiteful barb to its jerky rhythm (like gargoyles
with their tongues out), one lilting like some etherealized folk dance,
a chorale for trombones and finally a chirpy woodwind theme. The
music is mainly soft, but there are frequent loud interruptions and
changes of rhythm. It ends as mysteriously as it began, flickering to
swift extinction.

None of Vaughan Williams's major works requires such polished
playing as this symphony. Its pellucid textures, its finely calculated
balance between orchestral sections and its rhythmical elasticity
demand careful rehearsal, especially in the Scherzo. Yet an English
critic could write of it[1] that it was 'not music demanding great
finesse or delicacy of tone'. Is it any wonder English music is sometimes misunderstood by our neighbours abroad? Imagine the
wonderful 'Romanza' slow movement played without finesse! It is
in this movement—which can be placed alongside the Larghetto of
Elgar's second symphony as the high peaks of English romantic
symphonic art—that most of the Pilgrim music occurs. The cor
anglais theme and subsequent passages are all in Act I, Scene 2,
'*The House Beautiful*'. Here, however, is a symphonic commentary
on those themes, sufficient unto itself. The agitation at the centre of

[1] The *Daily Telegraph*, 26 March 1957.

the movement is Pilgrim's 'Save me Lord! My burden is greater than I can bear', but the opera contains nothing as reassuring nor as magnificent as the rich and sonorous restatement of the cor anglais theme by all the strings. This great flood of sound, coming after a passage which recalls the hesitant mood of the Scherzo, is the consummation of the mood of serenity which had found expression in the Serenade, Household Music and the fourth *Tudor Portrait*. It culminates in an impassioned declamation of a phrase said to be a quotation of the 'Alleluia' of 'Lasst uns erfreuen'. The resemblance is there, but the composer denied that it was intentional and said it was more like the second phrase of 'The First Nowell'. It is also extremely like a variant of 'Dives and Lazarus', and it seems feasible that, at this moment of high exaltation, Vaughan Williams should subconsciously echo a tune which had meant so much to him. The climax dies away with each section of the orchestra meditating upon this phrase in an air of still tranquillity while a solo violin has its own incantation, or 'Benedictus'. For rich polyphony, symphonic design and expressive content the movement is at once the reverse of and parallel with its fellow movement in the F minor—reverse in its more extrovert mood, parallel in its logic.

The last movement is a Passacaglia, though not a strict one. The broad, spacious theme has a counter-melody of which one phrase again echoes 'Nowell'. There is also resemblance of theme and mood to the last section of *Dona Nobis Pacem*, but self-quotation was not Vaughan Williams's method and these likenesses are merely examples of similar emotions evoking similar personal musical images from the composer. Throughout the Passacaglia there is a sense of journeying towards an appointed goal, and we reach it with the return, fervent and affirmatory, of the D major horn call from the beginning of the symphony. The ecstasy slackens, the strings briefly recall the violins' first phrase from the Preludio and then begin the benedictory coda (which is not given the term Epilogue because it is a logical part of the whole movement); this coda is based on the counter-melody of the Passacaglia, slightly altered rhythmically and extended, soaring effortlessly to top B as the strings weave and interweave their miraculous counterpoint.

This symphony is, in one respect, an epitome of the contemplative side of Vaughan Williams's muse. But it has a hard centre, the result of fertilization by the F minor, which makes the Sixth Symphony comprehensible as its logical sequel and gives the three works their close-knit unity. No one has yet had the courage to play all three in one concert-programme, but it would be a revealing spiritual and musical experience. They are at once the summit and the kernel of Vaughan Williams's art; and the greatest of the three—perhaps of all his works—is, in my opinion, this Symphony of the Celestial City.[1]

---

[1] That was my opinion in 1963 and sometimes it still is; but I now tend to the view that the greatest and most original of Vaughan Williams's symphonies is the *Pastoral*, which more than ever sounds to me to be his 'War Requiem'.

CHAPTER NINE

1943–1952

Principal Works[1]

OBOE CONCERTO . FANTASIA ON THE OLD 104TH PSALM TUNE
STRING QUARTET IN A MINOR . THE SONS OF LIGHT
SYMPHONY (NO. 6) IN E MINOR . THE PILGRIM'S PROGRESS
FOLK SONGS OF THE FOUR SEASONS . ROMANCE FOR HARMONICA
AN OXFORD ELEGY . SINFONIA ANTARTICA

THE FIFTH SYMPHONY was eagerly taken up by orchestras in Britain and played at concerts thronged by music-hungry members of the Services as well as by civilians. It was soon recorded, by the Hallé Orchestra conducted by John Barbirolli, who had returned to England in June 1943 to revitalize the musical life of the North. The United States swiftly showed an interest. A letter to Vaughan Williams from Olin Downes, music critic of the *New York Times*, dated 25 August 1943, discloses that he had been told by Artur Rodzinski, Barbirolli's successor as conductor of the New York Philharmonic-Symphony Orchestra, that application for score and parts had already been made.[2] 'I am particularly eager to hear this work,' Downes wrote. '. . . I am one of the unregenerates who has not been able perhaps to enter adequately into the essential quality of your fourth symphony, or fully to appreciate this work at its ultimate value.' The deeply spiritual and lovable qualities of the Fifth Symphony were welcomed by many musicians. An American writer in the *Christian Science Monitor* even suggested that its simplicity would 'shock young ears attuned to harsh discords'. A typical English response, although this letter was not written until April 1947, was from Arnold Barter of Bristol, an employee of W. D. and

---

[1] The works written by Vaughan Williams in the last fifteen years of his life are discussed in the second part of Chapter Ten, pages 347–70.

[2] Rodzinski conducted the first American performance of the symphony in Carnegie Hall on 30 November 1944.

H. O. Wills, who was a most enterprising amateur conductor and had given the third performance of *A Sea Symphony*.

'In the first three movements the work seems to embody the very core of what you have been saying to us in earlier days, but in a kind of sublimated form so that one finds that a single note more, or less, would spoil the whole thing. But towards the end of the last movement something supernatural seems to creep in . . . and the work finishes in another world. . . . The scherzo got well on to its legs though I was not sorry when it was safely over!'

With the anxiety of the first performance behind him, Vaughan Williams was able to concentrate on other projects. A discarded scherzo of the symphony was turned into part of an Oboe Concerto for Léon Goossens. It was due to be played at a Promenade Concert on 5 July 1944, but this particular concert was among those cancelled because of flying-bombs and the first performance took place in Liverpool on 30 September 1944. The Second String Quartet, written for Jean Stewart, was completed and played on the composer's seventy-second birthday. Some music from *49th Parallel* found a more permanent form in this work, as well as a theme from a film about Joan of Arc for which Vaughan Williams had been asked to write the music but which never materialized.[1] The B.B.C. asked for incidental music for Shakespeare's *Richard II*; the music was written but not used.[2] A new symphony began to take form in sketch-books, and there was always the Pilgrim opera to look over and revise. His principal task, however, in 1943–4 was completion of the choral work commissioned by the B.B.C. for use when Hitler was eventually overthrown. He and William Walton had already had a brush with the B.B.C. over this 'victory anthem'. Both declined a commission because they found it impossible to comply with the official condition that the composition should be 'symbolic of all the fighting freedom nations' and not take longer than five minutes to play. The difficulty was resolved in R.V.W.'s case, and by Christmas 1943 he had sent his 'libretto' to his old collaborator, Harold Child, for his comments. Child replied on Christmas Day, saying he had 'got very keen on it' although 'I always hated speakers to, or through,

---

[1] Mention of a proposed film of Shaw's *St. Joan* to be produced by Gabriel Pascal with Greta Garbo as Joan was made in the *Daily Telegraph* of 23 June 1943, but there is no evidence to show that this was the film concerned.

[2] This was stated by R.V.W. in a letter to Hubert Foss, and it has been confirmed for me by Mr. Val Gielgud.

music but that, of course, is outside my terms of reference here, so don't take any notice. The choice and arrangement of the book seem to me almost miraculously good. I'm enthusiastic. And they sort of progress in a way that makes me long to hear the music. What a chance for that "no wobble" soprano at the close!' The work, originally called *Thanksgiving for Victory*, was completed in 1944 and was recorded by the B.B.C. on 5 November of that year, ready for transmission when victory was achieved. Valentine Dyall was the speaker, Elsie Suddaby the soprano and Sir Adrian Boult the conductor. It was first heard on the Sunday morning of 13 May 1945.

Before the war ended, the Fifth Symphony's two 'satellites', the A minor Quartet and the Oboe Concerto, were performed. Dealing symphonically with themes from the Pilgrim opera seems to have enabled Vaughan Williams to concentrate again on the opera itself, which, by 1945, was nearing completion. The new symphony, too, was well under way. Its origins are curious. Vaughan Williams had enjoyed writing music for Jeffrey Dell's film *Flemish Farm* (and had derived amusement from the exiled Belgian Government's protest over a love scene in a barn which had to be altered to make it clear that the couple were married. This reminded him of French prudery in his youth, when the curtain was lowered just before Faust went into Marguérite's bedroom.) Two themes conceived for the film but not used in the final sound-track became the openings respectively of the second and fourth movements of the symphony. The former, because of its rhythm, was called by the film orchestra 'Two hot sausages' and the latter 'Miserable Starkey'.

Throughout his career, as has been shown, Vaughan Williams was always anxious to consult other musicians about his compositions, to seek technical advice and help. After Holst's death, Gordon Jacob was one such helper. From 1944 to 1958 Vaughan Williams consulted Roy Douglas, a brilliant musician, and sent most of his scores to him for perusal. Douglas first helped Vaughan Williams late in 1942 over some film music. In 1944 he made a reduced orchestration of *Thanskgiving for Victory*. On their first meeting R.V.W. asked gruffly, 'Did you go to the College or the Academy?' 'Neither; I'm afraid I'm one of those dreadful self-taught musicians.' 'Thank God for that,' R.V.W. answered. 'I get very tired of these young men from the College who think they know everything.'[1] Unfor-

[1] *R.C.M. Magazine*, Easter Term 1959, Vol. LV, No. 1, p. 49.

tunately, owing to Vaughan Williams's prolific creative activity at an advanced age and also to his habit of introducing Roy Douglas to people with the jocular comment: 'This is the man who writes my music for me,' certain people put the story about that Vaughan Williams did not orchestrate many of his last works. The allegation was made in print and over the radio by people who ought to have known better. It was even suggested that Mr. Douglas had himself professed to have orchestrated some of these works, a false and hurtful charge which he emphatically denied. This, therefore, seems the moment to quote from Mr. Douglas's own account of their work together:[1]

'There were . . . occasions when V.W. was unsure about the balance of his scoring—"will the tune come through?" was his constant concern— especially during recent years when his hearing played such unkind tricks; at these times he asked for, and genuinely wanted, a second opinion.[2] (He frequently said "I ask everybody's advice, but never promise to take any of it"). . . . I would receive a letter in R.V.W.'s delightfully illegible handwriting telling me that he had written another work . . . . and asking me to go and play it to him on the piano, so that he could see "whether any of it was worth keeping".'

The first play-through would be to a few close friends. Then R.V.W. would say he must 'put in a good deal of homework' on the score. The next play-through, some weeks later, would be to a gathering of musicians whose opinions he valued such as Sir Arthur Bliss, Frank Howes, Scott Goddard, Edmund Rubbra, Herbert Howells, Gerald Finzi, and others. All were asked to be frankly critical and he would listen to all they had to say.

'Sometimes,' Mr. Douglas wrote, 'a movement was much re-shaped in accordance with suggestions made on one of these occasions . . . I am inclined to think that the passages which he altered were probably passages about which he already had doubts. When he was quite sure that a movement was exactly the right shape and its component sections justly balanced, no amount of discussion could change his mind. More weeks would pass, and then I would go once more to play the work to him. . . . Now my work would start in earnest, for at this point the full score

---

[1] Op. cit., pp. 46–48.
[2] A letter from Vaughan Williams to Roy Douglas, 14 June 1950, about the *Fantasia on The Old 104*th said, for instance: 'There are some points . . . I want you to look out for. 1. The pitch of the piccolo. I sometimes think I write it too high and sometimes too low. Please alter that according to your own taste. 2. The pitch of the glockenspiel. The same thing applies.'

would be handed over to me so that I could begin "washing its face"—which was V.W.'s own phrase for my ministrations.

'R.V.W.'s manuscript being what it was, a more easily readable copy was considered to be kinder to conductors and to the copyists of the orchestral parts. This new score was by no means a "mere copying job", for a great number of details had to be tidied up and adjusted according to my own judgment or else queried with the composer. He wrote his scores in ink and apparently very quickly, and many unintentional discrepancies found their way on to the pages. Small things such as a missing bass clef after a tenor, *arco* missing after *pizz.*, "change to flute 2" missing after piccolo, clarinets in A mistransposed as in B flat,[1] trumpet passages written on the horns line for a few bars—all these were easily put right. At times, however, the complete woodwind or brass section or timpani would be playing up to the end of a right-hand page and over the page there would be blank bars; in these instances I would pencil-in what I thought he might have intended as continuation and send it to him. Sometimes my guess was right, and sometimes entirely wrong. Again, perhaps one of those curious scale-passages would have a G sharp in all the wind and a G natural in all the strings when it was quite obvious that they ought to be the same. On consulting the piano score I might find that it had F, or A, and not G at all. Another query for the composer to answer. There were also occasions when I just could not read the notes. . . . R.V.W. allowed me to refashion his harp, piano and xylophone parts because he liked to think that I could improve the layout for the pedals, fingers and sticks, thus making the parts more enjoyable for the players. Apart from this I think I can only claim to have "composed" one note of his music: for the benefit of the curious, this note is the last quaver of the solo cello, second bar of figure 21, second movement of ninth symphony. . . . The description which has sometimes been given of Vaughan Williams as a clumsy amateur whose scoring was incompetent and slipshod should be firmly contradicted now. . . . His scoring was indeed unconventional—which is hardly surprising—but he knew what he was doing and why he was doing it, and he spent a very great deal of time in getting the smallest details to his satisfaction; even to the extent of rescoring passages in works long after they had been printed and published. . . .'

The comments on the orchestration of his music were to reach a climax after the first performance of *Sinfonia Antartica* in 1953, when Eric Blom in the *Observer* derided the idea that any other hand could

---

[1] V.W. told Sir John Barbirolli: 'I always hate that damned A clarinet—I have never got on with it, and I have still got to count the transpositions on my fingers.'—*Music and Musicians*, October 1958, p. 15.

have scored this work. When Vaughan Williams received a letter of congratulation on the scoring from Neville Cardus, he wrote back, under the erroneous impression that Cardus was still in Manchester, invoking his aid in scotching the rumours. The letter, from The White Gates, was dated 28 January 1953:

'. . . I understand that a malicious rumour is going around Manchester that I had not scored it myself. The answer to this is obvious—that if Roy Douglas had scored it it would have sounded a great deal better. I can ignore these malicious tongues; but still, in case the matter does crop up again, I should like to tell you what Roy Douglas actually did do, for which I am very grateful to him: firstly he made a beautiful copy of the score (my writing is very bad) and in making the copy he discovered a lot of careless errors on my part (I am incorrigibly careless). For example, sometimes the oboe doubles the violin and when the end of the phrase goes over the page, I forgot to complete the oboe part, and various small things like that. And there were obvious mistakes which I made— wrong notes, and so on. These he corrected for me. He also made valuable suggestions as to the pianoforte and celesta parts. I am no pianist and he showed me ways of getting the same effect in a much more pianistic way. In one place he advised me to alter a passage because it reminded him of Elgar's *In the South*; but in no case did he make an alteration without consulting me first. We had long talks and letters over the whole matter. Sometimes I accepted his amendments and sometimes I did not. As I say, I am prepared to ignore all these idle tongues, but if the matter does crop up again I owe it to Mr. Douglas to explain what happened. He earns his living by orchestration and I should not like him to be blamed for my shortcomings.'

It cannot be too strongly emphasized that the only trustworthy full scores of most of the later large-scale works, from about 1947 to 1958, are those in the handwriting of Roy Douglas and the printed scores which were engraved from these. After Vaughan Williams had written out his final draft, or 'fair copy', it was carefully scrutinized, edited in close consultation with the composer, and copied by Mr. Douglas. When this task was completed, all further alterations and adjustments made *by the composer* after rehearsals and performances—dynamics, tempo markings, notes, changes in orchestration, interpolated or deleted bars—were inserted in the photographed copies of the Douglas scores and subsequently included in the printed scores, but were seldom added in the composer's manuscript scores. It is obvious, therefore, that the full scores in Vaughan Williams's handwriting, most of which are now in the British

Museum, do not represent these works as the composer wished them to be performed. In a different category are the Douglas full scores of *The Pilgrim's Progress*; these contain many alterations which were apparently made for reasons connected with the stage performances, but most of which were neither authorized by the composer nor supervised by Mr. Douglas.

To return to the Sixth Symphony: this was played through at The White Gates by Michael Mullinar on 14 July 1946. On 13 February 1947, Vaughan Williams wrote to Roy Douglas:

'I have been foolish enough to write another symphony. Could you undertake to vet and then copy the score? If in the course of this you have any improvements to suggest I wd receive them with becoming gratitude.'

Some time later he sent the full score and pianoforte arrangement to Douglas asking him:

'Please (1) correct all actual errors of notes etc.
      (2) correct all obvious errors of judgment
      (3) All other cases which may be a matter of opinion, but which you think are wrong make a list of from time to time. I shall value your opinion very much though I do not promise always to accept your advice. . . . I feel very happy leaving it in your experienced hands.'

On 5 June Mullinar played the symphony through four times at the Royal College of Music and 'magically turned an R.C.M. piano into a full orchestra',[1] Roy Douglas said. Howard Ferguson, James Friskin, Adrian Boult, Malcolm Sargent, John Barbirolli, Gerald and Joy Finzi and Ursula Wood were among those present, as was R. O. Morris who later wrote to Adeline:

'I was immensely impressed and thought the symph. unquestionably the finest thing he has done since the F minor. Whether I shall eventually like it quite as much as that remains to be seen, for the F minor remains for me about Ralph's high-water mark. The new one is less faithful to the traditions of classical symphonic structure (as far as I can judge) than the F mi., which is probably a merit in itself, but not for me personally, who am a slow and stupid listener and find it rather comforting to have certain expected things happen at certain places. But the sustained vigour and originality of the musical ideas is most imposing—truly astonishing to one who knows how incessantly Ralph has been labouring in one way and another since the war started.'

[1] *R.C.M. Magazine*, Vol. LV, No. 1, op. cit., p. 46.

Yes, but he thrived on incessant labour. Thinking ahead in 1944 to the time when the Leith Hill Festival would again be held, he found time to prepare an English version of Bach's B minor Mass, in which he was assisted in certain details by his friend Robert Müller-Hartmann, and work on this proceeded throughout 1945 and 1946. Vaughan Williams's purpose was to enable the music to be sung at Anglican services and to preserve the 'incomparable language' of the English liturgy. 'It seems, therefore, worth while occasionally to alter a crotchet into two quavers, to re-articulate a tied note or even (occasionally) to add a note, or (very occasionally) to omit one, for the sake of keeping the Prayer Book text unaltered,' he wrote in his programme note to the Dorking performances in 1947 and 1948.[1] His standing in English musical life in 1945 was that of the undisputed leader of his art and profession. Moreover, he was now dubbed the Grand Old Man of English Music, a phrase he cordially detested, saying that he was not grand and not old. It is indeed a hateful tag, perhaps inescapable in a country which tends to appreciate its great men only when they are over sixty-five. But it illustrates the special affection which everyone, musician and man-in-the-street, had for him. He was very conscious of his fortune in finding appreciation in his own lifetime. He was grateful, but not everyone remained unenvious. Holbrooke, for example, would write him vitriolic letters—in purple ink—railing at his success 'at others' expense'.

In April 1946 *Sir John in Love* had at last achieved professional performance at Sadler's Wells, with Roderick Jones as Falstaff, Anna Pollak as Mrs. Ford and Howell Glynne as Ford. The work still failed to impress itself adequately upon the audience, due chiefly to a tame and disappointing performance with a small orchestra, bad sets and staging which suggested to the composer that 'they had turned out their oldest costumes from the wardrobe'. November 1946 was a great month, with a concert of his music at Southwark Cathedral on the 16th, conducted by the faithful Dr. E. T. Cook, containing *Toward the Unknown Region*, the *Magnificat*, the *Tallis Fantasia* (which the composer conducted) and *Sancta Civitas*. Richard Capell, in the *Daily Telegraph* of 18 November, found the right words:

'The great music gained by the appropriate beauty of the setting. . . .

---

[1] Reprinted in *National Music and Other Essays*.

Sancta Civitas towers above its age. While in its starkness and the frostiness of its atmosphere the music is worlds away from Elgar, this apocalyptic oratorio is the culmination of that trilogy whose third part Elgar contemplated but never carried out. Among living composers, not only in England but even in the world, Vaughan Williams alone is of the stature, the superiority of mind and imagination, to rise to the sublimity of the text.'

On the 22nd, St. Cecilia's Day, the Pianoforte Concerto in its revised form for two pianofortes was played at the Albert Hall by Cyril Smith and Phyllis Sellick. The rearrangement evidently aroused the wrath of the original soloist, Harriet Cohen, for Vaughan Williams wrote, some months later, in pacification:

Dear Harriet,

I am sorry you feel cross about the concerto. But, you know, you had it all to yourself, I think, for a year. Most people for whom I have written things are content with a first performance and then are willing to have it thrown open. Since that time many other pianists have played it (including Cyril Smith himself)—and you know you cd. not have played it by yourself on 2 pftes (one hand on each?) any more than if I had arranged it for organ or ukelele. At the time of the 1st performance many people urged me to rearrange it for 2 pftes—they thought it too heavy going for one. But I held on so as to give the 1 pfte a good send-off before I did anything. Have a good time in U.S.A. and bring back plenty of dollars. I am so glad about the recording of the Gibbons[1]—I shall probably rearrange that for 4 bass tubas and a banjo.

                                                         Love from R.V.W.

Work on the rearrangement was roughed out by Vaughan Williams in August. He then sent his score for detailed work to Mr. Cooper who began his task at Castle Cary, Somerset, on 20 September 1946. It was completed in about three weeks. Any tricky passage was referred by post to Vaughan Williams who sent back his suggestions, and the final version was sent to Mr. Smith and his wife, Miss Sellick.

On the same night as the concerto was played in London, Clarence Raybould conducted the Finnish National State Opera Orchestra in Helsinki in the Fifth Symphony, and Jean Sibelius was at last able to hear the work dedicated to him 'without permission' at a time when England and Finland were technically

---

[1] *Hymn Tune Prelude on 'Song 13' by Orlando Gibbons*, recorded by Miss Cohen on Columbia DX 1552 (78 r.p.m.).

enemies. Although he had been silent since 1926, Sibelius's reputation was at its peak in Britain in 1945. The public saw in his work a combination of classical procedure and a ruggedness which appealed to them as being of the twentieth century although the harmonic language was largely of the nineteenth. He was still regarded as one of the giants of the musical world. Five other 'giants' were still active as the war in Europe ended. Richard Strauss, at eighty-one, was in his final, under-rated autumnal phase which produced the oboe concerto, *Metamorphosen*, the Duet Concertino and the Four Last Songs. In style and outlook he seemed very much a stranger stranded on the shore of a land to which he was alien, but his music's popularity with audiences was as strong as ever and when he returned to London to conduct at the Strauss Festival in October 1947 the old warrior was saluted accordingly. The other four 'giants' were living in exile in the United States. Nearest in age to Vaughan Williams but furthest away in musical style was Arnold Schoenberg (born 1874), whose 12-note system was still derided in English academic circles and was at this time the object of admiration principally by his American pupils in Los Angeles. Of the older generation of pupils who had fought his Vienna battles with him, Anton Webern was dead, the chance victim of war, and Egon Wellesz and Erwin Stein were working in Britain where eventually they were to influence a whole new generation of composers. To Schoenberg's adherents, Vaughan Williams is the antithesis of all that they believe. Yet these words of Schoenberg could as well have been written by the Englishman: 'If a composer does not write from the heart, he simply cannot produce good music. . . . I write what I feel in my heart—and what finally comes on paper is what first coursed through every fibre of my body. . . . Beauty is the result of intuition; when the one ceases to be, the other ceases also.' Stravinsky (born 1882) became an American citizen in 1945. He was producing at this date such varied works as the *Ebony Concerto*, the Concerto in D for strings and the masterly Symphony in Three Movements. In the restless variety of his output he is perhaps closest to Vaughan Williams of the five names under discussion, but in no other way. 'Composition is a daily function that I am compelled to discharge,' he wrote. 'I compose because I am made for that and cannot do otherwise.' Hindemith (born 1895) became an American citizen in 1946. He had hitherto enjoyed respect rather than popularity, but the last years of the war brought about a deeper note of feeling in his music culminating, strangely enough, in a setting of Whitman's 'When Lilacs last in the Dooryard Bloom'd'. Greatest of all, in Vaughan Williams's estimation and perhaps eventually in posterity's, was Béla Bartók, who died of leukaemia in New York aged sixty-four on 26 September 1945, neglected except by a few perceptive musicians, and almost in poverty. It is to the eternal credit of the American Society of Composers, Authors and Publishers that in the last tragic part of Bartók's life it paid all his hospital bills and eventually for his funeral. He had burned himself out in five years in America, trying to scrape a living from concerts and lectures, working on his folk-song collection (which he considered to be his most important activity), and in a burst of creative work undoubtedly impelled by homesickness for Hungary. The Concerto for Orchestra, the Sonata, the Third Pianoforte Concerto and the unfinished Viola Concerto are evidence not of decline but of a trend towards a more popular, more tonal style. He died, like Holst, with his work half done, for it seemed that he was achieving a synthesis of the component parts of his excitable and complex musical personality. His outlook was parallel with R.V.W.'s.

'The musical language of a "national composer" must be as natural to him as his native tongue' [he wrote]. '. . . It is always the composer with strength, purpose and individuality who puts his country on the map, and not the other way around. The appropriate use of folk-song material, the basis for national music, is not limited to the sporadic introduction or imitation of old melodies, or to the arbitrary thematic use of them in works of foreign or international tendencies. It is rather a matter of absorbing the means of musical expression hidden in them, just as the most subtle possibilities of any language may be assimilated. It is necessary for the composer to command this musical language so completely that it becomes the natural expression of his musical ideas.'

Bloch, Shostakovich, Copland, Falla, Honegger, Milhaud, Poulenc, Martinů, Prokofiev, and Malipiero are representative names of the immediate post-war international scene. In England, of Vaughan Williams's generation, Holbrooke, Cyril Scott and Havergal Brian had long been silent or neglected; Ireland, with his more restricted output, commanded a loyal but select following. Bantock and Ethel Smyth died in 1946, their work overlooked. Thomas Dunhill, whose early promise had not been fulfilled, also died that year. Arnold Bax, sixty-two at the end of the war, enjoyed immense prestige, although his music was progressively ignored after Sir Henry Wood's death in 1944. Of the next generation, Bliss and Howells were at the height of their powers and Moeran had produced, in the Violin Concerto of 1942, the work of lyrical beauty to which his whole career had been leading. The gifted group born in the early 1900s—Finzi, Rubbra, Walton, Wordsworth, Berkeley, Lambert, Rawsthorne, Tippett—were men of varied and distinctive talent who amply showed the richness of twentieth-century English music. But they were all surpassed by one a decade their junior, Benjamin Britten, whose *Peter Grimes*, produced at Sadler's Wells in June 1945, created a sensation to be compared only with those caused on their first appearances by Elgar's *Dream of Gerontius*, Walton's *Belshazzar's Feast* and Vaughan Williams's Fourth Symphony. From 1945 onwards, aided by an influential and persuasive band of admirers, Britten's reputation spread throughout the world and it is true to say that, in the period 1945–58, a new work by Vaughan Williams and a new work by Britten were the events in English music which attracted most attention from musicians and public. The war had brought about a boom in the appreciation of music. The Arts Council of Great Britain, developed from the wartime Council for the Encouragement of Music and the Arts, became the first firmly established link between British cultural life and the Treasury. Some local authorities slowly rose to their responsibilities in providing spiritual as well as material benefits. The B.B.C., by its establishment in 1946 of the Third Programme, performed the biggest single act of assistance and encouragement to composers and dramatists in the history of British social life. Cheltenham in 1945 took the bold step of inaugurating an annual festival devoted to British contemporary music. Some facts give an idea of the extent of the 'boom'. In 1944 alone, the Hallé, Liverpool Philharmonic and London Philharmonic Orchestras between them gave 722 concerts to audiences of over a million people; fees paid by chamber music clubs associated with C.E.M.A. rose from £800 in 1941 to £7,500 in 1944; in the two Promenade Concert seasons 1942–3 Sir Henry Wood gave forty-two works their first performances in England. The British Council sponsored a number of gramophone recordings of English music; and between 1942 and 1947 Elgar's *Gerontius*, Holst's *Hymn of Jesus* and *Planets*, Walton's *Belshazzar's Feast*, Vaughan Williams's *Job*, Fifth Symphony and *Flos Campi*, Moeran's

Symphony, Bax's Third Symphony, Bliss's Piano Concerto, Purcell's *Dido and Aeneas* and Britten's Serenade all became available on records, most of them for the first time. Although the impetus was to slacken and public enthusiasm to cool, the years of and after the Second World War offered the British composer a better chance for his work to be played and heard than he had ever before experienced.

In 1947, the year of his seventy-fifth birthday, Vaughan Williams had the pleasure of seeing one of the best performances of *The Poisoned Kiss*, given by students of the Royal Academy of Music on 15, 16, and 17 July conducted by Myers Foggin. Of the singers who took part, hardly any was to achieve professional fame, but the orchestra was a nursery of talent. Nona Liddell and Hugh Maguire (violins), Fritz Spiegl (flute), Janet Craxton (oboe), Maurice Handford (horn), and Osian Ellis (harp) were all to become distinguished orchestral players. Celebrations of this birthday were on a smaller scale than those for his seventieth in 1942; the chief event was at Dorking on 11 October when his old friend and admirer Alan Kirby conducted his Croydon Philharmonic Society and the London Symphony Orchestra in *A Sea Symphony* and the *Five Tudor Portraits*, with Ena Mitchell, Astra Desmond, and Roy Henderson as the soloists. Then, on the 15th in London, R.V.W. conducted the *London Symphony* at a B.B.C. Symphony Concert. A week later Beecham conducted the *Pastoral Symphony*, a work he is popularly supposed to have disliked. This is hardly borne out by the number of times he elected to conduct it, nor by the fact that he tried before the 1939 war to persuade a gramophone company to allow him to record it.[1] But these pleasant anniversary occasions were merely incidental to work in hand. Two short commissioned works were first heard in 1947, the motet *The Souls of the Righteous*, written for the dedication of the Battle of Britain Chapel in Westminster Abbey, and 'The Voice out of the Whirlwind', composed for a St. Cecilia's Day service at St. Sepulchre's. This latter was a vocal adaptation of the 'Pavane of the Sons of the Morning' from *Job* to some verses from *The Book of Job*. The Double Trio of 1939, revised in 1942, was now completely re-cast as a Partita for string orchestra with a new finale to replace the original rondo. This work had its 'face washed' by Müller-Hartmann, to whom it was dedicated.

[1] On 15 December 1948 Beecham revived *In the Fen Country* at a Royal Philharmonic concert.

With this piece out of the way and the Sixth Symphony in its final stages, there came at the end of June 1947 a letter from Ernest Irving, musical director since 1935 of Ealing Films Ltd., with whom Vaughan Williams had worked in happy friendship in composing music for *The Loves of Joanna Godden* (for which, to his amusement, he had had to compose music to illustrate foot-and-mouth disease). This letter mooted a more ambitious subject, as R.V.W.'s reply on 3 July showed:

'As regards the Scott film, I think before finally deciding I should like to have a conference with you and the producer, or director, whichever it is—I never know which is which—and see whether your, his and my ideas agree as to the sort of music required. I have very definite ideas and if they do not agree with his it might be rather difficult.'

So began the *Scott of the Antarctic* music. It is clear that, like *Job*, the subject immediately appealed to Vaughan Williams, for the music was written without his having seen any of the film except for a few 'stills'.

'I am not surprised that you have definite ideas about the music,' Irving replied on 9 July, 'that is what we expect and welcome from you.' Then came the advice of a truly musicianly friend: 'I would suggest that you insist on a definite agreement as to the points when music can be used in full volume without admixture, and if a contract is made that it should include a stipulation that alterations must receive your consent or mine, and that no third person should be brought in to amplify or replace your work. That is, of course, assuming you find me trustworthy in those respects.' And on the top of this typewritten letter Irving scribbled 'This is treasonable, therefore private!' An agreement was ready in October, and Vaughan Williams gave Irving an 'omnibus' permission to make necessary cuts and minor changes to fit the film. Irving, through their mutual solicitor, assured R.V.W. that his wishes would be respected 'down to the last tail on the last quaver and that this time I shall not arrange any carols for the penguins, but leave it to him'. The 'this time' evidently referred to some contretemps over *The Loves of Joanna Godden*. All this sounds very severe until R.V.W.'s letter to Irving on 8 October is read: 'Of course you can do exactly as you like without consulting me. I only thought that in a formal document my rights over the music ought to be maintained. . . . P.S. I want to make it quite clear that you have had my absolute permission to do what you like with my music, but this is not official.'

Irving, who in 1947 was sixty-nine, was on the committee of the Royal Philharmonic Society. Vaughan Williams had first admired him before the 1939 war when he heard him speak at a Philharmonic supper and say 'Many people ask, are you any relation to Sir Henry? To which I answer, my only connection with Sir Henry is that my name *is* Irving and his was *not*'. In 1943 in an article on 'Music in Films' in *Music and Letters*,[1] he had criticized Vaughan Williams's music for *Coastal Command* as 'not quite up to his best standard, neither was it particularly good film music'. In 1946, while working on *The Loves of Joanna Godden*, he 'literally went down on his knees and apologized for his former strictures', Vaughan Williams related, explaining that he had made a success of this music under Irving's guidance.[2] The two men enjoyed a similar keen sense of humour and both had remarkable and original minds. It is not surprising that they enjoyed their work together. Much of the *Scott* score was delivered before Christmas of 1947, evidently with an apologia, because Irving wrote on 16 December:

'The winter of your discontent seems to be due to two causes.
(*a*) The dislocation and subordination of the music to the "real noises" and dialogue of the film.
(*b*) The discrepancy between the sound you heard *vis-à-vis* the orchestra and the sound that proceeds from the track.
Regarding (*a*) I have put your views with my strong support to Mr. Balcon and the directors and have done a bit of lobbying also. They would be delighted if you would come and talk it all over. Your idea of an orchestral "prelude" is a daring novelty, and film directors are mortally afraid of anything new, but . . . we may bring it off, though I fancy it will not be over penguins or icebergs but with a black [blank] film. . . . I have only had time to glance at the sketches you send—they look fine to me. I was amused at your variation of "The Golden Vanity". . . . You'll have to tell me the tunes you want to hear, for, as you have discovered, where there is dialogue the music goes west.'

More of the music was delivered early in January 1948. So clearly did Vaughan Williams imagine the scenes that he composed the music well in advance of the scenes themselves having been shot.

---

[1] Vol. XXIV, No. 4.
[2] *Music and Letters*, Vol. XXXV, No. 1.

The Prelude (for the Main Titles) was written with the sole instruction that it was to last about eighty-four seconds. Irving wrote to him on 9 January:

'Regarding the Main Titles, there should be no difficulty whatever in making these sound exactly as they look. Considering that you have placed yourself *in statu pupillari* the orchestration is most promising. . . . I quite agree with your point about the military march. "Land of Hope and Glory", however, would be wrong for the situation, which demands a bright 6/8. I cannot think of any English march of the period sufficiently well known to the present generation of filmgoers to immunize you, but as the band is in dim perspective, we can photograph them to the rhythm of "The Queen's Birthday". Then, if you disapprove of the result, we can dub any 6/8 march of which everybody approves, or, alternatively, you could write one yourself if you feel in light-hearted or penguinesque mood. . . . Regarding the timings, I am afraid no amount of bullying on my part will produce measurements of film that has not yet been shot, so you will be "walking in darkness" (though not necessarily in B minor) for some while yet.'

Throughout the long and sometimes technical correspondence about the 'Scott' music, there is an awareness on Irving's part that the film score was of an extremely high and original order, inspired by the subject rather than merely illustrative although the scene-painting was brilliant. He had short recordings made as he went along, sending them down to Dorking as a guide to how work was progressing. It is evident that the use of a soprano and wordless chorus caused some consternation:

January 22, 1948.

'Dear V.W., Confirming our telephone conversation, I will carefully rehearse the music of No. 8 with Mr. Frend and Mr. Cole so that everybody concerned knows of your intentions and appreciates the significance of the music. We will record it with the voices on February 6th, and I will afterwards make what is known as a preliminary dubbing. In this the music will be mixed with the dialogue and shown to you and all concerned with the picture when shot. . . . There is no objection *per se* to the use of a vocal theme; it is purely a technical difficulty which has been empirically found to be insoluble. The parallel with "Carnet du bal" is not an exact one as the street music is naturalistic in its origin, the singer having been shown to the audience. We *did* have some singing, and very effective it was, in the Dungeness scene [*The Loves of Joanna Godden*] but there was no conversational dialogue. You may be sure that we shall do our best to bring the thing off, and if it fails it will be for the same reason that Scott failed!'

The next instalment was on 10 February:

'I have heard the tracks. The Antarctic Prologue with the voices comes out very well indeed, and I think we may be able to get away with the voice in the footstep scene. . . . The vocal effect is sufficiently disembodied to make it usable as a background even behind dialogue.' The penguins music, Irving reported, was 'highly admired by all . . . . I like it very much even if the birds are a little aristophanic. And finally about the Main Titles. Before I give you your next lesson there are some problems I shall have to solve for myself. In getting the horns well and truly on to the track they seem to have swallowed up the string tone altogether. . . . With your permission I will make an alternative score of the Main Titles, and send it to you for approval. It was very lucky (for me) to have had this preliminary recording, especially if I am to justify my reputation as a private tutor. . . . Meanwhile I am abashed.'

By June 1948 the film was rough cut, the score having been completed in April. Although on no film on which he worked did Vaughan Williams experience his ideal of composer and director working as a team and planning everything from the start, perhaps *Scott of the Antarctic* came nearest to it. How much was owed to Ernest Irving's tactful and understanding mediation can never be overstated. Moreover, while all the foregoing was occurring, Vaughan Williams was suffering the birth pangs of the Sixth Symphony. This was always a painful process not only for the composer but for his friends, for as the day of performance drew nearer he was assailed by doubts and fears, and threatened to 'tear it all up' or withdraw the work concerned. In the case of this symphony he knew that even some of those closest to him had their doubts about the strange pianissimo finale in which, as they thought, he peered over the abyss. The work was first played through orchestrally at the B.B.C. studios at Maida Vale on 16 December 1947. Its effect on one listener is preserved in the letter written that same day by Müller-Hartmann:

Dear Vaughan Williams,
    I left the rehearsal of your new symphony rather hurriedly because I would not have been able to talk to you. Although I had heard it twice before on the piano, and certainly excellently played, I never anticipated the overwhelming impression the real thing would make on me. I am sure the new symphony is a great work of yours and a great work of our

time. To my mind it seems even to transcend your symphonies in F and
D. . . .

Yours,

Robert Müller-Hartmann.

The first performance was not to be until 21 April 1948, at a
Royal Philharmonic Society concert and in the meantime the Partita
had its first performances in two Third Programme broadcasts by
the B.B.C. Symphony Orchestra conducted by Sir Adrian Boult on
20 and 21 March. When the symphony was first played, at the
Royal Albert Hall, there was no mistaking the audience's passionate
reaction, nor the critics' unanimous enthusiasm. The music's vigour
and power, coming from a man of seventy-five, evoked comparisons
with Verdi, but it was the mysterious finale which attracted most
attention. Richard Capell, in the *Daily Telegraph*, describing the
concert as 'a profoundly memorable event', said that the composer,
'true to the spirit of his whole career', had done the unpredictable
thing.

'While something of an enigma is present, the listener feels that the music
springs from a torturing pain, notably the indescribably poignant slow
movement. But there is no passive submission. The sardonic scherzo is
one of the composer's most active and crowded movements. This leads
to a finale like nothing else in music—a wholly pianissimo movement like
a long farewell.'

Capell expanded his views a few days later:

'Only the greatly superior artists have so tirelessly renewed the adventure
of the spirit. . . . The sixth symphony in E minor takes a new direction.
It will challenge every hearer. The adventurous energy is terrific; and,
whatever words may be resorted to as a clue, the sheer musical means are
compelling and engrossing. . . . The music says that the soul of man can
endure pain and face the thought of a remoteness beyond the outermost
of the planets.'

It soon became clear that, like the F minor, the symphony was to
be labelled as a political document. This time its finale was held by
some to be a vision of desolation, of a world laid waste by atomic
warfare. Frank Howes in *The Times* of 22 April wrote:

'His successor who annotates the symphony 50 years hence will however
certainly relate the symphony to the experiences of war, its challenges, its
sinister import for ultimate values, its physical bombardment even. But

what will he make of the ghostly epilogue? Here the composer seems to be seeking not answers but the right questions to ask of human experience. His career has been one long quest. . . . Now he has started off once more on his travels and has begun to prove greater mysteries.'

No vision of destruction was in the composer's mind. He wrote to me on the subject of this finale on 22 January 1956: 'With regard to the last movement of my No. 6, I do NOT BELIEVE IN meanings and mottoes, as you know, but I think we can get in words nearest to the substance of my last movement in "We are such stuff as dreams are made on, and our little life is rounded by a sleep".' In 1951, he set these very words in a superb part-song.

'It never seems to occur to people,' he told Roy Douglas, 'that a man might just want to write a piece of music.'[1] He was perhaps expecting too much, for of all his untitled works the Sixth Symphony most easily and temptingly lends itself to programmatic description. That it was a deeply-felt, personal and impassioned utterance is obvious enough from the composer's programme-note which studiously avoids any hint of emotional commitment.

An American who perceived the work's greatness was Leopold Stokowski. 'This is music that will take its place with the greatest creations of the masters,' he declared in the programme of the New York Philharmonic-Symphony Society for 30 January 1949.[2] Another American, Olin Downes, was equally enthusiastic: 'This is one of the most powerful and deeply felt symphonic writings to have appeared since the turn of the century. The sincerity of the expression blazes in every page. The virility and driving energy of it are companioned by pages of tenderness and mysticism.'

[1] In January 1957 he wrote to Mr. Maurice Reeve:
  'You kindly ask whether there is any meaning attached to my symphonies. I admit that I have called four of them *Sea, London, Pastoral* and *Antartica*—in the *Sea Symphony* the words locate the emotion, and the mottoes the *Antartica*, but probably the music would get on just as well without them. But I hope that the words and the mottoes set the right mood to listen to the music. That is *all* I wish and all I hope for . . . I feel very angry with certain critics who will have it that my 4th Symphony "means" war, and my 5th "means" peace—and so on. If people get help in appreciating music from this descent from the general to the particular, good luck to them. But the opposite can be equally true. It is said that Beethoven's tragic *Muss es sein* movement in his last quartet arose out of a quarrel with his landlady!"
[2] Stokowski insisted on the use of valve trombones for this symphony. He was not alone among American or America-domiciled advocates for Vaughan Williams. Toscanini conducted the *Tallis Fantasia* and *A London Symphony*, Mitropoulos was a magnificent interpreter of the Fourth Symphony, and since 1933 Vaughan Williams had enjoyed the friendship and championship of Bernard Herrmann.

The younger critics were as impressed as their elders. Desmond Shawe-Taylor, in the *New Statesman*, called the symphony

'an extraordinary and unpredictable burst of creative activity for a man of 75, in which he seems to have effected a kind of synthesis of the two preceding symphonies, indeed to have summed up the whole of his life-work, but, at the same time, to have directed a serene and courageous glance into the future, to have meditated on first and last things with a grasp and profundity worthy of Beethoven.'

It was many years since a new symphony had stirred so many people. As Scott Goddard wrote in the *News Chronicle* of 22 April, it was to 'that immortal force, the spirit of man', that the final question in the symphony was addressed. In the troubled and turbulent post-war world the music penetrated to that spirit as neither of its two predecessors had fully done, whatever their musical virtues. Two years after its first performance, its hundredth was given—by the Hallé Orchestra on 6 July at the 1950 Cheltenham Festival—an achievement only exceeded by the initial success of Elgar's A flat Symphony in 1908–9. America was anxious to hear the work. The first performance in the United States was given by the Boston Symphony Orchestra under Koussevitzky at the Berkshire Music Festival on 7 August 1948; the second by the Baltimore Symphony Orchestra, conducted by Reginald Stewart, on 13 October. Bernard Heinze conducted the first Australian performance with the Melbourne Symphony Orchestra on 29 October. Eduard van Beinum introduced it into the repertoire of the Concertgebouw Orchestra of Amsterdam. Despite this extraordinary success, the composer of this astonishing masterpiece still worried about ways of improving it and even after it had been recorded he altered the scoring of the Scherzo. Those who possess the 78 r.p.m. version of the symphony recorded on 23 February 1949, on H.M.V. C3875 and have the matrix numbers 2 EA 13627–1 and 13628–1 on the label of the Scherzo possess the original version of the movement. The revised version was re-recorded with the same catalogue number.

One particular performance of the Sixth Symphony resulted in the development of a long and intermittent acquaintanceship into a close friendship which lasted for the rest of Vaughan Williams's life. Vaughan Williams attended a rehearsal and concert by the Hallé

Orchestra, conducted by John Barbirolli, on 2 June 1949, in the Sheldonian Theatre, Oxford.

'He was obviously very impressed with the performance of the Scherzo,' Sir John related later,[1] 'and confessed he had some uncertainty about this movement: whether it was the orchestration or the actual form that produced this unsatisfactory impression—an impression which, he said, disappeared that afternoon—was not quite clear. But he decided that it was my slightly slower tempo that clarified it, and he paid me the great compliment of altering the metronome mark accordingly.'

The first conductor of the symphony, Adrian Boult, lost no time in including it in as many of the B.B.C. Symphony Orchestra's concerts as he could. One performance was at Oxford on 11 May 1948, during the Oxford Festival of Music from 9 to 16 May which celebrated English composers (including Handel) of five hundred years, especially Hubert Parry the centenary of whose birth had occurred on 27 February. R.V.W. had commemorated his master with a setting of Skelton's 'Prayer to the Father of Heaven' which was first sung in the Sheldonian on 12 May preceded by an oration by one of Parry's successors as Heather Professor, J. A. Westrup. The week brought back memories of Hugh Allen's days as Professor after the first war, especially when the festival culminated in *A Sea Symphony*, with Elsie Suddaby, William Parsons and the Oxford Bach Choir. Allen had died in 1946, but now there was Thomas Armstrong to continue his conducting activities. May 1948 was something of a *mensis mirabilis* for Vaughan Williams, for on the 20th *Job* was revived and staged at last at the Royal Opera House, Covent Garden, with new scenery, including an act drop, and costumes, all by John Piper (and all disliked by R.V.W.), revised choreography by Ninette de Valois and, best of all, the full score used for the first time in the theatre and conducted by Adrian Boult. Robert Helpmann was Satan, Alexis Rassine Elihu, and others in the cast were to make their mark in English ballet: Julia Farron, Alexander Grant, Donald Britton, Philip Chatfield, John Cranko, John Hart, Michael Somes, John Field, Nadia Nerina, Rowena Jackson, and Annette Page. Three members of the original 1931 cast were still working with de Valois in 1948: Ursula Moreton, Claude Newman, and Joy Newton. The composer conducted *Job*, with the Scene of the Comforters omitted, at the Worcester meeting of the

---

[1] *Music and Musicians*, October 1958, p. 15, op. cit.

Three Choirs on 7 September. On 29 November *Scott of the Antarctic* was shown at the Royal Film Show at the Empire, Leicester Square. Early in October Irving had delivered to Dorking a set of studio recordings of the music. 'My wife wants to thank you so much,' Vaughan Williams wrote. 'It is some consolation to me for her not being able to see the picture.'

When the film and the music were 'married', it was found that apart from minor adjustments of timing, the music and the scenes it evoked or illustrated 'fitted' perfectly. The film was not a public success; in its effort to be documentary and factual some of the human drama evaporated and certain episodes, such as Evans's death, were softened or glossed over. Nevertheless, it was a noble achievement to which the music made an unforgettable contribution, although few film critics chose to mention it. It opened to the public at the Odeon, Leicester Square, on 30 December and Vaughan Williams went to see it. He was horrified by the incongruity of Grieg's 'Homage March', which the cinema organist, Mr. John Howlett, played after the film had ended, so he wrote a 32-bar piece based on a theme from the film.[1] Meanwhile it had been decided to record some of the music, and this was done by H.M.V. on 30 December. The composer, in agreeing, expressed only one doubt to Irving: 'Will it prevent me later on writing an "Antarctic Symphony" using the same themes, which I have slowly revolving in my mind, though it may never come to anything?'

The *Scott* music and the finale of the Sixth Symphony inaugurated an 'experimental' phase in Vaughan Williams's compositions. The combinations of unusual and sometimes intractable sonorities attracted him. Since 1947 he had been at work on a setting of parts of Matthew Arnold's *The Scholar Gipsy* and *Thyrsis*. After *Thanksgiving for Victory*—which in its revised form had been tamely re-titled *A Song of Thanksgiving*—he was anxious to write another work employing a speaker. He said he was 'tired of choral works in which one couldn't hear the words'. All his life he had been haunted by *The Scholar Gipsy*, and continued to wish that he could devise an opera libretto based on it. In *An Oxford Elegy*,

[1] Mr. Howlett wrote to me: 'As I remember it, there was a modal type of melody for the left hand, a ground-bass for the pedals and a florid figure for the right hand (semiquavers). . . . Although this fragment certainly "fitted" the film it was rather harshsounding (as is "Hyfrydol" to my ears) and in my humble opinion did not "come off" as organ music.' The Leicester Square organ, Mr. Howlett pointed out, was 'not of the typical cinema breed'.

as the work eventually became, he told Cedric Glover he had used a tune he had written in 1901 which he thought was 'like Barnby though other people thought it was like Puccini'. This apart, it is a post-1945 work. Parallel with this he was writing a Fantasia on the metrical version of the 104th Psalm tune in Sternhold and Hopkins (1550), for pianoforte, chorus, and orchestra with the organ ad lib., an extraordinary work to which only Beethoven's Choral Fantasia and Lambert's *Rio Grande* can be compared in form. The new works were first played at a private concert at The White Gates on 20 November 1949.

He was perhaps relieved to have completed these short works, so that he could clear his desk for the Antarctic Symphony. On 29 June 1949 he had written to Irving asking for the score and sketches of the film music because 'it is about time I started thinking about the *Sinfonia Antarctica* [*sic*].' But on 28 September he wrote: 'I cannot get on at all with the "Scott" symphony, so it will have to wait a bit, I expect.' He still seized every chance to keep in touch with amateur groups for whom his latest works were possibly too difficult. He was glad to be asked in that year to write a choral work for the Women's Institutes national singing festival; it was an opportunity for a new folk-song work. Since the end of the war, his output of folk-song settings had ceased, although he took an active part still in the affairs of the English Folk Dance and Song Society and especially in its Journal. Now he wrote a cantata, *Folk Songs of the Four Seasons*, which had as a unifying factor the calendar, the passing of the months from spring to winter. His private joke during its composition was that he was delighted at the thought of 'all those matronly women singing "I wish I was in that young man's arms that once had the heart of mine" '. There were eliminating contests throughout the W.I. districts to decide which choirs should constitute the three thousand voices for the Albert Hall first performance on 15 June 1950. Frank Howes has described the result better than anyone else could:

'The effect of so many voices singing with simple sincerity melody that was bone of their bone, composed into a cantata specially for English women dwelling in the English countryside, by a composer who more than any other has steeped himself in our native traditions, was extraordinarily moving.'[1]

---

[1] *The Music of Ralph Vaughan Williams* (London, 1954), p. 196.

The texts used in the cantata occasioned some criticism for being too decorous. Vaughan Williams admirably set forth his views on a very vexed subject in a letter to Rutland Boughton—the letter of a man who was no prude and enjoyed a Rabelaisian jest as much as anyone:

'It is a mistake to suppose that ballads as far as I know are very "outspoken" about amorous things—you will look in vain for detailed physical descriptions of sexual contact; the folk singer has a due sense of proportion and does not imitate the modern novelist in a morbid preoccupation with these physical details of the natural functions of man.

'The folk singer when confronted with the collector has an exaggerated idea of what he will consider "rude"—of course it is absurd for the F.S. collectors to refuse to print such beautiful lines as

> "I wish that the night had been seven long years"

or "Undress yourself my darling said he
And come along to bed with me"

or "We spent that night in sweet content
And the very next morning to church we went"

'But these are positively reticent compared with what one gets in a modern novel—it is only the conventions of expressions are different. Of course there is a type of ballad words which *are* indecent in the true sense of the word—these though harmless (I am not one to cast a stone at anyone who relishes an improper story) are of no artistic or any other value and therefore are best left unrecorded. But these are not *outspoken* and their point (as in all "smutty" stories) depends on facetious and sly allusiveness. Possibly these are not genuine folk songs, but have drifted in from some other stratum. The whole question of genuineness is hopelessly confused—and collectors are always apt to think that all they value is genuine and all they dislike is a corruption.'

This subject was continually cropping up. One of the last things he wrote, the preface[1] to the *Penguin Book of English Folk Songs*, compiled in collaboration with A. L. Lloyd, dealt with it:

'We have not hesitated to include words, verses or whole texts which earlier collectors prudishly modified or omitted as being objectionable. The old habit of cleaning-up or even entirely re-writing the texts led to the false supposition that folk songs are always "quite nice". The folk singer has no objection to plain speech. He is likely to be forthright in his treatment of the pleasures and pains of love, though he may class some

---

[1] *The Penguin Book of English Folk Songs* (London, 1959), pp. 7-10.

songs as "outway rude" which we think quite harmless. In restoring song-texts that had hitherto been published only in bowdlerized form, we have referred to the collectors' original manuscripts.'

His interest in folk song continued to bring him new friendships. One he valued was that with the Rev. George Chambers for whose book on plainsong Vaughan Williams in 1955 wrote a preface—'call it preface, or introduction, please, but not that horrible word, foreword!'—in which he referred to musicologists unable to see that plainsong derived from folk song as 'bat-eyed'.

Four commissioned (or requested) works occupied parts of 1949, 1950, and 1951. For the twenty-first anniversary of the Rural Music Schools Association he composed a concerto grosso for strings, thoughtfully written for three classes of performers, the skilled, the semi-skilled and the beginners 'who prefer to use only open strings'. At the first performance in the Royal Albert Hall on 18 November 1950, over four hundred players took part, the majority of them of the third class. The Queen (now Queen Elizabeth the Queen Mother) was present but the composer excused himself the honour of a place in the Royal Box and sat among the second violins 'just to see how they are getting on'. His friend Bernard Shore, the viola player, was also chief music inspector of schools and he asked Vaughan Williams for a four-part work, for the Festival of Britain, for the choirs of the Schools Music Association which specialized in non-competitive festivals. At first the reply was 'No. I don't know enough about the job'. Later he said he was thinking about it and asked for samples of music which children could and could not sing.[1] The result was *The Sons of Light*, to a poem by Ursula Wood, first performed by eight hundred children conducted by Sir Adrian Boult on 6 May 1951. The third commission arose from R.V.W.'s attendance at a Wigmore Hall concert given by the harmonica virtuoso, Larry Adler. Mr. Adler asked Vaughan Williams to write a work for him, as several other modern composers had done. The result was the short Romance in D flat. The fourth commission which it gave him much pleasure to undertake was the 'Solemn Music' composed for the final scene of the Masque at his old school, Charterhouse, in 1950. The Masque, first produced in 1911, was revived with additions in 1919, 1922, 1929, and 1935. The 1950 revision was extensive and ambitious. Vaughan Williams attended rehearsals and was

[1] *R.C.M. Magazine*, Vol. LV, No. 1, 1959, p. 35.

present on Old Carthusian Day. An anonymous writer in *The Carthusian* of October 1950 said:

'Dr. Vaughan Williams, when he came to the rehearsal, and also at the performance itself, spoke very warmly of the quality of the playing; at the first rehearsal which he attended he openly congratulated the boys. He also greatly praised the singing of the choir. . . . In the last scene, the sudden entry of the choir after the dramatic climax of the orchestral introduction was truly stirring: the music of the *Carmen* rising suddenly out of the orchestral turmoil seemed like sheer creation. . . . The great dramatic moment when the whole school joined in the *Carmen* with Dr. Vaughan Williams's superb orchestration and the descants of the choir was the most thrilling of all. Dr. Vaughan Williams had told the school that when the Headmaster asked him to write the music for the masque he had stipulated that the *Carmen*, which he considers to be the greatest of all school songs, should be included and that the whole school should join in it. When he heard it at the rehearsal on the Sunday before the performance, he must have felt rewarded; at the wonderful performance in Chapel on the Saturday night, he was clearly very deeply stirred by it.'

Writing in *The Carthusian* in December 1952 Vaughan Williams repeated this view of the *Carmen* and added:

'In my time we all knew it and used to sing it on all big occasions. Later on it was apparently allowed to lapse, and it is a cause of great pride to me that I was partly instrumental in its resurrection at the recent Charterhouse masque.'

One work, however, took precedence in Vaughan Williams's thoughts over all others. In 1949 he had completed his opera on *The Pilgrim's Progress*. It was then forty-three years since the Reigate performance had given him the idea of an opera from the book which he thought had something in common with his favourite novel, George Borrow's *Lavengro*. One episode, *The Shepherds of the Delectable Mountains* had appeared in 1922. More music was sketched in the 1930s, but it was the B.B.C.'s commission of incidental music for the 1943 broadcast version which gave the stimulus to a revision of the libretto, with passages added from the Bible. Between the wars Vaughan Williams had been asked by W. Nugent Monck of the Norwich Maddermarket Theatre to write the music for a stage version, but nothing materialized. It is significant that the broadcast version acknowledged a debt to Monck, who had helped to produce the Reigate dramatization. By 1949 the music of the opera was written, except for the Nocturne, which was inserted in 1951, and some additions after the first performances, and the libretto was given to Müller-Hartmann to translate into German. Müller-Hartmann was by now living in Dorking.

This was to be almost the last task Müller-Hartmann was to do for Vaughan Williams. In September 1950, after Vaughan Williams had returned from Gloucester where he conducted the Sixth Symphony and the first public performance of the Fantasia on the Old 104th, he asked Müller-Hartmann to go through the Partita score before publication—'as the work belongs so much to you.' 'Harpo', as his friends called him, died suddenly on 15 December. 'R. will miss him,' Adeline wrote to her sister Cordelia Curle on 19 December. 'He had come to look upon him as a friend and to value his musical opinions.' This personal loss was the first of the shadows which were to be cast over the production of *The Pilgrim's Progress*. It had been announced as Covent Garden's principal contribution to the Festival of Britain which the Labour Government had planned as a centenary celebration of the Hyde Park Exhibition of 1851. R.V.W. had strong views on how his work should be staged but both he and the producer, Nevill Coghill, failed wholly to carry the day. Adeline's letter quoted above has a hint of strife:

'We had a wonderful time with the producer—such a friendly cultivated man—about 50—he couldn't have been more congenial to us all. I wish you could have seen him illustrating Apollyon with Ursula as the Pilgrim thrusting at his heart—it was to measure the timing of the thrusts to the music—Ursula was in her glory! and did it all very well. The hitch is that he will refuse to produce unless he has his own designer and the management are undecided tho' Steuart[1] thinks it can be arranged. They apparently want the designer to collaborate with *their* costume designer—perhaps it's financial.'

When 26 April 1951 came and the opera at last took the stage, it had what can only be called a *succès d'estime*. The applause, after a moment's respectful silence, was sustained but did not become rapturous until the composer himself appeared. Eventually he spoke a few words of thanks to the performers and added: 'Someone asked me who wrote the libretto! It was he' (pointing to Inia te Wiata, in the character of Bunyan). The worst aspects of the production were

[1] Sir Steuart Wilson was at this time Deputy General Administrator, Royal Opera House.

the appalling costumes and the unimaginative lighting. The critics, almost to a man, admired the music but failed to find the work suitable for a stage setting.

'Covent Garden undertook a prodigious task in presenting a work deriving from the traditions of the Morality, the English cantata and the pageant, but not opera,' Capell wrote in the *Daily Telegraph* of 27 April. 'Only genius could have saved, at Covent Garden, a production so wanting in the dramatic element—so anti-theatrical. The distinction of Vaughan Williams's music must silence the scoffers. . . . Such music largely but not wholly makes up for the dramatic want. In a word, the Pilgrim's ordeal is not realized.'

The next day he put forward a point of view which, though expressed since then, was his alone at the time:

'Can it be said that the long-standing promise has been fulfilled by this new "morality"? Hardly; for the truth is that fulfilment had already come. It came in the composer's symphonic works. The world, if it expected an expression of the Pilgrim's spiritual ordeal, his agony and his victory, of a final intensity and concentration, will be disappointed. Rather is *Pilgrim's Progress* an aftermath. How, indeed, could it be otherwise, when Vaughan Williams had already, in the diabolic music of the fourth and sixth symphonies, given us Vanity Fair and the battle with Apollyon with the highest intensity, and in the fifth symphony . . . the music of the heavenly haven gained after the soul's agonizing voyage? . . . His *Job* is his great achievement in the theatre. A ballet! This is something always to be wondered at—that he should have entered an arena traditionally meretricious and have imposed sublimity upon it! He ignored the tradition but observed the fundamental laws. In *Job* all that we see as well as what we hear contributes, as in *Pilgrim's Progress* it does not, to the sublime effect. The admirable score of *Pilgrim's Progress*, we may be sure, will find its niche, but this will not be in the theatre. It is trammelled by the stage.'

This was the reaction of a sympathetic and knowledgeable critic. Another, Herbert Murrill,[1] was possibly more perceptive:

'He [the composer] positively disregards theatrical and operatic convention; throws to one side the nice delineation of character, the careful balance and adjustment of climax-points, the pointed underlining of the dramatic situation; and with a sort of humble self-confidence writes a loose-knit and contemplative score that succeeds by its sincerity, convinces by its integrity and becomes a unity by its single-mindedness. So I say that if *Pilgrim's Progress* achieves greatness—as I think it does—it

[1] In *Music and Letters*, Vol. XXXII, No. 4.

achieves it *through* its disregard of stage convention, and not *in spite* of this. . . . We are given what Vaughan Williams, with his usual felicity, called a Morality. It could be played in a cathedral or before some great architectural façade. Yet it is not unsuited to the opera-house, where the more exotic religious dramas of Wagner, of d'Annunzio and Debussy, of Claudel and Honegger have been seen. . . . In [his] complete reverence for the sung word Vaughan Williams provides a parallel to Debussy's setting of *Pelléas et Mélisande*, where Maeterlinck's text is enabled to move with the naturalness and at the pace of speech itself.'

That very point had been mentioned to the composer by Ursula Wood, who told him that she found all the speech-rhythms so much in character as well as so good. 'So good,' he replied, 'that none of the critics noticed.' The production precipitated many letters from friends and colleagues. These and the composer's replies are perhaps more interesting than the critics' first reactions. Here is R.V.W.'s reply dated 17 May 1951, to Hubert Foss who had evidently criticized the production:

'I was on the whole very much pleased with the production and I think I ought to tell you so. There are one or two things I disagreed with. I still believe that the Apollyon fight could be done on my lines. Of course the fight as it appeared on the first night was a patched-up affair at the last minute, which was a pity.

'I still feel it is essentially a stage piece and not for a cathedral. To start with, it would have to be about twice as long for a cathedral. It probably takes about six bars of moderate time for a procession to cross the stage at Covent Garden, but it would take about 100 bars for a procession to walk down the nave of (say) Salisbury Cathedral, and the whole thing would have to be on a much longer scale.

'I am lengthening "Vanity Fair". I am sure it is too short at present. I am making one or two slight alterations. The end of the Arming Scene, Act II, Scene I, wants altering. This also was a last-minute affair. . . . They did not seem quite to realise that it was not a "Curtain" in the ordinary conventional sense of the word. What I wanted was a gradual black-out and then an Act Drop Curtain to prepare for the next scene, instead of which they dropped the House Curtain, which to my mind was a mistake.'

On 12 May, Rutland Boughton, who heard the work broadcast, had written an entertaining and provocative letter, a mixture of good sense, musicianship, prejudice, muddle-headed political dogma, and sheer wrong-headedness:

'It is the complete *YOU* disembarrassed of your age. Apollyon was less terrible than your Satan in *Job* and I was sorry that you had left out Mr. Valiant-for-Truth; but what gave me special satisfaction was the fact that in casting off the absurdities of opera you had discovered the reality of music as dramatic expression, as indeed you did in *Job*.

'I wrote to Willcocks[1] of Worcester, and to Steuart, asking if they could not arrange to have the Covent Garden crowd in the cathedral about the time of the next Three Choirs Festival, for the dramatic values of the work would come through more completely in such a building. . . . But Willcocks says that it couldn't be arranged in the time, which says little for their business capacity; and Steuart says that so much of the production (and even some of the actual music) would have to be altered, and that says little for the C.G. production staff. . . . But such excuses are just part of the topsy-turvy art world which prepares *Hugh the Drover* for concert performances and does the Chester Plays in a hall. The anti-Christians have got such a hold on our life that they are afraid of Christian vitality in Christian buildings (and by the way your Pilgrim seems to be afraid of his Christian name)—still more of admitting Christian thought into our theatres. That is where you have scored in a super-personal sense, for you have carried that thought to Covent Garden in spite of them.

'However, until C.G. is controlled in the service of the people wholly and without reserve, and not chiefly by Ricordi interests, they being controlled in their turn by American finance—until that time *Pilgrim's Progress* will continue to be a magnificent anomaly there, and will not yield up its true spirit until the whole set-up of our national opera is honestly national . . . .'

Vaughan Williams's reply neatly ignored some of the red herrings:

'Your long and interesting letter would take several weeks to answer properly, so I will content myself with a few points—the music is not published yet [Boughton had asked for a vocal score] because I wanted to hear it to make some revisions—and I am glad I did—principally technical questions. Even the libretto (enclosed) is by now out of date. The "nocturne" with "Watchful" is not there. [This beautiful episode had been inserted during rehearsals to cover a scene-change. R.V.W. wrote most of it in the train between London and Dorking.] I left out Valiant-for-Truth—one had to leave out many people (e.g. Faithful)—as his great speech wd not have gone well in the mouth of the Pilgrim (as a matter of fact I once made a musical setting of Valiant's speech). I on purpose did not call the Pilgrim "Christian" because I want the idea to be universal and apply to anybody who aims at the spiritual life whether he is Xtian, Jew, Buddhist, Shintoist, or 5th Day Adventist. As regards the cathedral

---

[1] David Willcocks, at this time Organist of Worcester Cathedral.

—it is, to my mind, essentially a *stage* piece and I said I wd not allow it in a hall or church till it was fully established on the stage. Thank you so much for writing.'

In *The Times*, Frank Howes defended the work's stage habitat. 'The stage can show the inner conflict of principles as well as the outer conflict of action,' he wrote, 'and music can depict states of mind even better than physical exertion.' Of the music in this case he was an unqualified admirer—'that astonishing ringing of changes on diatonic tunes and simple triads that lifts the heart to something beyond the power of language. Familiar yet ever new.'

The production itself was softly dealt with by the critics with the exception of an American, the late Cecil Smith, who was working in England at this time. His account in *Opera*[1] was not an exaggeration:

'It is hard to imagine a job worse done. The House Beautiful and the friendly landscapes amounted to no more than pale sentimental calendar art. Vanity Fair looked . . . like a scene from the Dick Whittington pantomime. . . . Mr. Coghill taught Arnold Matters, the Pilgrim, the gestures of a village vicar or perhaps of a provincial Elijah. . . . The delineation of lust and frivolity in the Vanity Fair scene was enough to send one to the nearest convent in the hope of a gayer time. As Madam Wanton, Audrey Bowman did, it is true, display one entire stockinged leg. . . . The lighting was uniformly atrocious. When Pilgrim was supposed to descry, with effort, a distant light he was hit full in the face by a blinding spotlight. . . .'

By far the most interesting set of letters[2] was from E. J. Dent, who remained a whole-hearted admirer of the Morality and said of it:[3] 'It is an opera and its only place is the theatre. . . . *The Pilgrim's Progress* is undoubtedly the greatest and the most deeply moving contribution of modern times to the building-up of a national repertory of musical drama.' His tributes to Leonard Hancock gave special satisfaction to the composer who, with typical generosity, had entrusted this major work to a conductor hardly known to the general musical public.

Vaughan Williams set to work at once on what he called 'alterations and repairs' to the opera and on 13 June asked Roy Douglas if he would 'as usual, be kindly willing to act as accoucheur for the

[1] Vol. 2, No. 7.
[2] These may be read in Appendix I of the hardback edition.
[3] *Musical Times*, October 1952.

new bits? There is nothing in Act I. There is a small addition and alteration in Act II, which I can send you now. The same in Act IV which will be ready very shortly. Act III will take rather longer, but I expect to be able to finish it in about a week.' He had in 1949–50 worked on revisions of *Hugh the Drover* with Douglas. Between them there existed a rare understanding.

R.V.W. did not mention to any of his correspondents who wrote congratulating him on the opera that the reason for his delay in replying to their letters was Adeline's death on 10 May. She had heard the broadcast of the work which, as she well knew, meant so much to Ralph. She did not live to see it dropped from the Covent Garden repertoire as soon as the second set of performances in the 1951–2 season was over. It received only one provincial performance, at Leeds on 12 July 1951. Its failure, and the misunderstanding of its nature, wounded the composer more deeply than anything else in his career. 'They don't like it, and they won't like it, and perhaps they never will like it,' he said to Ursula Wood, 'because it hasn't got a love story or any big duets and it's not like the operas they are used to; but it's the sort of opera I wanted to write, and there it is.' But that was said in a philosophical moment. I remember mentioning the opera while lunching with R.V.W. in the Grand Hotel, Manchester. 'The Pilgrim is dead, and that's that,' he said curtly, in a manner which allowed of no contradiction and manifestly concealed a bitter disappointment. Happily, Cambridge was to make amends in 1954.

The Festival of Britain was a magnificent opportunity for the propagation of English music, and it was seized. But even in a notable year like 1951 there were reminders that much still remained to be done for the cause of art in Britain, and that the dark age of prejudice and bigotry had not entirely given way to enlightenment. Plans for the programmes of the 1952 Leith Hill Festival provoked an astonishing illustration of this, and also provoked the following letter from Vaughan Williams to Mrs. Hooper, of Redhill, Surrey:

Dear Mrs. Hooper,

I am amazed to hear that some members of your choir [the Dorking Oriana] have taken exception to the beautiful words of Holst's *Tomorrow shall be my Dancing Day*, apparently on the grounds firstly that dancing and religion are something apart and consequently that it is wrong to use the words 'This have I done for my true love' in connection with a statement of the central doctrines of Christianity.

I had hoped that the killjoy and lugubrious view of religion which once obtained was now happily dead, but I fear there are still some people who have a degraded view of the dance and connect it only with high kicking and jazz, but the dance in its highest manifestations shares with music, poetry and painting, one of the greatest means of expression of the very highest of human aspirations. The dance has always been connected with religious fervour—that is, orderly and rhythmical movement surcharged with emotion.

What are the great Church ceremonies but a sublimation of the dance? What about the 150th Psalm, 'Praise Him with the timbrel and dances'? Surely Bunyan's *Pilgrim's Progress* is full of the highest religious fervour and he makes Mr. Ready-to-Halt celebrate his deliverance by dancing. One of the most beautiful books of the Apocrypha, the Gospel of Nicodemus, contains in *The Hymn of Jesus* an apotheosis of the dance, 'Divine Grace is dancing, dance ye therefore'.

As regards my other point, human love has always been taken as a symbol of man's relationship to divine things. *The Song of Solomon* has been treated in all the churches as a symbol of the relationship of God to man. And what about Isaiah and his 'beloved's vineyard'? And is not the Church in the Book of Revelations always symbolized as the bride?

Let me conclude with a practical suggestion. I should advise all those who do not feel themselves worthy to sing the beautiful words of this carol to vocalize, and to leave the words to those singers who have not this inhibition. But if they do this they will miss a great spiritual experience.

Yours sincerely,
R. Vaughan Williams.

How Holst would have applauded this blow on behalf of his little masterpiece![1] The episode ranks in absurdity with two later similar manifestations—the withdrawal from the choral competition in the 1960 Welsh National Eisteddfod by the Trimsaran male voice choir because one of the set pieces was the Drinking Chorus from *In Windsor Forest* ('Back and side go bare') to which they objected on temperance grounds, and the English choir, at the time of Suez, which altered the words of a chorus in *Aïda* because they were in praise of Egypt.

One of R.V.W.'s contributions to Festival Year was his setting of three Shakespeare songs, including the lines 'We are such stuff as dreams are made on' which were at the heart of his Sixth Symphony. The history of these songs is this: Armstrong Gibbs was asked to invite Vaughan Williams to compose a special test for mixed voices

[1] The performance took place on 2 May 1952.

for the June 1951 festival of the Federation of Music Festivals, of which R.V.W. was president.

'This I did [Gibbs wrote[1]] and I confess I was both surprised and put out when he replied that he did not agree with the idea at all, and that it would be much better to give them some established test. I wrote back and did my best to explain why we wanted fresh tests. . . . To this letter I got no reply . . . and at the next meeting we decided to defer the final decision till next meeting. I returned home and soon afterwards I was stricken down with some illness and was in bed when a fat envelope, registered and bearing the Dorking postmark, was brought up. Inside was the MS. of the *Three Shakespeare Songs* dedicated to me and the briefest of notes which ran:

Dear Armstrong,

Here are three Shakespeare settings. Do what you like with them.

Yours ever

R.V.W.'

The songs were first heard at the festival on 23 June 1951, in the Festival Hall.

As if to show his total disregard of the calendar, R.V.W.'s activities in 1952 were fuller than for many years. His energy seemed unlimited. A good cause would always find him ready to support it, especially if he scented harm to music and musicians. In February he wrote to *The Times* in protest over the abolition of the Crown Film Unit, 'a sentence damaging to our colleagues at home and our prestige abroad'. In April, as president of the Composers' Guild of Great Britain, he complained in an open letter, jointly signed by Guy Warrack, the chairman, about the 'meagreness' of publicity given to the activities of the contemporary English composer and the absence of a single work by a living English composer from the B.B.C. public symphony concerts of that season. Addressing the International Folk Music Council in London on 14 July 1952, he returned to an old theme—that the English were first-rate artistic snobs: 'We cannot believe that any artistic effort is good unless it comes from abroad.' In this case he was doing English cultural life an injustice, for the assimilation and absorption of foreign influences into native art (evident in his own music before the First World War) had raised standards generally. On 30 September, on the centenary of Stanford's birth, he laid a wreath on his grave in West-minster Abbey, having earlier in the month loyally defended his

---

[1] Letter to Ursula Vaughan Williams.

former master when Frank Howes wrote, after a performance at the Three Choirs Festival of Stanford's *Stabat Mater*, that 'everyone knows it was modelled on Verdi's *Requiem* and it should therefore have been tackled in an Italianate way'. Howes compared the finale adversely with *Sancta Civitas* which was in the same programme. From Hereford Vaughan Williams and Herbert Howells wrote jointly to *The Times* to protest about what they called the 'astounding criticism' of the Stanford work, which prompted them to the opinion that 'this magnificent work is one of the finest which have come from these islands' and that the only similarity with Verdi was that 'both composers wrote with mastery both for voice and orchestra'. Howes replied in *The Times* article on Stanford's centenary that these views did 'more credit to their hearts than their heads'.

During 1952 the Promenade Concerts included all six symphonies in the programmes. A similar tribute had already been paid during the 1951–2 Manchester season of the Hallé Orchestra, its first in the rebuilt Free Trade Hall. In preparation, Vaughan Williams wrote on 10 September 1951 to Roy Douglas:

'As there seem to be about to be a good many performances of my symphonies I think they ought to be overhauled. I am sending you "Pastoral" and "No. 5"—Will you help me by going through them carefully and suggesting alterations in any places where in your opinion the texture (and especially the orchestration) does not "come off". It is often difficult to decide whether one ought to score for the wireless, the concert room or the Albert Hall—also I am getting deaf and things which are probably all right sound all wrong to me. e.g. No. 5 V 1 and 2 p. 2 figure (1). I often over the wireless have literally *not heard* the violins and even in the concert room I have only just heard it—yet it *looks* all right! . . . Act III [*Pilgrim's Progress*] is ready for you whenever you want it.'

Apart from *A Sea Symphony*, the symphonies were played by the Hallé in chronological order and all, again except the choral work, were conducted by Sir John Barbirolli. The composer conducted *A Sea Symphony* on 20 March and again two evenings later at Sheffield, where an event occurred which he richly enjoyed and which is best recounted in Sir John's words:[1]

'In the afternoon we were a 'cello short, so I deputized. I had not thought

[1] *Music and Musicians*, October 1958.

of playing in the evening, for I did not want it to have the appearance of any kind of stunt. But after the rehearsal V.W. said: "Would you play tonight for me?" I said I would, and he went on, "I will tell you why exactly. I once conducted an orchestra with Kreisler playing in it, and I would like to boast that I conducted an orchestra with Barbirolli playing in it".'

The season ended on 8 May 1952 with a performance of the Sixth Symphony. The composer was present, and allowed Sir John to announce to the audience that a seventh symphony, the *Sinfonia Antartica* (as it was still called, following the English and not the Italian spelling) was completed and would first be played in Manchester in the following January, the Hallé's reward for its fine playing.

This public announcement was the culmination of the long gestation of the new symphony. When Vaughan Williams had been in Manchester in March, the score had been played through to him from the full score, at sight, by the Hallé pianist, Rayson Whalley, a feat which R.V.W. said was worthy of Arnold Bax. It had, of course, already been played through early in 1952 by Roy Douglas at The White Gates. R.V.W. wrote to him on 27 December 1951, 'I have a very rough full score and short score which is in my best handwriting which you know. I think it is legible, although not pretty.'

He next sent it to Ernest Irving. Vaughan Williams had dedicated the symphony to him, and in so doing had told him that Irving had in fact written some of it. Hence the following: 'Your worry about "my" three bars is *pure moonshine*. They are just a kittiwake imitating Mabel Ritchie, and you have not even stuck to my original! . . . It should be remembered that you were inspired by the story and its milieu, with only the script and a few actual photographs of the Antarctic scene; short of going there, a poet or composer's muse could not get closer touch with Nature. I have often recounted my amazement on finding that the Main Title Music, written out of the blue, exactly fitted the glacier climb. I am certain John Barbirolli will like it,[1] and give it the *sostenuto* playing it requires. I find the modern practice of turning non-*legato* crotchets into quavers increasingly distressing, and the new Festival Hall shows it up nakedly.'

[1] Sir John has related that V.W. 'was loath to show it to me, for he feared I might not like it and wanted to spare me the embarrassment of saying so'.

All this seems to show that Vaughan Williams had considerable doubts about how the work would be received and whether his purpose in writing it would be understood—doubts which were to prove to be abundantly justified.

On 14 June the Oxford Orchestral Society, of which Vaughan Williams was president, celebrated the jubilee of its foundation by Hugh Allen. He conducted the *Serenade to Music* and returned to Oxford five days later for the first performance of *An Oxford Elegy*, conducted by Bernard Rose, with Steuart Wilson as the speaker. Any work involving speaker and orchestra is a spur to critics to write at length, and this was no exception. Although most of them concentrated on the 'irreconcilable' nature of the medium, Ernest Newman devoted a *Sunday Times* article (12 April 1953) to complaints that the composer had deliberately distorted Arnold's poems in order to give extra emphasis, for his own purposes, to Arnold's emotion for Oxford. 'E.N. probably really wanted to show how much he knew about the poem,' Vaughan Williams commented privately.[1]

The harmonica Romance for Larry Adler, which reached London in September via New York and Liverpool, attracted much publicity from all sections of the Press. Mr. Adler himself said[2] that of the contemporary composers who had written for the instrument, Vaughan Williams exceeded them all in understanding of the instrument's capabilities, limitations and characteristic features and in writing just the music to suit it. At the Promenade Concert the work had to be immediately repeated. The composer sat among the violins for the second performance.

In October the tributes came thick and fast. Some of them have a lasting significance, for they will tell posterity in what esteem the men of his own time held the composer on his eightieth birthday.

'Vaughan Williams's invention and style are so powerful and personal [Richard Capell wrote[3]] that the bare mention of his name conjures up to the mind a kind of image, not to be defined in words without recourse to musical jargon (and perhaps not then!), but clear as a monument or mountain landscape. . . .'

But it was Neville Cardus in an article in the periodical *Illustrated* who summed up the man's work magnificently:

---

[1] Letter to the author.
[2] Conversation with Ernest Bradbury, reported in *Yorkshire Post*, 11 October 1952.
[3] The *Daily Telegraph*, 11 October 1952.

'His music is an atmosphere. It does not woo the impressionable senses; it does not satisfy all the moods of pleasure-loving and sinful man. The greatness of it comes from a certain order of our national way of living, independent and natural as a growth out of the earth, refreshed by all the weathers and humours and dispositions of the reserved but romantic English.'

Then there were the private letters—some fulsome, some comic, some dull, but all heartfelt. The deepest chords were struck by the oldest friends: John Ireland, Anne Gilchrist, now 88, Steuart Wilson and S. P. Waddington. It was to the last that R.V.W. allowed himself one of his few regretful glances at the past: 'I wish you were back in London. I feel lost without you and Gustav to look over my things and tell me where I get off. Nobody else has *both* the skill and the patience to tell me what I want to know.'

CHAPTER TEN

1953–1958

Principal Works

TUBA CONCERTO . HODIE
VIOLIN SONATA . SYMPHONY (NO. 8) IN D MINOR
EPITHALAMION . SYMPHONY (NO. 9) IN E MINOR
TEN BLAKE SONGS . FOUR LAST SONGS
THE FIRST NOWELL

I

THE *Sinfonia Antartica* was played for the first time at a Hallé Concert in Manchester on 14 January 1953. At the last minute it was discovered that the spelling 'Antarctica' was incorrect in Italian and was amended. The occasion attracted wide publicity and the hall was full. As Richard Capell succinctly wrote in the *Daily Telegraph*: 'The composer was present, and when his tragic but uplifting music was over he received one of the great ovations of his long career.' On the whole the critical verdict was favourable, although there was much debate whether it was a symphony. Colin Mason, in the *Manchester Guardian*, forthrightly called attention to the work's 'masterly and completely unified symphonic form' and stressed the originality of its design and the symphonic logic of the treatment of the material. 'Nothing,' he added, 'could better demonstrate the rightness of his attitude to his art than the new symphony.' Capell described it as 'yet another testament to the prodigious vigour and fertility of his old age . . . it represents Vaughan Williams in a superbly energetic state of mind, without a hint of weakness.' Frank Howes, in *The Times*, asserted that the composer had 'broken new ground, not in the fact that he uses a larger orchestra, but that he has found in sheer sonority devoid of thematic significance a means of conveying his vision and placing it within a symphonic scheme'. Howes especially

praised the performance—'a vividness and authority that conveyed
unmistakably the composer's intentions in this latest instance of his
uncompromising originality and endless fertility'—and the composer
himself declared it to be his 'first flawless first p rformance'. It was
in the artists' room after the concert that he first dubbed Barbirolli
'glorious John'. The work had been in rehearsal for weeks. In
November 1952 Vaughan Williams had travelled to Manchester for
a play-through. What he thought is evident from a letter from
Ernest Irving, who had been unable to accompany him:

'Fancy nine hours' rehearsal and the only complaint a matter of percussion! Wind-machines have always been feeble and bells are always
an octave too high. If I remember rightly I reinforced the bell resultants
with pianoforte harmonics [in the film]. I will ask James Bradshaw who
is, besides being our best timpanist, a great friend of mine, what we did
at H.M.V. and I will see that you get the right articles at Manchester.'

Irving, who was by now a dying man, attended the first performance in London, given by Barbirolli and the Hallé, at a Royal Philharmonic Concert on 21 January. He wrote on the next day:

My dear Ralph V.W.,
    What a grand night and a triumph for you. . . . At the risk of being a
bore I must thank you most sincerely for giving me the great honour of
the dedication which has tagged me A.1 at Lloyds in a way nothing else
could have done. . . . Perhaps you would like a few observations on the
Sinfonia. First, you have scaled down the main subject, starting it p.
I take it your object was to present to the ear a sad unpeopled white waste
instead of glacier-climbing energumen, and if so this is achieved in the
symphonic version. . . . The choir, I think, has too many voices; 3 on
each line would be enough and much more flexible than 30, and they
should be *all contraltos* (singing in their upper register). The wind
machine was badly played. It should be geared so that the player can
increase its speed suddenly so that it whistles. Now it only rattles. It is a
small matter, but has caused much talk. . . . I thought the whole of that
episode was held too rigidly on the beat; and that Margaret[1] was tethered.
Still, she sang magnificently. The rest of it I thought was very well
played indeed, except that the cymbals always came in a shade before the
beat (megalomania?). You said you wanted the organ to make a nasty
noise and I thought it unpleasant enough, but with insufficient 32-ft. tone.
The great climax was most moving, and in a metaphysical way rather than
a descriptive one. . . . The Sinfonia is a noble work in its own right, full

---

[1] Margaret Ritchie, who sang the soprano part.

of musical skill and orchestral virtuosity. It is fully worthy of your genius and only lower in standard than the Fifth in that it tends to describe things as well as thoughts. But who would compare Homer disadvantageously with Wordsworth? Only, I think, the people who did not understand either. . . .

Yours ever,   Ernest I.

Obtaining the correct quality of sound from the wind-machine was a persistent problem. When the symphony was conducted by Sir Malcolm Sargent in April 1953 the effect was tried of horn players' whistling into their instruments, but this was unsatisfactory.

Undoubtedly, though, it was Neville Cardus's notice in the *Manchester Guardian* of the London performance which encouraged Vaughan Williams to think that his doubts of his own wisdom in allowing the work to be played were unnecessary.

'The *Sinfonia Antartica* seems to me the most powerfully imaginative of all the composer's works,' Cardus wrote, '. . . For sheer brilliance, vividness and spontaneity in the moulding and releasing of tone, in a swift imaginative blending of instrumental colours, everything serving the composer's inner vision, Vaughan Williams has never equalled this latest of his scores.'

The visit to Manchester had also provided an opportunity for an extra-musical event. R.V.W. supported the idea of world government. He was a vice-president of Federal Union, and in 1939 had used the prize-giving at the Petersfield Festival as a platform from which to express a hope for an eventual United States of Europe. The Manchester branch of Federal Union gave a lunch in his honour on 16 January 1953, at which he again spoke of how to reconcile nationalism and internationalism.

'We should know and love each other through our art—and it must be our own art, not a colourless cosmopolitanism. I believe that one's own community, one's own language, customs and religion are essential to our spiritual health. Out of these characteristics, these "hard knots", we can build a united Europe and a world federation. But without local loyalty there can be nothing for the wider issues to build on. Everything of value in our spiritual and cultural life springs from our own soil.'

On 7 February, he married Ursula Wood in the vestry chapel of St. Pancras Church. In March, consequent upon their intention to live in London, Vaughan Williams resigned the conductorship of the Leith Hill Festival.

During that last summer as a Dorking resident two events principally engaged Vaughan Williams's attention, the Coronation and the production of *The Bridal Day* on B.B.C. Television. Dr. William McKie, the organist of Westminster Abbey, had visited The White Gates on 23 October 1952, to discuss the music for the Coronation of Queen Elizabeth II on 2 June 1953. His notes, made afterwards, state: 'I told him that a new Te Deum was desired, but he replied he did not wish to write another one. He was agreeable to the use of the Creed and Sanctus from the English version of the Mass in G minor, and he said he would like to write a short unaccompanied anthem. I told him it was quite likely that a very short motet would be required while the Queen was making her Communion, and he said he would be glad to write this. He spoke at some length of the music of the 1937 Coronation, complained of the length and loudness of the organ improvisations, said he thought it a great weakness that there was nothing for the congregation to sing and offered, if a place could be found for the "Old Hundredth" (with the long notes) to arrange this for choir and orchestra if needed.' His actual words in making the offer were: 'If you can persuade the Archbishop to have a hymn in the Coronation Service, I'll make a mess-up of "Old Hundredth".'

The 'short anthem' became the exquisite 'O taste and see'. 'Do you want the whole thing?' Vaughan Williams asked Dr. McKie on 24 November, 'with the bit about the lions? Or will that run too much into Sir John Goss?' By 8 December he had sent it off, with the question 'Will this do?' He had used the Prayer Book version of the words 'and also written blest instead of blessed. I hope the Archbishop will not mind'. But it was the 'Old Hundredth' which principally concerned R.V.W. 'I hope you will be able to put it through,' he had written on 24 November. The Archbishop, Dr. Fisher, agreed to the innovation and by 17 December R.V.W. had decided to make it an elaborate setting, with fanfares adapted from his 1929 setting of the Hundredth Psalm. Dr. McKie favoured, for practical reasons, a simpler version but wrote that 'if you prefer to use the elaborate version, I shall be perfectly happy. The Archbishop would prefer not to have *Amen* at the end'. For a time R.V.W. thought the 'elaborate version' would not be a good idea—('I think the Archbishop is liturgically wrong not to have an *Amen* after the Doxology,' he wrote, 'but of course he must have his way')—but by February 1953 he was rightly convinced of the splendid effect which could be made by fanfares of trumpets before the first and last verses. 'Now, will you ask the Archbishop two things,' he wrote. 'The earlier versions of words say "mirth" instead of "fear", which is a much better version of "Serve the Lord with gladness". The original edition had the word "folck" which was misread in later editions as "flock" but obviously meant "folk". Also it is a much better version of "We are his people".' By 11 February the arrangement was fully scored for large orchestra with 'all available trumpets'. Dr. Fisher allowed 'folk', but retained 'fear' although he conceded that there were arguments for 'mirth', which already occurred in some books. 'All the same,' he wrote to Dr. McKie, ' "fear" is the word in Hymns A. and M.—all editions—and in the *English Hymnal*, and is certainly the word which most people would expect. I think it would be wrong to make the change in the Coronation Service. I do not think you will disagree violently with me and nor, I hope, will Vaughan Williams . . .' There the matter rested. Vaughan Williams was extremely proud of introducing this democratic musical reform into the service, although the choice of tune did not meet with universal approval. Nor did the performance in the Abbey meet with the arranger's approval:

'The effect in the Abbey was largely spoiled because all the Dukes and Viscounts, who probably had not copies of the music, and anyway could not have read it, sang the old all-equal version, steadily, against the whole chorus and orchestra.'[1]

Here Vaughan Williams overstated the case, for the effect, as recordings prove, was overwhelming in its splendour.

A further contribution to the secular Coronation music was the part-song 'Silence and Music' which Vaughan Williams and his wife contributed to *A Garland for the Queen*, the set of ten songs commissioned by the Arts Council from ten English composers and ten poets as a twentieth-century equivalent of *The Triumphs of Oriana*. These were sung for the first time at the Festival Hall on the eve of the Coronation, when a selection from *The Triumphs* was linked with the new *Garland* by a performance of the *Tallis Fantasia*, which the composer conducted—a happy and sensible piece of programme planning, for few other works so successfully bridge the English centuries. When all the pomp was over, there was a letter from Ernest Irving to provoke an irreverent chuckle: 'I hope your false

---

[1] Letter to author, 20 August 1957.

relations in the "Old Hundredth" were not a reflection on the Duke of * * * —but perhaps you were thinking of Lord * * *.'

The Bridal Day had lain in a drawer since the 1939 play-through. In 1952 Stanford Robinson asked Vaughan Williams if he could look at the score and R.V.W. sent it although, as he wrote to Hubert Foss on 17 September 1952, 'I had some doubts about it after not having looked at it for so many years.' It was hoped to produce it either at Hampton Court Palace or on television. A play-through was arranged with Michael Mullinar at Foss's home, 60 Corringham Road, N.W.11, on 2 October and on 8 October Vaughan Williams wrote to Hubert Foss: 'I am quite in favour of the idea of Television. Kenneth Wright must point out where the music wants adding to or subtracting from. I do not mind quoting from my earlier works but when I find, as I do, that some of my later works quote from this one then I must alter this rather than alter my later ones.'

By the end of October it had been decided to proceed with the television production. Vaughan Williams revised the music and added extra songs. These were ready by January, a play-through took place in March and on the Friday of Coronation Week, 5 June, the programme was televised, with Cecil Day Lewis as narrator, Denis Dowling as baritone soloist and Sheila Shand Gibbs as the Bride. The composer's views on the final result are perhaps best expressed in this extract from a letter written to me on 10 June 1953: 'I hope you did *not* watch the television. It had *nothing* to do with what Ursula devised.'

Hubert Foss did not see this fruit of his labours, for he had died on 26 May. He had worked devotedly for the cause of English music at a time when it was very much a cause. He belonged to the generation of Bernard van Dieren, Philip Heseltine, Cecil Gray, E. J. Moeran and Constant Lambert, all of whom, like him, went to premature graves. Foss, in his publishing days, not only published composers' music, he gave advice and help and took a close interest. This attitude of mind, not always found, was also Vaughan Williams's, who would often put work into younger composers' ways if he could.

It is astonishing to assess the mental powers of Vaughan Williams at eighty-one. 'You are so full of energy,' George Trevelyan told him. Since his mid-seventies he had produced a large-scale symphony, supervised an opera production, written a concerto for a mouth-organ, experimented in *An Oxford Elegy* with the difficult form of melodrama, written several occasional pieces and fulfilled many conducting engagements. Now, as he approached his eighty-second year, he was at work on a big choral work for Christmas, a Concerto for Tuba and his first Violin Sonata. He attended, in October 1953, the Leeds Festival at which Josef Krips conducted what Vaughan Williams considered to be the finest performance he ever heard of *Sancta Civitas*. In the autumn, too, he published a collection of essays, several of them reprints[1] but headed by the hitherto unpublished essay on Beethoven's Ninth Symphony which he had written in the early part of the war. (One fascinating point about V.W.'s prose style is its similarity to that of his great-uncle Charles Darwin in the latter's autobiography. This bears out Frances Cornford's statement[2] that Wedgwood family letters could be mistaken for R.V.W.'s essays 'so absurdly alike is the tone of voice'.) Some of the wickedly provocative statements in the book amused an older generation, who appreciated the spirit and atmosphere in which they were written, and scandalized the younger, who failed sometimes to look beneath the flippant tone of the words for the wisdom. The man who took it hardest, however, was a fellow-octogenarian, Ernest Newman, who renewed his lifetime's hostility to Vaughan Williams. Two articles in the *Sunday Times* issues of 21 and 28 February 1954 showed that R.V.W.'s description of the final theme in Wagner's *Götterdämmerung* as 'hardly good enough for a third-rate German beer garden' had sunk deep into the target for which it was probably always intended.

'The truth seems to be,' Newman wrote, 'that deep down in Dr. Vaughan Williams's subconsciousness are some blind phobias that make him not only lacking in ordinary courtesy but capable of the rankest rudeness where certain composers are concerned.'

Another sentence, that 'there are orchestral miscalculations even in Wagner, which any composer less conceited than he would certainly have corrected in performance,' provoked another eruption:

'After seven years of conducting in one of the leading German opera houses—an experience that never came Dr. Vaughan Williams's way—Wagner might reasonably have been encouraged to place some faith in his inner ear. . . . Dr. Vaughan Williams should keep a closer eye than he seems to do at present on some of his phobias. . . .'

---

[1] Some were revised. The most substantial alterations were made in 'The Letter and the Spirit': cf. with its original version in *Music and Letters*, Vol. I, No. 2.

[2] *R.C.M. Magazine*, Vol. LV, No. 1, p. 12.

Sundays were lively in those days.

And while R.V.W. was lively, too, rejoicing in living in London again and being able to attend concerts and cinemas as much as he wanted, the years inevitably brought the passing of old friends. Colles, Edwin Evans, and Fox Strangways had been dead for some time; in 1954 Richard Capell died. Arnold Bax and Ernest Irving, as well as Foss, had gone in 1953. Vaughan Williams seemed curiously undismayed by death. It was not that it did not move him deeply, but he seemed to accept it in others, while never considering it for himself, and to retain his friends' spirits in his mind so that they continued their existence as a part of his. He lived for tomorrow. One 'tomorrow' which brightened the wintry beginning of 1954 was the staging of *The Pilgrim's Progress* by the Cambridge University Musical Society for seven performances between 23 and 27 February. Under Boris Ord's direction and in Dennis Arundell's production, Vaughan Williams's university made amends to him for the deficiencies of Covent Garden. Probably no other service to his music gave him more satisfaction. The Pilgrim was sung by John Noble, a young physicist who later abandoned science for music after his success in this production, and almost the entire cast and orchestra were composed of university musicians. The following Sunday, in the *Observer*, Eric Blom wrote:

'That there is a certain sameness about the work is undeniable, but it is due to consistency of style, not to lack of invention or limited imagination . . . He is not just exquisite, or gracious, or mellifluous; there is an unworldly nobility about many of those strains which are neither archaic nor modern, though they often sound both at once, but belong to all time or none. I am a keen Handelian, but when it comes to the Alleluias at the end of this work of Vaughan Williams's they seem to me authentically celestial, and those in *Messiah* only full of a fine courtly Georgian swagger.'

He certainly continued to fill every minute with sixty-seconds-worth of distance run. He missed the final Cambridge performances of his Morality in order to conduct the *St. John Passion* at Dorking. A month later he conducted the *St. Matthew Passion* and then, in April, the *Five Tudor Portraits*. The previous December he had attended all Decca's recording sessions in the Kingsway Hall when Sir Adrian Boult and the London Philharmonic Orchestra recorded the First, Fourth, Fifth, Sixth, and Seventh Symphonies so that, with the *London Symphony* issued in 1952 and the *Pastoral* as a Coronation tribute in 1953, the complete set of symphonies as it then stood was available on long-playing records.[1] Posterity, therefore, has the benefit of all the symphonies recorded by their most sympathetic and loyal interpreter, for the Eighth and Ninth were added in due course (the Ninth not, though, by Decca). The Tuba Concerto was accepted in the spirit in which it was written when it was first played on 13 June 1954, and on 8 September at Worcester Vaughan Williams conducted the first performance of the Christmas cantata *This Day*, for which he preferred his original Latin title of *Hodie* and agreed with some reluctance to its use as merely a subtitle. In fact it has become generally known as *Hodie*. He found it difficult to conduct, but despite this, the performance had a splendid assurance. Most people were entranced by the work's joyousness, its peace and goodwill, its tunefulness and its mellow wisdom. Typical —and most happily expressed—of these was J. H. Elliot, who wrote in the *Hallé Magazine* of December 1954:

'It seemed to me, and a study of the score has confirmed what my ears told me, that this music has the authentic quality of old age— not of weakness, still less of senility or failing power. There is as much vigour, of spirit and execution, as there was in the music of the V.W. of twenty years ago. But it has something else, which I can only call the fullness of wisdom—a spiritual tranquillity that is not mere resignation, and a simplicity that is grander than any intricacy of performance or bold and exultant splendour of expression. There is something here that is other-worldly, withdrawn from the hurly-burly—or, rather, transcending it. It is the music of old age in the truest sense, the final maturity of a great mind. It breathes a deep peace of soul.'

But it was this work, too, which provoked the first open expressions of a reaction against Vaughan Williams's music.

On 19 January Sir Malcolm Sargent conducted *Hodie* for the first time in London. The critics of *The Times* and the *Daily Telegraph* received it respectfully, but a more searching look at this and Vaughan Williams's work in general was directed in *Musical Opinion* (April and May issues 1955) by Donald Mitchell. He described *Hodie* as 'grossly over-praised and grossly under-composed'.

'If this is the kind of music that rouses cries of exaltation, then our

[1] Boult had earlier recorded the Sixth Symphony on L.P. for H.M.V. as well as on 78s, and the *London*, Fourth, and Fifth Symphonies had been available on 78s.

musical culture is in a worse condition than I thought possible. Of course, a good deal of the whooping is positively Pavlovian. . . . There is a level below which "directness" and "forthrightness" of utterance—qualities for which Vaughan Williams is praised—deteriorate into a downright unacceptable and damaging primitivity. . . . It is doubly damaging when his contemporaries are so blind (or deaf, perhaps) that they mistake patent coarseness as evidence of exuberant genius.'

There followed a scornful attack on the collection of essays—'verbal utterance . . . often reminiscent in their creaking humour of that arch-comical bore, though brilliant analyst, Sir Donald Tovey'—and Mr. Mitchell was quick to seize upon Vaughan Williams's own references to his 'amateurish technique':

'It has to be admitted that this self-criticism has more than a grain of uncomfortable truth to it. When listening to a work of the character of *Hodie*, where, I suspect, Vaughan' Williams's compositional conscience was at a low ebb, it suddenly becomes very noticeable how clumsy his technique can be, and how much he relies on his inimitable idiosyncrasies to pull him through. At the same time, one is reminded, rather disturbingly, of many a more masterful composition of his where his technique has not seemed fully adequate to his needs. . . . The composer who pioneers in the national field loses that very freedom of artistic expression which his pioneering activities confer upon his successors. In a sense he becomes the first—perhaps only—victim of his revolution. . . . I believe [Vaughan Williams] will be regarded as a major minor composer. . . . His very real and personal genius will keep his music alive, though I fear the limitations which circumscribe it will become increasingly apparent as time moves on.'

The mid-fifties were a time of revolt in English artistic life, in the theatre, literature, architecture and music. Old values were challenged, neglected causes (such as Schoenberg's theories) re-examined. Inevitably, some of the younger generation of critics questioned Vaughan Williams's stature. The irony of his last years, of which he was aware, was that he had, as Mitchell said, become a victim of his own pioneering endeavours. His principal aim had been to throw off the Teutonic shackles of the nineteenth century. This he had done. The generation which followed him—the generation of Britten and Tippett—had fertilized the national basis of their art with the eclectic influences of Continental developments—a procedure Vaughan Williams advocated and had himself followed in what he learned from the music of Ravel and Debussy. But now a younger generation seemed to him to be fettering itself to a new German tyranny—atonalism—encouraged by the influence of Schoenberg's followers who had settled in England and penetrated British musical life at many points. The wheel had turned back fifty years; but inevitably it would turn again.

Of all this the general public knew and cared little. Vaughan Williams was a national figure, and his presence at a performance of his music was a signal for a great demonstration of affection. He rejoiced in several chances to see performances of his operas. *Hugh the Drover* and *Riders to the Sea* were a frequent 'double bill' at Sadler's Wells; *Sir John in Love* was performed by several amateur groups and by Cambridge University Arts Club in February 1956. More revision of *Hugh the Drover* was incorporated early in 1956 into the Sadler's Wells production. *The Poisoned Kiss* was conducted by William Neve at Cheltenham Grammar School in April 1956. This production impelled Vaughan Williams to buy the copyright of the libretto so that he and his wife could make a thorough revision. The new version was first performed at the Royal Academy of Music in July 1957. Midway through 1955 the Gold Albert Medal of the Royal Society of Arts was awarded to Vaughan Williams 'in recognition of his eminent services to music'. This was the first time it had been given to a musician, and the presentation was made in November by the Duke of Edinburgh. It is, perhaps, appropriate here to quote some words written at about this time by Vaughan Williams to a close friend of his last years:

'If anything in my life, music included, has enabled anyone to have a fuller enjoyment of life then I feel I have not lived in vain. . . . I hope people feel this, but so few of them take the trouble to say so . . . I wish I could be all you think and say I am—but it gives me an ideal to live for. You write of being true to oneself. That is a thing I always try for and hope I may sometimes achieve it. . . . I wish I could start life all over again and really become, approximately at any rate, the sort of person you describe. Nevertheless I loved having your letter because the affection of a good man is worth having anyhow.'

In this same summer *The Making of Music* was published. The most perceptive review of these Cornell lectures was perhaps that by Martin Cooper[1] who saw through the bantering humour and the outrageous remarks to the heart of the writer. 'It seems to show,'

[1] The *Daily Telegraph*, 6 August 1955. The lectures were given during R.V.W.'s visit to America and Canada, September—December 1954.

he wrote of one of R.V.W.'s theories, 'that, for the writer, deep feeling and experiment are mutually exclusive, an unexpected revelation from the composer of Vaughan Williams's fourth symphony.' But not so unexpected now that we know the origin of that symphony. 'If you wish to know more about music,' Cooper concluded, 'Vaughan Williams's lectures will disappoint you. If you wish to know more about Vaughan Williams's music, read them.'

A circle of close friends knew that a new symphony was nearing its final stages. This work was dedicated to John Barbirolli who was shown the score in the summer of 1955. On 24 October, after a televised Hallé Concert, Sir John revealed publicly the existence of the work and the date of its first performance, in Manchester the following May. Vaughan Williams's eighty-third birthday was celebrated by a Festival Hall performance of *Job*. On 22 October he gave an address—from the chancel steps—at a special choral Evensong at St. Mary-le-Tower, Ipswich, in honour of his old friend and collaborator Martin Shaw, using the opportunity for a diatribe against un-musical clergy. On 17 November, he gave his famous talk on Parry and Stanford to the Composers' Concourse. He was glad of the opportunity to pay homage to the dead; he honoured the living, too, writing tributes in the *R.C.M. Magazine* and in the *Daily Telegraph* to Sibelius on his ninetieth birthday on 8 December 1955.

'I do not count as civilized those mid-Europeans who ignore Sibelius [he wrote[1]]. Why is he great? . . . It is because he has never deviated from the strait path that he is truly original and will remain so when the twelve-tone apostles have become mere commonplaces. . . . We must always remember that it was the same man, with the same outlook and the same mind, who wrote both Finlandia and the fourth symphony. Sibelius has his head and his heart in heaven but his feet are firmly planted on the ground. There is a popular element in all great music. . . . Great music is written, I believe, not by breaking the tradition, but by adding to it. Sibelius has shown us that the new thought which can be discovered in the old material is inexhaustible.'

That passage, which might almost have been written about Vaughan Williams himself, shows why Sibelius and Vaughan Williams admired each other. Both were almost feudal figures, dominating the musical life of their respective countries at a critical

[1] The *Daily Telegraph*, 8 December 1955.

emergent stage of their cultural history. Both were strongly influenced by a feeling for the traditions, the landscape, the history, of
their countries. They were proud to be mouthpieces for the artistic
and even the social aspirations of their times. They gloried in their
'insularity', in the knowledge that they found expression for what
their countrymen felt but could not say. They knew, too, that the
impatient youth of their countries would one day scrutinize their
reputations—and they were unafraid.

Early in February 1956 Vaughan Williams went to Manchester
for a day of rehearsals on the Eighth Symphony. He found the work
completely prepared: it could have been performed that evening.
He was also himself to rehearse the Hallé Choir for the performance
of the *St. Matthew Passion* which Sir John had invited him to
conduct in Manchester, the first time the work was to be performed
at the Hallé since Stanford had conducted it in 1904. The performance took place on 18 March, eight days after the Leith Hill Festival
performance. The hall was crowded, and few were unmoved by the
meeting of two great musical minds in the sublime music.

The first performance of the new symphony at Manchester on
2 May was a triumph, for the public enjoyed this uninhibited music
and accepted it in the right spirit. A spontaneous burst of laughter
sounded through the Free Trade Hall after the perky Scherzo,
which Martin Cooper happily described as 'as though Shostakovich
had become a Cockney with atavistic memories of the Cotswolds
rather than the Steppe'.[1] No one, however, was more perceptive of
the work's strength than Colin Mason in his long review in the
Manchester Guardian. He took strong exception to the vibraphone—
a sound one either likes or dislikes, with no half-measures—and was
not amused by the finale, but the first two movements impressed him
deeply.

'The new symphony does not quite satisfy as a complete musical form,
as the *Antartica* satisfied those who listened for its form as well as for its
antarcticness. Nor are all the sound-effects justified by any real musical
significance. In the earlier work they were an essential and thoroughly
integrated part of the musical content, but here they are often superfluous
and sometimes intrusive. . . . The first movement . . . is most beautiful
and original both in shape and content. . . . What is also refreshing in
this first movement is the modal variety and flexibility of the melodic
lines, which are more elegant, easy and graceful in motion, less tied to his

[1] The *Daily Telegraph*, 3 May 1956.

usual distinctive but rather lumpish modal formulas than any he has ever written, and show him at 83 still extending his musical range. As this is the most sophisticated, civilized and universal music he has ever written, so the second movement . . . is the wittiest. . . . This movement made the audience laugh, and in the old days, when audiences knew their own mind and did not hesitate to express it, an immediate encore would have been demanded.'

There was general agreement that this was an enjoyable work, likely to be popular, which the composer had enjoyed writing. Hardly anyone suggested that the finale needed no apologia, that only an unconventional and fearless composer would have dared to write it. At both the Manchester performances and at the Festival Hall on 14 May (for which Vaughan Williams thinned out the percussion in the finale) the audiences rose to their feet to greet the composer of this extraordinarily youthful and indiscreet symphony. Barbirolli lost no opportunity to further the claims of the new symphony, conducting it throughout England and Europe. Other conductors soon took it up, notably Ormandy and Stokowski in the United States. To the former belonged the privilege of the first American performance, with the Philadelphia Orchestra in New York on 9 October 1956. Its reception was such that the New York Music Critics' Circle voted it the best new symphonic work performed there in 1956. Within six months of the Manchester performance it was played in Lille, Brussels, Strasbourg, Zurich, Lisbon, Vienna, Gotesborg and Helsinki. The *Antartica* was played twice in Warsaw—and it should be mentioned that a recording of this symphony was played on mid-winter's day, 21 June 1956, at the Royal Society Antarctic Expedition's base at Halley Bay! Scores of congratulatory letters reached Vaughan Williams after the Eighth Symphony, and one which, though not congratulatory, was especially delightful. It was from a nine-year-old boy, Tom Whitestone, who had written to Barbirolli saying how much he had liked the Haydn Symphony which the Hallé had played and how little he had liked the V.W. Eighth Symphony. Sir John sent the letter to the composer, who wrote to the boy:

Dear Tom,
   Sir John Barbirolli has sent me your letter to him—I am glad you like Haydn. He was a very great man and wrote beautiful tunes. I must one day try to write a tune which you will like. '
                              Yours affectionately,   R. Vaughan Williams.

Yet another new work appeared on 4 June. As a present to Dr. Harold Darke on the fortieth anniversary of his appointment as organist at St. Michael's, Cornhill, R.V.W. had written a motet, 'A Vision of Aeroplanes', a setting of a prophetic passage in *Ezekiel*, which was played in company with tributes from Howells and Dyson. Vaughan Williams was a frequent attender at the Bach recitals at Cornhill. On 13 June he addressed the Hymn Society conference at Addington Palace, the beginning of celebrations to mark the fiftieth anniversary of the *English Hymnal*. Shortly afterwards, through rolling the lawn on a wet day after being advised not to mow it, he developed phlebitis in the leg. This caused him to cancel a proposed visit to the Cheltenham Festival. When I asked him if he had any message for his friends at the festival, which I was to attend, he said: 'Yes, tell them there's no need to inquire about me in hushed tones.' He recovered in time to go, for what was to be the last time, to the Three Choirs Festival at Gloucester, where the audience stood in silence as he went to the rostrum to conduct *The Lark Ascending*. It was forty-six years since he had first conducted there. Now the great frame stooped, the black hair was white, but the eyes were as firm in their gaze and the face even more striking. After the Festival he went to Majorca for a holiday, where news reached him of the death of Gerald Finzi.

Older friends also died in 1956; Isidore Schwiller on 28 May, aged seventy-seven, who had led the Leith Hill Orchestra for so many years and who had played in the First String Quartet in 1909; and, in November, Marie Hall. R.V.W.'s phlebitis attack sent a chill shadow across the hearts of his friends, for this was the first intimation of his mortality. He seemed indestructible, and his swift recovery banished gloom. He returned looking very fit from Majorca, where he had been glad to meet Robert Graves, and resumed his assiduous concert-going. A new 'Choral Flourish', dedicated to Alan Kirby, was sung on 3 November, and the F minor Symphony was a rather surprising choice for the St. Cecilia Festival concert on 19 November. For a concert to mark Casals's eightieth birthday he would have liked to be able to offer the Cello Concerto with which he was continually 'tinkering', but instead he arranged Bach's *Schmücke dich, O liebe Seele* for cello and strings. This choral-prelude for organ has also been orchestrated by Schoenberg. Its namesake, the Cantata No. 180, had first been performed in England under Gustav Holst fifty-two years before. It was a concert of Holst's less known works given at the Festival Hall, conducted by Sir Adrian Boult, which gave Vaughan Williams the greatest musical pleasure of 1956. He had helped to plan the programme and contributed financial support through the newly formed R.V.W. Trust whereby income from his performing rights was used for the benefit of other music and musicians.[1] He wrote to me afterwards on 23 December:

'. . . The Holst concert was, I believe, a success: excellent performances, the house not full, but not painfully empty. I hear that there were a lot of quite young people there who were much excited. I am confirmed in my opinion that the *Ode to Death* is his finest choral work. *Egdon Heath* is gradually clarifying in my mind—it is still a bit of a puzzle. Christopher Finzi, as representing the younger generation, admired it most of all. Then there is 'Assemble All Ye Maidens', which I had not heard since I conducted it years ago. [First performance, Bach Choir, 24 May 1927] It is very lovely. *The Morning of the Year* is a strange mixture—I like the tunes very much, and I like the choral part, when I can forget the words—but the two don't seem to fit. I am glad we did the Choral Fantasia, which again takes some knowing, as I believe it is fine. . . . I went to St. Martin's to hear the new Stravinskys and they frankly bored me.'

The last sentence is a reference to Stravinsky's *Canticum Sacrum*, Mass and Symphonies for Wind Instruments, and his arrangement of Bach's 'Vom Himmel hoch' Variations, performed at St. Martin-in-the-Fields on 11 December 1956. 'If he dislikes Bach as much as that, I don't know why he bothers to orchestrate him,' he said to Christopher Finzi.[2]

He spent the first weeks of 1957 at Joy Finzi's home, Ashmansworth, Newbury, where he worked on the Ninth Symphony, with which he had made good progress in Majorca. The symphony and a work for brass band were his chief creative preoccupations. He had written a Prelude on Three Welsh Hymn Tunes for the Salvation Army Band in 1956—he admired their musicianship and while in Dorking had endeared himself to them by attending a concert which they gave there. He presented the prizes at the National Brass Band Championship in 1956 when he was impressed by the competing

---

[1] The Trust, confirmed in Vaughan Williams's will, is administered by an independent Committee. The Musicians' Benevolent Fund acts as custodian trustee, but does not benefit financially.

[2] *R.C.M. Magazine*, Easter Term, 1959, Vol. LV, No. 1.

bands' performances. Almost at once he started work on a test piece, the Variations, which was used for the 1957 championship on 26 October 1957, and was described in *The Times* as 'unquestionably the best piece ever written for this unwieldy medium'. During this year, too, he began work on his sixth opera, to a libretto by his wife based on the two ballads 'Tam Lin' and 'Thomas the Rhymer'.

A recurrence of the phlebitis in the leg late in July was followed by a major operation in the Middlesex Hospital in August. R.V.W.'s rapid and vigorous recovery surprised everyone except himself, and he was in the Festival Hall on 30 September for the first performance of the cantata *Epithalamion*, which he had adapted from *The Bridal Day*. He fulfilled his promise to John Barbirolli to contribute towards the opening concert of the Hallé Orchestra's hundredth season and sent a 'Flourish for Glorious John' for full orchestra.

October brought the eighty-fifth birthday celebrations.[1] The Royal Philharmonic Society opened its season on 9 October with a V.W. concert at which the only unhappy note was the absence through illness of Adrian Boult. In his place another old friend, Basil Cameron, conducted the *Pastoral Symphony* and *Job*, and William Herbert sang the solo part in the orchestral version of *On Wenlock Edge*. On the 11th, the eve of his birthday, he attended a Macnaghten concert at which, by his request, none of his music was performed but there were six birthday-gift works from fellow-composers: Franz Reizenstein, Anthony Milner, Edmund Rubbra, Herbert Howells, Elizabeth Maconchy and Robin Milford. Nor was there any music at the Dorking celebration on 13 October, again by request, but, instead, a conjurer and the presentation of a landscape by John Nash. There was certainly nothing 'convalescent' in all this activity, nor in the week-end a fortnight later when he spent the whole day at the brass band championships and went next morning to Manchester for the Hallé's eighty-fifth birthday tribute where the *London* and Eighth Symphonies were balanced by

[1] In view of the widely held belief in the 'insularity' of Vaughan Williams's music it is instructive to read the list of overseas performances given between September and November 1957. The Fourth Symphony was played in New York, the Fifth on New Zealand radio; the Eighth in Helsinki, Malmo, Rotterdam (twice), Houston, Boston (10 times), Hilversum, New Zealand and Cape Town; the Serenade to Music in Cape Town, Auckland, Hilversum, and Kingsport, Tennessee; *Hodie* in Sydney N.S.W. and Youngstown, Ohio; *Job* in Toronto; the Harmonica Romance on Australian radio; the Piano Concerto on Danish radio with the original soloist, Harriet Cohen; the Oboe Concerto in Germany and Vancouver, and *The Sons of Light* and the Concerto Grosso in New Zealand.

The Wasps Overture, the *Tallis Fantasia* and the 'Old Hundredth', with the new 'Flourish' as an encore. 'I don't think I need to tell you what a joy it was to have you and Ursula with me for your Birthday Concert,' Barbirolli wrote afterwards. 'What wonderful news about No. 9. Let us know as soon as it becomes available (after its initial performances) and eager hands will be clutching for the score.'

The new symphony had been submitted to the private 'jury', and had been played through at his flat in Albert Hall Mansions to Malcolm Sargent, who was to conduct the first performance. On 14 November its existence was officially announced to the press—and the composer at once began revising it yet again. After Christmas he resumed his round of concerts and operas—*The Carmelites* by Poulenc and Tippett's Second Symphony in particular—and started rehearsals for the *St. John* and *St. Matthew Passions* at Dorking. On 8 February he went to Croydon to hear his S.A.T.B. arrangement of Patrick Hadley's *Fen and Flood*, a cantata which had originally been written for male voices to a libretto by Charles Cudworth, Librarian of the Pendlebury Library, Cambridge. Vaughan Williams had greatly liked the work and, because he thought it would be a pity if future performances were confined to male voices, asked if he might arrange it for mixed chorus—a situation somewhat analogous to Elgar's scoring of Herbert Brewer's *Emmaus*, though the circumstances were quite different.

The performance of the *St. John Passion* on 15 February was aptly described in the *Daily Telegraph* by John Warrack as 'a communal act of music worship' whose essence 'more nearly touches the whole purpose of the work than any amount of the circumstantial reconstruction he deplores. . . . It is not virtuosity, nor even some mystique attached to Vaughan Williams's presence—no conductor could be more practical, more self-effacing. It is rather his unblinking vision and realization of the work's aim as, in Bach's own words, "the glory of God and the recreation of the mind" '. A reference by Warrack to the 'odd sound' of the pianoforte continuo in place of the harpsichord stirred R.V.W. to write to the *Daily Telegraph*:[1]

'Surely this work should be produced in such a way as to give modern hearers the same emotional and spiritual effect which Bach himself produced on his contemporaries? I have no doubt that if the grand

[1] 20 February 1958.

pianoforte of our day had been available to Bach he would have used it in preference to the harpsichord. . . . There can be no doubt that the pianoforte, with its infinite gradations of tone, from an almost orchestral fortissimo to an almost inaudible pianissimo, performs the function of a continuo much better than the harpsichord with its hard unyielding tone. The same applies to our oboes with their lovely tone, which no one hesitates to use instead of the coarse-sounding oboes of Bach's time. . . . It seems to me that to use the resources which we now possess, reverently and with true musical insight, is right. . . . It is well known that Bach was dissatisfied with his orchestral resources, and was often obliged to put up with what he could get. A striking example of this occurs actually in the St. John Passion where the wonderful flute obbligato may, according to the composer's footnote, be played also on the organ! I believe it is our privilege and our duty to use all the improved mechanism invented by our instrument makers to do full justice to this immortal work.'

This began the kind of controversy dear to any editor's heart. 'Apparently my letter . . . has lit a candle which will not easily be put out,' R.V.W. wrote to me a week later. He was delighted by any chance to 'upset the purists', and it should be remembered that musicians of Vaughan Williams's generation formed their judgements at a time when harpsichords really were museum pieces of dubious musical worth, often insensitively played, and could not have compared with the splendid modern versions. Even so, there is no likelihood that he would have altered his deeply-held views, and what was remarkable about the Dorking Passion performances was that even Bach scholars to whose views those of Vaughan Williams were anathemata came away from them profoundly stirred. They went to scoff and left in admiration, for the whole performance was illuminated by one great composer's instinctive understanding of the mind of another. As the years went by, the performance of the *St. Matthew Passion*, in particular, grew in stature and deepened in interpretation. It was extremely dramatic. Nothing was left to chance, and he even 'timed' the pauses. The atmosphere in the Dorking Halls was unique and unforgettable. No applause was allowed, and woe betide any strangers who so far forgot themselves as to applaud Vaughan Williams's entry. His face would flush with anger and he would walk off and start again. This was no prima-donna-ish gesture: he felt it necessary that no element of ordinary concert behaviour should enter into the proceedings. This was Bach's night, not his, nor anyone else's. He liked to work with the same artists year after year if he could—Eric Greene as Evangelist, Arthur Cranmer as Christus, Norman Walker for the bass solos, in particular—but as death or retirement made their inroads he welcomed and encouraged numerous young singers. He knew that his views on the work might not always commend themselves to his collaborators—'I have a bee in my bonnet about the Passion'— and he had a charming way of allowing them to think that his opinions were eccentric but, nevertheless, while in Dorking they must do as the Romans do. Eric Greene himself was surprised by the pianoforte continuo when he first heard it, but he appreciated Vaughan Williams's belief that it lent more realism to the music ('I like the piano to sound like one and to support the Narration, instead of chords popping up here and there'). His quirks and comments, his sudden and terrifying outbursts of wrath, at rehearsal endeared him to the performers. 'It's *Bar*rabas, not Bar*ra*bas,' he would exclaim—'and try as I might,' Greene wrote,[1] 'year after year, I never achieved his pronunciation for he would simply pass on with the grunted comment "Wrong man". . . . No. 73 was another danger spot—"What do you want this in?" he would exclaim. "Four in a bar, please," to which he grunted he would prefer eight. At the fourth bar he made a rallentando during a downward scale passage for the cellos and double basses. This caused chaos, but after one or two attempts, some semblance of order obtained. "I never could beat four in a bar." ' He did not close his mind to the scholars' versions of Bach and went to one of the 'authentic' performances, listening intently in the front row. But it changed nothing. 'Boring,' he said. 'I can't see music, I can only hear it.' There is little doubt that in the twenty-three performances of the *St. Matthew Passion* and the twelve of the *St. John Passion* which he gave in Dorking he found the greatest musical pleasure of his life. Not only was it Bach's music, it was the type of music-making that he loved best: the devoted amateurs and the enthusiastic professionals joining together for the sheer joy and inspiration of performing a sublime masterpiece. The audience's participation in most of the chorales extended this sense of a corporate act. 'His presence was magnetic, his stature fearful in its power, and his sincerity beautiful to behold,' Eric Greene said. And afterwards there was a party and refreshments, and a kiss for all the female performers, when Vaughan Williams became Uncle Ralph.

[1] *R.C.M. Magazine*, Easter Term, 1959, Vol. LV, No. 1.

He conducted his last *St. Matthew Passion* on 5 March. Such was the demand for tickets for this annual event that, for the first time, two performances were given in 1958, the first, on 1 March, being conducted by Dr. Thomas Armstrong. The R.V.W. performance had a special quality of which those who heard it and those who sang in it were conscious. It was exciting, moving and serene. He himself thought that these 1958 performances of the two Passions were the best he had done. It is fortunate for future generations that that of the *St. Matthew* is permanently preserved in a recording, even though that recording is not at present available to the general public. Afterwards came the usual message of thanks to the choir:

'You covered yourselves with glory, having to follow that fine, but very different, performance by Dr. Armstrong without special rehearsal. I thank you heartily. You were assisted by a fine orchestra and by the inspiring and helpful continuo playing by Dr. Cole and Mr. Gritton. It is difficult to describe what both the conductors and performers owe to these fine artists. We also had the advantage of what I believe to be the best sextet of singers[1] we have ever had. Thank you once again: and may we repeat our triumphs next year.'

All his attention was now concentrated on the Ninth Symphony. As always before a new work, he was fidgety and nervous, full of doubts about its quality and whether he ought to 'let it out'. In his study hung a Nash landscape with lowering clouds in the background. 'Before a new work I always swear the clouds get blacker,' he said. A play-through under Malcolm Sargent was arranged in St. Pancras Town Hall on 21 March, at which the Royal Philharmonic Orchestra made their first acquaintance with the work. Conditions of work for London orchestras being what they are, there was no possibility, as there had been with the Hallé, of long and continuous preparation of a new work at regular rehearsals. The three-hour rehearsal on 21 March, paid for by the composer himself (over £250), was all the preparation the new symphony received before the rehearsal on the day of the first performance, 2 April, at a Royal Philharmonic Society concert. In the event, and hardly surprisingly, the first performance did not do the work full justice. But, this apart, there was no denying the coolness of the critics' reception of the music. Its enigmatic mood puzzled them,

[1] Pauline Brockless, Nancy Evans, Eric Greene, Wilfred Brown, Gordon Clinton, John Carol Case.

and more attention was therefore paid to the use of the flügel horn and to the flippant programme-note. 'Even in Vaughan Williams's youth there can hardly have been anybody left who thought the second subject of a symphony in E minor should necessarily be in G major,' Colin Mason wrote in the *Manchester Guardian*, 'and though there may still be a few academicians at the Royal College of Music who would be perturbed by the return to the home key without the principal subject, in the living world of music these bogeys have been laid these fifty years.' 'Chatting to the converted', was another verdict. 'It is composing for the sake of composing'. The themes 'plainly resemble the themes of his other works'. The adjectives 'silly' and 'asinine' were applied to the second movement.[1] A few detected a note of defiant despair in the music. Others found in it a tranquil leave-taking. Only a handful heard a new richness of sound and the beginning of what might have proved to be an extraordinarily fruitful Indian summer. The next morning a friend called and asked R.V.W. what he thought of the notices. 'I don't think they can quite forgive me for still being able to do it at my age,' was the reply. He knew that the tide had turned. But there was still the appreciation of old friends. Eugene Goossens, for instance, wrote 'to tell you how I sat spellbound by the lovely sounds of your 9th. . . . As always with you, the orchestral texture came as a perpetual delight. So did your refreshing programme-notes!'

For relaxation after the anxiety of the symphony, the Vaughan Williamses had decided to have their holiday early in the year and to go on 14 April to Ischia, staying in a small villa owned by the Waltons. But before they went there were post-performance revisions to the symphony to be attended to, and other matters:

'We had another excitement to-day.[2] Roy was here for a corrections session and played Scene I, Act 1 of *Thomas the Rhymer* to us. (i.e. sketches for our new opera, R.V.W.) I am very pleased and the music is exactly what I hoped for. It's great fun trying to think dramatically in terms of duet, trio and chorus, and generally of ensemble. I'm enjoying it enormously, Ralph is not over-tyrannical—all things considered. Roy feels it a pity that there will be no correspondence to publish between the exacerbated composer and outraged librettist.'

[1] R.V.W.'s attitude to criticism is typified by a sentence from one of his letters to Roy Douglas, written about 1951: 'I have not seen ——'s article. I usually feel about him what Whistler said: "I don't mind his blame but I cannot endure his praise".'

[2] Letter from Ursula Vaughan Williams to the author, 8 April 1958.

The visit to Ischia meant that he missed the Leith Hill Festival for the only time in his life, but he sent the choirs a message: 'I shall miss you, but you need not miss me; you have an excellent and experienced musical director and a splendid secretary—what more do you want? So, good luck to you, and sing beautiful music beautifully. This after all is what our Festival is for.'

On his return, in mid-May, Vaughan Williams went to Nottingham University to receive an honorary degree. He worked intensively on the opera, on the *Penguin Book of Folk Songs* and on music for a nativity play devised by Simona Pakenham, whose book on his music he had enjoyed and whom he had enrolled among the vast company of kissable 'nieces'. Postcards from Hanover Terrace during June and July invariably included a phrase such as 'opera going splendidly', but there was time for a visit in June to East Anglia, to Gunby, Spalding and Lincoln and to a folk-dance festival. On the 20th he addressed the annual conference of the National Association of Music Advisers at County Hall, Westminster, and gave a message to youth not to be satisfied with listening to gramophone records but to 'get about and do something'.

In mid-July he spent four days at the Cheltenham Festival, attending the rehearsals and concerts of the Hallé Orchestra and listening to the new music with patience and interest. 'I'm still oldfashioned enough to like a good tune,' he told Alun Hoddinott, whose harp concerto received its first performance. The 'good tunes' of his own *London Symphony* were eloquently re-created by the orchestra on the Thursday evening. 'Do you know, John,' he said to Barbirolli at the morning rehearsal, 'I wish I could score now like I scored then. I seemed to get a richer sound—don't quite know how.' Despite his difficulty with his legs, he astonished everyone at Cheltenham that week by his energy.

Back in London, he was soon at Sadler's Wells where, at the end of July the New Opera Company were to perform their president's *Sir John in Love*. He attended the early rehearsals. A few days before the first night he re-entered the Middlesex Hospital for a minor operation. 'It has meant his missing the dress rehearsal, which has *infuriated* him,' his wife wrote. In a few days he was back at home and in his seat at Sadler's Wells on 29 July and succeeding nights. He was pleased by the production and by the audience's reception of his music. The younger critics' sour, grudging note was maintained. 'If we avoid a blunt comparison [with Verdi], the work will be found to possess many genuine beauties and even subtleties of its own,' wrote one of them. 'There may be stretches of unproductive rum-ti-tum and the final junketings are rather clodhopping. But the lyrical side is strong. A production as lively and as full of witty details as Brian Trowell's shows the work up in its best light.' 'Folksy home-spun' was another oracular utterance. More important to the composer was the cast's obvious delight in the work and his own delight in Eric Shilling's Sir John and John Cameron's Ford. A few nights later, on 5 August, he was at the Promenade Concert in the Albert Hall to hear Sargent conduct the Ninth Symphony. This was in the first half of the concert. In the second half Peter Racine Fricker's *Dance Scene* was played. 'It was typical of him,' Fricker said in a broadcast a few weeks later, 'that he not only took the trouble to stay and listen, but also to come and say a few words to me afterwards.' This was to prove to be Vaughan Williams's last public appearance, and the last critical notice of his own music which he was to read was, happily, a perceptive and sympathetic one in the *Manchester Guardian* by that critic, Neville Cardus, whom he had once thought 'allergic' to his music:

'The Ninth Symphony of Vaughan Williams [is] an astonishing production for a composer in his 86th year. Much of the technical formula is familiar; his music is much an art of cadence, with blocks of harmony the supporting pillars. But this Ninth Symphony is not repetitive of the content of the immediately preceding ones. The changes go deeper than the externals of instrumentation—saxophones and flügel horn, and so on. The texture of musical brainwork is different and more direct, subtle yet simple. In an entirely different way, psychological and musical, Vaughan Williams in his latest period puts me in mind of Bruckner. . . . Both are noble without a single self-conscious attitude. And both are occasionally clumsy and hardly "professional". . . . Vaughan Williams's great achievement has been to dispense with the current musical coin of the period of his basic culture and maturity and to modulate to the contemporary tone and language without obvious iconoclasms. He is of our period, and yet he is full of harvest—which means to say that he is a master. At the end of a strong, convincing interpretation of the Ninth Symphony by the B.B.C. Orchestra and Sir Malcolm, the composer walked down a high stairway, bent precariously on his stick, as he made his way to the platform to acknowledge tumultuous applause—applause led by young people standing in the arena. It was a very moving sight; and somehow it epitomized all that we had just been hearing from the symphony.'

Early in the morning of Tuesday, 26 August, after a normal working day, Ralph Vaughan Williams had a heart attack. He died as he would have wished—suddenly, painlessly, with his wife beside him. It was the silent hour before dawn.

Another great composer, in a few simple words, described the void which Vaughan Williams's death left in English musical life:

The Red House,
Aldeburgh, Suffolk.
August 28, 1958.

My dear Mrs. Vaughan Williams,

I should like to send my deepest sympathy to you on the death of your husband, a very great man. He has been such a tremendous figure to me, all my musical life, that it is hard to realize he is no longer with us. We will miss him sadly—above all his wonderful, uncompromising courage in fighting for all those things he believed in—things which I personally believe to be some of the most important in life. You have the warmest thoughts of the countless people who loved him with you at this terrible moment.

Yours sincerely,
Benjamin Britten.

'A tremendous figure . . .' Vaughan Williams was a natural aristocrat, a born leader, and like all true aristocrats—aristocrats by temperament—there was not a trace of snobbery, condescension or class-consciousness in him. Most true artists live in a classless world. R.V.W. certainly did. He had an innate respect and liking for his fellow-men, and he automatically evoked respect in return. He 'got on' with everybody except poseurs or pseudo-intellectuals. Nobody was thoughtlessly familiar with him.

Was he a 'religious' man? If anyone told him he was, he protested, saying that it made him feel 'such a humbug'. The views he held on life and death he expressed in his music. He had no particular use for the outward and visible ceremony of organized religion, except as an opportunity for good music. He was an agnostic idealist, in his practical way, and he probably agreed with the Cambridge philosopher A. N. Whitehead that 'religion is what a man does with his own solitude'.

II

The last fifteen years of Vaughan Williams's life had an unexampled creative richness, for not even Strauss and Verdi wrote as much music at the end of their lives and both had periods of silence, whereas Vaughan Williams always had work in progress. In 1953 he told Evelyn Rothwell (Lady Barbirolli), 'I have so much music in my head I know I will never have time to write it down.' After the Fifth Symphony a new energetic note entered his work as well as a preoccupation with sonorities and an expansiveness of method. There was nothing so radical as a change of style, but most of the later works are recognizable as such by a certain steely glitter in the orchestral sound and an added pungency in the harmonic language. These new qualities may perhaps be partly attributed to his experiences in writing film music. Its discipline spurred his mind. The first work to be completed after the D major Symphony, however, was in its same lyrical manner and used some of its discarded material. The Oboe Concerto is not in every sense a very good concerto. It requires a master of the instrument, a Goossens or a Rothwell, to make the solo part sound effortless rather than awkward. Part of the trouble lies, no doubt, in the unsuitability of the oboe for a concerto rôle: its limitations are obvious enough. Yet few instruments can express poignancy as effectively, or chatter so merrily. Vaughan Williams's concerto exploits both these tendencies in music that is not as slight as it has seemed to some commentators, and in which the writing for strings is in his most effective vein and is a good example of his technical mastery. The first movement is pastoral in mood, the second more formal. The weight of the music is concentrated in the finale, which begins as a piece for virtuoso display and deepens as it proceeds, via a waltz, to a passionate and regretful episode which twice interrupts the soloist's attempts to bring the work to a pyrotechnical close. Very little of Vaughan Williams's music is nostalgic, but here he seems to be yearning for some lost and precious thing. Characteristically he has put what are some of his most intimate longings into a work which has generally been overlooked. For a few bars a veil is torn aside.

Some of the Fifth Symphony's sustained rapture overflowed, too, into the Second String Quartet though naturally on a smaller scale. Its character is determined by its sub-title, 'For Jean on Her Birthday', for the viola, Jean Stewart's instrument, has the principal theme in each movement and closes the first two. Moreover, in the Scherzo the viola is the only unmuted instrument, as in Brahms's B·flat Quartet op. 67. This scherzo is a fine movement, fast and light yet taut. The scheme of the work anticipates the Sixth Symphony, which was beginning to shape in the composer's mind, in its 'discussion' of the keys of E and F and its preoccupation with the interval of the augmented fourth. The Romance movement is yet another meditation on what is almost a chorale theme which is slightly varied as each instrument takes it up, so that satiety is never reached. The short Epilogue, with its beautiful 'St. Joan' tune

recalls the Fifth Symphony, or *Flos Campi*, in its tranquillity—and at the close the key changes to D major from F major and the direction 'tranquillo' is added. If 'nobilmente' means Elgar, 'tranquillo' means Vaughan Williams.

The *Thanksgiving for Victory* is an occasional work which transcended the occasion. There is no gloating in this music, only a sense of thankfulness and a quiet determination to build wisely in the future. The use of a speaker, always risky, gives in this case a solemnity to the words which a baritone soloist might have dissipated. Musical England in 1944 turned unhesitatingly to this composer for a statement of values. They were not disappointed. The trumpet fanfare, an echo from an earlier period, is a summons to action, not to display. The choral writing is diatonic and varied without being unduly difficult. Few more effective passages occur in any of the choral works than the antiphony of women's voices to the speaker's 'Beauty for ashes'—simple, yet original and daring. The work is full of good tunes, yet it has unity of mood. Not the least of the tunes is the setting of Kipling's 'Land of our birth'. The Pavlovian reaction to Kipling in smart circles is a fit of intellectual nausea. Vaughan Williams knew that the simple words were the proper climax of this work which, after all, was an expression of a nation's thanks. And what more natural to him than to give these words to children? As older voices join in, the tune is skilfully expanded preparatory to the final descant. The end is unexpected. No glowing apotheosis, but the soprano soloist, accompanied by a distant trumpet, sings 'The Lord shall be thy everlasting light; and the days of thy mourning shall be ended'. It is the same formula as in the *Pastoral Symphony* and *Dona Nobis Pacem*, but there is no feeling of mere repetition.

The radio music written in 1944 for Shakespeare's *Richard II*, but not used, has a theme for 'Richard's Night' in Act III which is first cousin to the principal tune of the slow movement of the Sixth Symphony, sketched in 1944. Has this, taken with a similar link with a theme for the *Flemish Farm* film, any hidden significance? None, except that melodic shapes which are prominent in the mind of a composer at a particular time find their outlet in various guises. Of all his works, the Sixth Symphony provokes most sharply questions about some undisclosed 'programme' behind the notes. Try as he might to quell the discussion, the composer could not really expect people to remain pure-musically-minded about so dramatic, vivid and eventful a symphony. The unleashed, jocular energy of the start, its jaunty, almost superficial saxophone episode, the sudden transformation of the relaxed theme in B minor 6/4 into the golden sonority of E major, with first violins playing on the G string and seconds playing on the D string, accompanied by harp chords and trombones—the only lyrical major-key moments in the whole symphony—the extraordinary second movement, at first remote and distant and later dominated and crushed by a three-note trumpet figure which is a crib from Holst's 'Mars', the hell's-kitchen Scherzo —sardonic, noisy, banal and savage—and the final slow-movement epilogue, all pianissimo, tenuous, inhabiting the atmosphere of Holst's 'Neptune' and of parts of Shostakovich's Fifth Symphony, yet touched at the end with a few warmer moments, as if the last rays of the sun glinted on a sombre landscape: all this is bound to arouse the inevitable reactions, what does it *mean*? First of all it means a closely and logically pursued musical argument on the conflict of major and minor thirds, and the interval of the augmented fourth which sets off more conflicts in keys separated by that interval. The precipitate opening—allegro, fortissimo, 4/4—clashes E minor with F minor.[1] Also, almost at once, the minor third (A flat) is shown as the major third (G sharp) and, with a further progression, can be related to Pilgrim's 'My God, my God, why hast thou forsaken me?', no doubt a fortuitous, but none the less significant, parallel. The syncopated passages for brass and saxophone

---

[1] The work's principal themes are illustrated in the composer's programme-note.

were strikingly anticipated thematically twenty years before in the *Toccata Marziale*. Augmented fourths dominate the adventures of the lyrical B minor and E major episodes. The movement ends in E, against which the trumpets' B flat alters the key, by an augmented fourth, to B flat minor. The three-note trumpet-and-drum figure ♪♪♩ , foreshadowed in the second bar of the strings-and-woodwind opening theme of the second movement, emerges after a further reminder of the E-F conflict in a brass fanfare. Alternating major and minor chords, a passage of tense expectancy for strings, and then the trumpet figure, repeated ninety-four times, begins its conquest. It works up to fortissimo and back again four times and is undeterred by the swirling strings-and-woodwind scales which try to block its course. At last it retreats, a cor anglais laments and the drums mutter the rhythm of the trumpet-figure before the Scherzo erupts in a fugal firework-display of augmented fourths. The progress is from B flat to E, with difficulty. Organized chaos, perhaps, with the xylophone lending an hysterical clatter to the proceedings. The trio section, in C minor, shows another facet of Job's comforter the saxophone, here not creeping in oily fashion but jauntily displaying its flashiest charms until a sequence of augmented fourths, accompanied by tremolando violins, leads back to the Scherzo. The trio, too, is repeated and the saxophone tune is augmented and played as vulgarly as symphonic brass know how. The Epilogue begins in F minor with a theme which has features of both the opening of first and second movements and the fall by augmented fourths of the Scherzo. Moreover it ends with indecision as to whether it is in E or F. The oboe theme, when it arrives, pursues the E-F conflict but its wide-spaced leaps, anticipating the fourth movement of *Sinfonia Antartica* and echoing the romantic end of the oboe concerto, are what give the movement its ray of hope, its relief from total desolation. For although the oboe tune is a ghostly, dissonant echo nonetheless it seems to be a human voice. As it departs, the music gets quieter and slower, the upper strings alternate minim chords of E flat major and E minor, ending with E minor, *niente*. (At the same time, the cellos and basses, pizzicato, are recalling the opening of the main theme of the movement.) So the conflict is never really resolved. The end is a question.

Thus this wonderful work exists solely in musical terms. But the composer's hint, already quoted, of Prospero's Farewell as the key to the Epilogue's enigma prompts further examination. One is reminded of another work, also in E minor, by another Englishman, Elgar's Cello Concerto, which its creator described as 'a man's attitude to life'. If an internal 'programme' to this symphony must be sought, Vaughan Williams might have approved Elgar's description. The trumpet-figure of the second movement can stand for any of the crises of life, not necessarily war; the hectic Scherzo covers the whole range of humour; who shall say what tensions and ambitions are consoled by the romantic E major episode of the first movement? The Epilogue, so daring a musical feat, is an attempt to peer into the dimmest recesses of the Unknown Region. The cold impersonal splendour of the universe, depicted by Holst in 'Neptune', here becomes the mystery of life's transitory nature and the unsolvable riddle of the 'sleep' of death. It is agnostic music, in the same sense that *Sancta Civitas* is: again one thinks of Socrates's 'the risk is honourable'. The oboe's final threnody echoes the tenor soloist at the end of the oratorio and the last bars of the symphony recall Maurya's last utterance 'No man at all can be living for ever and we must be satisfied'. Some have found a sense of submission in this Epilogue. Acceptance would be a truer word, for it is not nihilistic music. And, like all great art, it is capable of many interpretations. But there is no doubt about the effectiveness of the scoring, the organic identity of material and form. He had all the technique he wanted at his disposal, as the brilliant Scherzo shows. Its scoring is certainly thick and tortuous, but the material demands such treatment, and, in a good performance, the strands of theme stand out with a clarity which Ravel might surely have admired. This and the F minor Symphony are the works by Vaughan Williams most likely to make an appeal outside these shores. This does not make them greater or better-written works than their predecessors. In them he made more use of the common properties of the idioms of the day, relaxing the markedly personal style of the *Pastoral* and D major Symphonies. They are also, basically, the most 'classical' in manner and in the universality of their emotional appeal, once their harsher language has been accepted. The Fourth and Sixth Symphonies are imitable whereas the Fifth is inimitable. To comprehend fully the greatness of each, it is necessary to understand the greatness of them all.

Although it was not produced until 1951, *The Pilgrim's Progress* should be discussed after the E minor Symphony because composition of both works ran parallel for the crucial years of 1944-7.

With one exception, Vaughan Williams's operas are problem-operas, a fact which he acknowledged by giving the title 'opera' only to *Sir John in Love*. *The Pilgrim's Progress* is a stage Morality, the vocal equivalent in Vaughan Williams's output of the masque *Job*. No work by this composer more sharply divides even his admirers into opposing camps. Criticisms of its dramatic content cannot be discounted, but it may be countered that the word 'theatrical' has been in the writers' minds when they have put 'dramatic' on paper. It is true that the composer's modal and reflective style is not conventionally operatic nor does his rhythmical sense escape monotony. To the conventional theatrical onlooker, Pilgrim has too easy a progress. There is not enough 'action' in the sense of bustle—there are only robing scenes, monologues in prisons, a gentle dialogue with Shepherds, and a final scene in which the 'hero' does not utter a sound. There is no Slough of Despond; the fight with Apollyon seems perfunctory unless an imaginative producer works on it; the Lord Hate-Good episode is chiefly recitative; minor characters hardly establish themselves as people (a fact which, as the composer's letter to Dent shows, did not trouble him). It has not been sufficiently emphasized that the action is 'in the similitude of a dream'; and in dreams situations do not develop logically or symphonically but, usually, episodically. It is true enough to say that the Morality is a series of *tableaux vivants*, each showing an aspect of Pilgrim's progress rather as the composer in his symphonies shows aspects of tunes rather than developments. The characters and situations are presented as allegorical or symbolic; they are denoted by motto-themes which are repeated but are not subjected to Wagnerian metamorphoses. Like *Fidelio*, the work is a gradual emergence from dark shadows to the light—in this case, *lux perpetua*—and it has not yet received a production which would enable its virtues to surmount the very considerable obstacles placed by the composer in the producer's way.

A more serious criticism of the work is of its musical value. It has been suggested that the composer pondered too long upon the subject and that he used up in his symphonies the creative vitality which had been inspired by Bunyan. This cannot be upheld by the facts. The *Shepherds* episode was written in 1921 and was incorporated into the complete work as it stood, except for the ending. Most of Act I, which even the work's harshest critics often find the best, was completed in the 1930s. Most of the Fifth Symphony links occur in this act. The Prologue was added after 1942 and seems to have derived from the B.B.C.'s production, which was introduced by Bunyan's voice as narrator, and the self-contained Intermezzo was written in 1951 though it could have come from any period in Vaughan Williams's career. Act II was probably sketched in 1942 and written between 1947 and 1948. The bridge-passage between the Intermezzo and Act II belongs to the *Scott of the Antarctic* period. Act III was all composed in the 1940s and enlarged in 1951 and Act IV, apart from the pastoral episode, is also a product of the post-1942 resurgence of work on the opera. Thus, although the work is undoubtedly a fascinating amalgamation of many periods of the composer's long career, its component parts were written in concentrated spells not noticeably longer than those devoted to symphonic works. It is the long span from start to finish which gives the work its uneven passages, rather than any 'under-composing' of individual sections. Nor must it be suggested that because the Morality deals with a serious subject, the musical accomplishment must, *ipso facto*, be superior. The quality of a work of art is not necessarily determined by its theme. If that were true, *The Apostles* would be a greater work than *Falstaff*. A composer must rise worthily to his theme, and in *The Pilgrim's Progress* Vaughan Williams does. The musical splendours are many. The hymn-tune 'York' was always associated in the composer's mind with Bunyan's book because of its Roundhead associations. He had used it at Reigate Priory in 1906, and it is an inspiration in the opera to interrupt it with a fragment of the *Tallis Fantasia*, differently developed. This reminiscence of *Tallis*

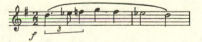

becomes an important theme in its own right in the Morality. Pilgrim sings 'Come fair, come foul' to a derivative of it in Act IV, Scene 1, and it is the whole basis of the Alleluias in the penultimate scene. It is, in fact, almost a *leitmotif* for the Celestial City. In Act IV, Scene 1, the Boy sings these very words to it, in a major version, and a few bars later it recurs when Pilgrim sings of 'the haven where I would be'. In the last scene of the work, the Epilogue, it makes a final appearance in Bunyan's aria to the words 'Holy land'. There can be little doubt that this association of ideas was intentional.

Bunyan's opening narration is finely set, and the entry of Pilgrim, back-stage, as the grinding theme representing his distress is played, is as theatrical as one could wish:

His cry of 'What shall I do?' has affinities, purely subconscious with the opening of the F minor Symphony. The Evangelist's E flat minor and D minor prefatory chords can only be a label, but little else is called for. Straightaway, E major triadic harmony represents the goal of the Progress, the salvation of the heavenly city, interrupted by the agitated and effective cries of 'Back, back' from the Neighbours. Act I, Scene 2, is a choral tableau at the House Beautiful. Here the music used in the slow movement of the Fifth Symphony assumes a different development and an extra dimension from vocal treatment. The whole scene, from Pilgrim's rapt

to the exordium by the Three Shining Ones, culminating in the ecstatic orchestral postlude, is extraordinarily beautiful, written by a master of choral and orchestral music. It is strange that the Intermezzo which follows it so perfectly should have been a fortuitous interpolation, for it makes a moving contrast between the serenity of Act I and the more militant Act II. As in *Hugh the Drover*, the romantic nightwatchman idea is again put to good service. Scene 1 of Act II is a mosaic of trumpet fanfares and the splendid virile setting of 'Who would true valour see' which is tantalizingly interjected into the dialogue of Pilgrim and the Herald before it bursts forth, strongly rhythmical and apposite. This whole scene, though static, would lose half its effect outside the theatre, for the pageantry is as essential an ingredient as it is in *Tannhäuser*. The 'allegro molto' section of the entr'acte depicts the advent of evil, characterized as in *Job* by an ascent of a seventh

p cresc.

The entr'acte conveys unerringly the chill atmosphere as Pilgrim leaves his friends and enters the Valley of Humiliation. The wind blows as searingly as in the Antarctic and the dissonant moans of the Doleful Creatures are sufficiently supernatural. Apollyon, chanting on one note through a megaphone, is a problem for the producer, but the 1954 Cambridge production by Dennis Arundell proved that a sense of indefinable horror can be adequately conveyed by use of shadows. The fight is certainly perfunctory, but there is a limit to the amount of fighting which an opera stage can successfully depict and which can be expected from singers, and to the kind of music needed for it. Again, the contrast of the cool music given to the Branch and Cup Bearer who sustain Pilgrim after he has been wounded is essentially of the theatre. Act III, Scene 1, is Vanity Fair. Here it has been said that the music is mild and banal; others, like Richard Capell, found it exciting and colourful. It is not valid to say that the Scherzo of the Sixth Symphony is 'Vanity Fair': that kind of music is not a practical consideration in the opera house, where the visual and vocal requirements demand something simpler. In any case Vanity Fair's wickedness might not be apparent to all eyes. It was a simple country fair, perhaps like Hampstead Heath on a Bank Holiday. Its sinfulness is pleasurable. The sense of bustle and the mood of leering enjoyment conveyed in Lechery's song are superb. This scene was extended after the first performances by nearly three hundred bars and has probably been seen in this new version by few of the people who have castigated it. Musically it is probably the most compact and unified in the opera and exposes the folly of any proposal to put this music into a cathedral. It is conceived solely for the stage, and very skilfully diversified; choruses, solo interjections, constant changes of tempo, a trial scene, a gradual ascent from low comedy to tragedy and a final ominous 'march to the scaffold'. The consecutive fifths and semitone octaves to delineate the nefarious traders, all in G minor, show how far Vaughan Williams had come along the operatic highway since *Hugh the Drover*. The waltz episode for Wanton, Bubble and Lechery, if well sung, is a good musical representation of seduction. The whole scene, culminating in 'Let us despatch him, out of the way' provides the central drama of the work, a chance for theatrical spectacle and a relief from the earlier meditative passages. All the greater, therefore, is Pilgrim's long monologue in prison (Act III, Scene 2) moving from despair (F minor) to radiant certainty (D major). The music is intensified in the theatre by the moonlight which shines on the King's Highway as Pilgrim sings his snatches from the Psalms over triads, harp arpeggios, rhythmic counterpoint and tremolo strings. This scene could have been written by no other composer. Its marvellous setting of the words, its combination of religious and romantic ardour and its ability to touch the heart for unanalysable reasons not necessarily connected with any kind of mystical communion are the prerogative of V.W. at his best. Hardly less good is Scene 1 of Act IV, as skilfully devised as Vanity Fair, but substituting tranquillity for vigour. This scene, too, is quintessential Vaughan Williams. The short prelude, with a reminiscence of the fanfare which opened Act II accompanied by familiar swaying triads, is magical and tells us that the end of the journey is at hand and that there will be no more night. The Woodcutter's Boy's enchanting song,

Pilgrim's comments, and the golden sound from the orchestra-pit give the scene a freshness and an innocence that shine like a good deed in a naughty world. No words can convey the beauty of the boy's indication of the Delectable Mountains: if the listener does not respond to this, no advocacy will persuade him. Critical analysis cannot penetrate the cause of such magic. Such a rapt air cannot be sustained and the delicious interlude of the By-Ends couple, with their mincing gait:

is welcome both for its humour and for the fanciful, *Poisoned Kiss* vein of the composer's style. As the dialogue becomes sterner, the bantering in the accompaniment is stifled. Now, the By-Ends departed, the Boy speaks of the Celestial City and Pilgrim sings

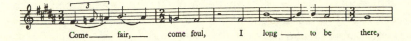

Come___ fair,___   come foul,   I   long ___ to be   there,

as who would not, seeing that the vision as here depicted is truly
delectable? The music at this point foreshadows the Alleluias of the
Celestial City. The change from this scene to the E modal minor
of the early Shepherds interlude which is now inserted, with some
revisions, as Act IV, Scene 2, is startlingly effective. The thinner,
rarefied air of the Scene is appropriate to Pilgrim's last halt on his
journey. The end is changed. The episode originally ended with an
E minor section of alleluias accompanied by harp and bells. The new
scene ends with the Pilgrim's descent into the River of Death.
Distant choral alleluias in B flat, preceded by a fanfare, herald his
arrival at the Celestial City. The imagery has produced music
similar to *Sancta Civitas* but less impersonal. Tenor, contralto, and
soprano soloists sing God's praises while the choirs exchange antiphonal alleluias. The effect is of majestic splendour. The alleluias
die away, the dream fades and the distant trumpet's last F natural
merges into 'York' and Bunyan's final offering to the audience to
'lay my book, thy head and heart together'. Truly, this is like no
other opera. Its day will come.

Of the smaller works of the immediate post-war period, two
motets, the 'Souls of the Righteous' and the 'Prayer to the Father
of Heaven', have an immediacy, a command of choral technique and
a sense of aspiration which give them an appeal likely long to
outlast the occasions for which they were written. The Introduction
and Fugue for two pianofortes is an example of impressive music in
a medium in which, try as he might, Vaughan Williams could never
convince us of his comfort. The chordal passages are often thick,
but there is no doubt that the music is an emulation of Bach's
preludes and fugues, and it achieves a power and substance which
make it worthy of the challenge to the pianists' powers and of its
exemplar. Another pianoforte work of this period is the under-
rated Fantasia on The Old 104th. This is an experimental work, and
its strange form—pianoforte, chorus and orchestra—limits its
chances of performance. Yet the pianoforte writing is as pianistic
as any that Vaughan Williams achieved, though the Lisztian and
Brahmsian decoration of the great tune sounds curiously perverse
at times. The prelude, hinting at fragments of the tune, and the

statement of the theme, with much ornamentation, are a splendid opening. If this standard is not consistently maintained, there is some elaborate and fine-textured polyphony and an eloquent conclusion. It is one more example of Vaughan Williams's response to 'the moral atmosphere implied by a fine tune' and another indication of a fine tune's stimulus to his ready imagination. As Frank Howes says, it 'sets the bells ringing'.

The Partita for strings is a solution of the problem which the composer failed to solve in the Double Trio. Even the revised version of 1942 failed to differentiate fully between the two trios, and Colles in *The Times* prophetically wrote that the music had still not found its true form. In laying it out for two string orchestras of different strengths, the aim seems to have been a constant blending of tone, with passages of antiphony, so that the original tendency for the two Trios to become a Sextet has not wholly been eradicated. The work is as far removed from the *Tallis Fantasia* as it is possible to go with somewhat similar forces. This is a highly sophisticated and cosmopolitan Vaughan Williams, as though on this occasion he had been having tea with Stravinsky. The cross-rhythms and syncopations of the Prelude merge into a Scherzo based on the following ostinato figure

which passes through various guises, including moto perpetuo, and is eventually transformed into the Intermezzo sub-titled 'Homage to Henry Hall', the dance-band leader. This attractive movement, with its off-beat pizzicato and its soft-shoe-shuffle motion, is an affectionate salute. The homage has the flavour of Mr. Hall's signature-tune 'Here's to the next time', though, as if to throw the listener off the scent, the resemblance is stronger when the tune appears in the preceding Scherzo. The finale, replacing the rondo of the earlier version, is a Fantasia of rather unsatisfactory scrappiness. It begins with a very obvious echo of 'Back, back', from *The Pilgrim's Progress*, and most listeners who know their V.W. will find scraps of the Fifth and Sixth Symphonies—including the main tune of the Epilogue of No. 6—and a hint towards the end of the F minor Symphony. The coda is a telescoped version of the end of the D major Symphony. The search for a better finale than the original was evidently a struggle and the result, though superficially effective, is not as clinching as the music of the previous movements required. A better work is *An Oxford Elegy*, for all that the combination of speaker and chorus is not as well handled as in the *Song of Thanksgiving*. It is not a major work, but to those who love R.V.W.'s music it will have a special place because it recaptures evocatively the spirit of his early songs and rhapsodies. It is music written for pleasure and from a lifetime's affection for Matthew Arnold's lovely poems. It is comparable with the Oboe Concerto in its nostalgic expression, a sadness tinged with mellow resignation. As in *Flos Campi*, the wordless tone of the chorus is handled poetically and one is grateful that when they are given words to sing, the lines beginning 'Soon will the high midsummer pomps come on' are set to a ravishing melody starting:

The end, too, is sweet harmony. 'The light we sought is shining still.' Thoughts, here, of Holst, of Butterworth? A stretching-out over the vanished years to those days in the Lakes with Trevelyan and Moore? It is difficult to banish the thought of these associations from the mind as one hears this spring-in-autumn music.

The music for *Scott of the Antarctic* and, to a lesser degree, that for *The Loves of Joanna Godden*, reveal an enlargement of Vaughan Williams's vocabulary. A freedom and virtuosity in the handling of a large orchestra are apparent in the sweeping cinematic-pastoral flourishes of *Joanna Godden*, and there is a new version of the phrase from *Pilgrim's Progress*

decked out for orchestra. But the most significant item is the music for the discovery of foot-and-mouth disease and the burning of the sheep which has a bleak, hollow and, eventually, a thunderous sense of catastrophe not far removed from the Epilogue of the Sixth Symphony and the howling of the Antarctic blizzard. A chorus of women's voices for a drowning sequence is another premonition of

the *Scott* music. It has already been described how this next subject
fired Vaughan Williams's imagination. The music must have been
taking shape in his mind: it only needed the right subject to bring
it into focus, and the heroic struggle of Scott and his men against
fearful odds provided the stimulus. Even while he was writing the
episodical film music Vaughan Williams knew that he wished to put
it into more permanent form. The film music is one of the outstanding achievements in the medium, and one regrets some of it that
did not survive into the *Sinfonia Antartica*—the wistful scene of
Kathleen Scott while she works on a sculpture, for example, and a
piquant Pony March sequence. But a re-hearing of the film music
was a forcible reminder of the rawness of the material compared
with the *Sinfonia Antartica* after it had been through the refining
fire. There was much discussion at first whether this work was a
symphony or a symphonic poem. What's in a name? That it is
programme-music is self-evident; but its nature is symphonic,
and its nobility and musical quality outweigh the purely descriptive
elements which at first attract attention. Where doubts arise is in
the final shape of the work, which has more of the design of a suite
and is inclined, by its episodic form, to seem diffuse if it is not
played and conducted with comprehensive skill such as it received
from its first performers. There is no attempt at conventional
symphonic development. More than in any other symphony,
Vaughan Williams relies on the quality of his themes to give the
work impetus and to sweep it forward from phrase to phrase. He is
assisted here by the astonishing virtuosity of his orchestration which
has resulted in some miraculous tone-painting. The writing for
percussion—which includes a vibraphone, a pianoforte often reinforcing the harps and itself supported by the xylophone, celesta
and a wind-machine—is that of a master. Equally fine is the employment of wordless soprano solo and women's chorus to suggest,
paradoxically, the inhuman wastes of the Polar wilderness, as though
they were the musical equivalent of Hardy's Spirit of the Pities.

Vaughan Williams set himself a major symphonic problem by his
invention of the main theme of the Prelude, a magnificent, aspiring
theme, but clearly not a tune which lends itself to development.

It has a nobler grandeur in the symphony than in the film, where tremolando strings gave it a 'cinematic' effectiveness and its tempo was faster. The composer solves his problem by the skill with which he places the theme, as a recurring *leitmotif*, to make its profoundest mark, and by varying its rhythm, as in the coda of the Prelude. This first movement, with its motto of heroic struggle, its depiction of ice, blizzard and the threat of death, sets the scene. The second (Scherzo) peoples it, first with the ships setting out on their voyage (a thematic resemblance to the scherzo of *A Sea Symphony*) and then with whales and penguins. It is light relief; the penguins theme is genuinely witty *and* musical, and is not overdone. Its quiet ending, 'on an indefinite chord', as the composer wrote, prepares for the 'Landscape' movement, that massive example of tone-painting, a rhapsody in ice-blue, which is the masterpiece of the symphony. The means are the simplest: whiffs of theme, the first of them based, like the opening of the Epilogue of the Sixth Symphony, on the rise and fall of a minor third,

and further 'Antarctic shimmerings' on a variety of percussion. Horns and flutes suggest frozen immobility; a descending brass theme binds all together and gives the music movement for, though it describes static nature, it must go forward. Not all the movement is inhuman: a rich, rolling theme on the lower strings, derived from the motto-theme of the Prelude, must stand for the bright gleam of heroism. The climax of the movement is the sensational blast of chords from the organ, an enigmatic moment suggesting either the terrifying impassability of the glacier or the 'mighty voice' of Coleridge's superscription. It has few parallels in music as an expression of man's awe in face of the unknown, natural or supernatural. The amazing feature of this movement is that although it is an essay in sonority it is, by the composer's victory of heart over head, pure music, in the same way that Bartók's Music for Strings, Percussion and Celesta is. 'Landscape' grips the imagination through its sheer atmosphere. Only afterwards does one care to discover how. The charming Intermezzo, with its folk-song-like ascending oboe tune associated in the film with Dr. Wilson's wife Oriana, is a moment of warmth after the numbness of 'Landscape'. In the film the tune had a beautiful dying cadence for solo viola, but here it passes to one instrument after another until the full orchestra plays it. A reminder of the true nature of the work is given by the intrusion of a passage associated with Oates's death and marked by a tolling bell. The bell's echo is in the trumpet challenge which opens the Epilogue, and provokes a magnificent tremolo for the whole orchestra, with pianoforte, before turning into a stoical march based on the motto-theme and quite different in rhythm from the film version of the music denoting the return from the Pole. The movement ends tragically. The somewhat hollow final apotheosis used in the film is abandoned, the opening of the Prelude returns and the voices and wind have the last word. It is not a work for the general repertoire, but for special occasions its heroic spirit, fine-grained sensitivity and grandeur give it a suitability both apposite and moving.

Sinfonia Antartica is also important for its powerful influence on the remainder of Vaughan Williams's work. It was as if Holst's interest in solving technical problems for their own sake had passed to his friend, who, being a man of instinct, brought his own rich humanity to bear upon these matters, for music was never, for Vaughan Williams, merely abstract problems of form and sound. Thus there is a series of works, mostly written for specific occasions or people, in which Vaughan Williams seemed determined to introduce new sounds into his work without destroying its traditional style. He also probably felt that in the *Antartica* he had leaned too heavily on pictorial associations for these new timbres. Some of the 1949–55 works, therefore, are 'dummy runs' for the Eighth Symphony. Best known is the Romance for Larry Adler's harmonica, a skilful concoction, its fluid harmonies in the orchestra making a pleasant background for the mouth-organ's ramblings. At the opposite end of the tonal scale is the Tuba Concerto, to which the general reaction was not to take it seriously, and to regard it as an elephantine romp, humorous and salty. This is too superficial a judgement. The finale, in which the tuba is surrounded by dancing strings, is surely Falstaff and the Fairies in instrumental terms. The composer took his idea seriously, as a challenge, to 'give a show' to an instrument which never was in the limelight. He went to great pains to discover the tuba's capabilities, and how successful he was in discovering its capacity for lyricism may be seen in the splendid

middle movement—another Romanza. It is a token of the composer's prodigality that he was able to expend so beautiful, fresh
and shapely a tune

on a work which he must have known would have limited hearings.
Several other *pièces d'occasion* are of varying quality. The Concerto
Grosso is prodigal of good tunes, including a Bunyanesque scherzo
and a march that might have graced *Old King Cole*: chippings from
a great man's workshop, but carefully and cunningly assembled. *The
Sons of Light* is, when well performed, a convincing piece of choral-
ism for the young, written by one who remained young in heart, as
this music proves. The *Folk Songs of the Four Seasons* is a labour
of love, an old and practised hand returning to his first enthusiasm.
It is an enchanting work, gay, touching, invigorating and timeless.
Perhaps its most beautiful section is the setting for three unaccompanied female voices of 'The Unquiet Grave'. This elaborate, moving
and skilful arrangement is almost an original composition, yet by its
very personal quality it somehow enhances the tune's ancient roots.
The Three Shakespeare Songs of 1951 open with a striking setting
of 'Full Fathom Five', in which the effect of submarine voices and
bells is unerringly conveyed. The setting of 'The Cloud-Capp'd
Towers' contains the lines which the composer associated with the
Epilogue of the Sixth Symphony. But what a different world it inhabits! Its simplicity and grave tranquillity, more moving and impressive with repeated hearings, make it a perfect little masterpiece.
Here is the peace which was sought but not found in the symphony.
The three Coronation works were superior to their 1937 equivalents.
The motet 'O taste and see' has outlived the occasion; 'Silence
and Music', in honour but not in imitation of Stanford, is a thing of
grave beauty; and the ceremonial setting of 'The Old Hundredth'
combines magnificence and splendour with a still, sad moment when
a trumpet descant carries the mind back to the slow movement of
the *Pastoral Symphony*. The 1954 *Te Deum* and *Benedictus* were
written perhaps in response to the 1951 report of the Archbishops'
Committee on Music in Worship which pointed out that, unlike the
other canticles, the *Te Deum* does not lend itself to chants. These

settings do not convey the impression that words and tunes were made for each other.

The big work of the 1953 period is the Christmas cantata *This Day*, more generally known by its Latin sub-title *Hodie*. In it, at eighty-two, Vaughan Williams produced a large-scale choral work filled with a grace, mellow naïveté and youthful exuberance quite unlike any of his previous cantatas. Its easy mellifluousness probably caused it to be underrated at its first appearance. It also undoubtedly lacks unity of style, since certain parts ('The Oxen' and the boys' narration, for example) might have been—but were not—written thirty years earlier than other sections. It is an 'anthology' work of the kind of which Vaughan Williams and Britten hold the secret. Here Vaughan Williams has done for Christmas what Britten has done for Spring. Like *The Pilgrim's Progress* it is a symposium of his style but within the smaller design the diffuseness is more satisfactorily contained, and also, perhaps, more obvious! Each poem called forth the type of music it required so that there is no sense of uneven invention, and the general effect is of a surpassingly happy lyrical flow of melody. The poems are linked by a modal narrative for boys' voices and introduced by a jubilant setting of 'Hodie, Christus natus est', which one might have expected from a man of twenty-five rather than from an octogenarian, so exhilarating and audacious is its precipitous course and so attractive its off-beat Nowells:

The soloists' songs are all high inspirations. The soprano's 'It was the winter wild' is a further demonstration that none of Vaughan Williams's imitators could approach the original in his ability to assume a pastoral style which never becomes sentimental but retains a slight astringency in its flowing triplets. The baritone is given a memorable setting of Hardy's 'The Oxen', introduced by sad-sweet woodwind and accompanied throughout by delicate orchestration which mirrors the poem's vein of nostalgic fantasy. This is, perhaps, the high-point of the work, a song for its season whose quiet beauty defies analysis. But much the same might with equal justice be said of the baritone's next song, 'The shepherds sing', a return after more than forty years to George Herbert, set without any kind of melodic repetition. Here again the accompaniment is of extreme delicacy. The tenor's song, 'Bright portals of the sky', is declamatory and harsh where the Herbert was smooth and consonant. The accompaniment is in 'Antarctic' style, with cold and glittering arpeggios from flute, oboe, clarinet, and celesta and a full battery of percussion. The singer must call on all his resources for this virtuoso piece of arioso writing which follows the soprano's Lullaby, a song of childlike faith such as the age-old wonder of Christmas evokes.

This same simplicity characterizes the two chorals, the first 'The blessed Son of God', undisturbed by so much as an accidental, a timeless carol. To write such music in 1954! The second, 'No sad thought his soul affright' is more complex. The episode of the Shepherds in the Fields, fixed musically in all English minds by Handel, is set without a suggestion of self-consciousness and with as much originality as in *Messiah* and making much more of the 'good will' phrases. As the choir's final 'Glory to God' floats on the air over flutes, glockenspiel, harp and brass, the male voices steal in with 'Let us now go even unto Bethlehem', an effect of extraordinary felicity. The March of the Three Kings has an oriental accompaniment, the choral writing is of a straightforward nature and the whole episode will seem, to the sophisticated, obvious and primitive. But music has a way of transcending the mere notes on the printed page, and in the context of this cantata this march is as right as the final, triumphant paean from Milton with which, amid pealing bells, the work ends. Whether the tune itself is strong enough to sustain the final grandiloquent apparel is doubtful—but a convinced and convincing performance can still the doubts at the time. *Hodie* is full of felicities which, in my opinion, outweigh the inconsistencies of style. Its affirmatory zeal was out of tune with the times in which it first appeared; but times can change, and it cannot be doubted that different generations may find in *Hodie* the musical and spiritual qualities which the world of 1954 overlooked.

A similar affirmation is discernible in the Eighth Symphony of 1956, although this work has its darker moments. It is a work quite unlike its seven predecessors and is the only one to which nobody made any attempt to fit an exterior programme. It is the most classical in form of the nine, and its first movement is the most intricately developed of any of his symphonic movements except the first of the F minor. The composer called it 'Seven variations in search of a theme'. In fact, the movement is based on transformations of three *motifs* of which the first—two rising fourths for trumpet, answered by vibraphone—is the most important.

The thematic material is richly diverse and is presented, with many changes of tempo, in kaleidoscopic form. Despite the very free and versatile treatment of the episodes, they are held together and they progress inevitably towards a splendid and positive hymn-like passage. This gradually thins down in a long diminuendo which is emotionally compassionate and emphasizes that this symphony is not quite as light and jolly as it might seem. The final soft restatement of the first *motif* is poetically managed. Each of the variations —the folk-song collector's 'variants' would be a better word—is a facet of Vaughan Williams's style, from the gently pastoral and the boisterous to the eloquent and jocular. Yet, despite its eclectic character, it is a new departure in his symphonic journey. The Scherzo, for wind, has a pawky wit and is derived thematically from the first *motif*. The penguins from the Antarctic have taken a course with Hindemith, or so it might seem until the gentle mockery of a folk-song inflection betrays the true composer. It has been customary to refer to the Cavatina for strings as 'In Vaughan Williams's most familiar vein', but this is only accurate up to a point. There are tensions and divine discontents here not reconcilable with mere recapitulation of the *Pastoral Symphony* and the *Tallis Fantasia*. There is also a remarkable display, as in the first movement, of sheer compositional prowess. The tunes are never repeated *exactly* as they first appeared; even the familiar use of a solo violin passage is anything but a reversion to type. It is the movement's uncertainty of mood which is its power and which prevents it from being simply an essay in relaxed meditation. Now follows the much-discussed Toccata, with its bells and gongs (the latter added after a visit to *Turandot* when the movement had already been completed). The tendency is to regard this rondo as a romp, of little significance and ill-judged in execution. Much is certainly placed upon the conductor—it was written, after all, for a virtuoso practitioner of the art—if the percussion is not to swamp the rest of the music. Again the form is deliberately episodical, each section being dominated by a special effect of tone-colour. To the composer, the opening of the movement was 'sinister', and if we are to accept this on its face-value it must be confessed that he failed to communicate this mood through the notes. The general effect is of an orchestral Psalm 150— 'Praise him upon the well-tuned cymbals: praise him upon the loud cymbals.' It is, in fact, a highly original movement, particularly strong in melodic invention, and an admirable finale to a work in which the composer's musical imagination is at work at a high level.

Something of the exuberance and vitality of the Eighth Symphony was carried over into the music for the short film *The England of Elizabeth* which Vaughan Williams composed in the last months of 1955. The film's historical basis evoked music in his bluffest and most lyrical vein, and the score is a fascinating kaleidoscope of familiar V.W. turns of phrase seen in a new and brightly burnished light. There are intriguing echoes of *The Wasps*, of the flute solo from the slow movement of the Fourth Symphony, charming orchestral 'fantasias' on 'The wind and the rain' and 'It was a lover and his lass', the former with a folk-dance counterpoint; and, significantly, the tune from the early unpublished tone-poem *The Solent* which became the 'limitless heaving breast' theme of *A Sea Symphony*, is called upon again, slightly varied. It was shortly to do duty again in the Ninth Symphony. What special spiritual significance, one wonders, did this melodic phrase have for its creator? As in all the film music, the impression is strong that the composer was thoroughly enjoying himself. The jaunty, swaggering opening music is extrovert enough; of deeper quality is the splendid melody for strings in the 'Tintern' sequence and the tune of 'The Road to London', which is the seed of the first of the ten Blake Songs. The great tunesmith still had a rich forge. The best of this music was arranged as a concert suite, *Three Portraits*, by Muir Mathieson.

The Violin Sonata in A minor of 1954 was unexpected at this stage in its composer's career. The last movement used a theme from the early pianoforte quintet, suggesting that the composer had looked through his unpublished works when they came to the surface at the time of his removal from Dorking to London. Again a criticism of the pianoforte writing must be made—there is too much unison work for the two instruments, the chords are thick. One wonders if an orchestral background to the violinist had been considered and discarded. But the sonata overcomes problems of texture by sheer musical interest. The large-scale Fantasia is structurally impressive and is followed by a brilliant Scherzo, one of Vaughan Williams's most rhythmically interesting movements although the closing bars are perhaps too easy a resolution of its problems. The theme-and-variations finale is not quite up to this standard, although the actual violin-pianoforte relationship is better reconciled. A better theme for variations is that in the set written in 1957 for brass band, a competition piece of considerable skill, which is even more convincing in its original form than in the orchestral version, and which contains in the adagio variation (IX) a last farewell to the world of the D major Symphony.

What remain now are a symphony, a cantata and two sets of songs. Marriage to a poet re-stimulated the lyrical gift which had been so pronounced at the start of his career and in the *Four Last Songs* there are fragments of song-cycles which might have been memorable. The restless 'Procris' is a fine achievement and one cannot but be moved by the tenderness of 'Tired', its fireside embers reflected by a last recollection in the pianoforte of 'Linden Lea'.

He also returned to the extracts from Spenser's *Epithalamion* which he and Ursula Wood, as she then was, had used as the basis in 1938–9 for their masque *The Bridal Day*. Now, in 1957, he arranged it as a cantata, restoring Spenser's title and adding some new music. In essence, though, *Epithalamion* is a pre-Second-World-War work and betrays its date in the very first bars, which belong to the silvery world of the Serenade to Music. There is, too, more than one reminiscence of 'Jane Scroop', including a catalogue of birds, and the music as a whole has that vein of tender, romantic lyricism which was so strong and so often overlooked a feature of his personality. The fine baritone solo, 'Ah, when will this long weary day have end', recaptures the strong mood of the *Five Mystical Songs*, a mood which was sure to be evoked by poetry of this sort, where love of woman and love of a deity are mystically commingled. The work is too uneven to be wholly satisfying, but the best parts are magical, and it is clear that much of it was written parallel with the Fifth Symphony.

In 1957–8 Vaughan Williams paid his last homage to Blake in a set of ten songs for voice and oboe which have, on the whole, been underrated. Here in the last year of his life he gave an astonishing display of melodic gifts and sensitivity to words. What a range is here! The utter simplicity of 'To Mercy, Pity, Peace and Love', the anguished 'Poison Tree' and 'Cruelty', the perfect melody for 'The Lamb', the imagery of 'London', the pastoral tenderness of 'The Piper' and 'The Shepherd', the naïveté of 'Infant Joy', and, best of all, the profound and compassionate 'Ah, Sunflower'—these are the constituents of a great masterpiece. Freed of the pianoforte, the composer was able, at the eleventh hour, to extend this branch of his art and to crown it with ten virtuoso songs, ending with the calm gaze at 'Eternity'.

Four months before Vaughan Williams died, his Ninth Symphony was played for the first time and coolly received. Already there were signs of a reaction against his music. An eagerness to look only for reminiscences of former works replaced any extended analysis of what is in some respects the most individual and enigmatic of the nine works. It is clear that this symphony was of great importance to the composer. It is rich in material, almost as if he was determined to incorporate all the symphonic ideas germinating in his mind. Its origin in an idea for a symphony about Salisbury, a city he loved and whose literary associations with *Tess* exerted a strong fascination on him, was soon abandoned but left its traces in a mood which, though not nostalgically regretful, has elements of the resigned regard of age for 'all things lovely' which must eventually be looked upon for the last time. The form of the work is unconventional within a conventional design. Whereas, for all its panoply of percussion, No. 8 was economic in construction, No. 9 is ample.[1] The upward striving theme of the first movement, inspired by the *St. Matthew Passion* and a cousin of the motto-theme of *Sinfonia Antartica*, at once denotes seriousness of purpose; the waywardness of the whole work is epitomized by the woodwind episode which

---

[1] The composer's programme note contains twenty-four music examples, but even this does not do full justice to the thematic profusion and complexity of the symphony, especially its great finale.

follows the first splendid tutti. The use of the flügel horn imparts a dark quality to the texture of the work; this is no eccentric experiment in sonority, it is absorbed into the fibre of the musical thought, and its timbre is an essential part of the appeal of the main theme of the second movement. This tune (derived from the early *Solent* tone-poem and having a kinship with the 'limitless heaving breast' motif of *A Sea Symphony*) is noble in itself and, coming in this context at the end of a splendid career, is profoundly moving. It is interrupted by the peculiar, 'barbaric' episode (originally designed for the ghostly drummer of Salisbury Plain) which, like some foreboding emanation of fate, haunts the movement. The constant changes of tempo, as in the Eighth Symphony, are a deliberate manifestation of restless energy and the extremely beautiful and tender episode, starting with strings only, is a last pilgrimage to the Delectable Mountains, but the gaze is wistful and brooding. The Scherzo, jaunty and noisy, has a sardonic edge to its humour, but treats the saxophone with more respect than it was accorded in *Job* or the Sixth Symphony so that its 'chorale' theme has a strange beauty thrown into relief by the little rhythmical tag which follows its main statement. The finale is the right and proper climax of the work, a large-scale, broad-spanned movement, in two distinct sections, beginning with a long and intricate theme for strings alone:

This movement is extremely complex, with many themes and fragments of themes, all interlocking and turning into each other, with turns of phrase which seem like derivatives from themes in the earlier movements. The music glows, not magniloquently nor autumnally but with an inner light. The closing bars, swelling and fading three times, have a curious quality of sound, unearthly and enigmatic. It would be wrong to read an elegiac intent into this symphony; rather is it as if he was opening a new chapter. Vaughan Williams, eschewing sentimentality, for the last time summons up those reserves which, for want of a better word, must be called visionary.

The nine symphonies of Vaughan Williams cover an extraordinary range of human experience far beyond any narrow nationalism. Each is a necessary and inevitable extension of the composer's personality, a momentous personal statement. Each has a distinctive character. The last of them asserts that he remained unpredictable and independent to the end and that his mental vigour was astonishing. He wrote symphonies, as did other Englishmen, at a time when European composers rejected the form as dead. He showed ways in which life could be poured into an old mould. It could be asked if his music might have had a more universal appeal if his life had been less materially comfortable and if he had been a more complex man, like Elgar. The question is surely unnecessary. Who can tell what emotions a man stores in the kingdom of his mind? Who can tell what gave rise to the fury of the F minor Symphony or the scorn of the Scherzo of No. 6? Beneath his outward controlled ease was an emotional and excitable temperament. The quality of a man's work is not affected by the universality of its appeal. Bunyan, Herbert and Skelton will not fade into oblivion because only those who are of English ancestry can get close to them. Vaughan Williams held throughout his life to that which he felt to be good. He could do no more. The music is there.

Between Elgar and the birth of Britten no other composer born in the British Isles can approach him in achievement, in the adventurousness of his mind and in the extent to which he touched musical experience at all points. He stamped his personality on all that he undertook. Like all the great masters, he is recognizable at once by one or two bars of his music. There is as much of the essential V.W. in 'Linden Lea', 'Down Ampney' and 'O how amiable' as in *Job* and *The Pilgrim's Progress*. It is rare in the twentieth century for an artist to enjoy the feeling of complete communication with the unsophisticated as well as with the professionals of his art. His style, therefore, became the perfect instrument for that communication. His so-called 'uncompromising' language is in reality an inspired use of simple effects, of blocks of chords, of keys bluntly juxtaposed— C major and E flat in *Hodie*, D flat against C in the Fourth Symphony, a device much favoured by another composer, Mahler, who had the secret of conveying his most personal thought in direct musical terms through the expressive use of 'false relations'. He did not sum up the complex changes of his period in musical history. He was not a pioneer in the sense of propounding some new great theory of composition which would make all earlier music obsolete and bring a new musical heaven to earth. He knew that salvation did not lie in atonality or serialism, any more than it lay in the exclusive use of modal or diatonic scales or any other procedures of past or present. It lay in the use of whatever means or method would enable the composer using them to produce music of beauty, significance and expressiveness. To him it was only the music that mattered and not the devices used to produce it. His mastery and his imaginative vitality outstrip many a 'cleverer' composer. He was a pioneer in the much more vital sense that he—and Holst with him—broke the subservience to Continental music, particularly German, which had stultified English music for most of the nineteenth century. Though he admired much of it, Vaughan Williams himself found no basis is German music later than Bach on which he could build a style in which to express his own musical thought. He found that basis, and he found inspiration, too, in the music of his own land. It is an over-simplification to ascribe his 'Englishness' solely to use of the modes and the pentatonic scale, for there is nothing exclusively English about them, as Debussy, Bartók, and Borodin can show us. It is safer to relate his style to the emotional character of his music—the reconciliation of opposites, of restlessness and tranquillity, of brusque, direct expression and serene, visionary meditation, of anger and humour.

He not only found freedom for himself but also was able to give freedom to his younger contemporaries, not to imitate him nor to adopt his methods, but to follow their own bents and to work out their own salvation, subservient to nobody, disciples of nobody, but true to themselves. Very largely owing to his example and his encouragement we have seen emerge not a school of English com-posers following a set pattern but a number of individuals whose work bears comparison with the best being produced anywhere in the world. Replying to eighty-fifth birthday greetings from the Com-posers' Guild, Vaughan Williams told his colleagues: 'Bach was behind the times, Beethoven was ahead of them, and yet both were the greatest of composers. Modernism and conservatism are irre-levant. What matters is to be true to oneself.'

Vaughan Williams eschewed glamour and sheen, but his music has a more lasting quality. There is nothing narrow or dogmatic in his choral works, no polished pulpit or glossy prayer-books. The musical thought behind the setting of the words is original, logical and noble. He was content to be thought 'parochial', which he regarded as praise not abuse. His music is a great gesture which cannot be repeated and its effect on the musical morale of his period in English life cannot be exaggerated. Its rich humanity is its surest stake for survival and can be expected to appeal to generations which did not know the man's strong personal magnetism and influence. But something of these will be understood by a sympathetic listener to a performance of the *Five Mystical Songs* or the Fifth Symphony in one of the cathedrals of the West Country, in the harvest-time of the year, when music, architecture, history, and aesthetic experience blend into one.

He never broke faith with his audience by condescension or by abdicating his high resolve. He was an extraordinary ordinary man, expressing the beliefs, fears, hopes, joys and delights of 'that divine average' in which, with Whitman, he believed. On his desk on the day of his death were an opera and a setting of carols. So it had always been: the personal adventure alongside the perennial enjoyment of traditional pleasures. 'Music is everything to him,' a Darwin relative wrote of him in his youth. That was the simple truth. If we would know him, it can only be through his music, for into it he put all that he knew.

Some Views on other Composers

CREATIVE artists are by nature absorbed by their own creative processes. It is therefore debatable whether their opinions on the work of others are particularly instructive as criticism. But the opinions certainly tell us much about their holder. Vaughan Williams's views on other composers were as forthright as Stravinsky's, Britten's, and Mahler's. Some, where germane, have been incorporated into the main section of this book. Others are well known from his writings. Bach was his musical god; Holst was in a special category; for Beethoven he had a love-hate relationship. Purcell he described in 1914 as 'not only our greatest composer but one of the greatest composers the world has ever seen'.[1] During the Festival of Britain, in the foreword to a series of Purcell Society concerts, he protested that Britain had for too long allowed 'one of the greatest geniuses of music to languish unwept, unhonoured and almost unsung'. The 'ecstatic fervour' of the Evening Hymn was one of Vaughan Williams's own most precious musical experiences. 'We all pay lip-service to Henry Purcell, but what do we really know of him?' In his case it was not lip-service, for his work for the Purcell Society in his youth had been a determining factor in his work, as parts of *A Sea Symphony* plainly show. For Wagner he retained a life-long admiration, and in his last years, when he attended the Covent Garden performances of *The Ring*, he recaptured the enthusiasm of his youth for the operas' bigness of conception and magnificence of achievement. He realized, too, how much better sung they were in the 1950s than in the 1890s—'The singing at Bayreuth in the old days was dreadful,' he said. 'You couldn't tell within three notes what was being sung.' I think he preferred Haydn to Mozart. (He called *Idomeneo* 'bad Gluck until the last act'.) He disliked intensely the mid-nineteenth-century group of composers such as Liszt and Berlioz. To both of them he preferred Meyerbeer,

[1] *The Music Student*, Vol. 7, No. 3, November 1914.

and claimed that Berlioz was 'just second-hand Meyerbeer'. For Verdi, especially for *Rigoletto*, he had an abiding love. Of his old teacher, Ravel, he liked best the songs and pianoforte music, and thought *Ma mère l'Oye* had been spoiled by orchestration. Stravinsky's music held no particular interest for him. He disliked the later works and admired the Symphony of Psalms. He regretted that Stravinsky had abandoned his *Fire Bird* vein, and found even *Petrushka* not to his liking. Of Mahler he made his celebrated remark about his being 'a tolerable imitation of a composer'. Once, while at work on the 'Scott' film, he asked his publisher, Alan Frank, to buy him some 'wrong-note' scores and also the score of Mahler's *Resurrection Symphony*—'not for its wrong notes; his all sound painfully right to me'. He had no use for atonalists—'When you see what they're getting at, it's the worst kind of German music'— though he thought Webern the best of them. His contribution to the *Music and Letters* symposium on the death of Schoenberg was unsympathetic but honest: 'Schoenberg meant nothing to me—but as he apparently meant a lot to a lot of other people I daresay it is all my own fault.'[1]

About his contemporaries and his juniors he was usually discreet. In the case of the new generation he reserved judgement, for he pretended he could not understand them and he complained of the lack of tunes. I remember his speaking of the 'promise' of Richard Rodney Bennett, and he listened with interest to Hoddinott, Gardner, Milner, Fricker, and others. Tippett and Rubbra he admired, particularly the latter's third symphony. Finzi, Moeran, Stanley Bate, Elizabeth Maconchy, and Howells were probably more on his 'wave length' than Britten, of whose works he particularly admired *Les Illuminations* and *Peter Grimes*. In 1932 in a letter to Holst he described as 'very lovely' the slow movement of Ireland's early violin sonata and added, 'The rest is a little spoilt by the desire to shine and show he understands the instruments. I wonder how much a composer *ought* to know of instrumental technique—do you remember we had a long talk about this last year—of course the deepest abyss of the result of writing "effectively" is Frank Bridge— but there is a slight *snobbishness* about Ireland's music which worries me, if you know what I mean.' Of his opinions of Stanford and Parry enough has already been said; there is no doubt that Parry, both as man and composer, was a major source of inspiration to R.V.W. throughout his life.

Elgar's music he admired rather than loved. He had practical knowledge of it and, in his youth, assiduously studied the scores. In the spring of 1934 he conducted *The Dream of Gerontius* at Dorking, a performance which had been planned months before Elgar's death but which became a memorial concert and drew this comment in a letter from Elgar's daughter, Mrs. Elgar Blake:

'I do want you to know what a wonderful performance I thought it and to thank you for all the love and care and the tremendous amount of work you put into it. The choir sang marvellously, and the whole atmosphere was so beautiful and what my father would have loved to feel. It means so much to me to know you are teaching this generation to know and love his works and above all teaching them in such a splendid way.'

In January 1935 Vaughan Williams contributed an article 'What have we learnt from Elgar?' to the memorial number of *Music and Letters*.[1] Amid the fog of words from other contributors this stands out by reason of its factual appraisal. Students of Elgar are recommended to read the whole article. One or two points should be repeated here:

'It is extraordinary that people writing in admiration of his orchestration have taken it for granted that he was not also a great choral writer. Such people should be taken to hear a pianoforte rehearsal of *Gerontius*; they would then soon change their minds.'

'I have found that with Wagner extra instruments could almost always be dispensed with altogether, with a little loss of colour it is true, but with no damage to the texture. But when it came to Elgar the case was quite different. Even in the accompaniments to choral movements there was hardly anything that could be left out without leaving a hole in the texture.'

'Several of us have been influenced by Elgar. By whom was Elgar himself influenced? . . . We must, I believe, look for the germs of the Elgarian idiom to the little group of organists who were writing small but rather charming music when Elgar was a young man, such as Henry Smart and John Goss. . . . Anyone who has any knowledge of aesthetics or musical history will know that this is the way things happen.'

Of Delius's music he had no very high opinion in his later years,

[1] Vol. XVI, No. 1.

although he admitted that it was a 'lovely sound'. At Leith Hill he conducted the two *Aquarelles* part-songs but always doubted if they had been worth the trouble because of their difficulty. 'Delius always sounds to me like the curate improvising, I'm afraid,' he said. 'His music doesn't grow. It is addition, not multiplication.' But Ralph Nicholson, of the London Symphony Orchestra, who played in the Leith Hill Festival Orchestra, recalled a performance of *On Hearing the First Cuckoo in Spring* under Vaughan Williams 'which seemed completely "right", not only in its setting in an English Spring festival but through the tempo and mood'.[1] In a letter[2] dated 13 January 1955, R.V.W. wrote: 'As regards Delius—I think to have written the Wedding Scene from *Romeo and Juliet* (*not* the "Paradise Garden") entitles Delius to be called a great composer. For the rest he smells rather too much of the restaurant.' More of his views on music are contained in the next Note.

Something further should be said here of Vaughan Williams as a conductor. He was not a good technician, but he had 'a way' with him, especially in certain of his own works, which enabled him to draw more from the players than many a professional conductor could. His conducting of the Fourth Symphony is fortunately preserved in a recording. He penetrated to the heart of *A London Symphony* and the *Tallis Fantasia* as no one else did, and his interpretations of the *Five Tudor Portraits* and *A Sea Symphony* had a special intuitive understanding which were strongly personal and inimitable.

[1] *R.C.M. Magazine,* Easter term, 1959, Vol. LV, No. 1, p. 44.
[2] To the author.

NOTE TWO

A Personal Note

I HAVE thought it proper to detach from the main narrative an account of my own relationship with Vaughan Williams, except where certain remarks which he made to me have been relevant to the context. He was fifty years my senior, although I was never conscious of his age, so alert was his mind, and I knew him only for the last twelve years of his life. From early childhood I had responded whole-heartedly to his music, and our friendship developed from a hastily written letter which I sent in a fit of homesickness while in the Royal Navy during the war. Had I been at home I should probably never have dared to write it, or should have torn it up before posting it if I had. It certainly never occurred to me that I would receive a reply, rather difficult to decipher, by return of post:

'I was much touched by your letter. One of the advantages of putting down black dots on paper is that it forms a means of communication and sympathy with people whom we may never meet in life (though I hope we may one day). . . . Please write again if you feel moved to.'

As was the case with most of his friends, I came to know the man after I knew his music. I think this pleased him, because he then could feel that opinions expressed to him about his music were not coloured by personal feelings—though there can have been few composers whose music evoked such personal affection even among people who perhaps had never met him or had only shaken his hand. I soon came to know how wrong was the journalistic impression of him given to the public. He was often described as 'a jovial farmer' or a country-dweller of pronouncedly bucolic character. Such an impression was grossly superficial and was, indeed, almost the exact opposite of the truth. True, he was a big man, heavy of gait and prone to wearing tweed suits of uncertain fit. (Sydney Grew[1]

[1] *Our Favourite Musicians* (London, 1922).

described meeting him in London in 1912 'dressed as for stalking the folk song to its home'.) But many an artist is careless about clothes and his untidiness was notable, apparently, even in early childhood. At the end of his life he rejoiced in new suits and ties and was rather amused to be called a dandy by his friends. Nobody with any power of observation could fail to notice the long, thin, delicate fingers of his smooth hands—the hands of an artist— the finely-cut nose and the beautiful grey eyes, so expressive and alert at some times, so withdrawn and visionary at others. They were the eyes of a thinker. To the end of his life his pale skin was fresh, his face unlined. No ravages of time or struggles of spirit showed there. Humour and serenity, kindliness and candour were his habitual expressions, with occasional flashes of sudden anger. As a friend once said, 'Even when he is telling you you are wrong you feel "What a pleasure!"' Of all this, Epstein's bust reveals nothing, but David McFall's is a strikingly true portrait of the man as he really was, like Sir Gerald Kelly's 1958 painting.

He was inspiriting company and seemed to have an inexhaustible supply of amusing stories about people and events. His quick precise manner of speech was very much of the period of his youth. He liked people to hold strong opinions even if he disagreed with them, and he quickly saw through any pretence at omniscience. After we had seen an exhibition of this failing he said to me: 'They used to say no one could be as wise as Haldane looked. . . .' In his dealings with others, he was thoughtful and lacking in self-interest. He found time for everything, and when I asked him how, he said: 'Only the lazy man has no time.' If inadvertently one interrupted his work, he would lay it aside saying, 'I like to be disturbed.' When Eva Hornstein, aged ten at the time, had to miss a performance of the *St. Matthew Passion* in her home-town, Dorking, because of mumps he 'found time' to send the following:

To Eva
I'm all in the dumps
To think you have mumps.
That's only for frumps
(With protuberant humps
Which stick out in lumps)
That growls and that grumps;
Not for EVA, who jumps
In elegant pumps

Surrounded by clumps
Of lovers that bumps
And stirs their young stumps
To the sound of bright trumps
While the drum loudly thumps.

Music was, of course, the mainspring of his being. He seemed to have heard it all (or gone to hear it, for from youth onwards he would fall asleep if bored). He did not care to discuss his own work except to praise somebody's performance of it. I do not agree with my friend Christopher Finzi that 'his interests apart [from music] were not very wide'.[1] I was constantly amazed by the extraordinary range of his knowledge on a tremendous number of subjects. He was alert to all that was going on in the world; the idea of shutting himself up in an ivory tower was abhorrent. His sense of humour was Rabelaisian at times; at others wickedly witty. He read the *Daily Mail*, including Rip Kirby, as avidly as *The Times*, and he was a devotee of *Vogue*. His knowledge of English literature was extensive and he was catholic in his tastes, enjoying Dodie Smith's *I Capture the Castle*, for example, as much as more serious and intellectual books.

At 10 Hanover Terrace—his 'plainly grand' home, as Frances Cornford described it—he enjoyed five years of golden harvest, happy, creative, and surrounded by friends young and old. Only a few months before he died he said, in writing to Herbert Byard to decline the offer of a lecture engagement, 'Rightly or wrongly I want to spend more time putting black dots on paper.' That he was able to do so was due in great measure to the wonderful sympathy and understanding of his wife, Ursula. 'One thing only you couldn't know about him at first-hand,' Simona Pakenham wrote to her, '—the look on his face when he spoke of you when you were out of the room.' It was a look which explained the glowing serenity of the works from *Hodie* to the last symphony.

Many besides myself will have their memories of particular facets of this remarkable man whose personality is still so strong that it colours our lives when he himself is physically no more. I hold many pictures of him in my mind, perhaps the most vivid being of his laughter, when his whole body shook in abandoned enjoyment of the joke. As I lived near Manchester, two hundred miles from him, we wrote many letters. Here is a selection from his to me which may be of interest, since they were usually about music.

[1] *R.C.M. Magazine*, Vol. LV, No. 1, p. 53.

Where I indicate omissions, it is usually of some day-to-day detail no longer of any moment, or a message of love to my wife. However I have left a few of the latter, not out of vainglory but because others may be as charmed and amused by them as we were:

> The White Gates, Dorking.
> May 22, 1952.

'. . . I think you are right in suggesting that to attach "meanings" to music is a mistake. Each person may attach their own meaning if they like, but it does not follow that their meaning will have the same meaning to anybody else—music is too universal for that. . . . By the way, do not "Doctor" me any more. I am Uncle Ralph to all the young people I am fond of.   Yours, R.V.W.'

> August 9, 1952.

'. . . I am glad you went to Down Ampney. Of course the interior of the church has been entirely spoiled by some local millionaire who was allowed by the snobbish ecclesiastical authorities to put in that terrible screen. . . .'

> August 27, 1952.

'Thank you so much for the photograph of Down Ampney Church. It is a lovely little church, is it not? I agree with you about Holst's carol. [*This have I done for my true love*] It is very beautiful. I wish you could persuade Barbirolli to do more of him. I think his finest work—at all events his finest choral work—is the *Ode to Death*, which is not very often done. . . .'

> October 19, 1952.

[After his 80th birthday] '. . . It is you young people's affection that prevents me getting old.'

> January 27, 1953.

'Thank you so much for the photographs. The one of John [Barbirolli] and me meeting looks just as if one of us had just been telling an improper story; but do I really look like a sick dog when I am listening to music? . . .'

> April 20, 1953.

'. . . Yes, after 40 years I think it is time to resign from the Leith Hill Festival before my hair comes off and the rest of my teeth drop out. But I will go on conducting the Passion if they ask me. . . . I know that the wind-machine [in *Sinfonia Antartica*] must remain. I know it's not a musical sound, but nor is the side drum, and no one objects to that. The most satisfactory version is in the record made of some of the music actually used in the film. The Manchester one didn't satisfy me entirely. The horns were my suggestion; [in place of the wind-machine, an effect made by the horns was used in one performance] you may remember that at one of the Manchester rehearsals one of the horns started whistling through his instrument and that gave me the hint; and when I didn't like the little tin trumpets that Malcolm Sargent produced I suggested the horns and they seemed all right at rehearsal. But for some reason at performance, at all events over the wireless, they didn't seem right.

'Do you know Haydn's *Imperial Mass*? A magnificent work. We did it at our Festival last week. I sympathize with your doubts over Larry's Piece [the *Romance* for harmonica]. I was surprised myself when it turned out a "best seller". I too am sorry that the Howells work [*Hymnus Paradisi*] is so difficult. I rather think that the double chorus is quite unnecessary. We couldn't possibly do it here in Dorking. . . .'

May 26, 1953.

'. . . Sancta [*Sancta Civitas*] is, on the whole, the one of my own choral works that I like best. Fancy *Antartica* getting into a popular concert! I must try and come up for the recording, and we *must* get the wind-machine right. . . . I never saw the controversy about the *Old Hundredth* in the *Telegraph*. I am rather proud of having persuaded the Archbishop to put it in, but I am afraid that the Viscounts will only know the equal note version, and with British doggedness will stick to it through thick and thin. I fear I cannot sympathize with "Dorabella's" effusions. She seems to think that hers is the only variation [in Elgar's *Enigma Variations*], and to my mind it is the worst and weakest of the lot. . . .'

10 Hanover Terrace,
London, N.W.1.
February 10, 1954.

'Thank you both so much for your wedding anniversary good wishes. We celebrated with lots of drink and a visit to a French film about an unhappy marriage. . . . As regards the pfte concerto the only thing that is published is the one pfte version, with the orchestra arranged for 2nd pfte. This is confusing, as some people think that this means the 2 pfte version, but it does not: to do the two pianoforte version with the pfte arrangement for the orchestra wd require 3 pftes! And to add to the confusion, I have altered the end since it was printed. I think both 1 pfte and 2 pfte versions are occasionally played, anyway in America. . . .'

March 2, 1954.

'. . . If you had been, as we were, at the earlier rehearsals [of *The Pilgrim's Progress* at Cambridge, to which we drove in the day, leaving for home straight after the performance] you would have been even more amazed at the almost miraculous final result. I am so glad about what you say, that it is essentially a stage work, and I am so frightened of its finishing up in the Parish Hall. But this was a stage performance in the best sense of the word, though not conventionally of the stage. . . . I feel more touched than I can say that you both undertook that long and arduous journey in order to hear a tune by me. We had a very good performance of *St. John* on Saturday. The chorus howled like Whipsnade where necessary.

January 17, 1955.

'P.S. I see that Mr. Milner [Anthony Milner, in *The Musical Times*, January, 1955, p. 29] said that neither Rubbra nor I had learnt the new chaos and that it was excusable for me owing to my advanced years—but that there was no excuse for Rubbra!!'

April 22, 1955.

'Thank you for all your news. I am sorry I could not answer before but I got cold after Dorking and am only just recovered. I must hear Rubbra's symphony [No. 6] again. I have liked it so much the twice I have heard it. Evelyn and John [Barbirolli] came to dinner last night. He looks better, I think—which reminds me that I had a jury (A. Bliss, Gerald Finzi, Rubbra, Roy Douglas, Scott Goddard and Howes) to sit on my new tune [Symphony No. 8] and decide whether I had better go on with it. They decided to put it on the "short list" with the proviso that it wanted a lot more revision (with that I entirely agreed). I showed it to John who took it away knowing that it is unfinished. I wish I liked *Troilus* [Walton's opera] more. I admire it coldly, but it never takes me by the scruff and shakes me. I must try again. . . .'

August 5, 1955.

[In reply to a request that he should write an article about Sibelius's 90th birthday for the *Daily Telegraph*.] 'When you and Sibelius pull together it is like the Spring tides. So I will do my best. As things are going at present, I don't think I shall have any more time in my life for composition! . . .'

October 15, 1955.

'. . . As regards the new symphony [No. 8]—I hope it is going to be all right. But I feel rather nervous. At all events it is simple and sets no problems, but at my age ("I speak as a fool") I cannot afford to let out anything 2nd rate—which is not really straight from the fountain-head. . . . I believe John is going to allow me a private run-through in Feb. which will settle its fate. . . .'

January 30, 1956.

'In great haste. I hasten to correct one error in your article [about his conducting of the *St. Matthew Passion*, in preparation for his performance with the Hallé. I had sent him a proof]. I have decided to keep the cor anglais for the *obbligati*. I can keep viola at Dorking—but have not the courage in Manchester.'

March 29, 1956.

'I am so glad you were able to listen to *Dona*. I only listened in, and it did not seem to me a very good performance. Several of the tempi were wrong. As far as I could judge on the first hearing the Rubbra was very good. But, as the man said "You should never hear Brahms for the first time," and this, I think, applies everywhere. I certainly want to hear it again.'

May 13, 1956.

'. . . I am still worrying a little about the last movement [of the Eighth Symphony]. I think the critics perhaps thought there were no tunes because they could not hear them! So I am thinning down the percussion a bit—if John will allow me to—because it may be the Hittites who obscure the tunes and a few bars less of phones and spiels won't do any harm. ['Hittites' was his jocular way of referring to the percussion in this symphony.]

July 1, 1956.

'I am dictating this from my bed. I am perfectly well, but the doctor says I must not put my foot down till I am cured of the phlebitis—or whatever it is I have got. You . . . ask so many pertinent questions in your letter that I will take them in order.

'*Merry Wives* (Nicolai): This is altogether delightful. I think it is the best of the operas on the Falstaff saga. There is a splendid buffo duet for Falstaff and Ford and a delightful quintet with Fenton and Anne making love in the middle of the stage and the rival lovers hiding behind bushes and making incidental remarks. . . .

'With regard to Parry and Stanford, I think Howes and the other critics are so frightened of not being up to date: but I believe they will come back into their own. Do you know an early choral work by Parry, *The Glories of our Blood and State*? It is a bit Brahmsy, but, I think, very fine. There is an interesting story about it which I believe is true. It had been put down in the programme of the Bach Choir in 1887: then it occurred to one of the committee that it would hardly do, seeing that the Royal Family were among the Patrons of the Choir, for them to sing a piece about Thrones and Crowns toppling down in the year of Queen Victoria's jubilee. So a friend, I think Stanford, went to Parry and asked him to write something else: whereupon, he wrote *Blest Pair of Sirens*. We must not judge, with all respect to you, the vitality of a composer entirely from the Press. Parry and Stanford may, according to Howes, be historic relics, but it would take a good many fingers of a good many hands to count up the number of annual performances, even now, of *Blest Pair*, *Songs of the Fleet*—not to mention a large number of part songs and other smaller works which continually appear on programmes.

'I fear I cannot put Mackenzie on a level with Parry and Stanford. He was a sound craftsman, and his *Benedictus* for violin solo is, I imagine, still popular, but that is all. As regards Bax, I am beginning to feel rather doubtful. He had, perhaps, more musical invention than any of his contemporaries but, as you say, it was quite undisciplined. I wish he had had some gruelling lessons from Stanford. But probably they would have quarrelled and nothing would have come of it. I agree with you that No. 3 is the best, and the last one. . . .

'. . . I could see no point in Beethoven when I was a boy—and I am still temperamentally allergic to him. But I am beginning to find out that he is nevertheless a very great man. I used to enjoy Schumann's sentimental songs very much when I was young, but I can't bear them now. Schubert has also gone off the boil as far as I am concerned. But Bach remains! I hope very much we can have a long talk about all these things at Cheltenham.

'I am so glad to hear about the cricket. I never could bear it myself, but I had to play when I was a boy, and one day I was out in the field and thinking about something else when a ball suddenly hit me hard on the shins. I awoke from my dreams to enthusiastic cries of "well fielded" and got a reputation as a cricketer!'

Both R.V.W. and Ursula were astonished at my perpetual horror that they lived a stone's throw from Lord's and never went near the place. His phlebitis prevented his visit to Cheltenham that year so we called to stay on our way there and then I sent him a full report of each concert by letter each night. I also sent him Colin Wilson's *The Outsider*, knowing what his reaction would be but knowing, too, that he would prefer to be provoked than soothed:

July 22, 1956.

'It was wonderful of you to send those long letters. . . . And many thanks for the book, which puzzles me at present; but I daresay I shall get to appreciate it, in spite of the approval of Edith Sitwell. . . . Our love to Eslyn [my wife], and there can be no doubt that she was the loveliest girl there in spite of the combined efforts of Gloucester and Cheltenham.'

July 29, 1956.

'. . . I find I am entirely ignorant of all the jargon of the wrong-note school: could you give me a short resumé? Telling me especially what the twelve-tone scale means and what a tone-row[1] means? . . . Postal tuition in theory and practice of wrong notery: conversational success guaranteed. Learn what all the learned reviewers mean: be contemporary! Enrol to-day as a Kennedy student. Love to Eslyn. R.V.W.'

August 18, 1956.

'I have much to thank you for. Firstly for the book. I have tried several

[1] He liked to pronounce 'tone-row' to rhyme with 'cow'.

rounds with Mr. Wilson, and have bitten the dust each time up to the present! But I am going to try one more bout, bloody but unbowed. He is apparently writing about existentialism, and he never explains what it is, and as I do not know, I feel I am fighting with one hand tied behind my back. At present the book seems to me almost entirely scissors and paste, with unexplained allusions to novels most of which I do not know and most of which, judging from the quotations, I do not want to know. But there, I am an old fogey, and it has apparently been much admired, though Edith Sitwell's praise is blame indeed.

'Secondly, thank you for your lucid explanation of the tone rows. If that is really all there is to it, it seems to me the most astonishing bit of mechanical pedantry which has ever been dignified by the name of art. I think I must try a tone-row myself and see what happens. But apparently one must not use any succession of notes which sounds agreeable to the cultivated ear. I remember Charles Wood giving a lesson to a young modern at the R.C.M. who thought he was going to show the old dry-as-dust how to do it. Wood looked at his work and said "It's all right, but it seems to me rather tame. Why didn't you do something more like this?" and sat down at the piano and played some outrageous stuff that the poor young man had never even dreamed of.

'Evelyn [Barbirolli] very kindly brought us a record of the new symph. Some of it seems a muddle to me, but then most records do and both Ursula and Gil said it was splendid. Poor Eslyn and her tooth. Give her our love and tell her that I am sure it was a sweet tooth."

December 23, 1956.

'Your selection of poems is splendid. [A collection of English poems on autumn which I hoped he might set.]· I am especially glad you have introduced the Tennyson lines about the full-juiced apple[1] which I sometimes think are, for pure beauty of sound, among the best things in poetry. But I don't know if I shall ever be able to get to your selection. I do not know whether I dare to set Hardy! . . .

'We had a very nice carol party here the other night—we sang all REAL carols, no Wenceslases or Silent Nights: we started at half past eight, had half an hour's break at about 10, and finished up with the *First Nowell* about 12, and then more drinks. Did you know the *First Nowell* goes in canon? Perhaps some people thought we sang it like that because of the very potent cup we had been imbibing. One thing we sang which was not traditional was the splendid tune sung to *While Shepherds Watched* in the West Country. (See *English Hymnal* Appendix 8). . . . You ought to read *The Lost Steps*, translated from .the Spanish, by Carpentier. . . .'

[1] *Choric Song:* Lo! sweetened with the summer light,
The full-juiced apple, waxing over-mellow,
Drops in a silent autumn night.

January 26, 1957.

'. . . Your question of who is the greatest man in my lifetime is very difficult to answer. I don't think Churchill, somehow, but a few names taken at random would include Brahms, Walt Whitman and General Booth . . . and of course there is also Sibelius. It took me some time to get accustomed to his No. 6, but I rather believe now that it is his greatest. . . . I have no particular use for Bruckner. I have never got over the first symphony I heard of his, in which 4 Wagner tubas played what sounded like old English glees. . . . My love, and three kisses please, to Eslyn, but perhaps she is La Belle Dame sans Merci, in which case it must be four. . . .'

February 15, 1957.

'I had already got a record of Nielsen 5, and had not made much out of it, but hearing it under John [Barbirolli] was quite a different thing and we both admired it very much though the first movement is perhaps rather too much what Tovey used to call a prelude-to-a-prelude-to-a-prelude. I've also heard the Walton [cello concerto], a fine work, finely played. . . . As regards Gerald's new songs [Gerald Finzi's 6 Hardy songs *I Said to Love*]—the first and the last hit the nail in my head right away, the others I should like to hear again, but this does not mean, as it usually does, that I do *not* want to hear them again! . . .'

March 3, 1957.

'I am so glad that you were able to come to the *St. John* . . . I think it was the best performance that we have given: I believe that it is our tenth year! I should like to see your article on *The Apostles*. . . . I am afraid that I have never cared about it, except the final Alleluias, which are beautiful. I always feel that he [Elgar] was oppressed by the fact that he was writing for the Church of England and could not get rid of the bombazine and bonnets of the Anglican Sunday morning service. On the whole I like *The Kingdom* better, though of course there is nothing so bad in *The Apostles* as the Lord's Prayer. . . .'

May 9, 1957.

'. . . With regard to that aria in the Matthew P. about bearing the Cross. I was told that at the first performance under Mendelssohn this was the hit of the evening—apparently then they used to encore things they liked at those early performances. I have an idea that I will put it into my next performance. But it will have to be rearranged for three cellos. I WILL NOT HAVE a viol da Gamba inside the building. I assure you we used to come to grief in early days over "He is guilty of death". It went right at rehearsal because I made the Evangelist sing the leading-in phrase in strict time, and then at performance he forgot. But they know it so well now that they would come in right even if the Evangelist sang the tune the old cow died of.

'I had lunch in the presence of the P.M. [Mr. Harold Macmillan] the other day, who was very pleasant and amusing. . . . As regards Third Programme, I do not quite understand Network 3 or whatever it is called. I entirely agree that the Third Programme wants improvement, but to shorten it will probably mean that the young pansies who run the B.B.C. will cut out all that we think worth while and have entirely Telemann and Blacher. . . .

'I think I only heard Richter conduct Elgar twice, first the *Variations*, when I was absorbed by the music, and naturally being the first time I heard it, did not know if it was being done well or badly. And then came that extraordinarily bad first performance of *Gerontius* which nearly killed the work. But it was not Richter's fault that the semi-chorus consisted of second-rate professionals from Birmingham and district, that the choir got hopelessly flat at the end of Part I, that Plunket Greene lost his voice, that Marie Brema had none to lose, and that Edward Lloyd sang it like a Stainer anthem in the correct tenor attitude with one foot slightly withdrawn. . . . Your letters make me sit up and think which I am too lazy to do usually.'

May 15, 1957.

'The quotation at the end of my Elgar talk was the opening of the first symphony: where the melody is given to violas and rather heavy woodwind, the bass to cellos and double basses, also playing rather heavily, while the inside harmony is given to two soft muted horns. By all the rules those horns ought to be inaudible, but they sound out all right, and that is the mystery and the miracle.'

This referred to an Elgar centenary broadcast tribute. I was fascinated by R.V.W.'s ambivalent attitude to Elgar's music. He delighted to shock me by suggesting that he would make an omnibus version of the two symphonies "keeping all the best bits".

I have excluded from this selection those letters which he wrote to me on personal occasions such as birthdays, but the one we received after his eighty-fifth birthday is revealing.

October 13, 1957.

Dearest Michael and Eslyn,

Thank you for your beautiful letter and for Max [a first edition of a volume of Beerbohm drawings] which will be a constant joy. I think that you both mean to each other as Ursula and I do.

Love from Ralph.

November 26, 1957.

'. . . I am ridiculously well except for this absurd leg: as a matter of fact there are one or two things I was glad to be able to miss . . . on the other hand, I have had to refuse an invitation to judge at a beauty competition (R.A.M. students!) which is sad.

'Most of Stravinsky bores me. I wish he even shocked me, especially the *Rite of Spring*. I do not think the scoring is masterly at all, he always makes a nasty sour sound with his orchestra, but I do like the *Symphony of Psalms*, *Les Noces* and the Suite for violin and pianoforte of which I once heard a record under very peculiar circumstances of which I will tell you one day. [A night-train-journey acquaintance invited him to hear this record, and others, in the early hours of the morning before R.V.W. caught the first train to Dorking.]

'Having "released" the new symphony [No. 9] I am proceeding to rewrite it! I shall then pass it on to Roy to "copy". I do not know if the last stage of that symphony will be worse than the first. We are going to hear Bartók's *Bluebeard* at Sadler's Wells on Friday, if the doctor will let me. I once heard it broadcast and disliked it extremely, but of course that is not a fair test of a stage work.' [In fact he admired it very much after seeing it.]

December 27, 1957.

'Thank you both so much for the books. I expect the metaphysical poets are more for Ursula, but I have a particular interest in Robert Graves as I know him slightly. [We had sent the revised edition of *Goodbye to All That* as a Christmas present.] I think I told you of our last meeting but will repeat it in case I haven't. (It sounds like a game of consequences!) We discovered that we had both been at Charterhouse, whereupon we both started singing the *Carmen Carthusianum* in a Majorcan restaurant in loud voices. This caused a thunderstorm, whereupon Robert Graves upset his coffee over Ursula and a cat.'

January 3, 1958.

'. . . Yes, I know exactly where *En Saga* ought to have stopped. The rest is a great pity, as the two ladies said of the lower part of Botticelli's Venus in Forster's novel.'

February 5, 1958.

'. . . We are now thick in John and Matthew, and as usual tenors are beginning to fail. For the John we have only four tenors left, two of whom can sing and two of whom can't. However I have managed to collect two outsiders who know it and are coming here for a special rehearsal beforehand. . . . I do not think we are going to *Peter Grimes*, but for our sins we are going to endure *The Carmelites*. . . .'

February 26, 1958.

'. . . I admired Tippett's symphony [No. 2] very much, but it is very hard; one of those things that will not get a really good performance till it has been done about 10 times. . . .'

March 6, 1958.

'. . . I think our performance of the Passion last night was the best we have done. . . .'

March 29, 1958.

[After a first play-through of the Ninth Symphony, in St. Pancras Town Hall on March 21, 1958.]

'. . . Thank you so much for liking the new symph. I have made a few alterations in the scoring and in the metronome marks—and specially the last movement where I have speeded it up a bit all through and made a short cut, of about 15 bars in the middle. I am sure it is an improvement. . . . I wonder if you disliked *The Carmelites* as much as we did? . . .'

Villa Cristabella, Forio d'Ischia.
April ??, 1958 (postcard).

'We had a bumpy flight, saw a very bad opera—a new one—in the Opera House at Naples and went to Herculaneum. The opera is said to be founded on Sardinian folk songs. If that is so, God help the Sardines!'

June 16, 1958.

[In answer to a question in my research into the history of the Hallé, for a book which I was writing.]

'Richter. When I was young the only orchestral concerts (except the Phil: which did not count) were Manns (Crystal Palace) and Richter, with Henschel a little later—so we had no real standard of comparison. But I felt that at all events in Wagner and Beethoven you heard not an "individual reading" but the music itself—and that was what mattered both to Richter and the audience. I felt with him as with no other conductor that he never got between you and the composer. It was always straightforward and no monkey-tricks and intensely satisfying—a feeling which no other conductor has given me. He used the old-fashioned walking-stick baton and a straightforward businesslike beat. I only once remember his using any showmanship—when he used to let the orchestra play the 5/4 Tschaikowsky without beating—of course he did a good deal of conducting in the movement with his eyebrows and little finger—but the audience thought it wonderful.'

I last saw Ralph Vaughan Williams when we stayed at Hanover Terrace for the August Bank Holiday week-end and went with him to *Sir John in Love*. On the Sunday, to avoid the traffic, my wife and I decided to drive home at midnight. While Eslyn was getting her coat he waited with me by the front door. Something impelled me to thank him, more forcibly than usual, for his music. I think he knew why I did so. I am glad that I did. A fortnight later he sent me, from Dorset, a postcard of the Cerne Abbas giant. For some reason I did not reply at once, but when I did I referred to a ribald limerick we both enjoyed and said that the giant had obviously not been to Keble. He received my letter on 25 August, and it apparently amused him greatly. I am glad that our last contact was a subject for laughter.

Vaughan Williams was cremated privately at Golders Green on 28 August, with only a few close friends present and the organ played by William McKie. On the day of his death, Dr. Don, Dean of Westminster, had offered burial in the Abbey and there, on Friday, 19 September, near to Stanford and Purcell, Vaughan Williams's ashes were laid in the North Choir Aisle. The Abbey was full on that late-summer morning with representatives of the whole world of music and with a host of R.V.W.'s friends. In their devotion to him, in their single-mindedness on that day, they made the great abbey feel like a village church: Westminster became Coldharbour. When the Dean and Chapter and other officiating clergy, wearing the robes made for the funeral of Charles II (a fact which would have immensely pleased R.V.W.) had taken their places, Adrian Boult began the Commemoration in Music which preceded the Service. Into the silence of the Abbey came the first notes of the Five Variants of 'Dives and Lazarus'. It was as if Vaughan Williams himself had spoken. The tune which he had loved all his life, which came from the soil of England, ageless and anonymous, which he had used in so many of his own compositions, was the perfect choice to create a mood of remembrance which will haunt those who experienced it to the end of their days. Frederick Grinke and David Martin played Bach's D minor Concerto for two violins, and a choirboy could not restrain his feet from tapping to Bach's dancing rhythms. How R.V.W. would have approved. Then, the Pavane, Galliard, and Epilogue from *Job*, majestic and tranquil. Three items in the music of the funeral had been chosen by Vaughan Williams: the Sentences from William Croft's Burial Service, Lord Mornington's chant for Psalm 104, and Maurice Greene's anthem 'Lord, let me know mine end'. While the bronze casket was taken to its resting-place, the hymn 'Come down, O Love Divine' was sung to the tune Vaughan Williams named after his birthplace, Down Ampney—sung, that is, by those who could conquer their emotions. The small party which went to the graveside comprised Ursula, his wife; Adeline's sister, Cordelia Curle; three of his closest friends—Maud

Karpeles, the folk-song collector, singer, and dancer, to represent all folk musicians; Steuart Wilson, who from youth onwards had sung his works, to represent all his friends in the musical profession; and Gilmour Jenkins, who also represented the R.V.W. Trust; and two of the younger generation—Christopher Finzi, who took the place his father Gerald would have taken had he lived, to represent the young professionals; and Robert Armstrong,[1] who had sung for some years in R.V.W.'s madrigal group, to represent all gifted and enthusiastic amateur musicians. He carried the insignia of Vaughan Williams's O.M. Many others might have been included, but the group had to be limited to six.

After the committal, the choir sang 'O taste and see', the voice of the Woodcutter's boy from *Pilgrim's Progress*, as it seemed. And then, as the sun blazed into the Abbey, irradiating the sombre scene with its golden warmth, the trumpeters of Kneller Hall sounded the great fanfare which opens the Coronation setting of 'The Old Hundredth'. 'Sing to the Lord with cheerful voice. . . .' It was not easy, but the triumphant note was the right one. 'Enter then His gates with praise, Approach with joy His courts unto'. . . . Praise and joy—these were right, too.

After the Blessing, Bach's St. Anne Fugue, R.V.W.'s choice; and as the congregation went out into the noonday sunshine, the bells of the Abbey rang out a half-muffled peal over the London in which Ralph Vaughan Williams had lived and worked, and which he had turned into music.

---

[1] Now Sir Robert Armstrong, Secretary to the Cabinet from 1979.

APPENDIX ONE
Letters to Ralph Wedgwood

ONE of the most important friendships in Vaughan Williams's life was that with his cousin Ralph Wedgwood (1874–1956), known to his family as 'Randolph', to whom two of the best of Vaughan Williams's early works were dedicated, *In the Fen Country* and *A Sea Symphony*. They were at Cambridge together and among their particular friends were G. E. Moore, G. M. Trevelyan, Theodore and Crompton Llewelyn Davies, and Maurice Amos, all to achieve distinction in various fields of endeavour. Wedgwood eventually became general manager of the London and North Eastern Railway.

The following recently discovered letters cover a period from 1895, when Vaughan Williams had left Cambridge and taken up a post as an organist in Lambeth (see pp. 41–42), until 1913.

> 2 St. Barnaby Villas
> South Lambeth Rd.
> [1895]

Dear Randolph . . .

Yes, before you wrote I had settled to stop on, at all events till next Xmas. I was persuaded by the curate, of all people, who pointed out that if I left at Easter I should just have finished knocking down the old building and not have started building the new, and that things would just slip back into the old groove. You see before I came they used to yell bad music much too quick. I make them sing good music rather too slow; and at first they don't like it. But the vicar is coming round. . . . Also we have started a choral society. First practice tonight—also I intend to start an orchestral society. . . . Now cannot you take your holiday *later*, then I could probably get off. Now Trevy and Moore can more or less choose their own time for holidays—and as to Amos, well we all know that a lawyer has six months vacation every other day. . . . If you want to read a really very good French novel read 'Madame Bovary' by Gustave Flaubert—an attempt was made in France to suppress it as being 'lascive' but I don't think this will hurt you—also 'Le Cousin Pons' by Balzac is very good . . . [Rest missing]

The next letter was written in April 1898. Vaughan Williams had married Adeline Fisher in October 1897, and they moved into 5 Cowley Street, Westminster, in July 1898.

Hotel Victoria
Prague

Dear Randolph,

My natural pedantry nearly led me to call this place Praha which the Bohemians call it. I don't suppose that you knew we were out of England. But firstly Mother gave us £50 to go abroad with, secondly I was out of employment, thirdly there seemed no chance of your ever coming to London, fourthly we have just taken a house. So that we decided now was the time for action. We first went to Berlin to keep up with the influential people there and incidentally hear some music, then we spent a night in Dresden, and now we are in this most delightful place where everybody talks Czeckish and Dvorák's operas are performed at the National Bohemian theatre—we are going to one tonight which is called 'Cert a Kaca' which the waiter tells us means 'The Devil and the Kitty' [*The Devil and Kate*]. I feel awfully national just now—though I have just written an article against national music which no magazine has thought fit to accept [see pp. 29–30]. *Monday*. We went to the opera—all the part of it which dealt with Bohemian village life was tremendously good. But when he got down to Hell and there were people being put into cauldrons by devils it got very dull—and much of the music was bagged from the Nibelheim in Wagner's *Rheingold*. When we get home I am going to make a really strenuous effort to get work to do without returning to Organism which I do not want to do even if any parson would have me which I doubt. . . .

Yours affectionately
R.V.W.

Burley, Ringwood,
Hants
[Summer 1898]

Dear Randolph . . .

We have a plan in store which is as follows—I have got, before October, to write a thing called a degree exercise which will take all my time till then but inasmuch as such work can be best done in a quiet country place we are thinking of taking a small place in the country. . . . The New Forest is a most wonderful place . . . not one of your horrid stern places where you feel you must discuss high themes but a warm comfortable beauty— though very wild. . . . Don't think me degenerate in my likes but you know I always *have* preferred soft scenery to stern uncomfortable scenery. I can admire it but I can't really enjoy it. I know that shows a craven spirit but I can't help it. My heart goes through the same manoeuvres as Words- worth's when he saw a rainbow when I see a long low range of hills—I suppose this comes from being born in Surrey S.W.[1] I am now working

[1] Evidently he forgot he was born in Gloucestershire.

at my degree exercise—I'm going to write a Mass—they're such fine words and you get such good climaxes out of them. I think I told you all this before, but this letter has been going for a week. . . .

Yours
R.V.W.

5 Cowley Street, S.W.1.
[Spring 1899]

Dear Randolph,
 . . . My name appeared yesterday on a programme—in an obscure corner of a programme of a second-rate performance of a fourth-rate play might be seen: The orchestra will perform the following selection—and then among numerous other things, *Scènes de Ballet*. . . . Williams.[1] That's all—but it's just a crumb to keep me going . . .

Yours affectionately
R.V.W.

During 1899, Ralph and Adeline moved into 10 Barton Street, Westminster. The *Bucolic Suite* was completed in November 1900. The magazine *The Vocalist* first appeared in April 1902. Among the songs published in it was *Linden Lea*.

10 Barton Street
[Undated]

My dear Randolph,
 . . . I've not very much to chronicle except that I've sold my soul to a publisher—that is to say I've agreed not to sell songs to any publisher but him for 5 years. And he is going to publish several potboiling songs of mine—that is to say not *real* pot boilers—but they are more or less simple and popular in character. They are to come out in a magazine called 'The Vocalist' and then to be published at 1s. which is a new departure—and I'm to get a penny halfpenny on each copy—so you see I'm on the high road to a fortune. . . .

Yours affectionately
Ralph Vaughan Williams

The next letter was written when Ralph Wedgwood announced his engagement to Iris Pawson in 1905:

O my dear Randolph,
I am so glad . . . You have everything to make a wife happy for ever and ever—and you have everything in you which *cries out* for it. . . . You call Adeline and me your best friends and I can't say what it means to me to have you say that. . . . I would venture to send a message to Iris (may I

---

[1] No trace of this work remains.

call her so?) if I dared, so if I may you can invent one from me—you will do it so much better than I shall! Bless you. This is quite illegible but my hand shakes from excitement.

Yours
R.V.W.

In November 1905, Vaughan Williams moved into 13 Cheyne Walk, where he was to live for the next 24 years. The view from his study partly inspired the *London Symphony*.

Leith Hill Place,
November 1905

Dear Randolph,

You must come and see the new house soon. I've got a grand study in the attic with a grand view of the river and a bridge and 3 great electric light chimneys and a sunset. Then I've also got a roll-top desk, a writing table and a new piano—so I ought to do! . . .

R.V.W.

on Board s.s. Wakool
Jan. 6, 1906

Dear Randolph,

You will be surprised to see this address. . . . The fact is that I am on my way to Canary to see my sister-in-law—we all felt that someone ought to go and none of her brothers could. I was free and wanted a holiday so I started off . . . It's certainly a most lazy life being on a steamer. . . . I'm getting a good deal of reading done—*Tom Jones* (for the 2nd time) and a book about hypnotism and Shakespeare's historical plays and a vol. of Browning. Yesterday we passed about 6 miles from C. Finisterre and the mountains in the N.W. of Spain. I thought of you and wondered what mountains they were. Fine arid-looking mountains.

It's a small boat going eventually to Australia—we have only 16 salooners aboard—a very dull and shoddy crew—I wish you were here to get something out of them, I can't. I can't even flirt with the ladies—there's only one who is *possible* from this point of view and she is fearfully dull. Also she much prefers the chief engineer who tells long stories about the various idiosyncrasies of various passengers. But it's very jolly and extraordinary getting gradually into summer—today the sun was actually too hot and we sat out on deck under umbrellas.

I had a dream about you last night that you and I were staying in a house together and we went out for a walk and I heard a folk song being sung by some schoolchildren. We went on for our walk (it was somewhere in the North of England among hills) and on our return I enquired at the school and found that the children had learnt it from an old man in the village (he had some funny name but I can't remember it) and that the old man knew some more, 'some of them beauties', so then I said 'You go home and start off on your motor and I will wait here'—but then I suddenly found, what I hadn't realised before, that I might come with you—so I gave up my folk-songing. Then somehow suddenly Adeline was with us and she and you and the chauffeur got in and made a trial trip, then you came back for me and I and the chauffeur got in behind and *you* drove—and I woke up. . . .

Yours affectionately
Ralph

P.S. The whole company discussed Marie Corelli last night—I realised for the 1st time what it means to be really out of it. The young man who is going out to be Governor at Fort Jameson started it by saying she was his favourite author—his brother objected that she was too far-fetched—but he said all good plays and novels *were* far-fetched. Then the chief engineer chimed in. *He* said that M.C.'s work had lasted while that of other chief women novelists (Sarah Grand and 'Iota') had *not*. The general opinion seemed to be that 'Sorrows of Satan' and 'Mighty Atom' were not *quite* nice. Indeed the dressy young lady who is going to the Cape to be married and is very high church went so far as to say that they were 'profane', casting down her eyes. But the general opinion was that 'Thelma' and 'Romance of Two Worlds' were 'very interesting'—indeed the parson said that one of them had made him think! Which, if true, is indeed a very high testimonial.   R.V.W.

Toward the Unknown Region was first performed at the Leeds Festival in October 1907 [see p. 88].

3 July 1907

Dear Randolph,

. . . I had a most amusing time at Leeds the other day—I went to take the chorus through it—first I was introduced in a little speech by the secretary and afterwards I was interviewed by the *Yorkshire Evening Post* —the young man begged me to tell him what my hobby was. When I assured him there was nothing interesting about me he said 'except your face'. Finally I was taken to a hotel to wait for my train and on the threshold I suddenly heard 'Hello Mester Williams' and found myself clapped on the back by two lusty Yorkshiremen—they turned out to be members of the chorus—they insisted on standing me drinks and one of them wanted to take me home with him promising me a spare bed and a 'Yorkshire stëak' cooked by his wife! . . .

Yours affectionately
R.V.W.

[October 1907]

My dear Randolph,

How nice of you to write. I wish you could have been there—they sang and played magnificently—but the 20 minutes I stood there conducting was like 1000 years of purgatory. *The Times* praised too much—several papers were sniffy and some good—the audience seemed to like it—but that may have been to encourage me. But after all it's only a step and I've got to do something really big sometime. I think I am improving. It 'comes off' better than my earlier things used to . . .

Yours

R.V.W.

Gloucester Hotel,
Weymouth
[March 1909]

Dear Randolph,

. . . We needn't fear that we are forgetting each other because we don't see each other. Luckily it doesn't depend on that. Now I'm blest if I haven't left the press notices of my fen piece in London which I meant to have sent you [*In the Fen Country* was first performed on 22 February 1909, conducted by Beecham]. By the way I don't think I ever told you that it was dedicated to you—to tell you the truth I had forgotten about it—but your initials are at the top of the score. I've been fearfully busy of late with some beastly lectures and trying to get *The Wasps* ready . . .

Yours affec.

R. Vaughan Williams

A Sea Symphony, first performed at Leeds in October 1910, was published in 1909.

13 Cheyne Walk
[1909]

My dear Randolph,

I send you herewith your own especial goat which has just come out. It is my best work I believe up to the present—and so however feeble it may be, I love to think of it with your initials at the top—it cd have no better fate. . . .

Yours

R.V.W

13 Cheyne Walk
[Undated]

Dear Randolph,

R. Curle [husband of Adeline's sister Cordelia] reports that you think that I think (this is rather Irish) that I don't admire G. Butterworth's compositions—so I want to put right anything I may have said which led you to this conclusion. Because I do think that he is one of our rising lights. I don't think that he has quite 'found himself' yet—but is rapidly doing so. . . .

Yours
R.V.W.

Hotel Suisse,
Ospedaletti Ligure,
Italy
[December 1913]

Dear Randolph,

How good of the gentleman from Killaloe to send me Lecky.[1] It will make me all the more prepared to volunteer (if they'll have me) on the side of law and order when the fight comes. . . . I am very well, but then I was never ill. And the opera [*Hugh the Drover*] is nearly finished. I come back in March. . . .

Yours
R.V.W.

[The fight did come, nine months later, and he volunteered at once, at the age of 41.]

---

[1] W. E. H. Lecky O.M., historian (1838–1903). Perhaps the book R.V.W. was lent was *Democracy and Liberty* (1896).

Letters to Henry J. Wood

THE following correspondence with Sir Henry Wood covers the years 1937–43. The first letter refers to the Fourth Symphony.

The White Gates, Dorking
Jan 22, 1937

Dear Sir Henry Wood,

I listened in with great interest to your performance of my symphony. It seemed to be an excellent performance as far as I could judge—I don't like the work itself much, but that is another question.

Yours sincerely,
R. Vaughan Williams

Early in 1938 Wood asked R.V.W. for a work for the concert on 5 October to celebrate his golden jubilee as a conductor. The result was the *Serenade for Music* for sixteen solo voices and orchestra [see pp. 256–7 and 277–8].

The White Gates
Dorking   Jan 24

Dear Sir Henry,

I should love to write—to have the honour of writing—a piece in your praise if I can manage it. Is there any poet you can suggest who could write me some words appropriate for the occasion? How about asking the Poet Laureate [John Masefield]?

Yours sincerely,
R. Vaughan Williams

25 January, 1938

Dear Dr. Vaughan Williams,

I cannot tell you the gratitude I feel that you should write me so kindly regarding my request. I do not for a moment however propose that this work of yours should be written as an ode to myself, for I would like it to be a choral work that can be used at any time and for any occasion. I would not think of asking you to write a work that might only be used the once, which would naturally be the case were it written round myself. Perhaps, for such a work you already have many poems by you.

With kind regards,
Sincerely yours,
Henry J. Wood

The White Gates
Dorking, June 2 1938

Dear Sir Henry,

I send herewith a copy of my 'Serenade' for you to look at and express your approval or otherwise. I am afraid I must ask you to send this copy back as this must be the one for the printer if it is printed.

Yours sincerely,
R. Vaughan Williams

The White Gates
Dorking, Oct. 11, 1938

Dear Sir Henry,

Very many thanks for sending me Rachmaninoff's delightful letter.[1] I am much gratified that he should have approved of my 'Serenade'. I return his letter herewith. I hear that the recording is to be next Saturday at 10. I will be there.

Yrs vy sincerely,
R. Vaughan Williams

The White Gates
Dorking. June 14, 1939

Dear Sir Henry,

Many thanks for your suggestion of making an orchestral piece out of my Serenade. It is certainly worth considering.

Yours sincerely,
R. Vaughan Williams

By 31 December, 1939 the orchestral version of the *Serenade* was completed. Wood conducted the first performance on 10 February 1940. Three years later the Fifth Symphony was ready for performance.

The White Gates
Dorking. Feb 5, 1943

Dear Wood,

I have come to the conclusion that my new symphony must now go forward for better, for worse. So would you like me to send it to you to see if you would like to do it. The orchestration may want a little revision (I am taking it to Gordon Jacob for that purpose, as usual). It plays about 35 minutes and though not technically difficult will I imagine want a good deal of rehearsal to make it 'come off'—so perhaps for that reason, if for no other, you may not think it suitable. . . .

Yours sincerely
R. Vaughan Williams

[1] Rachmaninoff had been the piano soloist at the Jubilee Concert.

The White Gates
Dorking. Feb 9, 1943

Dear Wood,
I am honoured that you will put my symphony into your programme without seeing it! As regards conducting it—of course I should be pleased and proud if you did it, on the other hand if it would take a burden off your shoulders I will willingly do it myself and though no conductor I think I have had sufficient experience not to let you down.

Yours sincerely,
R. Vaughan Williams

The White Gates
Dorking, March 15.

Dear Wood,
Would it be possible to place my symphony toward the end of the season—I have taken longer over 'washing its face' than I calculated and now that it is ready all my copyists have failed—do you know of any good copyist? If I can get it done in time Adrian Boult has kindly promised to run it through one morning at Bedford[1] so as to check the parts.

Yours sincerely.
R. Vaughan Williams

The symphony was first performed at a Promenade Concert on 24 June 1943. Wood was ill at the time.

The White Gates
Dorking. June 25

Dear Wood,
I cannot tell you how touched I was by your letter and how I felt about Lady Wood coming all the way to the Albert Hall to give it me. But, you know, it was very wrong of you—you have to spend every ounce of your energy getting well quick to come back and feed your hungry sheep at the Albert Hall. The orchestra were splendid—and as I made no serious mistakes we had a very fine performance.

Yours,
R. Vaughan Williams

The next letter was probably written late in January of 1944, when Wood was planning his next season of Proms.

The White Gates,
Dorking.

Dear Wood,
How good of you to write. I have by me at present a concerto for oboe and strings which has never been performed— but I think that you consider that oboe concertos do not do in the Albert Hall. Also I am making

[1] During part of the war the BBC Symphony Orchestra's headquarters was the Corn Exchange, Bedford.

the music I wrote for 'Flemish Farm'[1] into a suite. But I do not know if you would consider that as 'new' enough for your purpose—it would be of course first performance of the *Suite*.

Yrs
R. Vaughan Williams

The White Gates
Dorking Feb 5, 1944

Dear Wood,

I agree that the oboe concerto would not be suitable for the Albert Hall —would you tell me (quite at your leisure) whether you would consider a suite made out of my 'Flemish Farm' film as a 'new work' under the terms of the act. It is, I think, some of the best film music I have written and would make a good suite.[2]

Yours
R. Vaughan Williams

Wood evidently changed his mind about the oboe concerto:

The White Gates
Dorking
May 31

Dear Wood,

At last I am able to send you a fair copy of my oboe concerto. I am so sorry for the delay which is due (i) to the fact that when I had, as I thought, finished it I began to re-write it and (ii) my copyist fell ill in the middle. It is most kind of you to be willing to conduct it. I hope you will receive the score from the OUP simultaneously with this.

Yrs sincerely,
R. Vaughan Williams

Wood has written at the bottom of this letter 'Many thanks! I am going to find much pleasure in doing this, and hope you will be kind enough to run through it with me prior to rehearsal.' But he died a few weeks later. The work was scheduled for performance at the Proms on 5 July 1944, but the concert was cancelled because of the flying-bomb raids and the first performance was given in Liverpool in September of the same year.

---

[1] Film first shown in August 1943.

[2] R.V.W. conducted the first performance at a Promenade Concert on 31 July, 1945, the year after Wood's death.

SELECT LIST OF WORKS
Arranged in chronological order

The following list of works by Vaughan Williams is less detailed than that given in the hardback edition of this book, but it includes most of his published compositions and some of the more significant of his unpublished and withdrawn works.

1897

1. SERENADE in A minor, for small orchestra.
   First perf.: Bournemouth, 4 April 1901. Bournemouth Municipal Orchestra, cond. Dan Godfrey.

1898

1. STRING QUARTET in C minor.
   First perf.: Oxford and Cambridge Musical Club, 30 June 1904.
2. QUINTET in D major, for clarinet, horn, violin, cello, and piano.
   First perf.: London, 5 June 1901.

* * * * *

A. THREE ELIZABETHAN SONGS: *Sweet Day* (Herbert), *The Willow Song* (Shakespeare, *Othello*), *O Mistress Mine* (Shakespeare, *Twelfth Night*). Composed probably between 1891 and 1896.
   First perf.: Shirehampton, 5 November 1913, Avonmouth and Shirehampton Choral Society, cond. R.V.W. Published 1913.
B. HOW CAN THE TREE BUT WITHER? (Vaux). Song for voice and piano.
   First perf.: London, 5 June 1907, Francis Harford (bass). Published 1934.
C. CLARIBEL (Tennyson). Song for voice and piano.
   First perf.: London, 2 December 1904, Beatrice Spencer (sop.), Hamilton Harty (piano). Published 1906.
D. COME AWAY DEATH (Shakespeare, *Twelfth Night*). Part-song. Published 1909.

1900

1. BUCOLIC SUITE, for orchestra.
   First perf.: Bournemouth, 10 March 1902. Bournemouth Municipal Orchestra, cond. Dan Godfrey.

1901

1. LINDEN LEA (Barnes). Song for voice and piano.
First perf.: Hooton Roberts, Rotherham, 4 September 1902, J. Milner (bass). First London perf.: 2 December 1902, Frederick Keel (bar.). Published 1902. Several other arrangements.

1902

1. REST (C. Rossetti) Part-song.
First perf.: London, 14 May 1902. Published *c.* 1904.
2. BLACKMWORE BY THE STOUR (Barnes). Song for voice and piano. *First perf.:* Hooton Roberts, 4 September 1902, J. Milner (bass). First London perf.: 27 November 1902, Campbell McInnes (bar.). Published 1902.
3. ENTLAUBET IST DER WALDE. German folk-song arr. for voice and piano.
First perf.: London, 27 November 1902, Campbell McInnes (bar.).

1903

1. SILENT NOON (D. G. Rossetti). Song for voice and piano.
First perf.: London, 10 March 1903, Francis Harford (bass). Published 1904.
2. WILLOW-WOOD (D. G. Rossetti). Cantata for baritone or mezzo-soprano and piano.
First perf.: London, 12 March 1903, Campbell McInnes (bar.), Evlyn Howard-Jones (piano). Published 1909.
3. SOUND SLEEP (C. Rossetti), for 3 female voices and piano.
First perf.: Spilsby, Lincs, 27 April 1903. Published 1903.
4. ORPHEUS WITH HIS LUTE (Shakespeare, *King Henry VIII*). Song for voice and piano.
First perf.: London, 2 December 1904, Beatrice Spencer (sop.), Hamilton Harty (piano). Published 1903, prob. comp. 1901.
5. REVEILLEZ-VOUS, PICCARS. Song for voice and piano.
First perf.: Eastbourne, 19 October 1903, Walter Ford (bar.). First London perf.: 11 February 1904, Francis Harford (bass). Published 1907.
6. QUINTET IN C MINOR, for piano, violin, viola, cello, and double bass. Withdrawn 1918. Principal theme of finale adapted for finale of Violin Sonata (1954, no. 4).

1904

1. IN THE FEN COUNTRY, symphonic impression for orchestra.
   First perf.: London, 22 February 1909, cond. Thomas Beecham.
   Published 1969.
2. THE HOUSE OF LIFE (D. G. Rossetti). Cycle of 6 songs for voice
   and piano. No. 2 is *Silent Noon* (*see* 1903, no. 1).
   First perf.: London, 2 December 1904, Edith Clegg (con.), Hamilton
   Harty (piano). Published 1904.
3. SONGS OF TRAVEL (R. L. Stevenson). Cycle of 9 songs for voice
   and piano. 1 The vagabond. 2 Let beauty awake. 3 The roadside fire.
   4 Youth and love. 5 In dreams. 6 The infinite shining heavens. 7
   Whither must I wander? 8 Bright is the ring of words. 9 I have trod
   the upward and the downward slope.
   First perf.: London, 2 December 1904, Walter Creighton (bar.),
   Hamilton Harty (piano). Published in 2 books, 1905 and 1907, no. 9
   not included until 1960.

1905

1. PAN'S ANNIVERSARY. Masque by Ben Jonson, music arr. by
   R.V.W., dances arr. by Holst.
   First perf.: Stratford-upon-Avon, 24 April 1905.
2. DREAMLAND (C. Rossetti). Song for voice and piano.
   First perf.: London, 31 October 1905, Gervase Elwes (tenor),
   Frederick Kiddle (piano). Published 1906.
3. A CRADLE SONG (S. T. Coleridge). For voice and piano. Probably
   comp. 1894. Published 1905.

1906

1. THE ENGLISH HYMNAL. Music edited by R.V.W., who arranged and harmonized many tunes and contributed 4 original tunes:
   (a) Come down, O Love divine (Down Ampney); (b) God be with
   you till we meet again (Randolph); (c) Hail thee, Festival day (Salve
   festa dies); (d) For all the Saints (Sine Nomine). Published 1906.
   Revised and enlarged edition 1933.
2. NORFOLK RHAPSODY No. 1 in E minor, for orch.
   First perf.: London, 23 August 1906, cond. Henry J. Wood. Rev. *c.*
   1922, published 1925.
3. NORFOLK RHAPSODIES No. 2 in D minor and No. 3 in G.
   First perf.: Cardiff, 27 September 1907, London Symphony Orchestra
   cond. R.V.W. First London perf.: 17 April 1912, New Symphony
   Orchestra, cond. Balfour Gardiner. Withdrawn after 1914.

1907

1. TOWARD THE UNKNOWN REGION (Whitman). Song for
chorus and orchestra.
First perf.: Leeds, 10 October 1907, Leeds Festival Chorus and
Orchestra, cond. R.V.W. First London perf.: Royal College of
Music, 10 December 1907, cond. Sir Charles Stanford. Published
1907.

1908

1. 15 FOLK SONGS FROM THE EASTERN COUNTIES, collected
and set with piano acc. by R.V.W. Published 1908.
2. BUONAPARTY (Hardy). Song for voice and piano. Published 1909.
3. THE SKY ABOVE THE ROOF (Verlaine, *tr.* M. Dearmer). Song
for voice and piano. Published 1909.
4. THREE NOCTURNES (Whitman), for baritone, semi-chorus, and
orchestra. Unpublished. Theme in *Sancta Civitas* (1925) taken from
no. 3, 'Out of the rolling ocean'.
5. STRING QUARTET NO. 1 IN G MINOR. Revised 1921.
First perf.: London, 8 November 1908, Schwiller Quartet. Published
1923.

1909

1. ON WENLOCK EDGE (A. E. Housman). Cycle of 6 songs for tenor,
piano, and string quartet. 1 On Wenlock Edge. 2 From far, from eve
and morning. 3. Is my team ploughing? 4 Oh when I was in love with
you. 5 Bredon Hill. 6 Clun.
First perf.: London, 15 November 1909, Gervase Elwes (tenor),
Frederick Kiddle (piano), Schwiller Quartet. Published 1911. Version
for tenor and orchestra, first perf.: London, 24 January 1924, John
Booth (tenor), cond. R.V.W.
2. (a) THE WASPS (Aristophanes). Incidental music for tenor and
baritone soloists, male chorus, and orchestra, for Cambridge Greek
Play production. Overture and 17 items.
First perf.: Cambridge, 26 November 1909, cond. Charles Wood.
Published 1909.
(b) THE WASPS, Aristophanic Suite for orchestra: 1 Overture. 2
Entr'acte. 3 March-Past of the Kitchen Utensils. 4 Entr'acte. 5 Ballet
and Final Tableau.
First perf.: London, 23 July 1912, New Symphony Orchestra, cond.
R.V.W. Published 1914.
3. A SEA SYMPHONY (Whitman). For soprano, baritone, mixed
chorus, and orchestra. Composed 1903–09.
First perf.: Leeds, 12 October 1910, Cicely Gleeson-White (sop.),

Campbell McInnes (bar.), Leeds Festival Chorus and Orchestra, cond. R.V.W. First London perf.: 4 February 1913, Agnes Nicholls (sop.), Campbell McInnes (bar.), Bach Choir, Queen's Hall Orchestra, cond. Hugh Allen. Revised 1910, 1918, and 1924. Published 1909.

1910

1. FANTASIA ON ENGLISH FOLK SONG: STUDIES FOR AN ENGLISH BALLAD OPERA, for orchestra.
   First perf.: London, 1 September 1910. cond. Henry J. Wood. Withdrawn.
2. FANTASIA ON A THEME BY THOMAS TALLIS, for double string orchestra and string quartet. Revised 1913 and 1919.
   First perf.: Gloucester, 6 September 1910, London Symphony Orchestra, cond. R.V.W. First London perf.: 11 February 1913, New Symphony Orchestra, cond. R.V.W. Published 1921.

1911

1. FIVE MYSTICAL SONGS (Herbert). For baritone, opt. chorus, and orchestra, or for baritone and piano, or baritone, piano, and string quintet. 1 Easter. 2 I got me flowers. 3 Love bade me welcome. 4 The Call. 5 Antiphon (Let all the world in every corner sing).
   First perf.: Worcester, 14 September 1911, Campbell McInnes (bar.), Three Choirs Festival Chorus, London Symphony Orchestra, cond. R.V.W. First London perf.: 21 November 1911, Campbell McInnes (bar.), Hamilton Harty (piano). Published 1911.

1912

1. PHANTASY QUINTET, for 2 violins, 2 violas, and cello.
   First perf.: London, 23 March 1914, London String Quartet, with James Lockyer (2nd viola). Published 1921.
2. FANTASIA ON CHRISTMAS CAROLS. For baritone, mixed chorus, and orchestra.
   First perf.: Hereford, 12 September 1912, Campbell McInnes (bar.)., Three Choirs Festival Chorus, London Symphony Orchestra, cond. R.V.W. First London perf.: 4 March 1913, Campbell McInnes (bar.), London Choral Society, New Symphony Orchestra, cond. R.V.W. Published 1912.
3. 15 FOLK SONGS OF ENGLAND, Vol. 1 (Sussex). Edited by Cecil Sharp, with piano acc. by R.V.W. and Albert Robins. Published 1912.

1913

1. O PRAISE THE LORD OF HEAVEN. Anthem for 2 choirs and semi-chorus.
   First perf.: London, St. Paul's Cathedral, 13 November 1913, London Church Choir Association, cond. Walford Davies. Published 1914.
2. FIVE ENGLISH FOLK SONGS. For unacc. mixed chorus. 1 The dark-eyed sailor. 2 The springtime of the year. 3 Just as the tide was flowing. 4 The lover's ghost. 5 Wassail song. Published 1913.
3. A LONDON SYMPHONY. For orchestra. I Lento – allegro risoluto. II Lento. III Scherzo – Nocturne, allegro vivace. IV Finale: Andante con moto – maestoso alla marcia (quasi lento) – allegro – maestoso alla marcia – Epilogue, andante sostenuto. Composed *c.* 1911–13.
   First perf.: (original version): London, 27 March 1914, Queen's Hall Orchestra, cond. Geoffrey Toye; first rev. version: London, 18 March 1918, New Queen's Hall Orchestra, cond. Adrian Boult; second rev. version: London, 4 May 1920, Queen's Hall Orchestra, cond. Albert Coates; third rev. version: London, 22 February 1934, London Philharmonic Orchestra, cond. Sir Thomas Beecham. Published 1920 and 1936 (1933 third rev.).
4. INCIDENTAL MUSIC for Shakespeare's plays at F. R. Benson's 1913 season at Stratford-upon-Avon: *The Merry Wives of Windsor, King Richard II, King Henry IV, Part 2, King Richard III, King Henry V.* The music chiefly consists of folk-song arrangements. Unpublished.

1914

1. FOUR HYMNS. For tenor and piano with viola obbligato; or string orchestra and viola obbligato; or piano and string quartet. Composed 1913–14. 1 Lord! Come away (J. Taylor). 2 Who is this fair one? (I. Watts). 3 Come love, come Lord (R. Crashaw). 4 Evening Hymn (tr. R. Bridges).
   First perf.: Cardiff, 26 May 1920, Steuart Wilson (tenor), Alfred Hobday (viola), London Symphony Orchestra, cond. Julius Harrison. First London perf.: 19 October 1920, Steuart Wilson (tenor), A. Hobday (viola), chamber orchestra cond. R.V.W. Published 1920.

1919

1. EIGHT TRADITIONAL ENGLISH CAROLS, arr. for voice and piano and for unacc. mixed chorus. 1 And all in the morning. 2 On Christmas night. 3 The twelve Apostles. 4 Down in yon forest. 5 May-day Carol. 6 The truth sent from above. 7 The birth of the Saviour. 8 The Wassail song. Published 1919.

1920

1. THREE PRELUDES FOR ORGAN, founded on Welsh hymn tunes. 1 Bryn Calfaria. 2 Rhosymedre. 3 Hyfrydol. Published 1920.

2. O CLAP YOUR HANDS (Text from Psalm 47). Motet for mixed chorus and organ, or brass, percussion, and organ. Published 1920.

3. TWELVE TRADITIONAL CAROLS FROM HEREFORDSHIRE, edited and arr. for voice and piano or unacc. mixed chorus. 1 The Holy Well (1st version). 2 The Holy Well (2nd version). 3 Christmas now is drawing near at hand. 4 Joseph and Mary. 5 The Angel Gabriel. 6 God rest you merry, gentlemen. 7 New Year's Carol. 8 On Christmas Day (All in the morning). 9 Dives and Lazarus. 10 The miraculous harvest. 11 The Saviour's love. 12 The Seven Virgins (Under the leaves). Published 1920.

4. THE LARK ASCENDING. Romance for violin and orchestra (or chamber orchestra) or for violin and piano. Composed 1914, rev. 1920. *First perf.:* Shirehampton, Glos., 15 December 1920, Marie Hall (violin), Geoffrey Mendham (piano). First London perf.: 14 June 1921, Marie Hall (violin), British Symphony Orchestra, cond. Adrian Boult. Published 1926.

5. SUITE OF SIX SHORT PIECES FOR PIANO. Published 1921. Arr. for string orchestra by James Brown, in collaboration with R.V.W., as *The Charterhouse Suite,* published 1923.

6. SUITE DE BALLET. For flute and piano. Composed *c.* 1913, rev. 1920. I Improvisation. II Humoresque – *presto.* III Gavotte – *quasi lento.* IV Passepied – *allegro vivacissimo.* *First perf.:* London, 20 March 1920, Louis Fleury (flute). Published 1961 (ed. R. Douglas).

1921

1. LORD, THOU HAST BEEN OUR REFUGE. Motet for mixed chorus, mixed semi-chorus, and orchestra (or organ). Text from Psalm 90. Hymn-tune 'O God our help in ages past' is used as descant. Published 1921.

2. MERCILESS BEAUTY. Three rondels for high voice and string trio (or piano). Words attrib. Chaucer but doubtfully. *First perf.:* London, 4 October 1921, Steuart Wilson (tenor) and string trio. Published 1922.

3. A PASTORAL SYMPHONY. For orchestra, with soprano (or tenor) voice. Composed 1916–21. I Molto moderato. II Lento moderato. III Moderato pesante. IV Lento. *First perf.:* London, 26 January 1922, Orchestra of Royal Philharmonic Society, cond. Adrian Boult, with Flora Mann (sop.). Minor revisions 1950–1. Published 1924, rev. edn. 1954.

1922

1. DIRGE FOR FIDELE (Shakespeare, *Cymbeline*). Song for two mezzo-sopranos and piano. Published 1922, composed prob. 1895.
2. O VOS OMNES ('IS IT NOTHING TO YOU?'). Motet for mixed double chorus, with alto solo.
   First perf.: London, Westminster Cathedral, 13 April 1922, cond. R. R. Terry. Published 1922. Eng. version adapted by M. Jacobson, published 1950.
3. IT WAS A LOVER AND HIS LASS (Shakespeare. *As You Like It*). Part-song for two voices and piano. Published 1922.
4. CA' THE YOWES (Burns). Scottish folk-song arr. for tenor solo and mixed chorus. Published 1922.
5. MASS IN G MINOR, for SATB soloists and double chorus. Composed 1920–1. I Kyrie. II Gloria in excelsis. III Credo. IV Sanctus – Osanna I, Benedictus, Osanna II. V Agnus Dei.
   First perf.: Birmingham, 6 December 1922, City of Birmingham Choir, cond. Joseph Lewis. First London and liturgical perf.: Westminster Cathedral, 12 March 1923, Westminster Cathedral Choir, cond. R. R. Terry. First London concert perf.: 7 April 1923, Wolverhampton Music Society, cond. Joseph Lewis. Published 1922. Adapted by M. Jacobson (with English words), and rev. by composer, as *Communion Service in G minor*. Published 1923.
6. THE SHEPHERDS OF THE DELECTABLE MOUNTAINS. Pastoral episode founded on Bunyan's *The Pilgrim's Progress*, set in 1 act for 6 soloists, women's chorus, and small orchestra.
   First perf.: London, Royal College of Music, 11 July 1922, cond. Arthur Bliss. Published 1925. This episode was incorporated, with final section omitted, into Act IV, scene 2 of Morality *The Pilgrim's Progress* (*see* 1951, no. 1).

1923

1. OLD KING COLE. Ballet for orchestra and opt. chorus, scenario by Mrs Edward Vulliamy in assoc. with composer.
   First perf.: Cambridge, 5 June 1923, cond. Boris Ord. Published 1924.
2. ENGLISH FOLK SONGS. Suite for military band. 1 March: 'Seventeen come Sunday'. 2 Intermezzo: 'My bonny boy'. 3 March: 'Folk Songs from Somerset'.
   First perf.: Twickenham, Kneller Hall, 4 July 1923, Band of Royal Military School of Music, cond. Lieut. H. E. Adkins. Published 1924. Transcribed by Gordon Jacob in 1924 for brass band (pub. 1956) and for full orchestra (pub. 1942). Arr. for piano by M. Mullinar, 1949.
3. SEA SONGS. Quick march for military and brass bands.
   First perf.: probably at British Empire Exhibition, Wembley, April 1924. Published 1924. Transcribed for full orchestra by R.V.W. in 1942. Published 1943.

4. LET US NOW PRAISE FAMOUS MEN (*Ecclesiasticus*, Ch. 44). Unison song, with acc. for piano, organ or small orchestra. Published 1923.
5. TWO PIECES FOR VIOLIN AND PIANO. 1 Romance. 2 Pastorale. Published 1923.

1924

1. TOCCATA MARZIALE. For military band.
First perf.: Wembley, British Empire Exhibition, 1924, Band of Royal Military School of Music, cond. Lieut. H. E. Adkins. Published 1924.
2. (a) HUGH THE DROVER, or LOVE IN THE STOCKS. Romantic ballad opera in 2 acts for 9 soloists, mixed chorus, and orchestra. Libretto by Harold Child, revised by R.V.W. and by Ursula Vaughan Williams. Composed 1910–14. Revised *c.* 1924, 1933 (extra scene, later withdrawn). and 1956. Libretto further rev. 1977.
First perf.: London, Royal College of Music, July 1924, cond. S. P. Waddington; first professional perf.: London, His Majesty's Theatre, 14 July 1924, cond. Malcolm Sargent. Published 1924, 1959, 1978.
(b) A COTSWOLD ROMANCE. Cantata for tenor, soprano, and baritone soloists, mixed chorus, and orchestra, adapted 1950 by M. Jacobson from opera *Hugh the Drover*.
First perf.: London, 10 May 1951, S.W. London Choral Society, Olive Groves (sop.), James Johnston (tenor), Arnold Matters (bar.), cond. Frank Odell. Published 1951.

1925

1. TWO POEMS BY SEUMAS O'SULLIVAN, for voice and piano. 1 The Twilight People. 2 A Piper.
First perf.: London, 27 March 1925, Steuart Wilson (tenor), Anthony Bernard (piano). Published 1925. O'Sullivan was pseudonym of James Starkey (1879–1958).
2. THREE SONGS FROM SHAKESPEARE, for voice and piano. 1 Take, O take those lips away (*Measure for Measure*). 2 When icicles hang by the wall (*Love's Labour's Lost*). 3 Orpheus with his lute (*King Henry VIII*).
First perf.: London, 27 March 1925, Steuart Wilson (tenor), Anthony Bernard (piano). Published 1925.
3. FOUR POEMS BY FREDEGOND SHOVE, for voice and piano. 1 Motion and Stillness (comp. 1922). 2 Four Nights. 3 The New Ghost. 4 The Water Mill.
First perf.: London, 27 March 1925, Steuart Wilson (tenor), Anthony Bernard (piano). Published 1925.
4. THREE POEMS BY WALT WHITMAN, for voice and piano. 1 Nocturne. 2 A Clear Midnight. 3 Joy, Shipmate, Joy! Published 1925.

5. FLOS CAMPI. Suite for solo viola, mixed chorus, and small orchestra. Each of the six movements is headed by a quotation in Latin from *The Song of Solomon*, but chorus part is wordless.
First perf.: London, 10 October 1925, Lionel Tertis (viola), voices from Royal College of Music, Queen's Hall Orchestra, cond. Sir Henry Wood. Published 1928.

6. SANCTA CIVITAS (The Holy City). Oratorio for baritone and tenor soloists, mixed chorus, semi-chorus, distant chorus (boys' voices preferred), and orchestra. Text from *Revelation* with additions from *Taverner's Bible* (1539) and other sources. Composed 1923–5.
First perf.: Oxford, 7 May 1926, Arthur Cranmer (bar.), Trefor Jones (tenor), Oxford Bach Choir and Orchestral Society, cond. H. P. Allen. First London perf.: 9 June 1926, Roy Henderson (bar.), Steuart Wilson (tenor), Bach Choir, London Symphony Orchestra, cond. R.V.W. Published 1925.

7. VIOLIN CONCERTO IN D MINOR (originally entitled *Concerto Accademico*). For violin and string orchestra. Composed 1924–5. I Allegro pesante. II Adagio – tranquillo. III Presto.
First perf.: London, 6 November 1925, Jelly d'Aranyi (violin), London Chamber Orchestra, cond. Anthony Bernard. Published 1927.

8. DAREST THOU NOW, O SOUL (Whitman). Unison song for voice and piano (or strings). Published 1925.

9. MAGNIFICAT AND NUNC DIMITTIS (THE VILLAGE SERVICE). For mixed chorus and organ. Published 1925.

10. SONGS OF PRAISE. Hymn book, joint music editors R.V.W. and Martin Shaw. Contained original tunes composed by R.V.W. for *The English Hymnal* (*see* 1906) and the following new tunes: 1 Saviour, again to Thy dear name (Magda). 2 The night is come like to the day (Oakley). 3 Servants of God (Cumnor). 4 England arise! the long, long night is over (Guildford). 5 At the name of Jesus (King's Weston). Also several arrangements by R.V.W. Published 1925.

1926

1. SIX STUDIES IN ENGLISH FOLK SONG. For cello (or violin, viola, or clarinet) and piano. I Adagio. II Andante sostenuto. III Larghetto. IV Lento. V Andante tranquillo. VI Allegro vivace.
First perf.: London, 4 June 1926, May Mukle (cello), Anne Mukle (piano). Published 1927.

2. ON CHRISTMAS NIGHT. Masque with dancing, singing, and miming, freely adapted from Dickens's *A Christmas Carol* by Adolf Bolm and R.V.W., with music devised by R.V.W. as a quodlibet of folk tunes and country dances.
First perf.: Chicago, Ill., 26 December 1926, Bolm Ballet, cond. Eric Delamarter. First English perf.: (as suite) London, 17 December

1929, cond. A. Bernard; (as ballet) Cecil Sharp House, 29 December 1935, cond. Imogen Holst. Published 1957.

1927

1. ALONG THE FIELD (Housman). Eight songs for voice and violin. 1 We'll to the woods no more. 2 Along the field. 3 The half-moon westers low. 4 In the morning. 5 The sigh that heaves the grasses. 6 Goodbye. 7 Fancy's Knell. 8 With rue my heart is laden.
First perf.: London (7 songs), 24 October 1927, Joan Elwes (sop.), Marie Wilson (violin). Rev. before publication 1954 (9th song being destroyed at this time).

1928

1. TE DEUM IN G. For male voices and organ or orchestra.
First perf.: Canterbury Cathedral, 4 December 1928 (enthronement of Dr C. G. Lang as Archbishop of Canterbury), cond. Walford Davies. Published 1928.
2. THE OXFORD BOOK OF CAROLS. Joint music editors, R.V.W. and Martin Shaw. Contains many R.V.W. arrangements and the following original tunes: 1 The Golden Carol. 2 Wither's Rocking Hymn. 3 Snow in the street. 4 Blake's Cradle Song. Published 1928.
3. (a) SIR JOHN IN LOVE. Opera in 4 acts, based on Shakespeare's *The Merry Wives of Windsor*, with interpolations from other authors and other plays by Shakespeare, for 20 solo singers, mixed chorus, and orchestra. Composed 1924–28.
First perf.: London, Royal College of Music, 21 March 1929, cond. Malcolm Sargent. Published 1930. *Prologue, Episode and Interlude* added optionally for Bristol performance on 30 October 1933, *Prologue* being later withdrawn. Published 1936.
(b) IN WINDSOR FOREST. Cantata for mixed chorus and orchestra, adapted from *Sir John in Love*. 1 Sigh no more, ladies. 2 Back and side go bare. 3 Round about in a fair ring-a. 4 See the chariot at hand. 5 Whether men do laugh or weep.
First perf.: Windsor, 9 November 1931, cond. R.V.W. Published 1931.

1929

1. BENEDICITE (from Apocrypha and John Austin's 'Hark, my soul'). For soprano, mixed chorus, and orchestra.
First perf.: Dorking, 2 May 1930, Margaret Rees (sop.), Leith Hill Festival Chorus and Orchestra, cond. R.V.W. First London perf.: Southwark Cathedral, 21 February 1931, choir and orch, cond. E. T. Cook, with Joan Elwes (sop.). Published 1929.

2. THE HUNDREDTH PSALM (Psalm 100 and Doxology from Daye's *Psalter* of 1561). For mixed chorus and orchestra.
First perf.: Dorking, 29 April 1930, Leith Hill Festival Chorus and Orchestra, cond. R.V.W. Published 1929.

3. THREE CHORAL HYMNS (tr. from German by Miles Coverdale). For baritone (or tenor), mixed chorus, and orchestra. 1 Easter Hymn. 2 Christmas Hymn. 3 Whitsunday Hymn.
First perf.: Dorking, 30 April 1930, Ian Glennie (tenor), Leith Hill Festival Chorus and Orchestra, cond. R.V.W. First London perf.: Southwark Cathedral, 21 February 1931, William Groves (tenor), chorus and orchestra cond. E. T. Cook. Published 1930.

4. THREE CHILDREN'S SONGS FOR A SPRING FESTIVAL. (Frances M. Farrer). For voices in unison with strings. 1 Spring. 2 The Singers. 3 An Invitation.
First perf.: Dorking, 1 May 1930, Leith Hill Festival Children's Choirs, cond. R.V.W. Published 1930.

5. FANTASIA ON SUSSEX FOLK TUNES. For cello and orchestra.
First perf.: London, 13 March 1930, Pablo Casals (cello), Orchestra of Royal Philharmonic Society, cond. John Barbirolli. Withdrawn by composer.

1930

1. HYMN TUNE PRELUDE ON 'SONG 13' BY ORLANDO GIBBONS. For piano. Composed 1928.
First perf.: London, 14 January 1930. Harriet Cohen (piano). Published 1930.

2. PRELUDE AND FUGUE IN C MINOR FOR ORCHESTRA (also arr. for organ). Composed 1921, revised 1923 and 1930.
First perf.: Hereford, 12 September 1930. London Symphony Orchestra, cond. R.V.W. Published (organ version only) 1930.

3. JOB, a Masque for Dancing, founded on William Blake's *Illustrations of the Book of Job*, in nine scenes and epilogue. I Introduction. Pastoral Dance. II Satan's Dance of Triumph. III Minuet of the Sons of Job and their wives. IV Job's Dream. V Dance of the Messengers. VI Dance of Job's Comforters. VII Elihu's Dance of Youth and Beauty, Pavane of the Sons of the Morning. VIII Galliard of the Sons of the Morning. Altar Dance. IX Epilogue.
First perf.: (concert version) Norwich, 23 October 1930, Queen's Hall Orchestra, cond. R.V.W. First public perf.: in London 3· December 1931, Orchestra of Royal Philharmonic Society, cond. Basil Cameron. First stage perf. (orch. reduced by C. Lambert): London, 5 July 1931, Camargo Society (Anton Dolin as Satan, John MacNair as Job), scenario by Geoffrey Keynes and Gwendolen Raverat, designs by G. Raverat, choreography by Ninette de Valois, cond. Constant Lambert. Published 1934 (piano arr. by V. Lasker 1931).

1931

1. SONGS OF PRAISE (enlarged edition). Extra original tunes by R.V.W.: 1 Into the woods my master went (Mantegna). 2 Servants of the great adventure (Marathon). 3 I vow to thee my country (Abinger). 4 Let us now praise famous men (Famous Men). 5 Fierce raged the tempest (White Gates). Published 1931.
2. PIANO CONCERTO IN C MAJOR. I Toccata. II Romanza. III Fuga chromatica, con finale alla tedesca. I and II composed 1926, III 1930–1.
First perf.: London, 1 February 1933, Harriet Cohen (piano), B.B.C. Symphony Orchestra, cond. Adrian Boult. Finale rev. after 1st performance. Published 1936. Arranged for 2 pianos and orchestra. by Joseph Cooper in collaboration with R.V.W., 1946, with further revision of finale. First perf.: London, 22 November 1946, Cyril Smith and Phyllis Sellick (pianos), London Philharmonic and London Symphony Orchestras, cond. Adrian Boult.

1932

1. MAGNIFICAT. For contralto, women's chorus, solo flute, and orchestra.
First perf.: Worcester, 8 September 1932, Astra Desmond (con.), Women of Three Choirs Festival Chorus, London Symphony Orchestra, cond. R.V.W. First London perf.: 1 May 1934, Blodwen Caerleon (con.), Philharmonic Choir, London Symphony Orchestra, cond. C. Kennedy Scott. Published 1932.

1933

1. THE RUNNING SET. Traditional Dance Tunes for orchestra.
First perf.: London, 6 January 1934, National Folk Dance Festival, cond. R.V.W. First concert perf.: London, 27 September 1934, B.B.C. Symphony Orchestra, cond. R.V.W. Published 1952 (2-piano arr. by V. Lasker and H. Bidder 1936).

1934

1. FANTASIA ON 'GREENSLEEVES'. Arranged for strings and harp (or piano), with optional flutes, by Ralph Greaves, adapted from opera *Sir John in Love* (*see* 1928).
First perf.: London 27 September 1934, B.B.C. Symphony Orchestra, cond. R.V.W. Published 1934. There are numerous other vocal and instrumental arrangements of 'Greensleeves'.

2. THE PILGRIM PAVEMENT (Margaret R. Partridge). Hymn for soprano, mixed chorus, and organ.
First perf.: New York, late in 1934. Published 1934.
3. SIX TEACHING PIECES FOR PIANO, in three books. Published 1934.
4. SUITE FOR VIOLA AND SMALL ORCHESTRA. I Prelude, Carol, Christmas Dance. II Ballad, moto perpetuo. III Musette, polka mélancolique, galop.
First perf.: London, 12 November 1934, Lionel Tertis (viola), London Philharmonic Orchestra, cond. Malcolm Sargent. Published 1963 (orch. part arr. for piano 1936).
5. FOLK SONGS FROM NEWFOUNDLAND, collected and edited by Maud Karpeles. Contains 15 piano accompaniments by R.V.W. for following songs and ballads: Sweet William's Ghost, The Cruel Mother, The Gypsy Laddie, The Bloody Gardener, The Maiden's Lament, Proud Nancy, The Morning Dew, The Bonny Banks of Virgie-O, Earl Brand, Lord Akeman, The Lover's Ghost, She's like the swallow, Young Floro, The winter's gone and past, The cuckoo. Published 1934.
6. SYMPHONY NO. 4 IN F MINOR. I Allegro. II Andante moderato. III Scherzo – *allegro molto.* IV Finale con Epilogo fugato – *allegro molto.* Composed 1931–4, last note of II rev. *c.* 1957.
First perf.: London, 10 April 1935, B.B.C. Symphony Orchestra, cond. Adrian Boult. Published 1935.

1935

1. TWO ENGLISH FOLK SONGS. For voice and violin. 1 Searching for lambs. 2 The Lawyer. Published 1935.
2. SIX ENGLISH FOLK SONGS. For voice and piano. 1 Robin Hood and the Pedlar. 2 The Ploughman. 3 One man, two men. 4 The Brewer. 5 Rolling in the dew. 6 King William. Published 1935.
3. FIVE TUDOR PORTRAITS (Skelton). Choral Suite in 5 movements for contralto (or mezzo-soprano), baritone, mixed chorus, and orchestra. 1 The Tunning of Elinor Rumming, *Ballad* (contralto, chorus, and orch.). 2 Pretty Bess, *Intermezzo* (baritone, chorus, and orch.). 3. Epitaph on John Jayberd of Diss, *Burlesca* (male chorus and orch.). 4 Jane Scroop (her lament for Philip Sparrow), *Romanza* (mezzo-soprano or contralto, women's chorus, and orch.). 5 Jolly Rutterkin, *Scherzo* (baritone, chorus, and orch.).
First perf.: Norwich, 25 September 1936, Astra Desmond (con.), Roy Henderson (bar.), Norwich Festival Chorus, London Philharmonic Orchestra, cond. R.V.W. First London perf.: 27 January 1937, Astra Desmond, Roy Henderson, Croydon Philharmonic Society, B.B.C. Chorus, B.B.C. Symphony Orchestra, cond. Sir Adrian Boult. Published 1935.

1936

1. NOTHING IS HERE FOR TEARS (Milton). Choral song for mixed chorus and piano, organ, or orchestra, composed upon death of King George V.
   First perf.: B.B.C. broadcast, 26 January 1936, B.B.C. Singers, cond. Sir Walford Davies. Published 1936.

2. THE POISONED KISS, OR THE EMPRESS AND THE NECRO-MANCER. Romantic Extravaganza in 3 acts, with spoken dialogue by Evelyn Sharp, for 12 soloists, mixed chorus, and orchestra. Composed 1927–9, rev. 1934–5, 1936–7, 1956–7, dialogue rev. by Ursula Vaughan Williams 1957 and 1965.
   First perf.: Cambridge Arts Theatre, 12 May 1936, cond. C. B. Rootham. First London perf.: Sadler's Wells, 18 May 1936, cond. R.V.W. Orig. casts included Margaret Ritchie, Ena Mitchell, Margaret Field-Hyde, Meriel St. Clair, Trefor Jones, and Geoffrey Dunn. Published 1936.

3. DONA NOBIS PACEM (Liturgy, Whitman, and John Bright). Cantata for soprano and baritone, mixed chorus, and orchestra. 1 Agnus Dei. 2 Beat! beat! drums! 3 Reconciliation. 4 Dirge for Two Veterans. 5 The Angel of Death. 6 Nation shall not lift up a sword against nation.
   First perf.: Huddersfield, 2 October 1936, Renée Flynn (soprano), Roy Henderson (baritone), Huddersfield Choral Society, Hallé Orchestra, cond. Albert Coates. First London public perf.: 5 February 1938. Elsie Suddaby (sop.), Redvers Llewellyn (bar.), Royal Choral Society, London Philharmonic Orchestra, cond. Malcolm Sargent. Published 1936.

4. RIDERS TO THE SEA. Play by J. M. Synge set to music in 1 act for 5 soloists, women's chorus, and orchestra. Composed 1925–32.
   First perf.: London, Royal College of Music, 30 November 1937, cond. Malcolm Sargent. Published 1936.

5. TWO HYMN-TUNE PRELUDES, for small orchestra. 1 Eventide. 2 Dominus regit me.
   First perf.: Hereford, 8 September 1936, London Symphony Orchestra, cond. R.V.W. Published London 1960.

1937

1. FLOURISH FOR A CORONATION. For mixed chorus and orchestra. Text selected from Old Testament, Chaucer, and Agincourt Song.
   First perf.: London, 1 April 1937, Philharmonic Choir, London Philharmonic Orchestra, cond. Sir Thomas Beecham. Published 1937.

2. FESTIVAL TE DEUM IN F MAJOR (founded on traditional themes). For mixed chorus and organ or orchestra.
First perf.: London, Westminster Abbey, 12 May 1937 (Coronation of King George VI). Special choir and orchestra, cond. Sir Adrian Boult. Published 1937.

1938

1. ENGLAND'S PLEASANT LAND. Music for a pageant by various composers, incl. R.V.W.
First perf.: Westcott, Surrey, 9 July 1938. R.V.W'.s contribution contained themes from 5th Symphony on which he was working.
2. SERENADE TO MUSIC (Shakespeare, *The Merchant of Venice*, Act v, Sc. 1). For 16 solo voices and orchestra. Composed for and dedicated to Sir Henry Wood on the occasion of his golden jubilee as a conductor 'in grateful recognition of his services to music'.
First perf.: London, 5 October 1938. Isobel Baillie, Lilian Stiles Allen, Elsie Suddaby, Eva Turner (sopranos), Margaret Balfour, Muriel Brunskill, Astra Desmond, Mary Jarred (contraltos), Parry Jones, Heddle Nash, Frank Titterton, Walter Widdop, (tenors), Norman Allin, Robert Easton, Roy Henderson, Harold Williams (basses), B.B.C. Symphony, London Symphony, London Philharmonic, and Queen's Hall Orchestras, cond. Sir Henry Wood. Published 1938 (vocal score), 1961 (full score). Other versions: (a) for orchestra (first perf.: London, 10 February 1940, London Symphony Orchestra, cond. Sir Henry Wood); (b) for 4 soloists, chorus, and orch.; (c) for chorus and orch.
3. DOUBLE TRIO. For string sextet. I Fantasia. II Scherzo ostinato. III Intermezzo (Homage to Henry Hall). IV Rondo. Composed 1938.
First perf.: London, 21 January 1939, Menges Sextet. Rev. version, first perf.: London, 12 October 1942, Menges Sextet. Withdrawn and rewritten. *See Partita* (1948, no. 1).
4. THE BRIDAL DAY. Masque (by Ursula Vaughan Williams) for baritone, speaker, dancers, mime, chorus, piccolo, flute, piano, and string quintet, founded on Spenser's *Epithalamion*. Composed 1938–9, rev. 1952–3.
First perf.: B.B.C. television, 5 June 1953, with Denis Dowling (bar.), Cecil Day Lewis (speaker), chorus and Wigmore Ensemble, cond. Stanford Robinson. Published 1956. *See also Epithalamion* (1957, no. 1.)

1939

1. SERVICES IN D MINOR (Morning, Communion, and Evening). For unison voices, mixed choir, and organ. Written for Christ's Hospital, Horsham, Sussex. Published London 1939.

2. FIVE VARIANTS OF 'DIVES AND LAZARUS'. For strings and harp(s). Introduction, Theme, and 5 Variants.
First perf.: New York, 10 June 1939, New York Philharmonic–Symphony Orchestra, cond. Sir Adrian Boult. First Eng. perf.: Bristol, 1 November 1939, B.B.C. Symphony Orchestra, cond. Sir Adrian Boult. Published 1940.

3. SUITE FOR PIPES (treble, alto, tenor, and bass). I Intrada. II Minuet and Trio. III Valse. IV Finale. Jig.
First perf.: Chichester, August 1939, Pipers' Guild Quartet. Published 1947.

1940

1. SIX CHORAL SONGS TO BE SUNG IN TIME OF WAR (Shelley). For unison voices with piano or orchestra. 1 A Song of Courage. 2 A Song of Liberty. 3 A Song of Healing. 4 A Song of Victory. 5 A Song of Pity, Peace, and Love. 6 A Song of the New Age.
First perf.: B.B.C. broadcast, 20 December 1940, B.B.C. Chorus and B.B.C. Symphony Orchestra, cond. Leslie Woodgate. Published 1940.

2. VALIANT FOR TRUTH (Bunyan). Motet for unaccompanied mixed chorus (or with organ or piano).
First perf.: London, St Michael's, Cornhill, 29 June 1942, St Michael's Singers, cond. Harold Darke.

3. FILM MUSIC FOR '49TH PARALLEL'. Film first shown London, 8 October 1941. Score played by London Symphony Orchestra, cond. Muir Mathieson.
(a) Prelude, *49th Parallel*. For orchestra. Published 1960.
(b) Song, 'The New Commonwealth', adapted from Prelude *49th Parallel*, text by Harold Child. For unison voices with piano or orch. Published 1943.
See also The Lake in the Mountains (1947, no. 4).

4. HOUSEHOLD MUSIC: 3 PRELUDES ON WELSH HYMN TUNES. For string quartet, or alternative instruments, and optional horn. 1 Crug-y-bar (Fantasia). II St. Denio (Scherzo). III Aberystwyth (8 variations).
First perf.: London, 4 October 1941, Blech String Quartet. Published 1943.

1941

1. ENGLAND, MY ENGLAND (Henley). Choral song for baritone, double chorus, unison voices, and orch. (or with piano).
First perf.: B.B.C. broadcast, 16 November 1941, Dennis Noble (bar.), B.B.C. Chorus, B.B.C. Symphony Orchestra, cond. Sir Adrian Boult. Published 1941.

1942

1. FILM MUSIC FOR 'COASTAL COMMAND'. Film first shown,
   London, 16 October 1942. Score played by R.A.F. Symphony
   Orchestra, cond. Muir Mathieson.
   (a) Suite of 7 movements, arr. Mathieson.
   First perf.: B.B.C. broadcast, 17 September 1942, B.B.C. Northern
   Orchestra, cond. Muir Mathieson (6 movements only perf.).
2. FIVE WARTIME HYMNS (Briggs). For unison voices with piano
   or organ, by R.V.W., Martin Shaw, and Ivor Atkins. R.V.W.'s
   contribution was: 1 A hymn of Freedom. 2 A call to the free nations.
   Published 1942.
3. THE AIRMEN'S HYMN (Lytton). Unison song with piano or
   organ. Published 1942.
4. NINE CAROLS. Arr. for unacc. men's chorus. 1 God rest you merry.
   2 As Joseph was a-walking (Cherry Tree Carol). 3 Mummers' carol.
   4 The First Nowell (baritone and chorus). 5 The Lord at first. 6
   Coventry Carol. 7 I saw three ships (baritone and chorus). 8 A Virgin
   most pure. 9 Dives and Lazarus. Published 1942.
5. INCIDENTAL MUSIC FOR 'THE PILGRIM'S PROGRESS'.
   Composed 1942 for B.B.C. broadcast adaptation of Bunyan's allegory
   by Edward Sackville-West.
   First broadcast: 5 September 1943, John Gielgud as Christian,
   Margaret Godley (sop.), Margaret Rolfe (con.), Bradbridge White
   (tenor), Stanley Riley (bar.), B.B.C. Chorus and B.B.C. Symphony
   Orchestra, cond. Sir Adrian Boult. *See also The Pilgrim's Progress*
   (1951, no. 1).

1943

1. SYMPHONY NO. 5 IN D MAJOR. For full orchestra. Composed
   1938–43, rev. 1951. I Preludio – Moderato. II Scherzo – presto. III
   Romanza – Lento. IV Passacaglia – moderato.
   First perf.: London, 24 June 1943. London Philharmonic Orchestra,
   cond. R. V. W. Published 1946, rev. score 1961. Some of the themes
   of this symphony were adapted from the then unfinished opera *The
   Pilgrim's Progress* (1951, no. 1).
2. FILM MUSIC FOR 'THE PEOPLE'S LAND'. Film first shown,
   London, 17 March 1943. Score played by London Symphony Orchestra, cond. Muir Mathieson. Music founded on traditional tunes.
3. FILM MUSIC FOR 'FLEMISH FARM'. Film first shown London,
   12 August 1943. Score played by London Symphony Orchestra, cond.
   Muir Mathieson.
   (a) Suite, *Story of a Flemish Farm*. 7 movements.
   First perf.: London, 31 July 1945, London Symphony Orchestra,
   cond. R.V.W.

1944

1. OBOE CONCERTO IN A MINOR, with strings. I Rondo Pastorale – allegro moderato. II Minuet and Musette – allegro moderato. III Finale (Scherzo) – Presto – lento – presto.
   First perf.: Liverpool, 30 September 1944. Léon Goossens (oboe), Liverpool Philharmonic Orchestra, cond. Malcolm Sargent. First London perf.: 4 May 1945, Léon Goossens (oboe), Bromley and Chislehurst Orchestra, cond. Marjorie Whyte. Published 1947.
2. STRING QUARTET NO. 2 IN A MINOR (FOR JEAN ON HER BIRTHDAY). I Prelude – allegro appassionato. II Romance – Largo. III Scherzo – allegro. IV Epilogue. Greetings from Joan to Jean – andante sostenuto. I and II composed 1942–3, III and IV 1943–4.
   First perf.: London (National Gallery) 12 October 1944, Menges String Quartet. Note: 'Jean' is Jean Stewart, violist of Menges Quartet. 'From Joan to Jean' is reference to fact that theme of this movement was taken from music for projected film about Joan of Arc. Main theme of scherzo adapted from film music for *49th Parallel.* Published 1947.
3. THANKSGIVING FOR VICTORY. For soprano, speaker, mixed chorus, and orchestra. Words from Bible, Shakespeare, and Kipling.
   First perf.: B.B.C. studio, 5 November 1944, recording for transmission when victory was achieved (relayed on 13 May 1945). Elsie Suddaby (sop.), Valentine Dyall (speaker), B.B.C. Chorus, children's choir from Thomas Coram Schools, B.B.C. Symphony Orchestra, cond. Sir Adrian Boult. Published 1945. Work renamed *A Song of Thanksgiving* 1952.
4. FILM MUSIC FOR 'STRICKEN PENINSULA'. Film first shown October 1945. Score played by London Symphony Orchestra, cond. Muir Mathieson.

1945

1. TWO CAROLS. Arr. for unacc. mixed chorus. 1 Come love we God. 2 There is a flower. Published 1945.

1946

1. INTRODUCTION AND FUGUE FOR TWO PIANOS.
   First perf.: London, 23 March 1946, Cyril Smith and Phyllis Sellick. Published 1947.
2. FILM MUSIC FOR 'THE LOVES OF JOANNA GODDEN'. Film first shown London, 16 June 1947. Score played by Philharmonia Orchestra, cond. Ernest Irving.

1947

1. THE SOULS OF THE RIGHTEOUS (*Wisdom of Solomon*). Motet for treble (or soprano), tenor, and baritone, and mixed chorus (unaccompanied).
   First perf.: London, Westminster Abbey, 10 July 1947, dedication of Battle of Britain Chapel. First concert perf.: London, 30 April 1948. Tudor Singers, cond. Harry Stubbs. Published 1947.
2. THE VOICE OUT OF THE WHIRLWIND. Motet for mixed chorus and organ or orchestra. Adapted from 'Galliard of the Sons of the Morning' (Scene VIII of *Job*, 1930).
   First perf.: London, St Sepulchre's Church, 22 November 1947, combined choirs cond. J. Dykes Bower, with W. McKie (organ). First perf. with orch.: Dorking, 16 June 1951, Leith Hill Festival Chorus and Surrey Philharmonic Orchestra, cond. R.V.W. Published 1947.
3. SYMPHONY NO. 6 IN E MINOR. For full orchestra. Composed 1944–7, scherzo rev. 1950. I Allegro. II Moderato. III Scherzo – allegro vivace. IV Epilogue – Moderato.
   First perf.: London, 21 April 1948, B.B.C. Symphony Orchestra, cond. Sir Adrian Boult. Published 1948, revised impression 1950.
4. THE LAKE IN THE MOUNTAINS. For piano. Based on episode from music to *49th Parallel* (1940, no. 3). Published 1947.

1948

1. PARTITA FOR DOUBLE STRING ORCHESTRA. Rewritten version (1946–8) of Double Trio (*see* 1938, no. 3) with new finale (Fantasia).
   First perf.: B.B.C. broadcast, 20 March 1948, B.B.C. Symphony Orchestra cond. Sir Adrian Boult. First public perf.: London, 29 July 1948, B.B.C. Symphony Orchestra, cond. R.V.W. Published 1948.
2. PRAYER TO THE FATHER OF HEAVEN (Skelton). Motet for unacc. mixed chorus.
   First perf.: Oxford, 12 May 1948, Oxford Bach Choir, cond. Thomas Armstrong. Composed for centenary of birth of Hubert Parry and dedicated to his memory. Published 1948.
3. FILM MUSIC FOR 'SCOTT OF THE ANTARCTIC'. Composed 1947–8. Film first shown, London, 29 November 1948. Score played by Philharmonia Orchestra, cond. Ernest Irving. See *Sinfonia Antartica* (1952, no. 2).

1949

1. FOLK SONGS OF THE FOUR SEASONS. Cantata based on traditional folk-songs, for women's voices and orchestra. *Prologue:* To

the Ploughboy. *Spring:* Early in the Spring, The Lark in the Morning, May Song. *Summer:* Summer is a-coming in and The Cuckoo, The Sprig of Thyme, The Sheep-Shearing, The Green Meadow. *Autumn:* John Barleycorn, The Unquiet Grave, An Acre of Land. *Winter:* Children's Christmas Song, Wassail Song, In Bethlehem City, God bless the Master.

First perf.: London, 15 June 1950, Massed Choirs of National Federation of Women's Institutes, London Symphony Orchestra, cond. Sir Adrian Boult. Published 1950. Songs available separately.

(a) Suite for small orchestra from *Folk Songs of the Four Seasons,* arr. by Roy Douglas. I To the Ploughboy and May Song. II The Green Meadow and An Acre of Land. III The Sprig of Thyme and The Lark in the Morning. IV The Cuckoo. V Wassail Song and Children's Christmas Song. Published 1956.

2. AN OXFORD ELEGY (Arnold). For speaker, mixed chorus, and small orchestra. Words adapted by composer from *The Scholar Gipsy* and *Thyrsis.*
   First perf. (private): Dorking, 20 November 1949, Steuart Wilson (speaker), Tudor Singers, Schwiller String Quartet, Michael Mullinar (piano), cond. R.V.W. First public perf.: Oxford, 19 June 1952, Steuart Wilson (speaker), Eglesfield Musical Society, orch. cond. Bernard Rose. First London perf.: 22 March 1953, Clive Carey (speaker), St. Martin-in-the-Fields cantata choir and orchestra, cond. John Churchill. Published 1952.

3. FANTASIA (QUASI VARIAZIONE) ON THE 'OLD 104TH' PSALM TUNE. For piano, mixed chorus, and orchestra.
   First perf. (private): Dorking, 20 November 1949, Michael Mullinar (piano), Tudor Singers, Schwiller String Quartet, cond. R.V.W. First public perf.: Gloucester, 6 September 1950, Michael Mullinar (piano), Three Choirs Festival Chorus, London Symphony Orchestra, cond. R.V.W. First London perf.: 15 September 1950, Michael Mullinar (piano), Royal Choral Society, B.B.C. Symphony Orchestra, cond. Sir Malcolm Sargent. Published 1950.

4. FILM MUSIC FOR 'DIM LITTLE ISLAND'. Film first shown, Edinburgh Film Festival 1949. Score cond. John Hollingsworth.

1950

1. CONCERTO GROSSO FOR STRINGS. I Intrada. II Burlesca ostinata. III Sarabande. IV Scherzo. V March and Reprise. Written for three groups of strings: (a) Concertino, skilled. (b) Tutti, all who can play a 3rd position and simple double stops. (c) Ad lib., less experienced.
   First perf.: London, 18 November 1950, massed orchestra of Rural Music Schools' Association, cond. Sir Adrian Boult. Published 1950.

2. FILM MUSIC FOR 'BITTER SPRINGS'. Film first shown,

London, 10 July 1950. Score played by Philharmonia Orchestra, cond. Ernest Irving.

3. THE SONS OF LIGHT (U. Vaughan Williams). Cantata for mixed chorus and orchestra. I Darkness and Light – allegro maestoso. II The Song of the Zodiac – allegretto pesante. III The Messengers of Speech – maestoso.
First perf.: London, 6 May 1951, massed choir of Schools' Music Association of Great Britain, London Philharmonic Orchestra, cond. Sir Adrian Boult. Published 1951.
(a) SUN, MOON, STARS, AND MAN. Cycle of 4 songs for unison voices with accompaniment for strings and/or piano, based on sections of the cantata *The Sons of Light*. Poems by Ursula Vaughan Williams (Ursula Wood). I Horses of the Sun – allegro alla marcia. II The Rising of the Moon – Lento. III The Procession of the Stars – allegro moderato. IV The Song of the Sons of Light – maestoso alla marcia.
First perf.: Birmingham, 11 March 1955, City of Birmingham Symphony Orchestra and schools' choir, cond. Desmond MacMahon. Published 1954.

1951

1. THE PILGRIM'S PROGRESS (Bunyan). Morality in Prologue, 4 acts, and Epilogue, libretto adapted from Bunyan's allegory by composer, with interpolations from the Bible and verse by Ursula Vaughan Williams. For 34 soloists (11 sufficient with doubling, etc.), mixed chorus, and orchestra. Composed *c.* 1921–1951.
First perf.: London, Royal Opera House, Covent Garden, 26 April 1951, with Arnold Matters (Pilgrim), Inia te Wiata (Bunyan), Norman Walker (Evangelist), Bryan Drake (Watchful), Geraint Evans (Herald), Michael Langdon (Apollyon), Parry Jones (Mr By-Ends), Adèle Leigh (Voice of a Bird), Covent Garden Chorus and Orchestra, cond. Leonard Hancock, prod. Nevill Coghill. Published 1952.
(a) SEVEN SONGS FROM 'THE PILGRIM'S PROGRESS'. For voice and piano. 1 Watchful's Song. 2 The Song of the Pilgrim. 3 The Pilgrim's Psalm. 4 The Song of the Leaves of Life and the Water of Life. 5 The Song of Vanity Fair. 6 The Woodcutter's Song. 7 The Bird's Song. Published 1952.
(b) THE 23RD PSALM, arr. by John Churchill, for soprano and unacc. mixed chorus. Published 1953.
(c) PILGRIM'S JOURNEY. Cantata for soprano, tenor, and baritone, mixed chorus, and orchestra (or organ), devised by Christopher Morris and Roy Douglas in 1962 from the Morality *The Pilgrim's Progress*. 1 Cast thy burden upon the Lord. 2 Into thy hands, O Lord. 3 Who would true valour see. 4 Unto him that overcometh. 5 Vanity Fair. 6 He that is down. 7 The Lord is my Shepherd. 8 Alleluia.
First perf.: Dorking, 26 April 1963, Iris Kells (sop.), Kenneth Bowen

(tenor), John Noble (bar.), Leith Hill Festival Chorus and Orchestra, cond. William Cole. Published 1962.

2. THREE SHAKESPEARE SONGS. For unacc. mixed chorus. 1 Full fathom five (*The Tempest*). 2 The cloud-capp'd towers (*The Tempest*). 3 Over hill, over dale (*A Midsummer Night's Dream*).
First perf.: London, 23 June 1951, combined choirs of British Federation of Music Festivals, cond. C. Armstrong Gibbs. Published 1951.

3. ROMANCE IN D FLAT FOR HARMONICA, STRINGS, AND PIANO. Andante tranquillo – poco animando – allegro moderato.
First perf.: New York, 3 May 1952, Larry Adler (harmonica), Little Symphony Orchestra, cond. Daniel Saidenberg. First Eng. perf.: Liverpool, 16 June 1952, Larry Adler (harmonica), Liverpool Philharmonic Orchestra, cond. Hugo Rignold. First London perf.: 6 September 1952, Larry Adler (harmonica), B.B.C. Symphony Orchestra, cond. Sir Malcolm Sargent. Published 1953.

1952

1. IN THE SPRING (Barnes). Song for voice and piano. Published 1952.
2. SINFONIA ANTARTICA. For full orchestra, soprano, and women's chorus. Composed 1949–52. I Prelude – andante maestoso. II Scherzo – moderato – poco animando. III Landscape – Lento. IV Intermezzo – andante sostenuto. V Epilogue – alla marcia moderato (ma non troppo). Some of themes are derived from film music for *Scott of the Antarctic* (1948, no. 3).
First perf.: Manchester, 14 January 1953, Margaret Ritchie (sop.), women of Hallé Choir, The Hallé Orchestra, cond. Sir John Barbirolli. First London perf.: by same artists, 21 January 1953. Published 1953.

3. O TASTE AND SEE (Psalm 34). Motet for unaccompanied mixed chorus with organ introduction.
First perf.: London, Westminster Abbey, 2 June 1953 (Coronation of Queen Elizabeth II), choristers of Abbey, cond. Sir William McKie. Published 1953.

1953

1. SILENCE AND MUSIC (U. Vaughan Williams). For unaccompanied mixed chorus. No. 4 of *A Garland for The Queen*, in which 10 British composers and 10 British poets paid tribute to the Queen in the manner of the first Elizabethan *The Triumphs of Oriana*.
First perf.: London, 1 June 1953, Cambridge University Madrigal Society and Golden Age Singers, cond. Boris Ord. Published 1953.

2. THE OLD HUNDREDTH PSALM TUNE (All People that on Earth do dwell). Arr. for mixed chorus, congregation, orchestra, and organ.

First perf.: London, Westminster Abbey, 2 June 1953 (Coronation of Queen Elizabeth II), special Coronation Choir and Orchestra, with trumpeters of Royal Military School of Music, cond. Sir William McKie. First concert perf.: Manchester, 27 October 1957, The Hallé Choir and Orchestra, cond. Sir John Barbirolli. Published 1953.

3. PRELUDE ON AN OLD CAROL TUNE. For small orchestra. Founded on incidental music for radio adaptation of Hardy's *The Mayor of Casterbridge,* composed in 1950.
First perf.: King's Lynn, 31 July 1953, Boyd Neel Orchestra, cond. R.V.W. Published 1953.

1954

1. TE DEUM AND BENEDICTUS. Set to metrical psalm tunes for unison voices or mixed voices with accompaniment of organ, harmonium, or piano. Published 1954.

2. BASS TUBA CONCERTO IN F MINOR. I Allegro moderato. II Romanza – andante sostenuto. III Finale – Rondo alla tedesca.
First perf.: London, 13 June 1954, Philip Catelinet (tuba), London Symphony Orchestra, cond. Sir John Barbirolli. Published 1955.

3. HODIE (THIS DAY). Christmas cantata for soprano (or mezzo-soprano), tenor, and baritone, mixed chorus, boys' voices, organ (opt.), and orchestra. Composed 1953–4. 1 Prologue (Vespers for Christmas Day). 2 Narration (Bible). 3 Song, soprano, women's chorus, and orch. (Milton). 4 Narration (Bible). 5 Choral (Coverdale, after Luther). 6 Narration (Bible and Prayer Book). 7 The Oxen, baritone and orch. (Hardy). 8 Narration (Bible). 9 Pastoral, baritone and orch. (Herbert). 10 Narration (Bible). 11 Lullaby, soprano, women's chorus, and orch. (W. Ballet). 12 Hymn, tenor and orch. (Drummond). 13 Narration (Bible). 14 The March of the Three Kings (U. Vaughan Williams). 15 Choral (Anon. and U. Vaughan Williams). 16 Epilogue (Bible and Milton).
First perf.: Worcester, 8 September 1954, Nancy Evans (mezzo-sop.), Eric Greene (tenor), Gordon Clinton (bar.), Three Choirs Festival Chorus, London Symphony Orchestra, cond. R.V.W. First London perf.: 19 January 1955, soloists as above, B.B.C. Chorus and Choral Society, boys of Watford Grammar School, B.B.C. Symphony Orchestra, cond. Sir Malcolm Sargent. Published 1954.

4. VIOLIN SONATA IN A MINOR. I Fantasia – allegro giusto. II Scherzo – allegro furioso ma non troppo. III Tema con Variazione – andante – allegro.
First perf.: B.B.C. broadcast, 12 October 1954, Frederick Grinke (violin), Michael Mullinar (piano). First public perf.: Rochester, New York, 14 November 1955, Josef Szigeti (violin), Carlo Bussotti (piano). First public perf. in England: London, 20 December 1955, Grinke and Mullinar. Published 1956. Note: Theme of Finale taken from Piano Quintet in C minor (*see* 1903, no. 6).

5. HEART'S MUSIC (Campion). Song for unaccompanied mixed chorus.
First perf.: London, St Sepulchre's Church, 25 November 1954, St Thomas's Hospital Choir, cond. Wilfrid Dykes Bower. Published 1955.

6. MENELAUS ON THE BEACH AT PHAROS (U. Vaughan Williams). Song for medium voice and piano.
First perf.: New York, 14 November 1954, Keith Falkner (bar.), Christabel Falkner (piano). First London perf.: 26 May 1955, Keith Falkner (bar.), Michael Mullinar (piano). Published 1960. Incorporated into *Four Last Songs (see* 1958, no. 2) as 'Menelaus'.

7. THREE GAELIC SONGS. Arr. for unacc. mixed chorus. 1 Dawn on the hills. 2 Come let us gather cockles. 3 Wake and rise. (Gaelic words available). Published 1963.

1955

1. PRELUDE ON THREE WELSH HYMN TUNES. For brass band. Tunes are *Ebenezer, Calfaria,* and *Hyfrydol.*
First perf.: B.B.C. broadcast, 12 March 1955, International Staff Band of Salvation Army, cond. Bernard Adams. First public perf.: London, 19 March 1955, by same artists. Published 1955.

2. SYMPHONY NO. 8 IN D MINOR. For full orchestra. Composed 1953–5, rev. 1956. I Fantasia (Variazioni senza Tema). II Scherzo alla marcia (for wind instruments). III Cavatina (for strings). IV Toccata.
First perf.: Manchester, 2 May 1956, The Hallé Orchestra, cond. Sir John Barbirolli. First London perf.: 14 May 1956, by same artists. Published 1956.

3. FILM MUSIC FOR 'THE ENGLAND OF ELIZABETH'. Film first shown, London, March 1957. Score played by Sinfonia of London, cond. John Hollingsworth.
    (a) THREE PORTRAITS FROM 'THE ENGLAND OF ELIZABETH'. Concert Suite adapted by Muir Mathieson. I Explorer. II Poet. III Queen. Published 1964.
    (b) TWO SHAKESPEARE SKETCHES FROM 'THE ENGLAND OF ELIZABETH'. Adapted for concert use by Muir Mathieson. I Allegro moderato ('The wind and the rain)'. II Allegretto ('It was a lover and his lass'). Published 1964.

1956

1. A VISION OF AEROPLANES (*Ezekiel*). Motet for mixed chorus and organ.
First perf.: London, St Michael's, Cornhill, 4 June 1956, St Michael's Singers, cond. Harold Darke, with John Birch (organ). Published 1956.

2. A CHORAL FLOURISH (*Psalm 32*). For mixed chorus with introduction for organ or 2 trumpets.
First perf.: London, 3 November 1956, Royal Choral Society, Bach Choir, Croydon Philharmonic Society, St Michael's Singers, cond. Reginald Jacques. Published 1956.
3. TWO ORGAN PRELUDES, FOUNDED ON WELSH FOLK SONGS. I Romanza ('The White Rock'). II Toccata ('St. David's Day'). Published 1956.

1957

1. EPITHALAMION (Spenser). Cantata founded on masque *The Bridal Day* (1938, no. 4), for baritone, mixed chorus, and small orchestra. Text chosen by Ursula Vaughan Williams from Spenser's *Epithalamion*. 1 Prologue. 2 Wake now. 3 The Calling of the bride. 4 The Minstrels. 5 Procession of the bride. 6 The temple gates. 7 The Bellringers. 8 The lover's song. 9 The minstrel's song. 10 Song of the winged loves. 11 Prayer to Juno.
First perf.: London, 30 September 1957, Gordon Clinton (baritone), Goldsmiths' Choral Union Cantata Singers, Royal Philharmonic Orchestra, cond. Richard Austin. Published 1957.
2. VARIATIONS. For brass band. Theme and 11 variations.
First perf.: London, 26 October 1957, test-piece for National Brass Band Championship of Great Britain. Published 1957. Arranged for orchestra by Gordon Jacob, first perf.: Birmingham, 8 January 1960, City of Birmingham Symphony Orchestra, cond. Sir Adrian Boult. First London perf.: 5 May 1960, London Philharmonic Orchestra, cond. Sir Adrian Boult.
3. SYMPHONY NO. 9 IN E MINOR. For full orchestra. Composed 1956–7, revised 1958. I Allegro moderato. II Andante sostenuto. III Scherzo – allegro pesante. IV Allegro tranquillo.
First perf.: London, 2 April 1958, Royal Philharmonic Orchestra, cond. Sir Malcolm Sargent. Published 1958.
4. TEN BLAKE SONGS. For voice and oboe. 1 Infant joy. 2 A Poison Tree. 3 The Piper. 4 London. 5 The Lamb. 6 The shepherd. 7 Ah! sunflower. 8 Cruelty has a human heart. 9 The divine image. 10 Eternity. Written for film *The Vision of William Blake* (first shown London, 10 October 1958) only 8 songs being used (excluding nos. 2 and 3). Performed by Wilfred Brown (tenor) and Janet Craxton (oboe). First concert perf.: B.B.C. broadcast, 8 October 1958, Wilfred Brown and Janet Craxton. First public perf.: London, 14 November 1958, same artists. Published 1958.

1958

1. THREE VOCALISES. For soprano and clarinet in B flat. I Prelude. II Scherzo. III Quasi menuetto.
   First perf.: Manchester, 8 October 1958, Margaret Ritchie (sop.), Keith Puddy (clarinet). First London perf.: B.B.C. broadcast, 22 December 1958, Margaret Ritchie (sop.), Gervase de Peyer (clarinet). Published 1960.
2. FOUR LAST SONGS (U. Vaughan Williams). For medium voice and piano. Composed 1954–8. 1 Procris. 2 Tired. 3 Hands, Eyes, and Heart. 4 Menelaus (*see* 1954, no. 6).
   First perf.: as cycle B.B.C. broadcast, 3 August 1960, Pamela Bowden (con.), Ernest Lush (piano). Published 1960.
3. THE FIRST NOWELL. Nativity play for soloists, mixed chorus, and orchestra, adapted from medieval pageants by Simona Pakenham, with music composed and arranged from traditional tunes by R.V.W., with additions after R.V.W.'s death by Roy Douglas.
   First perf.: London, 19 December 1958, soloists and St Martin-in-the-Fields Concert Orchestra and Singers, cond. John Churchill. Published 1959.

POSTHUMOUS

Undatable: ROMANCE FOR VIOLA AND PIANO.
First perf.: London, 19 January 1962. Bernard Shore (viola), Eric Gritton (piano). Published 1962, ed. Shore and Gritton.

UNCOMPLETED

1. CELLO CONCERTO. Sketches 1942–3. Three movements: Rhapsody, Lento, Finale. Intended for Casals.
2. THOMAS THE RHYMER. Opera in three acts to libretto by U. Vaughan Williams based on ballads *Thomas the Rhymer* and *Tam Lin*. Completed in piano and vocal score, but not scored and not revised.

SELECT BIBLIOGRAPHY

National Music (text of lectures delivered at Bryn Mawr, Penn., 1932), by R. Vaughan Williams. (London, 1934, reprinted with other essays by R.V.W., 1963).

A Musical Autobiography, by R. Vaughan Williams, in H. Foss's *Ralph Vaughan Williams: a study* (1950).

Some Thoughts on Beethoven's Choral Symphony, with writings on other musical subjects, by R. Vaughan Williams (London, 1953), reprinted in *National Music and other essays*, London, 1963).

The Making of Music (text of lectures delivered at Cornell University, New York, 1954), by R. Vaughan Williams (New York, 1955, reprinted in *National Music and other essays*, London, 1963).

Heirs and Rebels, letters between Vaughan Williams and Holst. Edited by Ursula Vaughan Williams and Imogen Holst (London, 1959).

Ralph Vaughan Williams: a study, by Hubert Foss (London, 1950).

The Music of Ralph Vaughan Williams, by Frank Howes (London, 1954).

Vaughan Williams, by Percy M. Young (London, 1955).

Ralph Vaughan Williams: a discovery of his music, by Simona Pakenham (London, 1957).

Vaughan Williams (Master Musicians Series) by James Day (London, 1961, 2nd edn, 1974).

Vaughan Williams, by A. E. F. Dickinson (London, 1963).

R. V. W.: a biography, by Ursula Vaughan Williams (London, 1964).

Vaughan Williams Symphonies (B.B.C. Music Guide) by Hugh Ottaway (London, 1972).

Classified List of Works

(U = Unpublished)

CHAMBER MUSIC

CHORUS (and/or Solo Singers) AND ORCHESTRA

CHURCH MUSIC
(Motets, Anthems, etc., excluding Hymns and major works for chorus and full orchestra)

DANCING, WORKS FOR. (MASQUES AND BALLETS)

FILM MUSIC
(all unpublished in original form)

FOLK-DANCE ARRANGEMENT

FOLK-SONG AND CAROL ARRANGEMENTS AND COLLECTIONS, BRITISH AND GERMAN

HYMNALS AND HYMN-TUNES

INSTRUMENTAL SOLOIST WITH ORCHESTRA

JUVENILIA (1878–95)
LEITH HILL PLACE, CHARTERHOUSE, R.C.M. AND CAMBRIDGE
(All these works were unpublished with the exception of 'A Cradle Song')

MISCELLANEOUS

ORCHESTRAL MUSIC
(A) BRASS BAND

ORCHESTRAL MUSIC
(B) FULL ORCHESTRA OR STRINGS ONLY

ORCHESTRAL MUSIC
(C) MILITARY BAND

ORGAN WORKS

PAGEANTS

PIANOFORTE MUSIC (SOLO AND TWO PIANOFORTES)

RADIO INCIDENTAL MUSIC

SKETCHES OF UNFINISHED WORKS

SOLO SONGS AND SONG-CYCLES
(excluding Folk-songs and Hymns)

STAGE WORKS

VOCAL MUSIC
(Part Songs, etc., Unaccompanied or with Light Accompaniment)

INDEX II

General Index

Abinger, Surrey, Pageant at, 241–2

Adkins, Hector, E., 163, 413, 414

Adler, Larry, 308, 320, 428

Albani, Emma, 1

Allen, Sir Hugh, 17–18, 69, 98, 107, 154, 155–6, 240, 304, 320, 410, 415; liking for *A Sea Symphony*, 99; Director of R.C.M., 146–7

Amos, Sir Maurice, 17, 395

Ansermet, Ernest, 193, 212

Arkwright, G. E. P., 45

Armstrong, Sir Robert, 393

Armstrong, Sir Thomas, 304, 342

Arnold, Dr. J. H., 66, 197

Arnold, Matthew, 305, 320, 359

Arts Council of Great Britain, 295, 326

Arundell, Dennis, 329, 355

Asquith, Anthony, 259

Auber, Daniel, 1

Auden, W. H., 253

Austin, Frederic, 207

Austin, Richard, 431

Bach Choir, 146, 161, 178, 194, 210, 337, 410, 415; RVW as conductor of, 147; subscribes to *Job*, 229 n.

Bach, Johann Sebastian, 3, 15, 36, 70, 175, 336, 357, 375, 386, 392, 393; RVW on performance of, 339–40; RVW and *St. Matthew Passion*, 340–2, 384

Balcon, Sir Michael, 259, 298

Balfe, Michael, 1

Balfour, O.M., Arthur (1st Earl of), 162

Bantock, Sir Granville, 10, 54, 59, 95, 97, 110, 144, 145, 208, 243, 294

Barbirolli, Lady (Evelyn Rothwell), 347, 384, 387

Barbirolli, Sir John, 108, 207, 284, 288 n., 323, 335, 338, 339, 344, 382, 384, 417, 428, 429, 430; and 6th Symphony, 290, 303–4; plays cello in *Sea Symphony*, 318–19; dedicatee of 8th Symphony, 333

Barclay Squire, W. *See* Squire, W. Barclay

Baring-Gould, Rev. Sabine, 23–4, 25, 68, 72

Barnby, Sir Joseph, 3, 33, 34

Barnes, William, 77

Barrett, Dr. W. A., 24

Barter, Arnold, on 5th Symphony, 284–5

Bartók, Béla, 110, 188, 193, 209, 210, 236, 237, 262, 361, 372, 390; views on nationalism, 294

Baughan, E. A., 61

Bax, Sir Arnold, 76, 95, 105, 106 n., 145, 151, 159, 209, 243, 294–5, 296, 319, 329; association with *London Symphony*, 106–7; with *Pianoforte Concerto*, 236–7; gratitude for 4th Symphony, 247–8; RVW's view on, 385–6

Baylis, Lilian, 227

Beecham, Sir Thomas, 63, 91, 93 n., 95, 110, 144, 145, 166, 208, 239, 400, 408, 411, 420; forms L.P.O., 210; liking for *A Pastoral Symphony*, 296

Beethoven, Ludwig van, 13, 15, 18, 49, 103, 136, 175, 222 n., 265, 306, 375; RVW's essay on Choral Symphony, 328; RVW's 'allergy', 386

Beinum, Eduard van, 303

Bell, W. H., 54, 66, 69, 82, 110, 126

Benedict, Sir Julius, 2

Benjamin, Arthur, 258

Bennet, John, 162

Bennett, Richard Rodney, 376

Vaughan Williams, O.M., Dr. Ralph—
cont.
own music's value to others, 332;
Holst, 20–1, 86–7, 154, 186, 321,
336–7, 382; Housman, 439; hymn
tunes, 67–9; immortality, 194; inspiration from paintings, 221; lessons with
Ravel, 90–1; 'literary' music, 116–7;
Mahler, 376; 'meaning' of music, 211,
247, 302 and n., 382; Meyerbeer, 44,
375–6; 'national' composition, 29–30,
36, 37–40, 260; Nicolai's *Merry Wives*,
385; Nielsen, 388; obscene folk song
words, 307–8; Parry, 5–6, 13, 14–15,
146, 376–7, 385; performing Bach,
339–42, 388; phrasing of 'Silent Noon',
79 n.; Purcell, 375; Ravel, 376; religion,
42; Richter (Hans), 389, 391; Rubbra,
376, 384, 385; Russian Ballet, 202;
Schoenberg, 376; Stanford, 7, 18–19,
385; Stravinsky, 186, 337, 376, 390;
Tippett, 390; Verdi, 15–16, 376;
Wagner, 14, 16, 375; Walton, 384, 388;
world government, 324
   For his music, *see under* individual
entries in *Classified Index of Works.*
Vaughan Williams, Sir Roland (Lord
Justice), 62
Vaughan Williams, Ursula (*née* Lock),
179, 261, 290, 308, 312, 326, 339, 343,
346, 368, 381, 386, 387, 390, 392, 395,
420, 421, 427, 428, 429, 430, 431, 432;
meeting with RVW, 256; marriage
to RVW, 324; librettist of RVW opera,
338
Verdi, Giuseppe, 2, 176, 181, 218, 301,
318, 376; RVW on the *Requiem*, 15–16
Verne, Mathilde, 55 and n.
Verrall, Mrs. Harriet (folk singer), 75, 135
Vocalist, The, 50, 53, 397; RVW's writings
in: on English music, 29–30; on libretti,
47–8; on good taste, 48; on Brahms and
Tchaikovsky, 48; on Palestrina, Beethoven and emotion, 49; publishes
'Linden Lea', 51, 397
Vulliamy, Mrs. Edward, 413

Waddington, S. P., 166, 205, 321, 414;
advice to RVW, 20; letter to RVW, 261
Waghalter, Ignaz, 153 n.
Wagner, Richard, 2, 3, 8, 9, 15, 36, 42–3,
66, 70, 312, 328, 396; RVW's admir-
ation for, 14, 375; RVW on his libretti,
47
Walker, Dr. Ernest, 60
Walker, Norman, 341, 427
Wallace, William, 54
Walthew, Richard, 15, 51, 87, 163
Walton, O.M., Sir William, 192, 209, 243,
244, 263, 277, 285, 295, 343, 384, 388

Warlock, Peter. *See under* Heseltine,
Philip
Warrack, Guy, 317
Warrack, John, 339
Webern, Anton, 209, 293, 376
Wedgwood, Iris, Lady, 397–8; recollec-
tion of RVW in 1909, 96–7
Wedgwood, Dr. C. Veronica, 17
Wedgwood, Sir Ralph, 17, 96; RVW's
letters to, 395–401
Wedgwood, Sophy ('Aunt Sophy'), 11, 13,
395
Weelkes, Thomas, 135, 162
Weingartner, Felix, 44
Wellesz, Egon, 293
Wells, H. G.; his *Tono-Bungay* and the
London Symphony, 139–40
West, C. T., 11
Westrup, Sir Jack, 304
Whalley, Rayson, 319
Whelan, Winifred, 152
White Gates, The (RVW's Dorking
house), 188, 206, 290, 306, 319, 325
Whitman, Walt, 61, 64, 81, 92, 126, 190,
194, 254, 271, 294, 373, 388; RVW's
first setting of, 60; his appeal for English
composers, 82; RVW's liking for, 100
'*Who Wants the English Composer?*'
(RVW), 37–9, 101, 104, 136, 194
Wiata, Inia te, 310, 427
Wilbye, John, 50, 162
Willcocks, Sir David, 313 and n.
Williams, Grace, 234
Wilson, Sir Steuart, 42, 74, 105 n., 106,
107, 108, 148, 151, 152, 166, 178, 190,
196, 197, 310 and n., 313, 320, 321, 393,
411, 412, 414, 415, 426; in *The Wasps*,
96; and the *Magnificat*, 230
Wolstenholme, William, 110
Wood, Dr. Charles, 16, 82, 86, 96, 149,
159, 163, 387, 409; RVW's opinion of as
teacher, 16–17
Wood, Sir Henry, 10, 51 n., 52, 54, 58, 63,
95, 109, 110, 144, 242, 295, 408, 410,
415, 421; RVW's jubilee tribute to,
256–7, letters about, 402–3
Wood, Ursula. *See* Vaughan Williams,
Ursula
Woodgate, Leslie, 422
Woodhouse, Mrs. Violet Gordon, 104,
148 n.
Wordsworth, William (composer), 295
Wurm, Stanislas, 42
Wyss, Sophie; memory of RVW's 'fair
play', 253 n.

Yorkshire Post, 320 n.; on *Toward the
Unknown Region*, 88; on *A Sea Symphony*, 97–8